Solvency in Financial Accounting

Routledge Studies in Accounting

1 **A Journey into Accounting Thought**
Louis Goldberg
Edited by Stewart Leech

2 **Accounting, Accountants and Accountability**
Postructuralist positions
Norman Belding Macintosh

3 **Accounting and Emancipation**
Some Critical Interventions
Sonja Gallhofer and Jim Haslam

4 **Intellectual Capital Accounting**
Practices in a Developing Country
Indra Abeysekera

5 **Accounting in Politics**
Devolution and Democratic Accountability
Edited by Mahmoud Ezzamel, Noel Hyndman, Åge Johnsen and Irvine Lapsley

6 **Accounting for Goodwill**
Andrea Beretta Zanoni

7 **Accounting in Networks**
Håkan Håkansson, Kalle Kraus, and Johnny Lind

8 **Accounting and Distributive Justice**
John Flower

9 **Law, Corporate Governance, and Accounting: European Perspectives**
Edited by Victoria Krivogorsky

10 **Management Accounting Research in Practice**
Lessons Learned from an Interventionist Approach
Petri Suomala and Jouni Lyly-Yrjänäinen

11 **Solvency in Financial Accounting**
Julie E. Margret

Solvency in Financial Accounting

Julie E. Margret

Routledge
Taylor & Francis Group
NEW YORK LONDON

First published 2012
by Routledge
711 Third Avenue, New York, NY 10017

Simultaneously published in the UK
by Routledge
2 Park Square, Milton Park, Abingdon, Oxon OX14 4RN

Routledge is an imprint of the Taylor & Francis Group, an informa business

Typeset in Sabon by IBT Global.

Library of Congress Cataloging-in-Publication Data

Margret, Julie E., 1950–
Solvency in financial accounting / by Julie E. Margret.
p. cm. — (Routledge studies in accounting ; 11)
Includes bibliographical references and index.
1. Bankruptcy—Accounting. 2. Bankruptcy. I. Title.
HF5686.B3M37 2011
657—dc23
2011032795

ISBN13: 978-0-415-89582-8 (hbk)
ISBN13: 978-0-203-12968-5 (ebk)

This book is dedicated to Fiona, Sophie and Emilie. My three remarkable, beautiful and high achieving daughters of whom I am immensely proud and who I love unconditionally—thank you for your continued support, friendship and love

Contents

Figures

APPENDIX FIGURES

Tables

APPENDIX TABLES

Dramatis Personae

Abbott, Harold	Abbott was a director and reportedly one of the key players in the story of the Duke Group (in Liquidation). Originally a director of Kia Ora (from May 1983), Abbott was subsequently involved in the takeover of Western United that resulted in the 1998 case that became known as the "Duke" affair.
Adler, Rodney	Previous chairman of FAI and one time director of both HIH Insurance and One.Tel Limited. Married with four children, Adler had been part of the BRW Rich list since 1983. In 2002, he was banned from acting as a director for twenty years and ordered to pay substantial pecuniary penalties. In July 2003, Adler was committed to stand trial on three counts of stock market manipulation and two counts of false or misleading statements with regard to financial securities.
Adsteam	A 1980s conglomerate reportedly driven, until it collapsed—with entrepreneurial flair. At that time, the Adsteam Group structure was part of the Adelaide Steamship Co. Limited. The enterprise then operated as Adsteam Marine Ltd. Adsteam has long been a provider of harbour towage, lines, mooring, bunkering and agency activities in Australia.
Allco Group	The Allco Group was founded in 1979. By 2006, the Group listed on the ASX. Five years later it was under external administration. Allco was delisted from the ASX on September 1, 2009.
Ansett, R. (Bob)	Bob Ansett, the much publicised leader of the Budget Group in Australia and one of the founding directors of the ill-fated public float of BCL. BCL was structured as a subsidiary of the holding company, Budget Transport Industries.

Ansett (ATI)	Ansett Transport Industries Limited, originally founded and directed by Sir Reginald Ansett.
ASL	Associated Securities Limited; originally Australian Securities Ltd., incorporated in Sydney in 1926. It provided a range of finance services for transport, mortgage, operating, capital expenses and real estate.
BCH	Bond Corporation Holdings Limited. Founded in the 1960s and led to entrepreneurial stardom during the 1980s by Alan Bond before its ultimate demise in the early 1990s.
BCL	In 1988 Budget Corporation Ltd (BCL) was floated as a public company on the Australian Stock Exchange. It collapsed and was delisted in 1989.
BI	Budget Investments: An unlisted wholly-owned subsidiary of Budget Transport Industries.
BRACS	Budget Rent-A-Car Systems: An unlisted wholly-owned subsidiary of Budget Transport Industries.
Burns Philp	Burns Philp & Company Limited is a multi-national organisation founded around 120 years ago. The business is widely known as a leading producer of yeast products and manufacturer of other bakery ingredients and industrial vinegar. The company suffered a central business failure in the 1990s but survived and continues its business operations today.
Chambers, R. J.	Foundation Professor of Accounting at the University of Sydney. Enduring scholar, Chambers developed the fully integrated method of continuously contemporary accounting (CoCoa). He was a very well liked, greatly respected and admired man who amassed myriad accolades during his career—too numerous to list on this page. His works continue to be an inspiration to all and especially helpful to those who nurture an enquiring mind.
Duke	The Duke Group Limited, a conglomerate formed from a takeover and reverse takeover that initially involved Kia Ora and Western United and began in 1987. By 1989 the acquiring company was deemed insolvent and placed in liquidation by order of the Supreme Court of South Australia. Legal action commenced in 1992 with damages claimed for losses allegedly sustained as

a consequence of the 1987/1988 acquisition. The trial commenced in 1994 and concluded in 1998. The major issue in the case was "valuation."

Elliott, John — John Elliott is a high profile member of Melbourne society. He has substantial business acuity, having directed and been a non-executive director of many corporate entities during his career. He held the esteemed position (at least in Melbourne) of President of the Carlton football club for many years. A long-time antagonist of many, particularly regulators, Elliott was charged and convicted of insolvent trading at the culmination of the Water Wheel crisis in 2003.

Enron — Prior to its collapse in 2001, Enron was reportedly the seventh largest company in the US. It evolved from the pipeline company, Houston Natural Gas, which later acquired Florida Pipeline Company and then merged with Inter North Inc., apparently tallying at that point 40,000 miles of pipeline. The so constructed company changed its name to Enron in 1986 and soon after became a market leader in energy-trading operations.

Fincorp Group — Fincorp was founded by Eric Krecichwost. Twenty-one separate entities formed the Fincorp Group of companies. Fincorp was largely a fixed-interest investment provider. On March 23, 2007, Fincorp was placed in receivership.

Great Southern — In 1987, the Great Southern Group of companies was formed. In May 1999, the Group were publicly listed and 'changed its name from Templegate Services Ltd to Great Southern Plantation Limited' (Directors' Report, Annual Report, 1999, p.8). In 2007, the Group changed its name to Great Southern Limited. Until the 2000s, the mainstay of its business remained managed investment schemes (MIS), after which the group diversified its product and business activities to include cattle, olives, viticulture and almonds. By August 30, 2010, Great Southern Limited was delisted.

Hamley, Stuart — A company director of BCL. At the time of the BCL float, Hamley beneficially owned, with Bob Ansett, Budget Rent-A-Car Systems and another car rental business named Thrifty and was also a director of Quadrax Corporation and Oakminster Limited.

HIH	HIH Insurance Limited, a multi-national corporation, reportedly the second largest general insurance company in Australia prior to its collapse in 2001.
HIHRC	The HIH Royal Commission was set up to investigate circumstances surrounding the fall of the "titan." It commenced in May 2001 and ended in April 2003. The Commissioner was Justice Neville Owen of the W. A. Supreme Court.
Kia Ora	In 1987, Kia Ora Gold Corporation NL initiated a takeover of Western United. The acquisition led to a reverse takeover that resulted in the "Duke" affair—a case (in liquidation) where valuation of the target company was the major issue.
Minsec	Mineral Securities of Australia Limited—a group of companies in existence during the 1960s into the early 1970s.
Nelson Wheeler	The accounting firm Nelson Wheeler Perth prepared the initial and subsequently controversial valuation in the takeover of Western United. The valuation was a major issue in the case of the *Duke Group Ltd. (in Liq) v. Pilmer & Ors.*
One.Tel Limited	A telecommunications conglomerate that commenced operations in the mid 1990s. One.Tel's founders, Jodee Rich and Bradley Keeling, reportedly led its daily operations with entrepreneurial flair until its demise in 2001. Journalist Paul Barry's published "Rich Kids" provides an informative view of the rise and fall of One. Tel and its founders.
Owen, J. Neville	Justice Neville Owen was appointed as the HIH Royal Commissioner in 2001. Subsequently, he presided over myriad hearings and dealt with millions of pages of submissions throughout the term of the Royal Commission—from May 2001 until the final report was released in April 2003.
Reid Murray	Reid Murray Holdings Limited was a well known retail operation in Australia that unexpectedly was placed in receivership in 1963.
Scheutze, Walter	Former chief accountant of the Securities and Exchange Commission in the US.

Water Wheel	Water Wheel Holdings and its operating company Water Wheel Mills were mainly involved in the business of milling wheat and paddy rice. The Water Wheel board placed the company in voluntary administration in 2000. Later the courts found Water Wheel had been insolvent at least since 1999.
Westmex	Westmex Limited with Russell Goward as the man at the top was a multi-national short-lived success story during the late 1980s.
Williams, Ray	Founder and Chief Executive Officer of HIH Insurance Limited. The Group began in 1968, when Ray Williams and Michael Payne started an underwriting insurance business, MW Payne Liability Agencies Pty. Ltd. Subsequently, in 1971, the company was taken over by British listed C. E. Heath Insurance. In September 2000, Williams announced his intention to resign from the HIH Group and did so in December that year.

Glossary

Accounting data: Numeric information disclosed in the financial statements of an entity from which assumptions or inferences can be made with regard to the financial characteristics of conducting business.

Conventional financial statement: Accounting report prepared under generally accepted accounting principles (GAAP). Otherwise may be considered as a statement that follows accounting convention of what has been done generally and habitually for some time.

Dated financial statement: The term is used to draw attention to the date of the financial statement. The separate financial components of the statement should directly relate in monetary equivalents (financial worth) to its date.

Entity: A business unit, centre, department or a "being," in existence but separate and distinct from emotions.

Excellence: That which surpasses a standard accepted generally as good or of merit.

Financial: Of money and money related matters.

Financial attribute: A characteristic that directly relates to money and its purchasing power.

Financial data: Units that relate to money.

Financial information: Collective data that enlighten interested parties about money and what can be achieved with money. Data may be considered details that become truly informative only when they are serviceable to and for the recipient—particularly with regard to the problem at hand.

Financial statement: A report on money and money related matters.

Financial worth: An entity's accumulated wealth determined by its net monetary state.

GAAP: Generally accepted accounting principles.

Monetary fact: A statement pertaining to a cash balance or cash equivalent of a non-cash item—what it would be exchangeable for in a general, active and current market.

Monetary position: Money (financial) state of an entity at a certain point in time.

Monetary worth: Money equivalent.

Quality: A generally agreed 'degree of excellence.'

Quality financial information: Serviceable details that truly inform. Refer also to financial information.

Preface

This book examines one of the most contentious but little discussed areas in accounting. It analyses legal and accounting notions of solvency and demonstrates that conventional financial statements are deficient in terms of establishing the dated financial position of an entity and equally lacking with regard to the quantification of an entity's state of solvency. Much has been written recently about the quality of financial information available for economic decision-makers. The examination of solvency is juxtaposed with assessment of what is meant by the phrase 'quality financial information.' Quality is herein defined in terms of serviceable financial information—data serviceable in the sense of being generally relevant to the users of financial reports.

This work contributes to the literature by drawing on real-world observations of how the meshing of commercial and legal foundations creates the environment in which accounting must serve. The aim of this work is to provide insights into what changes to existing financial reporting systems might assist in mitigating continuing criticism of accounting in the aftermath of unexpected corporate collapses. Terminological deficiencies are revealed through the sometimes imprudent use of words in accounting. This is shown to be so especially with respect to accounting for an entity's financial position, a precondition of determining its solvency—its *financial state.*

It is argued that, frequently, constructs of conventional financial statements have no external referent of financial substance with regard to ascertaining an entity's financial state. Further, it is argued that quality financial information relating to real-time market referents is crucial for on-going business activities; it is *a prius* for stakeholders involved in commercial enterprise being able to properly assess future risks and rewards.

Using a common-sense approach to measurement, this study investigates practical aspects of accounting for business activities and reporting the financial results of business affairs. Drawing mainly on major Australian cases, links are found between each case highlighting associations between the language of accounting and the data contained in financial statements of an entity's worth. Although the cases are mainly Australian, there are situations that may be generalised; they have international significance. The circumstances of each case highlight implicit links between the language of accounting and the data contained in financial statements. In challenging times, from the many unexpected corporate collapses and related financial dilemmas throughout the twentieth century and beyond, this work is important from a public policy perspective as regulators grapple with a commercial environment heavily influenced by perceived scandalous corporate group activity. Solvency is a topical and on-going issue in financial accounting.

Acknowledgements

This book is based on my PhD thesis conferred at the University of Sydney. So primarily I acknowledge my PhD supervisors, Professor Graeme Dean and Professor Peter Wolnizer, who gave me seemingly endless support and astute guidance during those challenging years. Their wisdom, advice and encouragement provided a strong foundation for me to continue to learn and to explore ideas. During that time, I was most fortunate to meet Professor Ray Chambers. I thank Professor Wolnizer particularly for introducing me to Ray Chambers, the man and his work, and for providing the opportunity for me (and others) to study with him at Deakin University so many years ago.

I also thank Professor Graeme Dean for his kind permission to include in this book, as I had in my PhD thesis, extracts of a survey conducted by Dean, Clarke and Houghton (2003) from some of the top 200 publicly listed companies on the Australian Securities Exchange (ASX). The following papers are referenced in this book: 'Survey: Working Paper' (Dean, Clarke and Houghton, 2003) and 'Solvency Solecisms: Corporate Officers' Problematic Perceptions' (Dean, Clarke and Margret, 2008).

I also thank the editors of the *Australian Accounting Review* for publishing 'Insolvency and Tests of Insolvency: An Analysis of the "Balance Sheet" and "Cash Flow" Tests' (Margret, 2002). This article was based on Chapter 3 of my PhD thesis, a previous version of the now Chapter 2 in this book. I also acknowledge the Institute of Certified Management Accountants in Australia and the editors of *Journal of Applied Management Accounting Research* (JAMAR) for publishing 'Surviving Financial Distress: The Case of Too Many Herbs and Spices' (Margret, 2005). , This article was based on the case study of Burns Philp Company Limited included in my PhD, a revised extract of which is included here in Chapter 6.

To my family and friends who are tireless in their support of me in my continued pursuits, thank you. You are my rock. To my colleagues in the School of Accounting at La Trobe University, I extend my sincere appreciation for your friendship and support and the collegial spirit that underpins our working day. I have known some of you for many years, and I am thankful for our enduring friendship and productive coffee breaks. The anecdotes we share are good for the soul!

1 A Crucial Aspect of Financial Accounting

'Bad production management and bad sales management have slain their thousands, but faulty finance [leading to insolvency] has slain its tens of thousands.—Collin Brooks' (in Chambers, 1986, p.v).

THE PROBLEM

This book examines the notion of solvency as revealed in the legal and accounting domains. Inconsistent ways of determining solvency at law and in accounting are revealed.

Solvency is a critical commercial financial attribute. Quantifying solvency has been the focus of many of the concerns expressed across time with regard to business continuity and the financial reporting system. It has featured in myriad press headlines globally about major multi-national corporations. In Australia, the various inquiries—Liquidators', Royal Commissions' and Courts'—into HIH, One.Tel, Ansett, Water Wheel and others have deliberated this financial characteristic. Whilst this is not altogether new, there does appear to be a greater emphasis on solvency in the new millennium than in previous decades.

Arguably accounting data should provide a major input in any assessment of an entity's solvency. Hence, a major premise of this book is that *a precondition of ascertaining an entity's corroborable financial state, its dated financial position, is to determine its level of solvency.*

Although there appears increasingly to be recourse in the law and in commerce to solvency, its quantification has not been adequately considered, especially in financial accounting.[1] The AASB framework (para.16) [IASB framework equivalent] provides:

> The financial position of an entity is affected by the economic resources it controls, its financial structure, its liquidity and solvency, and its capacity to adapt to changes in the environment in which it operates. [and] . . . Information about liquidity and solvency is useful [arguably essential] in predicting [ascertaining] the ability of the entity to meet its financial commitments as they fall due. Liquidity refers to the availability of cash in the near future. . . . Solvency refers to the availability of cash over the longer period to meet financial commitments as they fall due.

Regardless of the rhetoric, however, given the content of conventional financial statements, including the cash flow statement in its current form, there is no apparent development on how best to quantify solvency. The primary focus on assets as expectations of future economic benefits is intangible and is arguably unhelpful. For instance, the AASB Framework states: 'An asset is a resource controlled by the entity as a result of past events and from which future economic benefits are expected to flow to the entity' (at para.49 (a)). The concept of expected future economic benefits allude to anticipation of gains, a hope—not assured financial facts.

The financial industry and its regulators have insisted on minimum solvency requirements—prudential limits—for financial institutions such as banks, superannuation funds, general and life insurers that 'maintain a prescribed excess of assets over liabilities.'[2] Similarly, the international balance sheet test of [in]solvency mandates that an entity's assets exceed its liabilities.[3] The HIH Royal Commission highlighted the notion of *regulatory solvency* and noted particularly the recognition and valuation treatment of assets as a prerequisite to determining an entity's state of solvency.[4]

Additionally, Commissioner Owen (2003, s.19, p.20) noted that during the HIH investigation 'a common theme emerge[d], . . . that the [minimum solvency] requirement was regarded by some as a requirement of form rather than substance, without due heed to its underlying prudential purpose,' for instance, assets shaped from the Cotesworth Group letter of credit arrangements.[5] In accord with the Insurance Act (1973), HIH (and other general insurers) included intangible assets such as goodwill in minimum solvency calculations. Since July 2002 and the release of new prudential regulatory standards, intangible assets are not to be included in determining a general insurer's regulatory solvency—namely, for reporting to APRA.[6]

On the other hand, preceding 2005, there were no such restrictions for external financial reporting purposes under the guidelines of generally accepted accounting principles (GAAP)[7] and the then AASB1023: *Financial Reporting of General Insurance Activities.*[8] Such inconsistencies at law and in accounting are shown below to be pervasive, much to the detriment of achieving an orderly, informed commercial setting.

By 2007 a revised AASB1023: *General Insurance Contracts* was released that incorporated amendments compliant with the international financial reporting standard IFRS 4: *Insurance Contracts.* The revised prudential standards were effective from July 1, 2008, and included focus on assets GPS 120, capital adequacy GPS 110 and measurement of capital GPS 112 and risk management including issues of balance sheet and market risk GPG 250 among others. Such standards are subsequent to the APRA Discussion Paper released on November 20, 2003, on "Stage 2 Reforms" of the General Insurance Industry—a bid to further strengthen prudential requirements on solvency issues.

Interestingly now, in accounting, financial assets for insurers are likely recorded at fair value[9] whereas operating assets for other corporate entities are not.[10] The reason for the difference remains unclear. Similarly confusing the AASB1023 provides: 'Where assets are not backing general insurance liabilities or financial liabilities that arise under non-insurance contracts, general insurers apply the applicable accounting standards making use of any measurement choices available' (at para.15.1.1).

Arguably in financial accounting little has changed, and the consequences may be dire; as Clarke *et al.* (2003, p.310) noted:

> HIH's published financials at 30 June 2000 brought to account nearly $1 billion dollars of Future Income Tax Benefits, goodwill and various capitalised expenditure [assets] all potentially in accord with the prevailing [accounting] Standards. Those balances are of highly contestable relevance to any assessment of the company's solvency at the time or of its overall financial position. That scenario is not unique to HIH.

Returning momentarily to the notion of "form over substance" or "substance over form," the AASB Framework (para.35) provides: 'If information is to represent faithfully the transactions and other events that it purports to represent, it is necessary that they are accounted for and presented in accordance with their *substance* and *economic reality* and not merely their legal form' [emphasis added]. The primary objective of financial reports is to provide financial information 'that is useful to a wide range of users in making economic decisions' (para.12). Relevance and reliability are principal qualitative characteristics of financial reports (para.24). Hence, to enable financial reports to depict *substance over form* entails that the content of those reports be *relevant* to the date of the report.

Therein lies a problem—for, to fulfil the stated 'objective of financial reports . . . to provide information about the financial position . . . of an entity that is useful to a wide range of users in making economic decisions' (AASB Framework, para.12) necessitates that financial information considered useful for making economic decisions is well-defined. If information on financial substance and economic reality are to be achieved, quality financial information is required. Quality is herein defined as "a degree of excellence,"[11] that which is "serviceable,"[12] with excellence apparent as that "surpassing merit."[13] Quality financial information is not achieved necessarily by following accounting rules and dictum. West (2003, p.6) showed that across time:

> [N]o demonstration has been made of how extant accounting rules redress the alleged "market failures". Indeed, examination of these rules reveals that they do not embrace any coherent quality specification for accounting information. Nor has any robust explanation been offered for why the "market failures" should necessitate a continuing expansion of the number of rules.

Historically, Chambers (1979b, p.74) 'described usefulness [in accounting] as a *vanishing premise* on the ground that every advocate of a rule or practice would contend that the product of it is (or would be) useful.' Later, with regard to public sector accounting, Carnegie and Wolnizer (1999, p.18) discussed briefly the difference between the use of accounting numbers and the concept of those numbers being useful therein. Chambers (1979b) noted also that accounting data should serve as a warrant—a form of quality control—quality in that sense would ensure that the data depicted truthfully and fairly the salient characteristics that all users require—namely, data about an entity's solvency, liquidity, profitability and adaptability.[14]

By 2010 the AASB Framework (para.46) asserted 'the application of the [four] principal qualitative characteristics [understandability, relevance, reliability and comparability] **and** of appropriate accounting standards *normally* results in financial reports that convey what is *generally understood* as a *true and fair view* of, or presenting fairly such information' (emphasis added). Arguably the assertion is confusing and actively, it is not possible. For all of these "principal qualitative characteristics" and "appropriate accounting standards" cannot be applied in all given situations because the standards direct one to disregard relevant financial details if they are deemed unreliable; refer for instance to AASB Framework (paras.26 and 32).

On financial details, Chapter 2 examines the asset test (balance sheet test) of insolvency and the commercial test (cash flow test) of insolvency and explores the various elements therein, and Chapter 4 investigates the constructs of conventional financial statements and their ostensible lack of substance on solvency. With focus on terminology and the sometimes "sloppy" use of words in accounting, Chapter 3 analyses the notion of directors' accountability with regard to knowing the actual financial state of the entity they direct.

In September 2003, CAMAC highlighted the importance of solvency in a group setting. CAMAC released a discussion paper on rehabilitating large, complex enterprises in financial difficulties. It emphasised that directors should know the level of solvency of the businesses they direct (at least) to enable those entities to continue 'in business as a going concern'[15] and to assist directors to fulfil their legal obligations in preventing insolvent trading.[16] Additionally, under the concept of a *financial stress test*, CAMAC indicated that directors should determine the extent of the entity's 'actual or likely insolvency' prior to initiating any rehabilitation process.[17]

Interestingly the law has defined solvency. For instance, in Australia the *Corporations Act* (2001), s.95A (1) describes solvency as the ability of an entity 'to pay all . . . [its] debts, as and when they become due and payable.' Similar definitions are used in the legislation of other countries.[18] Nonetheless the concept of solvency, especially in the area of commerce, remains deficient, as there is a lack of consonance between law and accounting as to its meaning. Similarly, dissonance exists in the requirements of prudential standards and legislatively-backed accounting standards with regard to quantifying solvency. This is likely to result in practical problems for decision-makers during the ordinary course of commercial activity, a point explored throughout this book.[19]

Of specific concern here is the quality of financial information supplied to decision-makers through accounting reports.[20] This is because conventional audited financial statements about an entity's financial position do not contain time and circumstance specific financial facts about the entity.[21] Importantly, both dated financial position and solvency are conditions that require recourse to estimates of the monetary worth of the entity's assets and liabilities as they relate to money and the worth of money at a particular point in time. Hence, financial data contained in the current suite of publicly available and audited financial reports are of concern. Especially where audits are considered a 'kind of quality control, control of the quality of the information on which managers, investors and creditors will make judgements about the performance and prospects of companies' (Chambers, 1973b, p.144).[22]

Following a long-standing perspective, this study analyses an integral aspect of accounting, namely, the matter of quantification—especially in determining an entity's solvency. Crosby's (1997) analysis of what differentiated the *Renaissance* from earlier times highlighted the need for knowledge about quantification. This knowledge is equally pertinent today. The deliberations of the HIH Royal Commission in Australia (related *inter alia* to FAI and HIH's affairs), the Bond Corporation/Arthur Andersen S.A. Supreme Court case and others, for instance, the Enron saga in the US all rely on an understanding of when an entity is (in)solvent.[23] These and other similar cases and the financial dilemmas they entail, in Australia and overseas, make this story topical and important from a public interest and a public policy perspective.

Notably in examination of the demise of Enron in the US, capitalised and deferred expenses were identified as a key risk area producing misleading financial statements.[24] Similarly, HIH reported \$304.3 million deferred acquisition costs as a current asset in its June 30, 2000, balance sheet along with \$738.8 million of intangibles that included goodwill and future income tax benefits (FITB). Of course this is not new. Bond Corporation's \$453.4 million FITB is a good example (see Clarke *et al.*, 2003, for many other instances). The amounts recorded, in all those cases, were arguably legitimately shown as "assets" under conventional accounting and GAAP, then supported by AASB1023.

Subsequent to, but not necessarily because of, the collapse of HIH, the Australian Prudential Regulatory Authority (APRA) redefined its concepts of assets and (as noted earlier) in July 2002 released prudential standards that excluded intangibles such as those described above, from prudential calculations of an entity's solvency. Further, the Institute of Actuaries of Australia supported the decision and strongly asserted, for instance, that deferred acquisition costs as an asset 'has no place in the APRA assessment of solvency' (IA Aust., 2002, p.28). If such vision were to become universal, the need for general public policy reforms related to accounting would be lessened.

AIM

The principal aim is to reconsider the solvency notion and to demonstrate through analysis and case data that *conventional financial statements are deficient in terms of establishing the dated financial position of an entity and equally lacking with regard to quantifying an entity's state of solvency.*

Consider revelations in the December 2002 "stage one" and April 2003 "stage two" reports of an accounting regulatory surveillance project conducted by the Australian Securities and Investment Commission (ASIC).[25] The former revealed that of approximately 1,000 listed companies, 215 had 'audit qualifications and/or "emphasis of matter" paragraphs . . . [and] six companies had audit qualifications relating to their continuation as going concerns.' In addition, '[a]nother 160 companies had an "emphasis of matter" in the audit report which related to significant uncertainty about going concern' (ASIC, 2002, p.2).[26] The ASIC (2003) report particularly focused on previously identified (and sometimes problematic) accounting issues of capitalised expenses, deferred expenses, revenue recognition and recognition of controlled entities and assets—discussed in some depth in Chapter 4 and then from Chapter 5 to Chapter 7 with emphasis on case analyses. Reportedly investigations continued on unresolved issues such as the practice of deferring expenses as assets, applying [or not] "fair value" to an acquisition and the process of writing off expenses to retained earnings.[27] The concept of fair value is contentious.

Such practices are cause for some concern—not least because, for a business to continue as a *bona fide* commercial going concern, it must have the financial capacity to adapt to changing market conditions. Yet, as will be demonstrated, conventional financial statements based on historical cost accounting methods (such as those previously mentioned) do not provide up-to-date financial information on a business entity's financial state or its ability to change—its capacity for adaptive (economic) behaviour.

In commerce, changes to business operations are commonplace, the *sine qua non* of markets, resulting in the mix of an entity's assets and liabilities continually altering as the entity adapts to its fluctuating trade arrangements. This continuous adaptation dictates that decision-makers repeatedly examine the entity's level of debt to equity, debt to asset structure and constantly monitor the strength of its financial capacity to conduct business. Chambers (1966, p.195) noted, '[t]he differential effects of changes in prices and price levels on the measurement from time to time of assets and equities makes it necessary to distinguish between monetary and non-monetary items.' This knowledge assists in determining the magnitude of an entity's debt obligations against its ability to pay that debt and its financial capacity to adapt to ever-changing circumstances of business. Such information is critical in assessing a firm's flexibility. Indicated previously, financial flexibility and adaptive (economic) behaviour in business are herein considered to be the same.

An entity's ability to adapt will ultimately decide its commercial strength, its competitiveness and its prospects for survival in the commercial world. Perhaps surprisingly, the notion of adaptive behaviour with regard to firms conducting business activities has been pursued in the accounting literature by relatively few writers—such as Chambers and Sterling.[28] Nevertheless, authors in cognate disciplines have discussed it.[29] Beer (1959, p.17), for example, stated, '[i]t is essential to the company that it develops techniques for survival in a changing environment; it must adapt itself to its economic, social and political surroundings.' An objective of this book is to further advance the notion of adaptation in business and to highlight the necessity for accounting reports to include this concept in the structure of financial statements.

Numerous actions by managers support this. Frequently their actions alter the financial state of the business entity in one way or another.[30] Strategies and tactics, applied by management to ensure the entity's continuity of business, might include changes to products, services, manufacturing operations and capital structure. Such activities may lead to rationalizations within organizations like retrenchments, elimination of specific retail outlets or manufacturing departments; or, perhaps a change in the source for, or type of, raw materials used in the production, or the sale, of subsidiary operations. Changes of this type alter the way in which an organization conducts its business operations, in addition to the inevitable adjustments to its financial structure.

Hence, adaptive behaviour in commercial enterprise is synonymous with economic behaviour. Economic decisions that promote dynamic business operations—proactive as well as reactive—directly relate to the concept of adaptation. Pfiffner and Sherwood (1960, p.407) asserted 'organizations are interacting entities in which the desires of the individual, the group and the organization are in a continued state of adaptation.' These decisions may result in structural change for the entity, for instance, expansion of its core and/or non-core areas of operations or diversification into broader areas of interest.[31] An increase in the entity's debt obligations or its aggregate cost of debt is most likely to occur; that in turn may adversely affect its capacity to be competitive and its ability to remain in business.

On the other hand, entities that act promptly and decisively and seize economic opportunities as they arise increase their chances to be, or become, market leaders. They usually attain a competitive advantage over other organizations, a position that is likely to heighten their chance for financial success and reduce their risk of business failure. It is not unreasonable to posit, therefore, that such circumstances dictate that decision-makers receive up-to-date financial facts about the relevant business entity.[32] Data would enable management to monitor continually the entity's financial state and more likely promote proactive and viable business activities that would in turn support profitable operating results that had real-market referents.[33]

That a business can fail is not of itself of significance. Many have noted the need in a market economy for the efficient to weed out the inefficient—recall Schumpeter's winds of "creative destruction." But there are often unexpected consequences of failure, especially unexpected failure![34] This suggests the possibility of economically damaging circumstances for the broader community. Chapters 5 and 6 elaborate selected case studies that illustrate what will be argued are widespread accounting practices that ultimately gave rise to deficiencies in financial statements; flawed financial information had been published to the detriment of users of conventional accounting reports. Those investigations demonstrate that accounting defects identified, examined and evaluated by Chambers (1973b) using national and international case studies and also Clarke *et al.* (1997/2003) and Clarke and Dean (2007) in their primarily Australian case analyses suggest those deficiencies have existed from the 1960s, throughout the 1990s and continue in the new millennium. Writers in other countries have provided similar case analyses as examples of anomalous behaviour—for example, Briloff (US) and Stamp (UK).[35]

Whether case studies are selected or not, fundamentally '[t]he present [and past] large [and small] *unexpected* failures have continued the flow of evidence that conventional accounting as it is enshrined in the Accounting Standards is inherently defective' (Clarke *et al.*, 2003, p.331). The cases examined in this book further support this view. In addition, the case analyses will demonstrate that accounting as an instrumentation system—a means of determining the financial state of a business—is not proving to be an effective mechanism under conventional accounting. It is only by chance that they contain up-to-date market-based financial data concerning the economic results of conducting business. Anthony (2004, p.51) asserted:

> [T]he balance sheet [for instance] is literally a "sheet of balances". . . . Individual items may be useful, but the totals do not mean anything. Informed users know this and pay little attention to those totals. They disregard the non-monetary amounts as a guide in measuring solvency.

Of concern is that not all users, economic decision-makers, are likely to be so informed. A crucial aspect of business nonetheless is to know, continuously, the actual financial results of particular activities undertaken. Consequently, only time specific financial information can be argued as being relevant for business and beneficial to the health of the economy.[36] This indicates that accounting reports hold a critical position in providing decision-makers with information on an entity's financial state, and so the spotlight is once again on the content of financial statements especially in terms of relevant definition and quantification of the elements contained therein.[37]

In accounting, over time, definitions of particular items like assets have altered, but the basic concept of defining what it is we speak about, in a general sense, has remained a constant. Bacon (1620/1891, p.397)[38] stated, 'men imagine that their reason governs words, whilst, in fact, words react upon the understanding.'[39] It appears that (some) decision-makers use conventional financial statements as a basis for economic actions in business, yet the quality of information likely contained therein is contestable.[40] Over the past sixty years in, for instance, Australia, there is repeated evidence of unexpected corporate collapses that have in turn produced professional and legislative enquiries, with direct reference to solvency now appearing in the Corporations Act.[41]

The scenario continues into the new millennium notwithstanding an extended boom period in economic activity halted abruptly by the May 2000 tech-wreck, its aftershocks and later the global financial crises continuing through 2010. Systematic evidence is not yet in on this period. In 2001 the collapse of HIH and One.Tel in Australia sent more shock waves throughout the national business community, and by December 2001 the tension had increased. And it became internationalised in the aftermath of the April/May telco meltdown, when the major US energy conglomerate Enron buckled under the weight of its massive debt and non-existent cash flow—'[t]he numbers were a sham and the portrait was fake. . . . Enron's profits were a mirage.'[42] More on this and others is revealed later.

The flow of corporate disasters did not stop with Enron's demise. By August 2002, around eight months after Enron's ruin, 'a growing list of companies . . . followed it on scandal's path, led by WorldCom, Global Crossing, Tyco International, Adelphia Communications and Qwest Communications.'[43] But the sagas continued with the Parmalat (Italian) affair emerging in late December 2003.

In Australia, by June 2003, Professor Berna Collier (ASIC Commissioner) spoke of increased budget support for ASIC to examine issues on corporate insolvency and to act promptly on matters related to directors and their duties, insolvent trading and corporate collapse. One initiative, from early 2003, was a project that involved 'trading surveillances . . . [run] in Sydney and Melbourne. . . . During this time, ASIC . . . conducted solvency reviews of 169 companies and 56 directors.'[44] Even with increased concentration on [in]solvency issues, the system of accounting for business activities and reporting its financial outcomes to stakeholders remained relatively unscathed—the focus persisted primarily on the individuals. Of course some individuals and their actions warranted the attention.

Chapters 2 and 3 will reveal that court judgements previously have generally considered the continuity of business as a "going concern." This suggested the courts only alluded to issues of solvency. More recently, focus has considered the significance of, and for, accounting and its output. Hence, the production of quality financial information was deemed necessary to assist users in making economic decisions about a business and its outcomes.[45] This shift was augmented by judgements in court cases concerned with the definition of solvency and operational tests of how to determine solvency, namely, the "balance sheet test" and "cash flow test" of [in]solvency, discussed in Chapter 2.

It is clear that, if an orderly commercial environment is to exist, the dictates of the law cannot be ignored. Under the legal tests of solvency, the joint limbs 'as and when they [debts] become due and payable' (ACA, s.95A) in the definition of solvency suggest that both an entity's state of liquidity and its level of solvency need to be considered. This study demonstrates this point analytically and through empirical case analyses.

William Paton (1922) described, as long ago as the 1920s, the corporation as the *par excellence* business form of a market economy. In Australia, Ramsay and Stapledon (2001) had shown that corporate groups were the dominant form. Accordingly, corporate groups and issues of solvency will form the basis of what follows.

METHOD AND METHODOLOGY

> Our coordinated knowledge, which in the general sense of the term is science, is formed by the meeting of two orders of experience. One order is constituted by the direct immediate discriminations of particular observations. The other order is constituted by our general way of conceiving the universe. They will be called the observational order and the conceptual order (Whitehead, 1933/1948, p.183).

For over thirty years, academic works have relied on the capital markets/empirical studies to seek better financial reporting. This followed several decades of what has been labelled "*a priori* reasoning." Each has been shown to have problems. The capital markets positive accounting literature mainly based, for instance, on Watts and Zimmerman (1978) has attempted, over time, to explain accounting practice by observing what accountants do to predict accounting choices. Earlier references begin with the work and deliberations of Ball and Brown (1968).

It emphasises contracting costs in accounting theory, for example, agency costs and lobbying costs, and their perceived relevance in explaining accounting phenomena. It highlights links between the capital markets and the role of contracting costs pricing models. Fundamental to this paradigm are assumptions based on the notion of costless information and the use of, for instance, the capital asset pricing model and the arbitrage pricing model in conjunction with the efficient market hypothesis.

As Watts and Zimmerman (1990, p.150) explained, 'The positive accounting literature takes as given the proposition that the accepted set maximizes the wealth of the contracting parties and then seeks to understand how wealth is affected by specific accounting methods.' An alternative approach to accounting and accounting theory, referred to generally as normative, preceded the rise of positivism in accounting literature. This prescriptive (yet also positive) method has been criticised mainly for its subjective, value-laden propositions. Sterling (1982, p.75) rebuked the notion:

> [A]ll propositions can be stated in normative form or in positive form . . . [and] all scientific propositions are normative in the sense that you can use them to achieve objectives. If you cannot use them to attain objectives, then they are useless. But the original statements of such propositions are positive.

To achieve its objective, this study employs multiple methods of analysis. Procedures based on the conceptual and observational orders of events are used to explore qualitative and quantitative aspects of the problem addressed herein. Ultimately, the problem dealt with herein concerns financial accounting processes in compiling financial reports—in particular, with regard to how best to define financial statement elements generally used to quantify an entity's financial capacity to pay its debts; and to determine whether after paying its debts the entity would be financially able to continue to conduct its business activities. Fundamentally, this work is concerned with terminological deficiencies—the sloppy use of words, especially those relating to the process of accounting for an entity's financial position and determining its level of solvency.

In accounting, a fundamental process requires that the extent of an entity's financial capacity to pay its debt and continue to operate as a business be periodically determined and reported in a statement of its financial position, otherwise referred to as a balance sheet. The outcome is disputed.

Deductive reasoning is used to assess the validity of the use of certain terminology in accounting due to the likelihood of confusion for users of accounting reports. In addition, some preliminary survey data (of Dean *et al.*, 2003) relating to "group" solvency issues are evaluated.[46] The problems of interpreting consolidated financial data of corporate groups are shown to be exacerbated by the constructs of abstract reporting entities with special regard to either "closed group" or "opting in" arrangements.[47] The analyses investigate practical aspects of accounting for business activities and subsequently issuing financial reports on those activities to interested parties and the likely flow of information that results. In this respect, several case analyses provide instances of what Chambers (1973a) described as 'observation—a method of enquiry'—they draw on the view that examinations of detailed instances are the definitive empirical form of data or observations.

Hence, two circumstances combine to underpin this study: first the conceptual nature of business and its language,[48] and second the practical aspects of elements in financial statements.[49] Together these result in a flow of data from accounting to society. The crucial outcome is to consider matters specifying the quality of financial information contained in the data given to decision-makers and how that quality might be measured. Basically the ideas here expressed concentrate on conditions of common sense, reason and logic. Homans and Curtis (1934/1970, pp.27, 28) explained, '[t]he first conceptual scheme for all the sciences is the common-sense world.' This is one of the main foundations of Chambers' (2000) views on accounting that are well illustrated in a posthumous article, "Common sense, science and technology." Throughout this book, there are extensive references to the work of Chambers and to quotes from his *Thesaurus* (1995), described by Clarke (1996) as 'an accounting chartulary.'

Figure 1.1 provides an outline of this book. The following elaborates the underlying theoretical framework for the story.

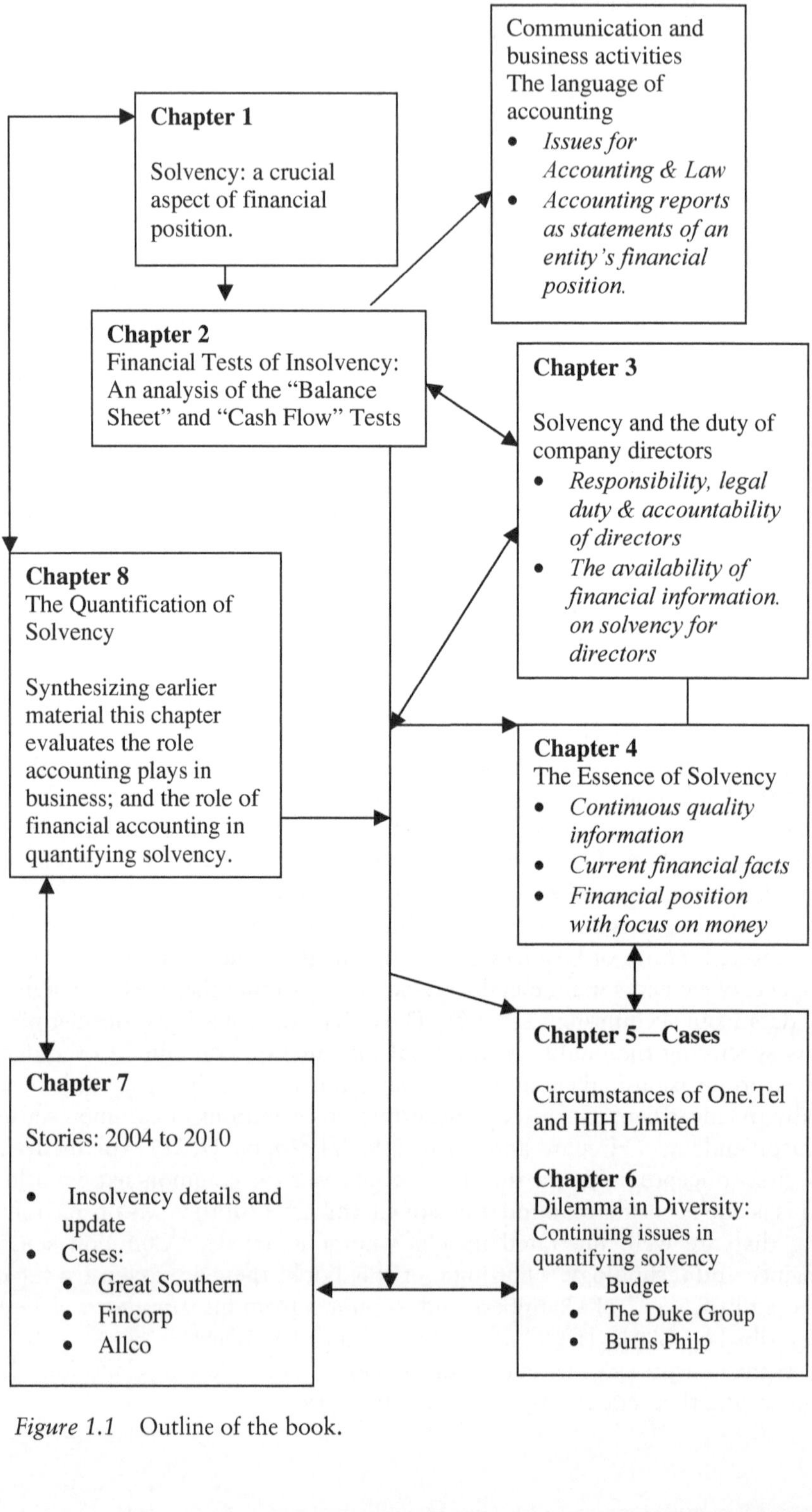

Figure 1.1 Outline of the book.

This study draws on ideas from phenomenology (Husserl 1859–1938) and hermeneutic phenomenology (Heidegger, 1889–1976; Gadamer, 1900–2002).[50] Although the two philosophies are similar and somewhat inter-connected, the differences between them are evident. Both assist in developing the framework of this study. Essentially phenomenology refers to a study of matter (things) that are observable, and hermeneutic phenomenology expands that philosophy to clarify minutiae and points of view to understand that which otherwise may be taken for granted. Perhaps this is why "beings" sometimes indulge in habitual behaviour, taking for granted the reliability (perceived common sense) of their actions, without assessing the relevance, suitability and serviceability of the outcomes of same. Briefly:

> Phenomenological research is descriptive and focuses on the structure of experience . . . to elucidate the essence of these structures as they appear in consciousness . . . Hermeneutic research is interpretive and concentrated on historical meanings of experience and their developmental and cumulative effects on individual and social levels (Laverty, 2003, p.27).

Previously, Lincoln and Guba (1985) discussed such research in terms of ontology (the nature of being and what can be known), epistemology (the nature of relationships between the one with some knowledge and that which may be accepted or discovered) and methodology (how one sets out to discover what may become known). Bochenski (1965, p.16) explained, '[t]he phenomenological method is a special cognitive procedure,' an intellectual observation of objects where the focus rests on the object of concern and peripheral ideas, hypotheses are excluded. There are a number of objects of concern highlighted in this book—and all are with regard to the basic premise of quantifying solvency. Hence, this book explores communication and measurement issues with regard to the use of language and action in accounting, focusing on quantifying an entity's financial state. In that context, semiotics as the study of language,[51] with focus on the meaning of words and the use of words in communication, is relevant.

Bagranoff *et al.* (1994, p.3) asserted, accounting is 'a communicative process,' and that process expresses the necessity for communication theory in accounting research. They emphasized previous works that focused on the measurement of meaning during the twentieth century. For instance Osgood *et al.* (1957) developed a later widely used instrument to measure semantic discrepancies in language. Its use in accounting was somewhat disputed after Haried (1973) implied significant disparities in meaning were missed, but later Houghton (1988) indicated the instrument discriminated between denotative and connotative aspects of meaning and distinguished the expected variations with regard to the latter. This is important in deliberations on accounting. Adelberg and Farrelly (1989) contrasted both aspects of meaning and concluded that 'connotative meaning . . . has the most significance in accounting' (p.39).

Expanding on Karvel's (1979) concern with the meaning of auditor opinions, Houghton and Messier (1990) examined the measure of meaning attributed to auditor reports pre and post audit changes whereas Bagranoff *et al.* (1994) investigated cross-cultural shared meanings of accounting concepts. Here, the consciousness of lived experiences comes to mind, as Heidegger (1927/1962) proffered with regard to our individual histories and the way we interpret, and understand, that which is formed on what went before. Thus background, personal history and culture all combine to affect understanding of meanings of words, events and lived experiences—in context, cultural, social and historical elements are indissolubly related (Munhall, 1989).

Communication theory emphasizes the relationship among the symbols, words and use of words. '[It] is perhaps hardly realized how widespread is the habit of using the power of words not only for *bona fide* communications, but also as a method of misdirection; and in the world as it is today the naïve interpreter is likely on many occasions to be seriously misled if the existence of this unpleasant trait . . . is overlooked' (Ogden and Richards, 1923/1960, pp.18, 19). In phenomenology, Husserl 'focussed more on the epistemological question of the relationship between the knower and the object of study, [whereas] Heidegger moved to the ontological question of the nature of reality and "Being" in the world' (Laverty, 2003, pp.26, 27).

Ultimately, in this book, it is argued that the point of convergence is the quantification of an entity's dated financial state wherein it illustrates its degree of solvency. Hence, several chapters discuss, examine and evaluate practical concerns of managing and measuring an entity's financial state at a given point in time, its financial position. Emphasized is that which is practical. Pareto (1916/1963, p.2024) asserted, '[t]heories are . . . what people say about the things they do or experience,' and theory underpins practise.

STRUCTURE

This book is basically divided into two parts. On issues and observation, Chapters 2 and 3 deal with the conceptual order of events. Further, Chapter 2 to Chapter 4 emphasise the significance of communication between and the interaction of business stakeholders and the role of accounting in a market-based economy. Issues relating to solvency, tests of [in]solvency, duties and responsibilities of directors and corporations are examined; financial details and the quality of financial information available in the public domain are investigated. It is argued that to enable informed investment, financing and operating decisions necessitate that directors and management are able to determine, continually, their business entity's ability to pay its debts when due and payable while maintaining the financial capacity to continue to conduct their business operations.

Then, Chapters 5 and 6 analyse five major Australian solvency cases from the 1980s to 2004. The circumstances of each case highlight that quality financial information, as earlier defined, is not readily available to stakeholders—and has not been for some time. Further, disclosure requirements of a business entity's periodic financial results, as required by law and professional accounting regulations, warrant continued investigation. Although, at a cursory glance and due to the continued and unexpected collapses of business ventures across time '[o]ne would have thought it obvious that the present regulatory framework has failed to achieve . . . [an] overall quality of accounting data' (Clarke *et al.*, 2003, p.330).

Four of the main cases analysed there illustrate unexpected corporate collapses—namely, HIH Insurance Limited and One.Tel Limited (Chapter 5), Budget Corporation Limited and the Duke Group Limited (Chapter 6). The fifth case, Burns Philp and Company Limited (Chapter 6), entailed a financial dilemma for an otherwise strong corporate group that experienced financial stress that led ultimately to a corporate restructure, and the group survived. The major point highlighted is that in all cases the demise of central business was unexpected.[52]

The penultimate Chapter 7 examines solvency from an insolvency perspective. Briefly, it reviews three insolvency cases post 2004 to 2011—namely, circumstances of Great Southern Limited, the Fincorp Group and Allco Finance Group Limited. As in previous chapters, the cases are mainly Australian—but arguably have international significance. Further, argument for a quantified solvency statement is elaborated. All cases examined, from Chapter 5 through Chapter 7, link analysis to previous reasoning and views expressed in Chapter 2 through Chapter 4. Significant indicators of concern to financial accounting are emphasised. Noteworthy is that they commonly persist in cases of insolvency.

Throughout this book, it is demonstrated that accounting as financial instrumentation—proved to be faulty—is in need of repair. It is also apparent in analyses that the demands of law cannot be ignored. Of equal import is that directors, corporate officers and other parties interested in the financial results of business activities need to have ready access to financial information that is relevant to their needs and reliable for use as a basis for business decisions—in other words, serviceable financial information that likely benefits all business stakeholders. Directors and the board of directors are significant stakeholders in business and as Kendall and Kendall (1998, p.224) stated, 'the board of directors is responsible to the [other] stakeholders for achieving . . . agreed goals . . . by its actions, and [all] the stakeholders are made aware of its progress by the communications it receives from them.'

To enable directors to communicate serviceable up-to-date financial information to other stakeholders, they must have access to quality financial details to keep them well-informed on the performance outcomes and ongoing financial capacity of the business they direct. In that context, analysis herein supports previously expressed views such that conventional accounting practice may camouflage, and it frequently does, the actual financial condition of a corporate entity to the detriment of stakeholders (see for instance, Chambers, 1973b; Briloff, 1972, 1976, 1981; Clarke *et al.*, 1997/2003, 2007).

The cases here are mainly Australian, but there are certain situations that may be generalised. The circumstances of each case highlight implicit links between the language of accounting and the data contained in financial statements. Those statements based on conventional accounting practice, supported by accounting standards having the force of law, are intended to provide users with financial information useful for making economic decisions. Yet, some argue: 'Missing is the link between the prescribed [financial accounting] practices and the quality of the end product' (Clarke *et al.*, 1997/2003, p.328).

With this in mind, each case study herein is evaluated with regard to financial accounting, financial reporting and governance issues such as directors' duty of care and responsibilities to stakeholders, and that includes reporting on the financial state of the business. The Corporate Law Economic Reform Program (CLERP) previously embraced such concerns under the name of Corporate Governance.[53]

Additionally, government regulators, the ASX, shareholders, creditors and all corporate stakeholders increasingly demand that directors and corporations pursue corporate governance activities and reporting. That some require corporate entities *en masse* to comply with for instance ASX guidelines on corporate governance concerns is not enough. It is essential for the continuing conduct of business that we differentiate between the "tick the box" approach to corporate governance and governance generally, which truly considers the effect of outcomes of business activities on the environment.

In concluding, Chapter 8 elaborates the integral role of market-based accounting data, quality financial information and directors' responsibility to report on the authenticated financial state of the business they direct. And that together they facilitate effective governance in the conduct of business. Worldwide, attentiveness to governance reform has been a relatively recent development in boosting demands on directors and the activities of corporations—with an ever quizzical eye on those unexpected corporate failures. Such changes have increased the inevitability that financial accounting needs to quantify solvency.

In synthesizing earlier material, Chapter 8 evaluates the role accounting plays in business. The principal aim of the study is appraised, concluding that conventional financial statements are deficient in terms of ascertaining the dated financial state of an entity and equally lacking in quantifying an entity's state of solvency. Clearly this story is, and has been, influenced by the previous work of many scholars, particularly those concerned with rational, reliable, logical and empirical content of accounting reports, about the financial position of business entities. The story continues.

2 Financial Statements and Tests of Insolvency

An Analysis of the "Balance Sheet" and "Cash Flow" Tests

'The conflict between theory and practice is a false one, for practice to be sound [it] should be related to sound theories' (Hatfield, 1939/1982, p.5).

INSOLVENCY AND ACCOUNTING REPORTS

Chambers (1973b) and Clarke *et al.* (1997/2003) have shown that companies sometimes collapse unexpectedly and often not long after they have published financial statements showing a sound financial position. This is of considerable concern to accountants and others, for example, directors, managers, the investing public and regulators, not least because these reports contain financial details prepared under the guidance of professional accounting standards and statutory requirements (often described as generally accepted accounting principles [GAAP]). This chapter considers the extent to which the courts and others use conventionally prepared accounting reports to determine an entity's financial state and establish its level of solvency.

Evidence detailed in Mescher (1996) and Margret (2002) supports the proposition that the courts go beyond the content of financial statements for information to determine an entity's ability to realise its assets and be granted extension of time for payment by creditors. Although the courts may go beyond the content of financial statements for such information, if accounting reports are used in insolvency decisions this necessitates examination of those reports. To this end, two accounting reports-based financial tests of insolvency are discussed herein, namely, the *balance sheet test* and the *cash flow test*. These tests have been used by financial analysts and courts from various countries since the nineteenth century. Nonetheless, it is argued that only one financial statement, hence one financial test, is necessary (albeit not always sufficient) to determine an entity's solvency.

A major proposition explored is that an entity's *factual* financial state can be sought at a nominated date through the process of accounting. However, it is asserted that present GAAP will not assist in generating the required information because resulting financial statements do not necessarily contain the required financial facts.[1] Moreover, financial facts are essential in the calculation of an entity's financial capacity to pay its debts when they are due and payable. Increasingly, the ability to quantify this financial state of an entity is being demanded by society.[2]

Thus it is proposed that the reported financial position of a business entity should indicate its financial capacity to pay its debts and still be able to continue its business operations. Following Loftus and Miller (2000, p.105), the main financial statement to provide the necessary information to enable informed assessments about solvency matters is most likely to be a statement of financial position and that over time has been referred to as a balance sheet. Arguably a statement of financial position is not a balance sheet. The former implies an entity's ability to pay its debts and maintain its capital and capacity to adapt to ever-changing commercial situations. And this view is consistent with the idea of commercial realism.[3] A balance sheet is a list of ledger balances that remain after an entity's profit (loss) is determined. Of primary concern are the concept and definition of assets and liabilities represented in the balance sheet.

Following, a brief summary of the balance sheet test and the cash flow test of insolvency precedes analysis of a number of selected insolvency cases. The cases illustrate problems that courts have encountered across time when deliberating an entity's financial state. The third section explores insolvency with reference to corporate regulations of common law countries such as the US, Canada, United Kingdom (UK), Australia and New Zealand. Findings suggest that those laws present similar financial information with regard to quantifying [in]solvency. Finally it is denoted that a financial test of insolvency has two distinct parts:

(1) that all debt incurred by the entity in the course of conducting its business be identified and incorporated in the quantification of its financial position, and
(2) that current market values of the entity's tangible, realisable assets be used in the calculation of its net asset worth.[4]

JUDICIAL TESTS OF INSOLVENCY

Around the world, courts primarily use two financial tests of insolvency: the balance sheet test and the cash flow test.[5] However, Keay (1995, pp.307, 308) and others noted that Australian courts use the cash flow test of insolvency only. The emphasis therein is on the entity's ability to pay its debts *as they fall due*. This idea implies focus on an entity's liquidity, its short-term financial state; and even though the concepts of liquidity and solvency are related, there is ample literature noting they are different. Anthony (2004, p.13), for instance, asserted, '[t]here are two ways to measure an entity's financial viability: liquidity and solvency.' Heath (1978, p.2) explained:

> [L]iquidity is closely related to solvency. The term, *liquidity*, is often used in at least two different ways. First, it is used to describe the nature of a company's asset holdings, that is their nearness to cash in some (often unspecified) sense. . . . Second, it is used to describe some relationship between a company's liquid assets and its short term liabilities.

Similar ideas are often found in financial analysis texts, as Foster (1978, p.28) remarked: 'liquidity refers to the ability of a firm to meet its short-term financial obligations when and as they fall due.'

In contrast, solvency, in a purely financial sense, more precisely requires longer-term calculations of an entity's ability to pay. This is because the concept of solvency includes (but is not limited to) the need to identify whether the entity has a short-term financial problem or not. Solvency extends to the future—'debts as and when they fall due'—some debts may not fall due in the immediate sense; hence, both the short- and long-term are envisaged. Later it is shown that difficulties have arisen (and continue) for the courts when using the cash flow test of insolvency, especially in deciding what debt to recognise at a particular point in time.[6] The following section investigates some of these difficulties, but first a brief explanation of both tests of insolvency is given.

The Cash Flow Test of Insolvency

The cash flow (or commercial) test refers to the entity's capacity to finance its current and near future operations, with emphasis on its "immediate" financial circumstances.[7] The main consideration of the test is whether the entity in question can pay its debts when due and payable.[8] This concern accords with the requirements of s5(2)(3) of the Australian Bankruptcy Act and s95A of the Australian Corporations Act. Essential elements in the use of this test include the entity's cash on hand, access to cash, items held that have a cash equivalent and the level of debt incurred by the entity. A major problem for the courts, over time, has been to determine what debt to include in this particular method of testing an entity's level of solvency.[9] Mescher (1996, p.842) expanded this point when referring to *Standard Chartered Bank v. Antico* (1995) 18 ACSR 1, where the judge held it was necessary to consider 'the company's financial condition in its entirety, including its activities, assets, liabilities, cash, money which it could procure by sale or on the security of its assets, and its ability to obtain financial assistance by way of loan or subscription for share capital.'

The Balance Sheet Test of Insolvency

In its simplest form, the balance sheet (or asset) test deems an entity to be insolvent if the book values of its assets (as reported on the conventional balance sheet) are less than its reported liabilities.[10] Hence, '[i]f the assets exceed the liabilities, the firm is solvent, that is, able to pay its debts in full. If the total of debts due to creditors . . . is greater than the liquid assets . . . the position of the firm may be financially unsound' (Carter, 1923/1956, p.43). At issue are the constituent parts, assets and debt; and their substance—in quantifying an entity's solvency.[11] This chapter re-examines the concept and definition of assets and debt in relation to financial tests of [in] solvency. Carter's reference to liquid assets above, for instance, highlights that not *all* assets on a balance sheet could be readily exchanged for money as they are not severable and may not have observable monetary exchange cash equivalents. This is the case especially with respect to conventionally-prepared balance sheets, for example, and bookkeeping constructs like *provision for deferred taxes* and *capitalised expenditures.*

APPLICATION OF THE BALANCE SHEET TEST

To apply the balance sheet test of insolvency, logically each element of the test should relate to things that are tangible and have a current and observable monetary equivalent. Under these conditions and contrary to conventional accounting wisdom,[12] *exchangeability* becomes an essential element in the definition of an asset.[13] With exchangeability inherent in the definition of an asset, the ability of an entity to cover all debt incurred could be objectively ascertained.

However, debt that is based on a contract or an agreement is usually an observable, contractually verifiable fact.[14] The associated contractual liability, in terms of the amount to pay, could be immediately due, payable at some future date or contingent on some possible event occurring.[15] The concept of a liability proffered currently by the AASB and the IASB Framework differs in that it is more ambiguous and emphasizes the expectation of outflows.[16] This definition is more problematic. It leads to a presumption of what is likely to happen in the future (an unknown element) and what may constitute an economic benefit to the firm (a subjective decision). Criteria for the recognition of liabilities in an entity's periodic financial statements emphasise the probability that a future sacrifice of economic benefits is required and that the amount recorded must be able to be reliably measured.

At times, the courts also consider contingent liabilities in conjunction with insolvency determination, but frequently these are disregarded. Nonetheless, the transcripts of *Sandell v. Porter* and *Expo International v. Chant* suggest that contingent liabilities should be taken into account. New Zealand company law now requires that contingent liabilities be included in the assessment of a company's ability to pay its debts.[17] Ambiguity in liabilities is also evident in the use of accounting "provisions," such as provisions for restructuring that many have suggested are used as a smoothing of earnings mechanism.[18] Restructuring 'is a programme that is planned and controlled by management, and materially changes either: (a) the scope of a business undertaken by an entity; or (b) the manner in which that business is conducted' (AASB137, para.10)—IAS37 equivalent.

Provisions for liabilities associated with environmental factors, such as litigation for environmental remediation, adds a further dimension. The Financial Accounting Standards Committee of the American Accounting Association when commenting on the IASC Exposure Draft E59, Provisions, Contingent Liabilities and Contingent Assets stated:

> [S]uch events and activities are typically firm specific in nature and difficult to assess using general information available from sources other than firms' financial statements . . . the committee believes that accounting for provisions and contingencies under E59 would reduce related uncertainty and enrich the information available to financial statement users (Linsmeier *et al.*, 1998, p.193).[19]

Monetary amounts attributed to liabilities (except contingent liabilities), however, are generally based on agreements; contracts and their details are identifiable. But this is not necessarily the case in relation to assets.

Assets are defined by the Australian professional accounting bodies with regard to *future* economic benefits.[20] The nebulous nature of these definitions of assets and liabilities results in unsupportable and unrealistic financial statement entries when, or if, used to determine an entity's solvent or insolvent state. This has long been a dilemma for interested parties. Hence, re-focus on the cash flow test of insolvency. The following elaborates.

HISTORY OF THE CASH FLOW TEST

The cash flow test 'has been in equity jurisprudence for hundreds of years and is a classical concept of civil law' (Keay, 1995, p.308). Its focus is on sufficiency of money to pay debts. Determining, however, when a debt is due for payment is not always an easy task for the courts, and myriad case law exists on this point.[21] Yet it has been ascertained that '[i]f a company fails the test it means, in effect, that it has insufficient resources available to pay creditors' (Keay, 1995, p.308). Although the cash flow test and balance sheet test are two separate means of assessing an entity's state of solvency, similarities and links between them are demonstrable.[22]

According to Keay (1995), the 1869 decision in *Re European Life Assurance Co.* (1869) L.R. 9Eq. 122 may be said to have employed the use of the balance sheet test. But that judgement also emphasized currently due and payable debt as the primary concern when deliberating on solvency, and this is a cash flow approach. In that case, specified future liabilities were considered extraneous to the issue of whether the company was in fact meeting its debt obligations when due. Similar decisions have been made in subsequent cases, including *Re A Debtor (No.17 of 1966)* [1967] 1 All E.R. 668.

The problem of what debt to examine in deciding an entity's [in]solvency is conceptual. When a court decides to recognise only presently payable debt in the calculation of an entity's financial position, debt to be paid at a future date is effectively ignored, hence treated indifferently. Thus, deciding what debt is payable, or not payable, and at what time payment is due is contestable.[23] For an entity to meet its debt obligations, all debt must be managed, and that entails a continual review of its financial state to ensure sufficient funds are available to meet those required payments when due. That is, all debt must eventually be paid or else forgiven.[24]

Where a business has committed itself to *bona fide* debt contracts that are due and payable at some distant time, regardless of the time factor, the obligations are agreed facts and change the financial structure of the enterprise. The crucial point in deliberating solvency (in contrast to liquidity) is not the date the payment is due necessarily, but rather the fact that debt has been incurred and must be paid.[25]

Further, the notion that an entity *must have and be seen to have* sufficient money available to pay its debts and continue business operations was illustrated in *Cornhill Insurance plc v. Improvement Services Ltd.* (1986) 1 W.L.R. 114. There it was held that the plaintiff could present a winding-up petition with respect to failure to pay a due debt even though the petition contained no evidence of insolvency, because the defendant, a large public company, ignored repeated demands for payment of the agreed debt by the plaintiff's solicitors. Those case circumstances indicate that a business entity cannot incur debt in the normal course of its business and then ignore its obligation to pay that debt.[26] Besides, unless a prior agreement exists between the parties, creditors may not have the patience or willingness to wait for payment. Changing business and environmental circumstances could mean that creditors require payment due to them earlier than initially agreed.[27] Such a situation could then alter the due date for payment of debts.

This brief review, confirmed by a detailed consideration in Mescher (1996) and Margret (2002), serves to illustrate some of the difficulties facing courts in deciding what debt is relevant to a test of insolvency. Debts are short-term and/or long-term obligations that require payment. That payment may be currently due or payable at some time in the future, or payment may be contingent on some predicted or unknown event occurring. These are identifiable monetary amounts. Bentley (1911, p.22) stated that 'the liabilities of a business include all debts owed by it, and such other obligations as it is legally liable for.'

Such responsibilities may at any time impinge on an entity's state of solvency but may not necessarily affect its liquidity position. Short-term funds may be readily accessible to pay debt due in the immediate sense (liquidity), while the financial capacity to cover present and future debt commitments remains questionable or appears non-existent. The cash flow test is meaningful in deliberations on liquidity, but its degree of usefulness in cases of insolvency remains contestable. As Loftus and Miller (2000, p.35) stated:

> A primary concern of many users of a financial report is the ability of the reporting entity to survive [and that implies an ability to pay present *and* future debts]. Accordingly, [it would seem an imperative that] financial reports should help users to identify both insolvent entities and those still solvent but experiencing financial distress [liquidity crises].

The balance sheet, which presents a business's assets, liabilities and resulting equity, arguably is the main source of information for users about the financial state of the business and, hence, its ability to survive.[28] Clearly, the accounting process used to recognise and report an entity's assets and liabilities will affect the financial information subsequently reported in that financial statement. The following discussion considers the sort of financial details users are likely to view in a balance sheet as opposed to those details that are likely to inform them on financial matters—given the use of extant accounting methods.

SOLVENCY: FINANCIAL FACTS OR CONJECTURES

The financial representation of items in the balance sheet is based on the assumption that the entity is a going concern and that the business will continue its operations, in the same style, into the future.[29] This assumption is likely independent of financial facts with regard to those elements. In the academic accounting literature, much has been written on the notion of a firm as a going concern, but authors such as Storey (1959), Chambers (1966), Fremgen (1968), Sterling (1968) and Yu (1971) have specifically questioned conventional wisdom in accepting the idea of a going concern as an untested assumption underlying practice.[30]

This notion, of an entity as a going concern, is the rationale for numerous accounting procedures, resulting in spreading costs over multiple accounting periods and representing assets periodically by unamortised costs that have no external monetary referent. This process can lead to some absurd results. Products of such cost allocations do not necessarily relate to any real-world referent; they are not indicative of a business's solvency, debt-paying ability or general purchasing power. Yet, it is these real-world characteristics that determine whether a business has the financial capacity to continue trading. As Fremgen (1968, p.656) stated, '[t]he going concern concept may be a valid description of the accounting entity, if it is justified by evidence in the particular case but not if it is offered as an untested general assumption.'

If the basis on which financial statements are compiled is incorrect, then it may be argued that the statements in their entirety are also incorrect. At times the conventional balance sheet lists assets at historic cost, replacement cost, director' or expert's revaluation or a combination of these or other valuations. In fact, conceptual frameworks around the world endorse this practice (see AASB Framework, paras.99–101).[31] Depreciation by formula of some of an entity's assets is required in current accounting practice.[32] This approach allocates a proportion of the assets' initial cost over the deemed useful life of the assets, so periodically reducing the recorded amount in the balance sheet.[33] Such carrying amount of assets also includes any amount deemed to be accumulated impairment losses.[34] However, if the depreciated item is actually appreciating in current monetary terms within the asset's normal market (see Chambers, 1966; Sterling, 1970), this change is not recognized unless the business considers a revaluation of a class of its assets, and then the revaluation may or may not relate to current market values.[35]

These factors add to previous reservations that the balance sheet test of insolvency in its current form is inadequate, mainly because too many accounting numbers are discretionary. Of course such reservations are not new.[36] As Gilman (1939, p.245) contended, 'many of the accounting errors that have been made by the courts, lawyers, economists and business men have been due to their failure to realize the fictional element in accounting conventions.' Canning (1929, p.11) made similar observations some ten years earlier.[37]

The survival of a business entity depends on its financial capacity to trade and its ability to respond in a timely manner to consumer demands, industry competition, technological improvements and other environmental changes. McCracken's (1948, p.28) observations apply equally today:

> [T]he chief concern of the successful businessman is that of watching daily the moves of his competitors and the possible or prospective changes in mood or habit of prospective customers. Every new move made by a competitor or customer makes imperative some new move or considered adjustment in his own business to meet the new contingency.

To this end, evidence, rather than assumptions, of financial capacity to meet debt obligations would at least provide some assurance of an entity's financial solvency and its ability to continue in business. Vickers (1981, p.174) also supported the necessity for continual change in managing a business when he stated, 'the firm today is not the same firm as it was last year. . . . Firms change their technologies, factor intensities, operating structures, financing mix, market penetration, product outputs, activity diversification, and expansion policies.' Conventionally prepared financial statements may be accurately compiled as per guidelines set by the accounting profession and law in the form of accounting standards, but it is doubtful whether they provide evidence that a business entity is solvent or insolvent.

The use of GAAP ensures financial statements include a mixture of monetary estimates, speculations, arbitrary allocations and operating outcomes derived by method. They do not provide up-to-date financial facts on an entity's financial capacity to pay its debts and continue to conduct its business. Financial desiderata such as dated solvency, dated debt to equity relations and dated rates of return all contribute in the analysis of an entity's potential to survive as a going concern.[38] These are effectively ignored in traditional financial accounts. Jones (1993, p.135) stated, '[t]he financial statements are, of course, prepared for the shareholders . . . [but he continued] this argument does not help the court when considering whether or not a company is insolvent.' Seemingly, conventional financial statements may not help shareholders in deliberations on [in]solvency—mainly because most elements therein have no external monetary referent.

Of concern, then, is the extent to which courts may depend on, or consider, the financial data contained in conventionally prepared accounting statements of an entity's financial worth, particularly when ascertaining conditions of insolvency. The previous discussion on the definition of assets and liabilities as well as the above discourse on the elements of financial statements based on GAAP suggest that the courts' use of these details in tests of insolvency be examined. Analysis follows on how various jurisdictions have interpreted insolvency.[39]

FINANCIAL TESTS OF INSOLVENCY BY AUSTRALIAN AND OVERSEAS COURTS

Numerous legal cases in Australia and overseas illustrate problems that courts have encountered when dealing with issues of insolvency. Examining such cases can show whether the courts state or imply dissatisfaction with the cash flow test and balance sheet test of insolvency. Also, it may suggest a model for providing financial information that would be more appropriate in assessing an entity's ability to pay its debt when due and payable.

According to Goode (1990, p.39):

> In most cases there is little or no doubt as to a company's insolvency, but in marginal situations the basis of valuation and the assessment of values upon that basis can be crucial. Here lie the seeds of a potentially difficult problem. For the purposes of insolvency legislation the court has to be able to decide whether on a balance of probabilities a particular company is or was at a particular time unable to pay its debts.

Essentially, the role of accounting is crucial in determining the appropriateness of 'the basis of [financial] valuation and the assessment of [financial] values.' Other considerations relevant to particular case details are matters for the courts to decide.

Table 2.1 depicts areas of interest that have been stressed by the courts and highlights similarities among the cases.[40] Although many factors may be considered, the cases are specifically relevant to the insolvency test that determines whether the entity is able to pay its debts as and when they become due and payable.

Table 2.1 Financial Tests of Insolvency

	Specific Debt or Timing	*Consider: All Assets &/or Debt*	*Ability to Pay Debt When Due*	*Focus on Assets/ Liabilities*	*Pay Debt & Stay a Going Concern*	*Realizable Assets*
Rees v. Bank of N.S.W. (1964) 111 C.L.R.		*	*	*		*
Sandell v. Porter (1966) 115 C.L.R.		*	*	*	*	
Timbatec Pty. Ltd. (1974) 24 F.L.R.		*	*	*	*	
Aust. Co-op Develop-ment society (1977) QD.R66			*			
Dunn v. Shapow-loff (1978) 2 N.S.W. L.R.235		*	*	*		*
Minion v. Graystone (1986) 1 QD.R66	*		*			

Note. This table is a brief review of legal criteria from selected twentieth-century cases.
Source. Characteristics of individual cases extracted from case references.

Clearly the courts have concentrated particularly on assets, liabilities and an ability to pay debt when due. These considerations gained momentum especially during the latter half of the twentieth century. This is evident in more recent legal cases where arguably the courts test an entity's state of solvency using both the elements of a cash flow and a balance sheet test of insolvency. An example is *Leslie & Anor v. Howship Holdings Pty.Ltd.* (1997) 133FCA, 459 (at p.466) where proceedings focussed on whether Howship would be wound up in insolvency due to the entity's failure to comply with a creditor's demand for payment (at p.465).[41]

Howship's failure to pay led to a presumption of insolvency, and the onus fell on Howship to show otherwise. Howship was found to be solvent. In the process, unaudited financial statements for the years ended June 30, 1994, 1995 and 1996 were used in evidence as well as a profit and loss statement for the six-month period ending December 31, 1996, and a balance sheet as at December 31, 1996. A cash flow chart was also constructed to reflect Howship's financial position as at January 17, 1997. The court considered the chart 'extremely helpful in assessing whether Howship [had] discharged the burden of establishing that it [was] solvent' (at p.473).[42] It was the cash flow chart that mainly suggested Howship was able to pay its debts when they fell due 'at least in the short term' (at p.473). In addition, cash flow charts were used to try to establish the financial position of Howship into the future considering the debt it had and would incur and its obligation to pay that debt. The asset and liability valuations used in the chart were at 'Estimated Real Value [for] January 97' rather than recorded figures in the entity's financial accounts (at p.473).

In this regard, a crucial observation was made by Loftus and Miller (2000, p.105):

> Users need information on the relative liquidity of the assets (their nature and function in the entity's activities including whether they are held to increase financial flexibility or for use and recovery in the normal course of operations, and the rate at which specific types of assets turn over). The relative proportion of debt (liabilities) in the capital structure is important as the lower the reliance on debt, other things being equal, the lower the risk of insolvency (through an inability to pay interest or other amounts falling due) and the greater the capacity to restore a weak cash condition by additional borrowing. Not only is the extent of the debt in the capital structure important but the timing of debt's required payment (its relative liquidity) is also important. A high proportion of debt with a near due date may result in insolvency, particularly if the entity's assets are relatively illiquid and economic conditions result in a shortfall in cash flow from operating activities.

In the case of Howship Holdings, J. Sackville found:

> [C]learly [Howship is] a company with substantial assets which, on the evidence, exceed its liabilities. However, its principal assets are in the form of land holdings which the company's directors wish to develop for sale. There is [however] no immediate prospect of the land being sold (at p.476).

This implies recourse to the elements of a balance sheet test of insolvency. The court also considered the entity's history of raising finance through loans (presumably dependent on asset collateral) to meet its commitments along with the evidence that its assets were greater than its liabilities. This is an example of combining the concepts of both the cash flow and balance sheet tests of insolvency when examining financial credibility.

Sackville determined that it was probable Howship would be able to pay all its expenses when due, at least until the end of that current financial year, but he concluded:

> This, of course, is not to say that the company's future is secure. The evidence suggests that its financial position is precarious and that further delays in developing the land that constitutes its principal asset may well result in the failure of the company. But the question is not whether the company will survive for the foreseeable future. It is whether the company has discharged the burden of showing that it can pay all of its debts as and when they become due and payable (atp.476).

Supporting the claim made previously that emphasis in Australia is primarily on the cash flow test of insolvency,[43] Sackville further remarked, '[i]t follows that the mere fact that the company's assets exceed its liabilities does *not establish* solvency' (at p.465; emphasis added).[44] It is a necessary but not sufficient condition. Nonetheless, it is clear that the balance sheet may be and is used in many cases to establish if an entity's assets exceed its liabilities. So it seems arguable that elements of the cash flow test and the balance sheet test ought to be combined to provide the courts and other interested parties with one more comprehensive financial test. Such a test may be based on a statement of solvency.

Figure 2.1 illustrates primary aspects of both financial tests of insolvency and highlights particular problems that have continued to arise for the courts. As shown the courts consider the extenuating circumstances of each case.[45] Analysis presented here, however, focuses only on the concept, definition and identification of an entity's assets, liabilities and its financial capacity to pay its debts.

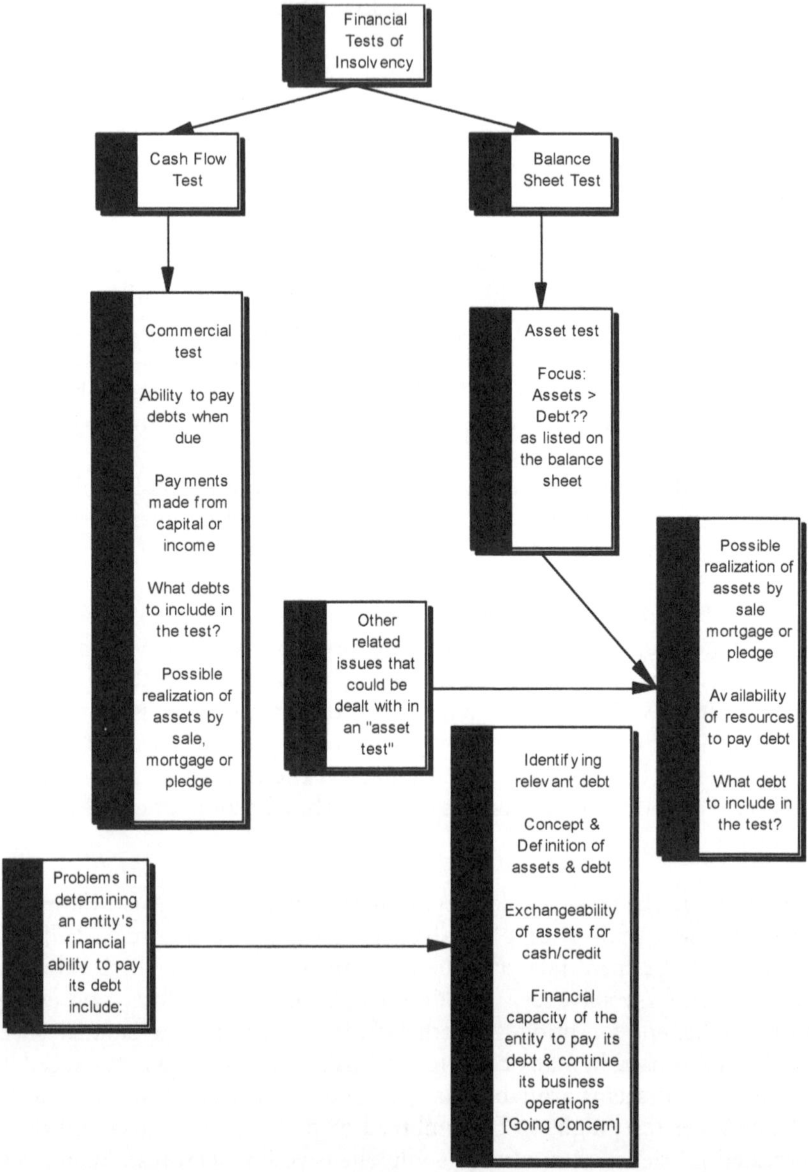

Figure 2.1 The cash flow and the balance sheet tests of insolvency.

Cases That Illustrate the Cash Flow Test of Insolvency

The following cases are similar in that the main concern is to ascertain the entity's ability to pay its debts. The situations are different. They cover circumstances such as the financial effect on the entity when payment of debt is made from capital, when dividend payments are made from capital and when the inability of an entity to pay its debt is due to a non-financial event that restricted the entity's ability to trade. The link between the cases is the use of the commercial, or cash flow, test of insolvency.

In Jones and Aiken (1994, pp.196–227), the significance of identifying corporate profit and the methods used to determine profit were discussed with emphasis on an entity's ability to pay dividends and whether payment was made from surplus funds or capital. Stressing accounting issues like the categorisation of assets, liabilities and their valuation to be included in the balance sheet when ascertaining corporate profit,[46] they highlighted two main concepts of profit. For instance, one method to determine an entity's profit or loss is to calculate the difference between total revenues less all expenses. In contrast, emphasis may be placed on the surplus of assets to liabilities, a balance sheet approach.

The concept of distributable profit or surplus funds is paramount in deciding an entity's ability to pay its debt, its dividends and its financial capacity to continue in business. Jones and Aiken (1994, p.201) remarked, '[t]he balance sheet is arguably a more significant document than the profit and loss account depending on the concept of profit accepted.' To decide what constitutes a relevant concept of profit, or surplus funds, requires recourse to the prevailing circumstances. In any test of insolvency, an entity's capacity to access cash, however, is always paramount. This is arguably a view of total assets over total liabilities, valued with regard to their monetary equivalent at a particular point in time.

In *Re Oxford Benefit Building and Investment Society* (1886) 35 L.R. Ch.502, the entity conducted much of its business by lending money to builders on mortgages. It was held:

> [T]hat the directors having treated estimated profits as realized profits, and having in fact paid dividends out of capital, on the chance that sufficient profits might be made, were jointly and severally liable, as upon a breach of trust, to repay, and must repay, the sums improperly paid as dividends (at p.146).

Technically, conventional accounting practice and the ACA, s254T do not permit dividends to be paid out of capital to safeguard the basic capital structure of the business entity. Yet, paying debts incurred in the ordinary course of business out of capital could have a more damaging effect on the financial structure of the entity. It is evident from examples to follow that legal thought concentrates on many aspects of the cases brought to trial; but in such situations, accounting remains primarily concerned with the financial circumstances of business and how best to determine and report on that financial state.

Other nineteenth- and early twentieth-century cases that emphasise the necessity to determine an entity's ability to pay debts when due include *Parker v. Gossage* (1835) 2 C.M. & R.617;150 E.R. 262 and *London & Counties Assets Co. Ltd. v. Brighton Grand Concert Hall and Picture*

Palace Ltd. (1915) 2 K.B. 493,501. These cases were cited, for example, in *Minion v. Graystone Pty. Ltd.* (1986) 1 Qd.R.157,169 as support for the idea that insolvency means commercial insolvency, an inability to pay debts when due. Nonetheless, a major dilemma remained and that was deciding what debts to consider relevant to the issue of insolvency.

L. J. Buckley in *London & Counties Assets Co. Ltd. v. Brighton Grand Concert Hall & Picture Palace Ltd* cited many authorities[47] with regard to insolvency and that it means an 'inability to pay *certain* debts as they become due' (emphasis added). J. McPherson in *Minion v. Graystone* referred to *Sandell v. Porter* (1966) 115 C.L.R. 666,670 where emphasis was given to utilizing all assets to command cash resources to pay debts when due, which is in accord with the reference to certain debt by L. J. Buckley and a selective view of liabilities. His Honour, J. McPherson, stated, '[f]or my part, I am not persuaded that later variation of detail have either added much or detracted from the original basic proposition that insolvency exists where a debtor is not able to pay his debts as they fall due' (at p.157). This opinion implies that the cash flow test of insolvency is adequate because of its emphasis on an entity's ability to pay its debts when due. However, as previously discussed, this disregards the entity's fundamental obligation to pay all the debt it has incurred.

The phrase 'ability to pay debts as they fall due and payable' draws attention to both the *time* when payment of debt is due and the entity's actual *ability* to repay its debt. In the previous cases, the court's unease centered mainly on the entity's payment of debt when due. But in *Sandell v. Porter*,[48] for instance, one issue was that all assets be utilized as a means of raising cash to pay the entity's debts, and emphasis was given to the financial capacity of the business to pay *all its debts*.

Later in *Re Australian Co-Operative Development Society* (1977) Qd. R66, at 79; (1976) 2 A.C.L.R 207,218, it was held that solvency was proved due to the respondents' ability to pay its debts at the relevant time. The applicant's claim was based on s122 of the Bankruptcy Act 1966 (Cth), which specifically refers to 'a person who is unable to pay his debts as they become due.' The Society paid its debts out of capital, but this was not considered to be of significance; the main point of concern was that payment was made and that payment was made in a timely fashion. Senior counsel for the respondent stated:

> [T]hat on the evidence the Society was at all material times in fact paying its debts with its own money as they fell due, so that it cannot be said that it was "unable" to do this. It was, no doubt, using capital (depositors' subscriptions) to make payments, but s122 does not make ability to pay creditors out of revenue the test. It seems tolerably clear—having regard to the Society's latest failure—that for some time

(including the period under consideration) the Society invested other capital improvidently and unwisely (at p.78).

In such a situation, many accounting theorists would argue that payments out of capital erode an entity's financial state and that this would in turn adversely affect its long-term financial capacity to trade. Clearly, there are different conceptual interpretations of what constitutes a surplus or available funds for an entity to pay dividends or its debts. Legal opinion in the *Re Australian Co-Operative* relied not so much on that debts were paid out of capital but rather that they were paid when due. The emphasis in the cash flow test is on the entity's ability to pay its debts when they are due and not necessarily that the entity will continue to operate into the future. This point is disputed here.

J. Dunn determined that even though the Society was actually using capital to pay its debts, this did not mean it was unable to pay its debts. The nature of its business was borrowing and an entity 'whose business is borrowing seems to me to be in a category of its own. In such a case, money which is borrowed cannot realistically be regarded as having been borrowed in order to stave off creditors' (at p.79).[49] The court applied the commercial test of insolvency to determine ability to pay debts incurred. Depositor's subscriptions were considered monetary loans (liabilities) to the Society, used by the Society in order to conduct business, make money (assets) and increase the rate of return to investors. The investigation focused on the immediate financial ability of the entity to pay its debts and not on its financial capacity to continue to pay debts and operate into the future.

However, arguably accounting reports should concentrate on determining whether the entity has the financial ability to conduct its business and still keep its capital intact—an essential feature of any going concern.[50] Critically, an entity is obligated to pay depositors all that is owed to them when due or perhaps earlier on their demand (see *Minion v. Graystone* below). In order to continue its business activities, the entity must have the money or access to money sufficient to meet its commitments and still be able to pay its debts. The role of accounting is to provide these financial details to assist decision-makers. Yet this has not always been achieved.[51] 'Conventional accounting practices complying with the prescribed Standards have been shown . . . to have contributed to masking impending failure, exacerbated losses to creditors and shareholders and provided regulators with a recurring dilemma' (Clarke *et al.*, 2003, p.329).

In *Minion v. Graystone Pty. Ltd.* (1986) 1 Qd.R. 157,169, it was held that 'the expression "becoming insolvent" was prima facie to be taken as meaning an inability to pay debts as and when they fell due, not the doing of something which caused . . . [an inability] to trade without restriction' (at p.157). The respondent had been unable to complete a contractual arrangement because property required to do so had been seized by another party. The entity's inability to complete the contractual arrangement altered its financial state and its ability to pay debt. Judgement in this case held that inability to pay debt was only part of the requirement to determine insolvency; another consideration was the length of time creditors were willing to wait for payment that was due.

Accounting is a communication system with social and organizational functions. Hence, there is a responsibility that the process provides users of accounting statements with financial facts that relate to the type of report issues; for example, an entity's cash flow, ledger account balances, production capacity, cost of production, environmental responsibilities, periodic accounting profit for taxation or internal management purposes, solvency or financial position. Although the cash flow test of insolvency extends the concept of the balance sheet test, it seems more precisely to be a test of liquidity. In contrast, the balance sheet test is implemented within a context of data based on a conventionally prepared general purpose financial statement that does not contain contemporary financial facts.

It is questionable, then, whether this accounting report, prepared using prescriptive formulae and discretionary valuations, can serve usefully the purpose of the judiciary or any interested party when determining an entity's state of solvency. This may be a reason why Australian courts, at least, implement the cash flow test of insolvency and reject the balance sheet approach.

The major work of Canning (1929) detailed a critical analysis of accounting theory and conventional accounting practice. Drawing on the work of Irving Fisher, Canning's forward-looking approach emphasised concepts of economics to link the two disciplines. The significance of this was detailed by Zeff (2000). Tweedie and Whittington (1984, p.25) proffered:

> [Canning's] critique of contemporary accounting practice . . . offered alternatives which were designed to bring the accountant's practices more in line with the economist's forward-looking methods of valuation . . . [and that Canning observed, that accountants were] fully aware of the difference between dollar accounting and a conceivable purchasing power accounting, and would prefer, just as economists do, a purchasing power accounting (p.196).[52]

Canning's position was that an entity's financial position as disclosed in the balance sheet would specify its financial capacity to procure future funds with due regard to its dated valued assets. As Canning (1929, p.20) stated, 'to include in the statements, e.g., the balance sheet, mere expectancies, would be to introduce items the value of which is highly speculative among items the value of which can be measured with much greater reliability.' Zeff (2000, p.21) explained that Canning was interested 'in applying theories of capital and price so that accounting information would yield a more rational basis for business decisions.'

The following cases indicate a balance sheet test of an entity's state of [in]solvency. A primary concern is shown to be the concept and definition of assets and liabilities represented in the balance sheet. Further noted are the various adjustments necessary to those reported details in order that they more readily determine factual financial circumstances.

CASES TO ILLUSTRATE THE COURTS USE OF THE BALANCE SHEET IN FINANCIAL TESTS OF INSOLVENCY

The basic nature of the balance sheet and the fundamental characteristics of assets listed in the balance sheet affect the extent to which those assets are able to assist in determining an entity's purchasing power, its debt-paying ability. Drawing on the notion of severability mentioned earlier in this chapter, it is stressed that the exchangeability of an asset is relevant under such circumstances.

Cases That Imply a Balance Sheet Approach to Testing Insolvency

The following cases reveal the importance of understanding Shackle's notion of "fortune"—more specifically of the necessity for a business entity to have and *have access to* cash, sufficient to cover its accumulated debt obligations, in order to be considered and in essence to be solvent.

In *Rees v. Bank of New South Wales* (1964) 111 C.L.R. 210, *Bank of Australasia v. Hall* (1907) 4 C.L.R. was cited in relation to the meaning of the phrase 'inability to pay debts as they become due' (at pp.1514, 1528,1543). At that time, barrister W. B. Campbell stressed that '[t]he phrase "as they become due" does not mean that simply because a man cannot put his hand on ready cash the day the debts fall due, he is insolvent'(at p.216). Moreover, in *Sandell v. Porter* (1966) 115 C.L.R. 666, opinion was that '[i]t is the debtor's inability, utilizing such cash resources as he has or can command through the use of his assets, to meet his debts as they fall due which indicates insolvency' (at p.670). C. J. Barwick stressed, 'It is quite true that a trader, to remain solvent, does not need to have ready cash by him to cover his commitments as they fall for payment, and that in determining whether he can pay his debts as they become due regard must be had to his realizable assets' (at p.218). The accent placed on realizable assets in *Re D'Onofrio* (1983) 76 F.L.R. 136 implied properties with a monetary equivalent, marketable character.

Such ideas stress the concept of severability and exchangeability in defining assets. Other cases follow that also support this view. The cases emphasise that it is tangible assets that are also readily realizable; in other words, marketable assets more precisely form part of a *bona fide* test of insolvency.

In *Re Timbatec Pty.Ltd.* [1974] 24 F.L.R., the company was held to be hopelessly insolvent from a certain date because it was unable to pay its debts from its own money. The mix of assets and liabilities as listed on the company's balance sheet were considered in this judgement. The court determined that the company was under-capitalized from its inception and had always carried an inadequate liquidity position. The decision of C. J. Barwick in *Sandell v. Porter* was applied, in that the court extended the cash flow test of insolvency to include realization of assets by sale, mortgage or pledge in order to determine capacity to pay debts when due. Although the courts specifically relate this move to a cash flow test of insolvency, the further consideration of realizable assets includes the concept of a balance sheet approach.

A further point made in the case was that a business should be able to continue as a going concern after meeting its debt obligations. C. J. Barwick stated that this 'test as regards ready realization of cash resources has regard, as I understand it, to the debtor who is conducting a business, and is applying his cash resources, and selling or mortgaging assets readily available to inflate these resources, while continuing his business' (at p.36). This idea asserts that a business will, or should, utilize all its available resources to survive in a competitive commercial environment as a going concern.

The reference above by C. J. Barwick to 'assets readily available' is worth considering in some depth because not all assets on the balance sheet are readily available or available at all to assist in payment of debt. In *Re Timbatec Pty. Ltd.*, other authorities were cited that show further complications. For instance, in *Rees v Bank of New South Wales* (1964) 111 C.L.R. 210, where C. J. Barwick 'emphasized that stock-in-trade in that case was clearly not an asset which was available to be realized to meet current debts except in the ordinary course of the company's business, a course which had proved itself inadequate' (at p.218) due to the company's insolvent state.

In *Dunn v. Shapowloff* (1978) 2 N.S.W. L.R.235, an officer of the company knowingly contracted more debt when the company was apparently unable to pay the debt it had already accumulated. This indicates a management problem and at least two separate accounting issues: first, whether the company's assets were in fact greater than its liabilities, in a monetary sense; and second, whether management was privy to this financial information and, if so, why it was unable to pay its debts. J. Reynolds remarked, 'The figures in the balance sheet were not a compelling guide to realisable figures' (at p.241). Further, the court discussed the effect of contingent liabilities to the extent, for this entity, of a possible future income tax obligation. The balance sheet and profit and loss statements were submitted as evidence, and it was decided that with an adjustment for the contingent debt and valuation of some shares, company assets would exceed its liabilities. J. Mahoney alleged:

> The fact that, e.g., the company's obligations, as to payment or otherwise, are contingent, does not, in my opinion, alter the position. If this be so, then the fact that, as the result of the contingency or otherwise, the debt never falls due for payment, does not mean that there was no contracting of it (at p.243).

It seems, at least in this case, that the court's preference was for the inclusion of all debt when deciding the entity's financial ability to pay. So the term *ability to pay* would then relate to the amount of money held by the entity, its access to money in the short and long term and its capacity to continue trading into the future. Perhaps if management had this information or had been given this information earlier, the financial dilemma may have been avoided.

CORPORATIONS' LEGISLATION AND CORPORATE SOLVENCY

Corporations' legislation around the world shares similar concerns, including the need to know whether an entity's asset accumulation is greater than its total liabilities and whether this knowledge is readily available. Loftus and Miller (2000, pp.23–58) explore this topic, noting that financial flexibility directly relates to the concept of solvency.[53] Seemingly the problem for countries, as well as for business entities, with regard to solvency is how best to determine assets, liabilities and the residual equity of an entity.

Figure 2.2 illustrates specific issues dealt with by courts in the US, UK, Canada, Australia and New Zealand when determining an entity's state of solvency, and it identifies relevant sections of the corporations' law of these countries. It shows that features emphasized in tests of solvency are similar in all countries.

Figure 2.2 refers to sections of law in the Uniform Fraudulent Transfer Act (UFTA), Bankruptcy Reform Act (BRA), New York Business Corporations Law (NYBCL) and Californian Corporations Code (CCC), the British Insolvency Act (BIA), Canada's Bankruptcy and Insolvency Act, the Australian *Corporations Act* (2001) and the New Zealand Companies Act (NZCA). Duns (2000) examined in more detail the insolvency legislation in the US, UK, Canada and Australia. A comprehensive discussion on New Zealand legislation is provided by Loftus and Miller (1996).

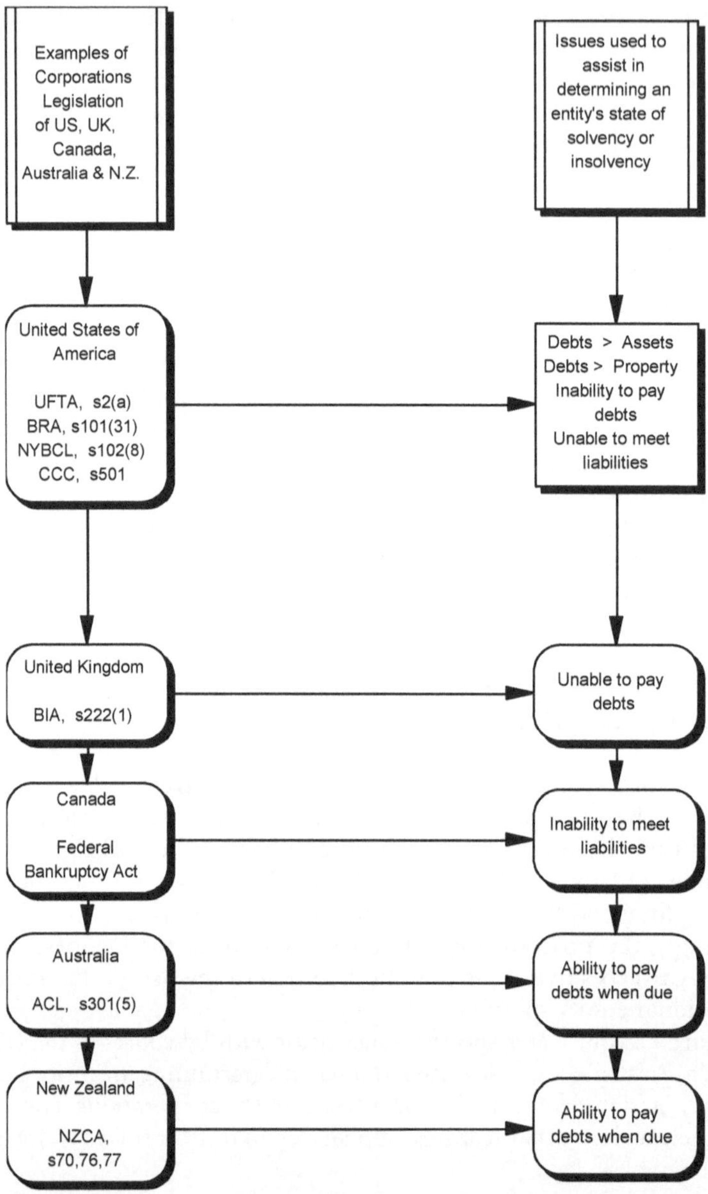

Figure 2.2 Legal requirements on issues of solvency. A concentrated view of statutory requirements of the US, UK, Canada, Australia and New Zealand.

In addition to specific areas of concern for accounting and law, there are a number of overlapping issues with regard to calculating and finally determining the extent of an entity's solvent or insolvent position. Figure 2.3 highlights and summarises these issues.

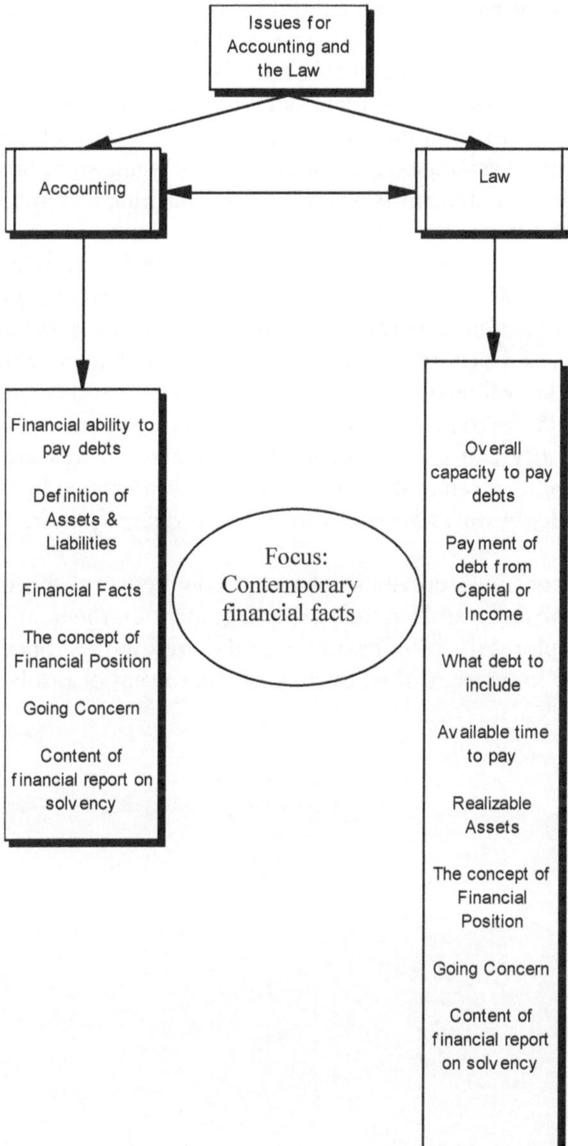

Figure 2.3 Calculating solvency—issues for accounting and the law.

CONCLUSION

This chapter investigated the use of conventional accounting reports in financial tests of insolvency. Two tests—the "cash flow" and the "balance sheet" tests—were examined. The balance sheet test of insolvency, which compares an entity's reported assets to its reported liabilities, has the potential to be a sound financial test of insolvency but not in its current form, primarily because of the vagaries of the GAAP definition of assets and the monetary equivalents ascribed to them in financial statements. In contrast, the cash flow test of insolvency has been shown to be currently better, mainly due to its emphasis on ascertaining the current market worth of assets and the exchangeability of assets. It is suggested, however, that only one financial statement is necessary to determine an entity's financial state and its ability to pay its debts at any point in time.

Two main premises were examined. The first proposed that a financial statement used to determine an entity's solvent or insolvent state should be compiled with particular regard to the definition and measurement of the elements contained therein. Specifically, the notion of assets with a current realizable market value—in an active general market—was considered necessary if assets were to be legitimately aggregated for purposes of assessing whether an entity can extinguish its debt. Second, it was argued that a financial test of insolvency should include all debt incurred by the entity in the course of its business activities in order to quantify more precisely its financial state.

Chapter 3 continues previous debate on how best to determine an entity's financial position and extends prior argument on the quantification of solvency. It explores the responsibilities and duties of directors with special regard to their knowledge of when an entity is solvent or insolvent.

3 Solvency and the Duty of Company Directors

'To observe, to reason and to report with care is nothing more than common sense applied to common experience' (Chambers, 2000, p.330).

THE DUTY OF DIRECTORS

The role of company directors in Australia and overseas is becoming increasingly more complex. This position is exacerbated especially by the changing structure of corporate groups[1] and how these changes create increased responsibilities for company directors to account financially for, and control, organizations. This chapter extends the argument in Chapter 2. It further examines issues related to financial information and the quality of the same contained in accounting reports albeit from a different perspective.

Chapter 2 investigated the use of conventional accounting reports in financial tests of [in]solvency. Herein, the responsibilities and duties of directors generally, but especially with regard to their knowledge of when an entity is solvent or insolvent, are examined.

Directors, in fact all corporate officers, have legal and ethical obligations to their business entity and to its stakeholders. This necessitates that they know exactly what their duty entails. The Corporate Law Economic Reform Program (CLERP) (particularly CLERP9 and the related CLERP 9 Bill, 2003) refers to the level of tort, debt obligations, responsibilities for financial accounts and other factors of control as entailing corporate governance. CLERP 9 supports the emphasis more apparent after further unexpected collapses like HIH in Australia and Enron in the US, on truth in financial reports. Notably, '[i]f any deficiencies in accounting standards have a general, unintended result that compliance with the standard would not result in a true and fair view, the appropriate response would be reform of the standard' (CLERP9, para.16).[2]

Also, the Joint Committee on Public Accounts and Audit (JCPAA) recommended that, '[t]he Financial Reporting Council develop a set of corporate governance standards, which would be given legislative backing in the *Corporation's Act 2001*' (2002, p.6). This idea is of concern and gains significance in the wake of the introduction of International Accounting Standards (IAS) in Australia from January 2005.[3] Furthermore, the Australian Securities Exchange (ASX)—Corporate Governance Council—under their guidelines released in March 2003, required that the true and fair view of an entity be presented in that entity's financial statements to '[s]afeguard integrity in financial reporting' (recommendation 4.1, principle 4). The eight principles are referred to throughout this work:

ASX Corporate Governance Council's Principles of Good Corporate Governance

- Principle 1: Lay solid foundation for management and oversight
- Principle 2: Structure the board to add value
- Principle 3: Promote ethical and responsible decision-making
- Principle 4: Safeguard integrity in financial reporting
- Principle 5: Make timely and balanced disclosure
- Principle 6: Respect the rights of shareholders
- Principle 7: Recognise and manage risks
- Principle 8: Remunerate fairly and responsibly

To this end, directors are increasingly being held more accountable for their actions, or non-action, relating to business and its operations. Solvency cases like Enron and WorldCom in the US and HIH, One.Tel and Water Wheel in Australia are seminal examples. As well, penalties imposed by the law have become more severe. Organizational and social duties of company directors have changed over time, and society's demands on them have been extended—recently in the guise of corporate governance.[4] This is notwithstanding the recognition by regulators that determining solvency at any time is difficult—just as they recognise difficulties in determining a true and fair view of an entity's financial state of affairs.

Hence, this chapter examines the type of financial information likely to assist directors in satisfying their apparently ever-increasing governance obligations. The main purpose is to emphasize that the quantification of solvency, indeed an entity's financial position, is essential information to (i) assist directors to organise business activities, and (ii) enable directors to meet their requirements under the Act. In addition, it will be shown that there are other aspects of accountability to consider.[5]

Directors perform multiple tasks.[6] They are strategists and policy makers who observe and form opinions on the physical and financial capacity of a business's management and control systems. Shareholders, creditors and other external parties have the right to seek from directors considered answers to business related questions at various times. Clearly, directors rely, to some extent, on information given to them by other corporate officers who are perhaps not quite as visible to shareholders. Hence, directors should be aware of and so have some involvement in the processes used to accumulate and compile data for preparing financial reports on the results of business activities. The argument of being unskilled in financial affairs, or unaware of actual financial circumstances, is not (and perhaps never was) a legitimate defence for directors.[7]

Directors' responsibilities include knowing that the entity under their governance is able financially to continue operating and to continue to pursue its business opportunities. Clearly they should be able to rely on accounting reports for this information. Accordingly, '[t]he objective of financial reports is to provide information about the financial position, financial performance and cash flows of an entity that is useful to a wide range of users in making economic decisions' (AASB Framework, para.12). In this book, the view that conventionally prepared financial statements enable directors to discharge their accountability obligations effectively is contested.

With reference to the Australian *Corporations Act 2001*, s292(1), '[a] financial report and a directors' report must be prepared for each financial year,' and s295(4)(c) stipulates that directors make a declaration that 'whether, in the directors' opinion, there are reasonable grounds to believe that the company, registered scheme or disclosing entity will be able to pay its debts as and when they become due and payable.' Augmenting this, s299 and s300 specify the details to be included in the annual directors' report on the operations and activities of the business as well as specific details on, for example, dividends, share issues and insurance premiums. The *Corporations Act 2001*, s588 provides defences and penalties where breaches of the provisions occur, but s588G of Pt 5.7B specifically demands that directors prevent insolvent trading.

Moreover and with further regard to the concept of an entity's financial position and performance and embracing recent changes to company law, it *is* still required, in Australia, that '[t]he financial statements and notes for a financial year must give a true and fair view' (*Corporations Act 2001*, s297(a) and (b)), and this requirement encompasses consolidated financial statements. Recently, the Royal Commissioner's report into the demise of HIH Insurance Ltd. stressed the necessity for published financial statements to heed the true and fair override in corporations' law.[8] Legislation provides some assistance, some relief, for directors as in s588, but how directors are to meet the demands of the legislature is problematic.

In the case of determining an entity's solvency, particularly with respect to a consolidated corporate group, the information directors require to comply with the statutes may simply not be readily available to them. In fact the JCPAA *Report 391* (2002, para.3.67, p.81) considered that, 'in light of the deficiencies in [accounting] standards . . . compliance with accounting standards cannot guarantee that overall financial statements will reflect a true and fair position' as the statutes mandate.[9] This point is pursued and examined in later chapters, where there is consideration of what is meant by corporate group solvency (or insolvency) and how it can possibly be determined using conventional financial statements.

Four sections follow. The first section defines the notion of a company director and discusses the director's fundamental role in business. In the second section, an overview of corporations' legislation in common law countries such as the US, Great Britain (UK), Canada and Australia follow to enable one to compare certain legislative requirements related to company accounts and directors' duties from each country. Differences among countries are highlighted in order to identify diversity or similarities that may exist in practice. Section three examines details of selected legal cases to explore penalties imposed on directors for circumstances related to corporate governance issues. A brief discussion on the benefits of "good" corporate governance rather than "compliance" governance is incorporated into the penultimate section, followed by concluding remarks.

So who is, or may be, deemed at law to be a company director?

COMPANY DIRECTORS

Company directors may be formally appointed to the position or deemed to be in the position because of involvement in the activities of the business.[10] Potentially this poses a problem for those who act in an advisory capacity to the operations of the business, especially when that business is suffering some form of financial distress. Moreover, the role of those who work with the entity from time to time, but otherwise are not an integral part of the internal management team, is contestable. Consider activities such as those provided by financial analysts, bank managers, accountants or other professionals acting as advisors or consultants.

A crucial aspect of a director's work is to ensure that the business entity remains viable in the continuing, ever-changing market environment. Hence, the capacity of a business to adapt to consumer wants, government decree, industry competition and other demands is *a prius* for directors and all corporate 'officers.'[11] Directors have a duty of care to ensure that all corporate officers within the organisation are held accountable for their actions and to do so with regard to maintaining sufficient business risk within operations for a given profitability and growth of the business enterprise.

Logically these aspects require a financial reporting system that renders precise up-to-date financial information to enable the directors to discharge those responsibilities properly, subject to legal and ethical considerations. Consequently, directors are required to be knowledgeable about all aspects of the business they supervise and lead. Such are the constraints of corporate governance, a system of management and control, and one that holds directors accountable for their actions.[12] Nevertheless, as Clarke *et al.* (2003, p.299) recalled, '[n]o sustainable evidence has emerged to the effect that corporate managers' ethical behaviour was less acceptable [in recent times] than that of any other cross-section of the Australian (or UK) community. . . . It is wrong to consider the current problems as new phenomena.'[13]

Case analyses in Chapters 5, 6, and 7 further illustrate the seemingly repetitive circumstances inherent in unexpected corporate collapses through several decades. Notwithstanding all the talk, alterations to accounting standards and deviations in accounting practice over time, there has been minimal change to the reporting system that produces deficient outcomes. One might speculate whether this new-age emphasis on corporate governance ideals will produce a different result.

Directors have, in the past, been required to meet the test of what could reasonably be expected of a person having the knowledge and experience to hold the position of a company director. But during the latter part of the twentieth century, expectations and demands changed, due in part to economic crises like those experienced throughout the 1980s and beyond.[14] Moreover, penalties for inadequate performance of directors have increased in accord with societal pressure arising from the many corporate collapses that occurred throughout the 1960s, 1970s, and 1980s.[15]

Now, with similar unexpected corporate collapses in the 1990s and 2000s, it would appear that company directors are increasingly expected to be pro-active in business affairs and are more likely to suffer severe penalties for non-performance. Nonetheless, regulators are conscious of the fact that directors need an element of freedom to express good business judgement, otherwise commercial decisions may be too conservative and essentially be to the detriment of shareholder wealth.[16] As Wallis (2000, p.17) explained, a worthwhile argument is 'for a little more balance on the basis that a good board [of directors] is required to be more than a policeman watching over management. It is supposed to agree the strategy, to monitor performance, approve investments and ensure risks are managed.' These tasks require a diverse set of skills from directors, with a more hands-on approach to guiding the moves of a corporate body than has been likely in the past.

Particular aspects of the statutory requirements to be satisfied by directors on a national and an international level follow. These include legislative demands that have become increasingly pertinent given the trend towards globalisation of commercial activities during the latter part of the twentieth century and continuing into the twenty-first century.

COMPANY DIRECTORS, THE LAW AND ACCOUNTING

Primarily this section emphasizes the use and meaning of words in the legislation and, as such, draws on phenomenology. Drawing on *Pinner v. Everett* ([1969] 3 All E.R. 257, pp.258, 259), for instance:

> In determining the meaning of any word or phrase in a statute the first question to ask always is, what is the natural and ordinary meaning of that word or phrase in its context in the statute? It is only when that meaning leads to some result which cannot reasonably be supposed to have been the intention of the legislature that it is proper to look for some other possible meaning of the word or phrase.

Chambers (1973a) appositely addressed this in an article seeking to determine the meaning of the corporation legislation's "true and fair view" phrase. More recently, the JCPAA (2002, p.5) sought to 'clarify the relationship between the need for financial statements to comply with accounting standards and provide a true and fair view.'

The use and meaning of words and terms in business communication are shown to be crucial to the continued development of worldwide commercial opportunities. This is especially so because directors and other corporate officers, either willingly or unwillingly, have the capacity to misrepresent the financial state of a business entity due, in part, to the wording of statutes. However, directors need to be ever-flexible and prepared to adapt to ever-changing business circumstances to enable their enterprise to move forward in a dynamic yet socially conscious style.[17]

"Good" corporate governance then may be seen to encourage confidence in market participants and increase the productive, pro-active involvement of directors in business activities.[18] As long as it does not simply become more regulation for directors and other corporate officers to contend with, as in accounting, where 'the push for a formula approach to financial disclosure . . . [p]erversely, . . . reveals a fatal attrition of professional judgment—the greater the regulation, the less reliable accounting has become' (Clarke *et al.*, 2003, p.298). Business can do without any more jargon, trendy words or phrases, blithely complied with as per the regulators dictum.[19] As Clarke *et al.* (2003, p.298) explained:

> Definition of the principles of good practice in corporate governance has entertained analysts of corporate failure even more so in the 2000s than it did in the 1990s. Individuals are to be controlled rather than the system rectified. Scant attention is being given to accounting and auditing as instruments of corporate regulation . . . it is mainly as a side issue to the focus on the allegedly recalcitrant behaviour of accountants and auditors.

Table 3.1 provides a brief overview of words used in the corporations' legislation and/or the Corporations Act of common law countries with regard to the preparation of financial statements. It is evident that areas of country similarity can be drawn from the data. The table serves to compare words and terms used in the statutes of the US, UK, Canada and Australia, specifically with regard to the responsibilities, duty and accountability of directors.

Table 3.1 reveals the degree of flexibility—albeit recently reduced especially after the *Sarbanes-Oxley Act 2002* in the US—that corporations' legislation tends generally to provide for corporate decision-makers. For instance, British Companies Legislation (BCL) appears more regulatory-based and demanding of directors than its counterpart in the US, but it still lacks definition. One difference is in the amount of legal reliance on GAAP. Seemingly, there is more reliance on GAAP in the legislation of the US than in the BCL, where specific section reference is made to the concepts of *true and fair*.[20] Following the release of the *Sarbanes-Oxley Act 2002*, however, the situation has altered slightly, where, for instance, s401(b) of the Act requires that financial details of publicly listed companies 'be presented in a manner that (1) does not contain an untrue statement of a material fact.'

Table 3.1 Corporations' Legislation—Directors and Financial Reports

Words and Terms Used in Statutes	*US*	*UK*	*Canada*	*Australia*
GAAP	*		*	
TRUE		*		*
FAIR		*	*	*
Emphasis on Financial Position/Financial State		*	*	*
Emphasis on State of Affairs		*		*
To Perform Their Duty in Good Faith	*	*	*	
To Act Honestly			*	*
Duty of Care	*	*	*	*
Defence	*	*	*	*
Penalties	*	*	*	*

Source. Corporations' legislation of each country as mentioned in s4.3 above and further explained the sub-section 4.3.1 below.

Explanation

Thoughtfully, in the US, national regulation appears to be minimal, mainly because the focus rests on the perceived requirements of each separate state jurisdiction. For instance, the Revised Model Business Corporation Act (the Act) applies to each state in the US, but s1.02 allows for any state to make its own amendments. The Act in general (and this section in particular) gives directors, managers and accountants substantial flexibility in choosing accounting procedures they deem appropriate to provide financial information to all stakeholders.[21] Nonetheless, legal requirements emphasize the use of regulations or accounting principles (GAAP), and since the *Sarbanes-Oxley Act 2002*, there is a stipulation to report on the true (alternatively "materially untrue") financial position of the business.[22] Financial accounts representing the true financial position of an entity, however, are not necessarily (frequently are not) the same as that reported under GAAP.[23] Even with the increased demands of Sarbanes-Oxley, there remains an anomaly in financial reporting due to the continued and heavy reliance on professional accounting standards and GAAP.

Arguably, it is essential, for clarity, to define carefully the words of language used to convey information from one party to another—in order to communicate effectively. And merely abiding by GAAP does not necessarily fulfil the fundamental objective of financial reports.[24] Consider, in *Re Associated Gas and Electric Company* (11 SEC 974 (1942), pp.1058, 1059), the Securities and Exchange Commission held that:

> [T]he question whether financial statements formally complied with principles, practices and conventions accepted at the time should not be permitted to blind us to the basic question whether the financial statements *performed the function of enlightenment* which is their only reason for existence (emphasis added).

This was reinforced in subsequent *Bar Chris v. Escott and the Continental Vending* cases, and it has been restated in post-Enron SEC announcements.[25] As Harvey Pitt, Chairman of the SEC, reportedly stated:

> In the US, the SEC has proposed to significantly expand its review of financial and non-financial disclosures to focus on disclosure that is important to understanding the companies financial position and results and which, at least at face value, seems to conflict with accounting standards or be materially deficient in explanation or clarity (JCPAA, 2002, p.86).

More than a decade ago, Chambers and Wolnizer (1991, p.198) examined a number of eighteenth- and nineteenth-century statutes with regard to private and public companies to assess, among other things, the basic role of company officers in view of the content of financial accounts. Their investigation illustrated that terms were used regarding the duty of officials 'to ensure that accounts were properly kept as a basis representing the financial affairs of public bodies and business firms.' They detailed many instances where words such as truly, true state, fairly, impartially, exact and perfect account were used to explain or attest to the financial condition of a business entity. The primary point made was that, 'whatever their technical classification may be, these couples [e.g. "true and fair", "full and fair", "true and correct"] forcefully express the idea of conduct of financial affairs with the utmost circumspection' (Chambers and Wolnizer, 1991, p.199).

The words used by the legislature, over time, have not seemed to digress from an expectation of quality of financial information being presented in the content of financial reports aimed at depicting an entity's overall financial state.[26]

Canadian Corporation's Law makes similar demands on company directors. It differs from the UK, but, like the US, there is a preference for GAAP. Other requirements concentrate on the duties and accountability of directors.[27]

By contrast, the Australian *Corporations Act 2001* s297(a) and s297(b), respectively, demands that company directors prepare financial statements that present a true and fair view of the entity's financial position and performance and of the consolidated entity. Company directors are also required to state 'whether, in the director's opinion, there are reasonable grounds to believe that the company, registered scheme or disclosing entity will be able to pay its debts as and when they become due and payable' (s295(4)(c)). The necessity to comply with accounting standards and ensure that a true and fair view of the financial position of the entity has been reported is also stipulated in s297, s304 and s305. The juxtaposition in legislative mandates on reports of an entity's solvency and financial condition are clearly evident in these sections.

Those legal requirements would appear necessarily to draw on accounting data. They specifically require that corporate officers have relevant financial information readily available to them, and that they communicate reliable, contemporary financial details to users of accounting reports. Consequently, attention again turns to the quality of financial information contained in accounting reports and the capacity for corporate officers to determine the financial state (condition, position) of an entity from the information so available. The worth of that information to users, however, depends on the *degree of excellence* (Chapter 1) of the accounting data first given to the corporate officers.

The actual merit that may be attributed to accounting data is dependent on the underlying principles and procedures used to amass it—and words (and other symbols) that are used to describe and explain such procedures. In accounting, as in other disciplines, words are frequently used in a technical manner, thereby providing users with accounting information that may have a different meaning than would be conveyed in general conversation. Depreciation is an apt illustration in accounting. Whereas in general parlance the word means a reduction in an item's financial market value (following the linguistic root, *de pretium*—fall in price), in accounting it often means an allocation of cost over time. These are two different meanings for a word that has been in common use for aeons. Additionally, according to GAAP, an entity may report its deferred tax debits as assets in its statement of financial position.[28] Many such bookkeeping debit examples pervade conventional accounting practice. This is an issue discussed further in Chapter 4 and beyond.

Returning to the plight of directors, especially to examine actual consequences that have and might continue to befall them,[29] the following section briefly reviews a small but pertinent number of legal cases, where the actions of corporate directors have been examined. There are many other similar cases—financial *causes célèbres* on which one could have drawn. The cases discussed mainly concentrate on issues related to dividend payments, but other circumstances are covered mainly from the UK and Australia. They illustrate that, although society may hold the position of director in esteem, directors are liable perennially for their actions. Additionally, and due in part to the corporate collapses of recent times, society's expectations of directors and the role they play in managing or steering a business have become more demanding. For instance, directors are more frequently asked to explain their actions, and ignorance of circumstance is less likely to be accepted as a defence. We see evidence of this, recurrently, in the lay and financial press.

It may well be worth contemplating the change suggested by Wallis (2000, p.17) that:

> At present we tend to think in terms of all directors being the same, but in future we will think more of the portfolio of skills we might need around the table. . . . This may mean more executive directors and more directors who have had industry experience or involvements. . . . We need to accommodate entrepreneurs around our board tables, not suppress or eject them.

If one accepts this view, all directors definitely require up-to-date financial information on the capacity of a business to function, as is illustrated by the entrepreneurial activity and corporate collapses of the 1980s and beyond.

ACCOUNTABILITY AND THE COMPANY DIRECTOR—CASE *BON MOTS*

Accountability is a term that affirms that those in positions of authority and trust have duties to attend and that they may be held liable for their actions.

Although this idea is not new, it has been expanded in recent times.[30] During the late 1800s, the liquidator of a banking company sought compensation from certain directors of that company for their apparent inadequacy in managing the company's affairs.[31] The main concern was related to the payment of dividends and whether financial accounts were structured to ensure that dividends could be paid to shareholders. The level of responsibility attributed to directors, including their involvement in company management, is a continually debated issue, as highlighted in *AWA Ltd v. Daniels*.[32]

Mescher (1996, p.839) explained, 'Rogers J noted that one of the most striking features concerning directors' duties was the insistence that directors accept more and more responsibility for overseeing a company's affairs at the same time as these affairs were becoming more complex and diverse.' *AWA Ltd* explored the capability of internal management systems[33] when dealing with foreign currency transactions that were regarded as being beyond the understanding of many directors. The responsibilities of directors, in a general sense, were deemed to include taking an active role in the guidance and monitoring of the company's business operations, in this case including the foreign currency hedging operations. Directors were to play an active part in the affairs of their company and particularly in its financial affairs.[34]

A similar point was emphasized in *Turquand v. Marshall*[35] more than 125 years earlier when dealing with the company's apparent loss of capital. There, the problem was an overstatement of assets due in part to accounting procedures used for recording bad and doubtful debts, distribution of profit, the differences between prices paid by the company for shares, their nominal value and the dividends on those shares. The significant point of concern was loss of capital, which ultimately caused the company to fail.[36] Lord Romilly held that if the directors had instigated improper payment of dividends and 'if the payment has occasioned any loss to the company, the directors may be liable for that.'[37]

An opinion reported in Mescher (1996, p.840) also noted that:

> Directors now have an obligation to discover in sufficient detail the company's *financial position* to enable them as members of the board of directors to stop, if possible, the company's activities when the company is no longer able to pay its debts as and when they fall due (cmphasis added).

Recent illustrations of such obligations include the fate that directors of Enron, HIH, One.Tel and Water Wheel faced as a result of their entity's collapse or insolvent trading charges. Mescher cites P. Kirby:

> The time has passed when directors and other officers can simply surrender their duties to the public and those with whom the corporation deals by washing their hands, with impunity, leaving it to one

> director or a cadre of directors or to a general manager to discharge their responsibilities for them (1996, p.840).[38]

Similar examples are to be found in the nineteenth century in the *City of Glasgow Bank v. Mackinnon* (1882) 9 Court Session Cases, 4th Series, 535, where a claim was sought against director Mackinnon for what was then a significant figure: £311,666 16s 9d.[39] It was argued that this amount had been paid as dividends to shareholders out of the bank's capital and not profits earned.[40] It was held that the balance sheet contained misleading information. In this case, the director was charged some twenty years after instigating a questionable act in his role as a company official and eight years after resigning his position as a director of the firm.

The transcript explains that an interest payment due but not received for £7,552 had been debited to the bank and credited to the profit and loss account.[41] The main point of contention at that time was the authorization of a dividend payment when interest due to the bank had not been received but was included in the calculation of profit. Subsequently, it was deemed necessary to establish whether the unpaid profits were secured or unsecured. The record stated that:

> [I]f the unpaid profits are fully secured, they become a part of the capital of the company, as a *surrogatum* for the cash of equal amount taken from the floating capital and paid as dividend; and thus the capital is not diminished, but a certain part of the floating balance of capital becomes invested in the securities which the company hold for the earned but unpaid profits in question (at p.115).

In this case, it was considered necessary to prove, against the directors:

> (1) that they knew that the interest on the American railway investment, though due, was not paid, and (2) that it was brought to the credit of profit and loss, and so divided as clear profit; . . . [and] (3) that they had not reasonable ground for believing that the interest was well secured and would ultimately be recovered. If they had reasonable ground for so believing, they [would have] acted in good faith (at p.115).

Hence, the directors would not have committed any breach of trust. The court displayed an expectation that the directors would act with diligence, skill and care. Subsequently, their actions would be measured in terms of what could be reasonably expected from them given their knowledge and experience.

By 1870, the bank held 'securities of the nominal value of £974,000 for a debt, principal and interest, amounting to £905,000' (at p.118). This was eventually held to be a sound investment by the court, one that was shown to yield a 4% rate of interest from 1870 to 1878 when the bank finally folded. This investment had grown over time, but the total amount included the £311,666 that Mackinnon was charged with misappropriating by paying dividends from capital, not profits, during this time. The crucial factor was to decide whether the interest earned but not received was well *secured* and so a reasonable part of the calculation of profit.[42] This requires identification of collateral, a financial concept. This is where accounting plays a crucial role.

Distinction was made between the actions of Mackinnon and other directors, particularly those who held office after his resignation in 1870. The court acknowledged Mackinnon had acted in a manner befitting his office and stated:

> For what took place after 1870 the respondent is of course not answerable. New directors and a new manager came into office between that date and the stoppage of the bank, and in this liquidation we have only too good reason to know that their management of the affairs of the bank was of the worst possible description (at p.119).

However, of the decision made and action taken by Mackinnon, the following remark may be used as an analogy, across time, to serve as a warning when accounting procedures are applied to cover hopes, speculations or estimates of future happenings. Lord Deas stated:

> I do not doubt that Mr. Mackinnon and his co-directors believed that the interest for all the years in question would be recovered in the end, nor do I doubt that they had reasonable grounds for believing so, but I have great difficulty in seeing why the directors, however much they expected and believed that all interest would be so recovered in the end, should have done that which they might have left undone—namely, paid the dividends for so many terms, in place of waiting till they had first received the interest out of which they were to pay them. I should be sorry to see the course adopted drawn into a precedent—and I hope it may prevent it from being so—*that although it may not lead to personal liability in this case, it must be seen to have been so sufficiently perilous as to make it rather a danger to be avoided than an example to be imitated* (at p.120; emphasis added).

Some years later, in *re City Equitable Fire Insurance Company Limited*, No.0048 of 1922, C.A. 1924,[43] the managing director's actions, which amounted to fraud, resulted in his conviction. The allegation against the other respondents was one of negligence, and the test applied was that of a reasonable man.[44] This lengthy case involved the court in the winding up proceedings of the insurance company. 'The summons came on for hearing before Romer J. on February 4, 1924' (at p.415). During examination of the entity's financial affairs, a shortage of funds was discovered in excess of £1,200,000. The transcript states that this circumstance was 'due in part to depreciation of investments, but mainly to the instrumentality of the managing director and largely to his deliberate fraud, for which he had been convicted and sentenced' (at p.407). Deliberate action entailed certain accounting procedures that had been implemented by the company in addition to the dishonesty of the managing director.

A later example is *Australian Securities Commission v. Fairlie*, as noted by Mescher (1996, p.840):

> [A] managing director was charged under a number of counts including failure to keep proper accounts. Steps taken by Fairlie to overcome problems with the accounts included employment of experienced accounts staff and engagement of a major accounting firm. While the magistrate found these were adequate steps, Zeeman J found that reasonable steps involved far more, particularly when the respondent knew the accounting records were in chaos.

The main link between the cases is the use of generally accepted accounting procedures to help determine by calculation the financial state of each company, using the accounts kept by each company. After all, action taken by directors may be deemed *adequate* at a point in time given prevailing circumstances but may not be considered *reasonable* by the courts at a later date—and directors may find themselves subsequently held accountable. Such circumstances are evidenced some sixty, seventy or eighty years after the City Equitable case.[45]

In City Equitable, however, the 'liquidator sought to make the respondent directors, all of whom (except the managing director) had admittedly acted honestly throughout, liable for negligence in respect of losses occasioned by investments and loans, and of payment of dividends out of capital' (at p.407). In explanation, J. Romer deliberated on the duties of directors and the meaning attached to words such as wilful, neglect and default. He considered the distribution of duty and work between the board of directors and other staff members of the company to be a business decision made with regard to the nature and operations of the entity.[46]

It was acknowledged, however, that directors of large corporations could not reasonably be expected to supervise personally all business transactions, including safe custody of investments. Directors were held to be not necessarily responsible for the outcome of unwise behaviour, like the declaration of a dividend when a more informed business judgement would be to retain the funds within the company. They would, however, be liable if payment was out of capital, but the onus of proof would then fall on the accuser. Notwithstanding these allowances, J. Romer held that '[it] is the duty of each director to see that the company's moneys are from time to time in a proper state of investment, except so far as the articles of association may justify him in delegating that duty to others.'

Nonetheless:

> Before presenting their annual report and balance sheet to their shareholders, and before recommending a dividend, *directors should have a complete and detailed list of the company's assets and investments prepared for their own use and information, and ought not to be satisfied as to the value of their company's assets merely by the assurance of their chairman, however apparently distinguished and honourable, nor with the expression of the belief of their auditors, however competent and trustworthy* (at p.409; emphasis added).[47]

Another such circumstance occurs when a director or other corporate officer continues to transact business and knowingly incurs a debt when the business entity is unable to pay its debts.[48] In *Dunn v. Shapowloff*, the respondent was found guilty and convicted. It was held that he had contracted a debt when at that time he had no reasonable grounds to consider that the company was able to pay the debt. This was determined after taking into account the other liabilities of the company at that time. The conviction was appealed, but subsequently the appeal was not allowed. The conviction remained.

Argument there emphasized whether a reasonable man in the position of director could be expected to know the financial capacity of the company to pay its debts. The main concern was not whether the company's liabilities and contingent liabilities exceeded its assets but that 'a director may have knowledge of what has happened, or is likely to have happened, which will bear upon the company's capacity to pay the debt in question, notwithstanding its present solvency' (at p.240). The director was found to knowingly contribute to the inappropriate action of incurring more debt when the company was already overly burdened with liabilities.[49]

Corporation's law may allow directors to rely on information provided by other officers of the corporation, their knowledge, experience and technical ability to prepare reliable reports (*Corporations Act 2001*, s588X), but ultimately responsibility for the outcome rests with the director. If directors permit their company to continue to incur unsecured debts when the company is insolvent or the company becomes insolvent by incurring a debt, the protection of directors provided by the corporate veil is removed.[50] The focus of the law is then on the protection of creditors. Directors, for example, are made personally responsible for those debts (Mescher, 1996, p.837).[51]

In the Shapowloff case (1978), a significant point was made by J. Mahoney as to whether the director had:

> [N]o reasonable or probable ground of expectation that the company would be able to pay the debt, i.e., if there was no such ground in existence objectively. If, subjectively, he had an expectation that the

> company would be able to pay the debt, he would still be open to conviction, if there was no such ground objectively' (at p.243).

Twenty years later, a case of different proportions was heard in the Supreme Court of South Australia that discussed and evaluated, at length, the role and duty of company directors. This case emphasized the degree in which society's expectations of directors and other company officials have changed and increased over time. The *Duke Group Ltd. (in Liquidation) v. Pilmer & Ors* (1998) 27 ACSR 1, which commenced in June 1994, was reportedly one of '[t]he longest case[s] in Australian legal history' (Evans, *Australian Financial Review*, 1998, p.3). This case is explored further in Chapter 6.

Briefly, the circumstances were that the plaintiff, the Duke Group Limited formerly named Kia Ora Gold Corporation NL, made a bid for a target company named Western United Limited. That bid was based on a valuation of issued capital. Accountants of the firm Nelson Wheeler Perth provided the valuation. At that time, the firm operating under the name of Nelson Wheeler conducted business throughout Australia with partners in each of the mainland states.

The plaintiff sought damages from both, the partners of Nelson Wheeler and the directors of Kia Ora Gold, which was later called the Duke Group Ltd. Neither all company directors nor members of the national partnership of Nelson Wheeler were held to be responsible, but of those who were, the judgement required compensation (at least) to the total of $93,863,796.81, including interest. The directors were held to be accountable. This case illustrated that directors were likely to be held answerable to all stakeholders for their actions—their governance of a corporation.

DIRECTORS' PERFORMANCE AND CORPORATE GOVERNANCE

Corporate governance entails duty of care, and that care encompasses all the facets of managing a business. This corporate responsibility is a charge on those in positions of power to act in an ethical, thoughtful and practical demeanor. How to perform and achieve best practice in business may cause directors to ponder at times, especially where there seems to be a disproportionate emphasis placed by regulating authorities on rules and performance measurement of corporate governance issues.[52] Certainly, the level of *good governance*[53] achieved by directors of corporate entities cannot be totally judged or measured by their adherence to a set of rules. Why? Because corporate governance is more, or should be more, than compliance with mandates set by regulating (including professional bodies) authorities.[54] Justice Neville Owen in his report into the HIH failure was strongly of this view.[55]

The Cadbury Report (1991/1992) defined corporate governance as 'the system by which companies are directed and controlled' (para2.5), whereas Tomkins and Vass (1998) stated that corporate governance was '[t]he act of thinking and acting strategically by setting the parameters and establishing the values within which an organisation's executive body and all staff are free to act.' It was further implied by Tomkins and Vass that this included alliance with external regulations, accounting standards, audits as well as constructing internal conditions to ensure management control systems were competent. Herein dwells a conflict especially if it is accepted that corporate governance issues far exceed the tenets of compliance.

Company executives and managers make business decisions for a variety of reasons, but generally, as a working premise, it may be assumed that the overriding aim of business is to make a profit. Further, business decisions are usually based on strategies and plans formulated by directors, and typically directors seek continuity and growth of business operations. Hence, directors are concerned with many facets of business—for instance, the increasing wealth of investors, organizational growth for the enterprise in addition to achieving stability and security of employment for staff at all levels. This necessitates that directors know their role in business as well as have knowledge of the business they direct. It is also incumbent of directors that they know continually the financial state of the business they direct and its degree of operations—to assist them to devise business strategies and plans for future activities.[56] It is hardly adequate for directors to simply meet the requirements of the regulators in order to accomplish what may be termed good corporate governance for business. The reasons are many, including, as Longo (1999, p.19) stated, '[c]orporate governance has been a central business issue of the 1990s. To a large extent, the excesses of the 1980s ensured that it would be the focus of public and shareholder attention.'[57]

Such a focus, however, will not be appeased by mere compliance with rules and regulations. Society expects that directors and corporate officers of today and into the future will take a more hands on approach to involvement in business and that they will know the financial and organizational capacity of the business to be a part of the world of trade.[58] In the US, Fairfax (2004) acknowledged the increased responsibilities imposed on directors post Sarbanes-Oxley (2002) but remarked on the lack of 'direct legal penalties [imposed] on directors who breach those responsibilities' (2004, p.395). She also argued that without somewhat stringent legal liabilities imposed on directors for misconduct their duty of care—their fiduciary duty—might be impaired. For instance although '[c]ongressional testimony has confirmed that . . . [some] directors understood their obligation to monitor the corporation and its financial affairs . . . some directors have admitted to signing off on company reports with limited or no knowledge of their content' (2004, p.399).

Notably, Fairfax (2004, p.398) asserted:

> Investigative reports indicate that directors at Enron Corp. ("Enron") and at other corporations embroiled in financial accounting scandals failed to fulfil their fiduciary duties. The reports not only reveal defects in directors' individual behaviors, but more importantly reveal their failure to monitor adequately and remain sufficiently informed about the behavior of others upon whom they bestowed power.

Earlier, with focus on corporate behaviour, the Cadbury Committee (1991/1992) made recommendations that could be applied to circumstances prior to and those existing at the turn of the twentieth century and beyond—moving into the new millennium. Specifically, the recommendations were related to a "Code of Best Practice" with which all listed companies, at that time, were to comply.

'The Code was based on three principles:

- *openness* (subject to commercial confidentiality);
- *integrity* (honest, balanced and complete financial reporting);
- *accountability* (the requirement for directors to provide quality information, and for shareholders to exercise their powers as owners responsibly)'

(Cadbury Committee, 1991/1992, paras 3.2–3.4).

The principles arguably are still most relevant. In particular, the third principle, *accountability*, is highlighted throughout this work, focusing on how best to determine an entity's financial state and what is meant by quality financial information for economic decision-makers—for instance, in quantifying solvency.

CLOSING REMARKS

> [W]e can . . . know the exact state of our affairs . . . what goods of every sort we have in hand; what payments we have to make, and what cash we can command; by which means we are . . . to prepare for any demands which can be made upon us, and can extend or curtail our trade as we find our capital will admit of, or the nature of our affairs require (Thompson, 1777/1984, p.2).

This chapter examined the role and duties of company directors. It was shown that, over time, failure to adhere to legal demands has incurred severe penalties for directors and other corporate officers.

Case *bon mots* in this chapter highlight the ignominy that directors have confronted when they failed to perform their duties as expected and required by law. The cases show that from the nineteenth century, throughout the twentieth century and into the twenty-first century, directors have been, from time to time, held accountable for their actions. Further, society's expectations with regard to directors' duties and their responsibilities have intensified, and penalties for non-performance have increased.

A number of the cases revealed that courts have emphasized the necessity for directors to know the financial capacity of the business they direct—hence, its financial ability to continue to conduct its business. Contrary to this perspective, conventional financial statements are shown throughout this work to provide a distorted view of a firm's financial position. Especially if one accepts that users expect those reports to provide up-to-date, factual, financial details on its wealth, changes thereto, and an entity's ability to pay its debts. This point especially holds if accounting procedures are meant to fulfil legislative requirements and assist directors and other corporate officers to comply with the demands of statutes related to financial matters, like assessing solvency. Chapter 4 examines this argument further.

Chapters 5, 6 and 7 investigate the circumstances of major case studies of business failure and financial distress. Although the cases examined therein are mainly Australian, the circumstances analysed are applicable globally. Continually, this is a topical issue for business. As into the new millennium, Barton (2000, p.300) remarked:

> It is now generally accepted that accounting systems ought to be financial measurement and communications systems which provide useful information to various users of the information, as advocated by Chambers ([1966], p.102). Most professional accounting bodies have adopted this approach in their statements of accounting objectives which are used as a basis for the formulation of [international] accounting standards. . . . Thus, accounting information must (a) assist management, investors and other stakeholders in making decisions to use resources efficiently and effectively in the firm's operations in the furtherance of its profit goals, and (b) provide appropriate information to assist stakeholders in evaluating the profit performance and financial position of the firm resulting from the use of those resources.[59]

But do conventional accounting reports so assist? Following a number of somewhat startling corporate collapses post 2000, some examined herein, West (2003, p.186) on "financial position" proffered:

> The consequences of a statement of financial position failing to embrace a single temporal dimension are profound. First, it means that the statement is incoherent and unintelligible. The aggregate figures it presents are neither descriptive of what was nor what is and are therefore not empirical. Nor however are the aggregates prospective. Instead, items of information pertaining to each of the past, present and future are combined as if they could be presumed to be substitutive. [Further] . . . conventionally prepared balance sheets have no logical connection to decision-making processes. Individual elements in the statement variously describe past actions, define present circumstances, or anticipate

> future outcomes. The aggregation of those elements cannot yield a factual and up-to-date guide for financial choice and action.

Chapter 4 continues to investigate relevant phenomena.

APPENDIX: A3.1

US

The *Sarbanes-Oxley Act 2002* followed shortly after the demise of Enron. Major reforms focussed on international harmonisation and a renewed emphasis on *truth* in financial statements. Statutory requirements, however, continued to support the implementation of US, GAAP. Seemingly, there is a move by 'the Financial Accounting Standards Board and the International Accounting Standards Board to work together toward greater convergence between U.S. Generally Accepted Accounting Principles and international accounting standards' (media release, 2002/154, SEC).[60]

Corporations and Business Associations—Statutes, Rules, and Forms by Eisenberg (1991/1993) is a major source of information for the following details. Seemingly, there is an Eisenberg (2010) edition, but as this book goes to print, it was unavailable to me. Hence, this may be a limitation to the details presented. For brevity, specific examples have been restricted to excerpts from the statutes of Delaware, California and New York. Reference is also made to supporting sections of the Securities Exchange Act of 1934.

The Revised Model Business Corporation Act (the Act) applies to each state in the US, but s1.02 allows for any state to make its own amendments. The Act encourages preparers of reports to comply with generally accepted accounting principles (GAAP) when compiling an entity's dated financial statements. It does not explicitly state what is meant by, and there is no definition for, GAAP in s1.40, which provides interpretations for other expressions used in the Act. There is no direct requirement to report the true or correct—financial position or state of affairs of the entity. Furthermore, auditors are not bound to attest to the firm's true financial position or state of affairs, as s16.20(b) states:

> If the annual financial statements are reported upon by a public accountant, his report must accompany them. If not, the statements must be accompanied by a statement of the president or the person responsible for the corporation's accounting records:
>
> (1) stating his reasonable belief whether the statements were prepared on the basis of generally accepted accounting principles and, if not, describing the basis of preparation.

With the *Sarbanes-Oxley Act 2002*, however, there is a resurgence of the notion of *truth in financial reporting*, but truth that aligns with the use of GAAP. The Senate Committee on Banking, Housing and Urban Affairs noted: 'The Committee seeks to address problems attendant to pro forma financial disclosures by requiring that issuers publish pro forma data with a reconciliation to comparable financial data calculated according to GAAP and in a way that is not misleading and does not contain untrue statements.'[61] Such ideals run deep as '[i]n 1973, the Commission [SEC] issued Accounting Series Release No.142, warning of possible investor confusion from the use of financial measures outside of GAAP.'[62] Then, 'more recently in December 2001, [the SEC] issued cautionary advice regarding the use of "pro forma financial information" in earnings releases . . . concerned that "pro forma" financial information, under certain circumstances, can mislead investors if it obscures GAAP results.'[63]

This book argues conversely that the use of GAAP (with a focus on capitalised costs and intangibles as assets) is more likely to result in uninformative, even misleading, financial information for economic decision-makers.

Returning to Eisenberg, the following excerpts from the statute show there are similar requirements and defences for companies, directors and managers within Delaware General Corporation Law and the California Code. New York legislators also seem to deal with the demands of corporation law in like fashion. This chapter acknowledges that a broad generalization of the statutory demands of corporations' law within the US cannot be made from these few examples. The statutes are included to illustrate that comparable points of law with regard to solvency and the duties of directors are likely to exist within the code of each state.

Directors and Their Duties As Required By Statute

The Securities Exchange Act of 1934 s13(b)(1) and (2) allows that '[t]he Commission [SEC] may prescribe . . . items or details to be shown in the balance sheet and the earning statement . . . methods to be followed in the preparation of reports, in the appraisal or valuation of assets and liabilities.' This section gives power to the Commission to ensure details in the financial statements of an entity provide the information required by the SEC. In addition, 'every issuer . . . required to file reports . . . shall (A) make and keep books, records, and accounts, which, in reasonable detail, accurately and fairly reflect the transactions and dispositions of the assets of the issuer,' and 'transactions are recorded as necessary (I) to permit preparation of financial statements in conformity with generally accepted accounting principles . . . and (II) to maintain accountability for assets' s13(b)(2)(B)(ii).

Subsequent to 2002, retaining the focus on GAAP, the SEC emphasises the significance of a ' "non-GAAP financial measure" [that] is a numerical measure of an issuer's historical or future financial performance, financial position or cash flows.' This term seeks to 'identify the types of information targeted by Section 401(b) of the Sarbanes-Oxley Act. The *Sarbanes-Oxley Act 2002* sought to eliminate the manipulative or misleading use of non-GAAP financial measures and, at the same time, enhance comparability associated with the use of that information.'[64] Hence, concentrated effort is on the application of GAAP. This action insinuates that the use of GAAP promotes comparability of accounts and truth in financial reporting. In fact, the consistent and accurate use of GAAP likely results in financial reports true to the mandates of accounting standards and the anomalies contained therein.

Further, in all states, the statutory demands with regard to financial statements are similar in that the focus is to adhere to GAAP. For instance, s114 of the California Corporations Code (CCC) states:

> [B]alance sheets, income statements and statements of changes in financial position of a corporation and all references to assets, liabilities, earnings, retained earnings and similar accounting items of a corporation mean such financial statements or such items prepared or determined in conformity with generally accepted accounting principles then applicable, fairly presenting . . . the matters which they purport to present.

Specifically, Delaware General Corporation Law (DGCL) requires directors and other committee members designated by the board of directors *to perform their duty in good faith.* CCC also requires directors to fulfil their obligations and perform their duties in good faith and demands they act 'in the best interests of the corporation and its shareholders and with such care, including reasonable inquiry, as an ordinarily prudent person in a like position would use under similar circumstances' s309(a).' Likewise, New York Business Corporation Law (NYBCL) requires in s717(a) that '[a] director shall perform his duties . . . in good faith and with that degree of care which an ordinarily prudent person in a like position would use under similar circumstances.' The notion of how directors perform their duty in good faith is not explained. Onus of interpretation rests with the individual, group or court.

In addition to acting in good faith, the law demands that directors be involved with daily business operations. This implies that directors should have continuous knowledge of the entity's trading activities, financial details and actual results of periodic business transactions. This may be viewed as a statutory demand for directors to play a dynamic role in business management. For instance, in s141(a) of DGCL, it is stated, '[t]he business and affairs of every corporation . . . shall be managed by or under the direction of a board of directors, except as may be otherwise provided in [legislation] or in its certificate of incorporation.' To this end, Paul Atkins, Commissioner of the SEC, stated that, '[t]he role of directors is to monitor and oversee. . . . Directors are not and can never become full time employees. There will always be a natural tension between directors as business advisors . . . and their role as monitors of management' (Speech on Sarbanes-Oxley Act, 2002).[65]

Under s141(e), DGCL directors will 'be fully protected in relying . . . upon the records of the corporation and . . . opinions, reports or statements presented to the corporation . . . as to matters the member reasonably believes are within such other person's professional or expert competence.' Similarly, CCC provides that, '[i]n performing the duties of a director . . .

[the directors] shall be entitled to rely on information, opinions, reports or statements, including financial statements and other financial data' (s309(b)). Protection also exists under s717(a) of NYBCL, where it is stated, 'a director shall be entitled to rely on information, opinions, reports or statements including financial statements and other financial data . . . prepared or presented by . . . (1) one or more officers or employees of the corporation . . . whom the director believes to be reliable and competent in the matters presented . . . (2) counsel, public accountants or other persons . . . within such person's professional or expert competence . . . (3) a committee of the board upon which he does not serve.' It may be argued that the provisions of these sections place increased responsibility on accountants to ensure that they provide company officials with specific financial information that will assist them to adequately perform their duties. Additionally, in relation to an entity's dated financial state, this would demand precise financial details regarding a current market situation.

Along with the degree of protection the law provides for directors, there is also provision in the statutes for legal action to be initiated against them. Officers, directors or stockholders may be held accountable under s325(a) of DGCL, where it states that, 'any person to whom they [officers of the corporation] are liable may have an action, at law or in equity, against any one or more of them.' The same corporate officers have a safeguard under s325(b), where it is stated, '[n]o suit shall be brought against any officer, director, or stockholder for any debt of a corporation . . . until judgment be obtained . . . against the corporation and execution thereon returned unsatisfied.' CCC under s309(c) also provides for no liability where the person has performed 'the duties of a director in accordance with subdivisions (a) and (b) of s309 of the Code.' Furthermore, s719 of NYBCL states certain circumstances where directors are to be held liable, but in s719(e), all liability is removed 'if, in the circumstances, [the director] performed his duty to the corporation under paragraph (a) of section 717.'

It may be that directors and other company officials are more likely to be held accountable for the outcome of their business decisions in the future than they have been in the past. However, there are defences in the statutes to assist directors who act honestly and in good faith. For example, s18(a) of the Securities Exchange Act provides a liability for misleading statements made by officers of a corporation 'unless the person sued shall prove that he acted in good faith and had no knowledge that such statement was false or misleading.' Such a defence should not be wholly relied on, however, as previously shown in the body of this chapter, where the outcome of specific legal cases were examined.

UK

The British Companies Act 1985 states that directors shall in each financial year prepare a report 'containing a fair review of the development of the business of the company and its subsidiaries during the financial year and of their position at the end of it' (s235(1)(a)). Corporations' legislation does not explain the meaning of fair review or the characteristics of the term "position." These are expressions in general use and so are of concern as such expressions in general communication can be misinterpreted when used, without explanation, to communicate technical details. This idea is not new. For instance, 'Language in itself and the interpretation of language are to some extent independent. . . . Different interpretations can usually be applied to the same formalized language' (Bochenski, 1965, p.35).

On the role of auditors, s.236(2)(a) requires, 'whether in the auditor's opinion the balance sheet and profit and loss account . . . have been properly prepared in accordance with this Act' and 'whether in their opinion a true and fair view is given . . . (i) in the balance sheet, of the company's affairs . . . (ii) in the profit and loss account . . . of the company's profit or loss . . . (iii) in the case of group accounts, of the state of affairs and profit or loss' (s.236(2)(b)). The section stipulates that auditors are to comment on whether the balance sheet provides a true and fair view of the company's state of affairs. In order to comply, auditors require financial information pertinent to the entity's dated financial state. The statutes emphasize words that demand a true and fair view of the entity's financial state. Consequently, users of financial statements could expect to be provided with a factual account of the entity's financial position.

Previously, Chambers and Wolnizer (1991, p.198) examined a number of eighteenth- and nineteenth-century private and public statutes to illustrate terms used regarding the duty of officials 'to ensure that accounts were properly kept as a basis representing the financial affairs of public bodies and business firms.' The authors detailed many instances where words such as truly, true state, fairly, impartially, exact and perfect account were used to explain or attest to the financial condition of a business entity. Primarily the point was made that 'whatever their technical classification may be, these couples forcefully express the idea of conduct of financial affairs with the utmost circumspection' (1991, p.199). The words used by the legislature, over time, have not digressed from such an expectation of quality in the content of financial reports.

Similar to legal requirements of other countries, a director's non-compliance with requirements of the Companies Act is reported as an offence. This occurs under s.245 of company legislation in Britain. If the accounts do not comply with the companies Act and are presented at a general company meeting or delivered to the registrar of companies, then 'a director of the company is guilty of an offence and, in respect of each offence [is] liable to a fine' (s.245(1)). A director may offer as a defence 'that he took all reasonable steps for securing compliance with the requirements in question' (s.245(3)). The fact remains that those different directors may apply different interpretations to the legal requirements relating to company reports and director's duties. This means the onus of interpretation is placed on the courts when a malfeasance occurs and directors or auditors come before the court.

Canada

Canadian corporation's law makes similar demands on company directors in the execution of their duties. The following details have been taken from the Canada Business Corporations Act (the Act), Canada Business Corporations Regulations[66] and the Ontario Business Corporations Act, the latter annotated by Ames and Lettner (1990). The law, like in the US and the UK, also provides that directors may rely on the expertise of auditors, or officers of the corporation, in preparing financial information reports for users.

As stated in s122(1) of the Act, '[e]very director and officer of a corporation in exercising their powers and discharging their duties shall,

(a) act honestly and in good faith with a view to the best interests of the corporation; and
(b) exercise the care, diligence and skill that a reasonably prudent person would exercise in comparable circumstances.'

Section 135(4) of the Ontario Act provides that:

> [a] director is not liable under section 130 or 134 if he relies in good faith upon, (a) financial statements of the corporation represented to him by an officer of the corporation or in a written report of the auditor of the corporation to present fairly the financial position of the corporation in accordance with generally accepted accounting principles.

This section highlights an expectation that during the process of accounting for an entity's financial status, preparers of reports will provide users with information to enable them to fulfil their duties.

Similarly, s.123 (4) of the Act, under 'Reasonable diligence,' provides that [a] director is not liable under section 118 or 119 . . . [or under] subsection 122(2), if the director exercised . . . care, diligence and skill . . . including reliance in good faith on (a) financial statements of the corporation represented to the director by an officer of the corporation or in a written report of the auditor of the corporation fairly to reflect the financial condition of the corporation.

And s.123 (5) provides for a defence when the director has acted in good faith.

> The provincial (Ontario) regulations and the national Act are seemingly in unison.

Further, s.154 of the Ontario Business Corporations Act states, '[t]he financial statements required under this Act shall be prepared as prescribed by regulation and in accordance with generally accepted accounting principles.' Whereas Part 8, s.70 of the Canada Business Corporations

Regulations states '[t]he financial statements . . . shall . . . be prepared in accordance with generally accepted accounting principles as set out in the Handbook of the Canadian Institute of Chartered Accountants.' The implication is that by so doing, the directors will provide a fair presentation of the entity's dated financial position.

Directors are required to access information that provides details of the entity's financial position. This entails that they first know how to interpret the term. For instance, under the Ontario Business Corporations Act, s144(2), it is stated, 'there shall be kept at the registered office of the corporation or such other place as is authorized under this section such records as will enable the directors to ascertain quarterly with reasonable accuracy the financial position of the corporation.' Hence, directors need clear understanding of the term financial position in order to fulfil legislative requirements, and the notion of "reasonable accuracy" also requires clarity. Additionally, s.153(1) of the Ontario Act stipulates that directors, at an annual meeting of shareholders, shall provide the corporations with financial statements that comply with the requirements listed under s.153, which includes an auditor's report and 'any further information respecting the financial position of the corporation and the results of its operations required by the articles, the by-laws or any unanimous shareholder agreement' (s.153 (1)(d)).

It seems incumbent on the providers to ensure the information they compile is relevant and in fact relates to the dated financial position of the entity.

Australia

The Australian *Corporations Act 2001* demands that company directors ensure that financial statements present a true and fair view of the entity's financial state. Pre-2004 'a company's directors shall . . . cause to be made out a profit and loss account for that accounting period that gives a true and fair view of the company's profit or loss for that accounting period' (s.292). Also, that 'a company's directors shall . . . cause to be made out a balance-sheet as at the end of that accounting period that gives a true and fair view of the company's state of affairs as at the end of that accounting period' (s.293). Post 2004, relevant sections are now s.297 and s.298.

Additionally, from the review conducted by the Joint Standing Committee on Public Accounts and Audit (JCPAA) in 2002, a renewed emphasis on risk management surfaced, not least because the Committee considered that '[c]urrent audit practice is limited to an attestation that financial statements have been prepared according to accounting standards.'[67] Such practice tends to ignore other risk related issues with regard to the financial capacity of the entity to continue operating as a viable business into the future. Hence, the committee asserted that closer scrutiny of an entity's level of compliance with the accounting standards was essential to ensure stakeholders were not misled, 'even though such practices may be in accordance with current black letter requirements.'[68]

The JCPAA (2002) recommended amendments to the *Corporations Act 2001*. For instance, that 'the Chief Executive Officer and Chief Financial Officer of a company [be required] to sign a statutory declaration that the company's financial reports comply with the *Corporations Act 2001* and are materially truthful and complete.'[69] Currently, this is required under s.295 (4) and s.297. These requirements emphasise the *true and fair override* contained in the legislation. An emphasis similarly made by Justice Neville Owen in his final report on the Royal Commission into the demise of HIH Insurance Ltd., is discussed later, in some depth, in Chapter 5.

Recommendation 5 of the report provides around twenty-five paragraphs (3.53–3.77) specifically related to issues of truth and fairness in view of the content of financial statements. The Committee recognised 'deficiencies in the accounting standards' and noted its concern that 'it received conflicting interpretations of the application of true and fair view requirements in the *Corporations Act 2001*' (para.3.53, p.78).[70] Some respondents were of the opinion that compliance with accounting standards were the primary concern whereas others advocated the necessity to report 'a true and fair view, rather than compliance with the accounting standards or that the *Corporations Act 2001* should contain what is commonly termed a true and fair override' (para.3.57, p.79).

> ***'In other words, the Committee considers that directors and auditors must separately consider whether the financial statements comply with accounting standards and, at the same time, provide a true and fair view'*** (para.3.69, p.81; emphasis added).

Company directors are required, however, to state 'whether, in the directors' opinion, there are reasonable grounds to believe that the company, registered scheme or disclosing entity will be able to pay its debts as and when they become due and payable' (s.295(4)(c)). The implication is that published financial reports should contain information that directly relates to a firm's state of solvency. Earlier it was noted that s95A defines solvency as an entity's ability 'to pay all . . . [its] debts, as and when they become due and payable.'

Recall discussion in Chapter 2 with regard to cash flows and the cash flow test of [in]solvency—how cash flows *vis-a-vis* a cash flow statement may illustrate liquidity, but to determine an entity's state of solvency demands a more in-depth review. The structure of the balance sheet, for example, has the capacity to provide the required details on solvency but not in its current form, the substance of which is an issue in determining solvency.

Moreover, the term "state of affairs" has *not* been defined in the statutes, and so like the US, Canada and the UK, the burden of interpretation has been placed on the courts when confronted with specific cases. Mannix and Mannix (1982, p.31) stated that 'the courts have . . . tended to accept evidence of any established practice of sound commercial accounting, as long as it is applied consistently.' This is of little help, however, in determining whether a conventional accounting statement of financial position is synonymous with the legal requirement for company directors to provide users with dated financial information on a company's state of affairs.

Regarding the meaning (in use) of words and terms at law, Maxwell (1883, p.69) stated that, '[i]n general, statutes are presumed to use words in their popular sense.' This refers to their accepted, approved and recommended use, which may illustrate an anomaly in the communication of ideas and financial information among accounting, corporate officers and the general public. On communication, the following, Figure A3.1.1 provides a chronology of corporate governance issues.

Financial Services Act 1986 (major effect on the regulatory role of the Stock Exchange)
Publication of the Treadway Report (US) 1987
SEC update listing requirements (US) 1988
Polly Peck business empire collapse (1.3 billion pounds) 1990
Establishment of the Cadbury Committee on Financial Aspects of Corporate Governance 1991
Discovery that 480 million pounds had disappeared from Maxwell Group pension fund 1991
BCCI collapse—multi-billion international collapse—early 1990s
Internal Control—Integrated Framework Report pub. COSO: 1992
Cadbury Report and Code published 1992
Citizen's Charter published 1992
UK Stock Exchange amends its Listing Rules 1993
(Companies were to show the extent of compliance with Cadbury Report effective July 1993)
Publication of the South African 'Cadbury,' King Report,1994
Rutteman guidance on Internal Control and Financial Reporting published 1994
Establishment of the Greenbury group on Executive remuneration 1995
Publication of the First Nolan Report 1995
Publication of Greenbury proposals 1995
Publication of the French 'Cadbury,' the Viénot Report 1995
UK Stock Exchange amends its Listing Rules 1995
(Companies were to show extent of compliance with Greenbury)
Establishment of Hampel Committee on Corporate Gov. 1995
Publication of the Second Nolan Report 1996
Publication of the Dutch 'Cadbury,' the Peters Report 1996
Stock Exchange amends its Listing Rules in the light of Greenbury's recommendation 1996
(re: phasing of share options)
Publication of the Third Nolan Report 1997
Publication of the Fourth Nolan Report 1997
Publication of the Hampel Report 1998
Publication of the Hampel Combined Code 1998
Publication of the Turnbull guidance on internal control 1999

Source. CIMA, Corporate Governance: history, practice and future, Executive Summary, p.3.

Later references to Corporate Governance include those issues discussed in the JCPAA, Report 391, August 2002 and in reports of the US Securities and Exchange Commission subsequent to the Sarbanes-Oxley Act 2002 available at www.sec.gov/rules and the Australian Securities Exchange at http://www.asx.com.au/governance/corporate-governance.htm

Figure A3.1.1 Chronology: The development of corporate governance issues.

4 The Essence of Solvency

> 'The scientific method . . . relies on an assumption of the possibility of objective knowledge, reductionism and mathematics. It is rooted in a realist ontology' (Gaffikin, 2000, p.291).

TO BE OR NOT TO BE—SOLVENT!

Ostensibly for a commercial enterprise to conduct and to continue to conduct its business it needs to have and have access to money. This is necessary to enable the venture to manage payment of its accumulated debt and still continue to conduct its business. In other words, the entity would be solvent. To quantify solvency necessitates not least of all that business stakeholders understand and agree to its definition.

Previously, Chapter 2 examined, in some depth, solvency as a primary point of interest of the *Corporations Act 2001* in Australia and various legislation overseas, namely, whether a business has the ability to pay its debts when due and payable.[1] In this vein, Chapter 3 explored the role of company directors on a national and international basis, including legal and social aspects of their responsibilities to business and the community. This chapter investigates difficulties in quantifying solvency from conventional accounting reports. It shows that the current application of conventional accounting procedures does not assist necessarily to ascertain an entity's financial capacity to conduct its business or pay its debts.[2]

Critically, conventional accounting reports are used as a basis for determining an entity's ability to meet its immediate and future financial commitments.[3] Professional concepts statements like Australia's SAC2 note that general-purpose financial reports are intended to 'meet the information needs common to users' (para.5), in particular those users who 'must rely on the information communicated to them by the reporting entity' (para.7). Given this, the content of general-purpose accounting reports prepared in accord with generally accepted accounting practice (GAAP), professional accounting standards, corporations law, the various elements they contain and the financial amounts attributed to those elements are contestable.[4]

It is herein emphasised that an inherent part of an entity's financial position is its level of solvency. It has been demonstrated that to determine whether an entity is solvent requires specific information on the entity's ability to pay all its accumulated debts and additionally its financial capacity to continue to conduct its business activities. To achieve both necessitates a definitive account of relevant financial facts—data that provide a sound basis for calculating the entity's state of solvency.

To ascertain rather than to assume an entity's level of solvency and its capacity to trade requires that the reported amounts of its assets and liabilities relate to money and the dated worth of money in the trading environment. With this information, the financial outcome from the continual process of liquidating assets in the *ordinary course of business operations* would be calculable. Importantly, it would be the financial result of the entity's business activities in current terms; it would not be the financial result from a forced trading situation for a management under duress. In this context, it is worth noting that the debate in the accounting literature has often floundered by referring to exit values generally as *fire-sale* prices.[5]

Following, the concept of solvency is examined with emphasis on determining what is meant by quality financial information, especially that which is available for economic decision-makers and those charged with managing debt.[6] Secondly, implications of calculating an entity's state of solvency from conventionally prepared financial statements are explored. The third section considers the increasing complexity of financial reporting in the context of consolidating group accounts by investigating, in particular, effects of the ASIC Class Order Deeds of Cross Guarantee. This part explores the financial implications to parties affected by the Deed covenants within the group. Concluding remarks precede case study reviews and analyses from Chapter 5 through Chapter 7 inclusive.

SOLVENCY AND MANAGING DEBT

Business continuity necessitates controlled management of an entity's financial capacity to support its accumulated debts.[7] From time to time, managers incur debt to facilitate trade, to decide between business opportunities or swiftly to secure a financially viable business advantage. Subsequently, judgements are made concerning access to money, the use of money, the amount of money required, immediate financial circumstances of the entity and its likely future financial state. Whether conventionally-prepared financial statements are useful for such judgements is disputable. It has been shown earlier that those financial statements contain many arbitrary financial data that have no relationship to money or its use in business.

In order to transact business, an entity requires money or access to money (cash equivalents). To compare an entity's debt with its stock of money and ability to access money, the two parts of the comparison must logically be of the same property, of like kind. This complies with the basic rules of arithmetic.[8] Yet generally accepted accounting procedures confuse this logic.[9] By way of explanation, the amount of money represented by cash in the bank is comprehensible because it is a commodity that symbolizes a current financial amount. Debt is usually a contracted amount that has been agreed on by the involved parties for provision and receipt of goods or services. The financial amount, the money that will conclude the transaction, forms part of the contract and will not alter if the agreement remains intact. Other denominated assets in financial statements, which comprise an entity's stock of wealth, require more thought.

Consider a business entity's mix of assets and liabilities in conventional accounting terms. The net financial balance (the entity's net worth), by and large, represents the owners' claim on the business. Yet in financial terms it is not possible to establish the extent of that claim unless each item represents a common attribute, money. Furthermore, the expression of each item as money, money's worth or cash equivalent, necessitates that monetary amount to be expressed in the same numerical dimension. This is not achieved using conventional accounting methods.[10] Such aspects of accounting have further implications for business practice. Consider, for example, that managers are more likely to make adverse investment and financing decisions if the entity's up-to-date financial resource details are not readily available.

The concept of assets is to some people indeterminate. GAAP defines assets in a broad way, often in economist Irving Fisher's terms, with respect to a future economic benefit to the entity.[11] Assets so defined may not exist in any tangible, severable sense and hence may have no exchangeable monetary equivalent in relation to the trading community. Assets defined that way arguably may not offer any immediate material support or monetary relief in the payment of debt or in the determination of a business entity's net financial worth. Yet, such information is *a prius* in analysing an entity's financial state. Critically, managers should acknowledge the possible inadequacies inherent in conventionally prepared financial accounts when involved in planning and investment decisions.[12] The next sub-section explores this idea further.

Measurement Issues

Determining what method is best used to identify and value an entity's assets has been a controversial issue in the accounting literature throughout the twentieth century. And the debate continues.[13] Value in this context is often mistakenly interpreted to mean "measure." The aggregate reported financial amount attributed to an entity's net assets is considered by some to be an indication of the entity's worth.[14] As Fetter (1937, p.6) stated, 'the worth of any kind of business asset or investment, is a purely financial conception.' To others, the value of many assets is the resultant of determining an income figure, a residual—of those periodic costs not expensed, but capitalised. Carter (1910, p.561) remarked, 'it is customary to adopt more or less arbitrary rules for valuing assets each year in order to arrive at a profit that can be accepted for practical purposes.'[15] In contrast, Montgomery (1927, p.206) asserted that '[t]he best definition of value is purchasing power.' Such opinions remain evident today.

The extant accounting definition of assets provides a guide for identification in practice. But the result is usually a financial illusion created by the process of using GAAP accounting. Applying various GAAPs with the use of an ambiguous definition for assets and the variety of ways those assets can be valued in financial terms will likely produce an illusion of a financially useful "net asset" outcome.[16]

Across time many writers have recognized that there are myriad contexts for examining measurement—for instance, Campbell (1921/1952), Canning (1929), Stevens (1946), Margenau and Murphy (1943/1956), Chambers (1965), Sterling (1970) and Brown (1987). Herein, reference to measurement issues is with regard to quantifying solvency. The measurement of an asset and its reported quantification are often used synonymously in accounting. Yet they are not necessarily the same. Chambers (1998, p.41) explained:

> It is conceivable that one may seek to *quantify* a particular property of some former but now non-existent object, and to *quantify* a particular property of some (expected) future but not yet existent object. The question is, whether such quantifications can properly be described as measurements . . . its importance lies in the freedom or constraint with which numbers purporting to be measures may be added and otherwise related.[17]

Earlier Canning (1929, p.319) similarly remarked on the economists' grievance 'that the balance sheet valuations of accountants are of mongrel origin.' May (1936, p.17) stated, 'people who would not dream of adding together a cart-horse and a saw-horse and speaking of the result as two horses, have no compunction at all about adding together a book figure (or, as they call it, a book "value") and a market value, and speaking of the result as a "value." ' Moreover, 'the balance sheet, as a statement of affairs, remains a mixture of historical and current costs, face values, conventional valuations and arithmetical estimates, all of which have to be reconsidered in greater or less degree when it comes to a current assessment of the present value of proprietorship worth' (Editorial, *the Accountant*, 1946, p.293).

Martin (1984, p.392) continued this theme, explaining that 'the balance sheet is not additive because it contains amounts representing different properties of the assets . . . to add a current market value to a written down historic cost, a market value prevailing two years ago and a current market value . . . must be misleading for analytical purposes.'

More recently, Clarke *et al.* (2003, p.328) proffered a more critical observation of conventionally prepared accounting information:

> In a reasonably well-ordered society, one would expect, indeed demand, regulation be directed to achieving quality, reliability, fitness for use—serviceability of the product rather than mere standardisation of the

> processing rules . . . the accounting profession appears to have led the field in the pursuit of standardisation divorced from the pursuit of serviceability.

Clearly, diverse methods to determine asset monetary values continue, even within a class of assets with similar attributes. Although inventory, for instance, entails a major business asset, the way an entity's inventory is quantified and subsequently expressed in financial terms within financial accounting statements is disparate. The inventory balance, however, is often significant with regard to the entity's overall net asset position.

Under conventional accounting procedures, with regard to determining asset monetary value, inventory is stated at the lower of cost or market rule. AASB102, para.9 states, 'Inventories shall be measured at the lower of cost and net realisable value,' and '[t]he cost of inventories shall comprise all costs of purchase, costs of conversion and other costs incurred in bringing the inventories to their present location and condition' (para.10). In contrast, '[t]he cost of inventories of items that are not ordinarily interchangeable and goods or services produced and segregated for specific projects shall be assigned by using specific identification of their individual costs' (para.23). Nonetheless:

> The cost of inventories, other than those dealt with in paragraph 23, shall be assigned by using the first-in, first-out (FIFO) or weighted average cost formula. An entity shall use the same cost formula for all inventories having a similar nature and use to the entity. For inventories with a different nature or use, different cost formulas may be justified (para.25).[18]

The standard is convoluted.[19] It demands a technically possible but subjective and perhaps too flexible and confusing a method. It is a method that will only by chance result in an accurate assessment of the inventory's current financial worth. It can hardly assist *on average* in reliably calculating, in actual money terms, an entity's debt paying capacity.[20]

Alternatively, the full extent of an entity's inventory (assets) could be quantified and established by observation, physical count and marking its financial value to an active current market. Recent encouragement for this proposition is given by Scheutze (2001a, p.3) when he stated, 'there is no question that mark to market produces relevant information that investors and creditors can use to make investment decisions. Not only is the information relevant, its quality is undisputed. The two ideas—relevance of information and quality—go hand in glove.'[21] Notably, "mark to market" is different to "mark to model," although some confuse the two. This point is discussed later. Meanwhile, a market, for instance, is symbolic of an active general trading market (not necessarily, but may include, a securities market) whereas a model is a calculation of, for example, net present values (NPV).

Importantly, the *bona fide* "mark to market" model herein stressed is with regard to an ongoing general active market, NOT a market under duress, and not related to the hubris associated with some entity's manipulation of accounting numbers to confuse or blatantly mislead the public. While some continue to confuse the concept of mark to market and further expound the historic appeal of cost based "values," the SEC was insightful in emphasising that the mark to market model necessitates an active market:

> In October 2008, in response to the effects mark-to-market accounting had on the subprime crisis, the SEC began a study on MTM, and the Financial Accounting Standards Board proposed FAS 157-d, an accounting rule that would regulate the use of mark-to-market accounting on assets with no active market (for related reading, see *Policing The Securities Market: An Overview of the SEC*).

With due regard to solvency, business entities require current details that inform on changing circumstances within the markets in which they trade. It is arguably silly of directors and managers to believe in a book figure that denotes an inflated asset monetary equivalent when it is essential that they determine their entities financial capacity to pay its accumulated debt. It is particularly so when they determine to enable the entity they direct to continue to conduct its business after payment of debt.

Further to adversaries' concerns on market-based monetary equivalents of operating assets are inventories. The method historically and currently prescribed for the measurement of inventories does not result in a financial attribute of anything. The process involves the aggregation of a number of dissimilar amounts. If all the numbers are similar in that they represent costs to the business entity, it remains that those costs would have been incurred at different times, and over time the value of money, the worth of that money in the changing economic environment, would have altered. It becomes evident as time passes that costs, in relation to money, are not *of the same kind*. It is clear that costs, in relation to monetary asset values are, as Scheutze (2001b) lamented, 'awful.'[22]

Measurement requires that the magnitude of a particular attribute corresponds to an accepted and a uniform scale. When the financial amount of inventory is reported in a statement of worth (financial position, solvency), the properties, characteristics and qualities of the money amount used to represent the inventory items must be constant. There are numerous examples throughout the literature specifying the necessary characteristics of measurement, for instance:

> The essential character of any attribute belonging to the category of quantity is . . . [e]ach state of a quantity's magnitude may always be formed through addition by means of other smaller states of the same

> quantity; each quantity is the union through a commutative and associative operation of quantities smaller than the first *but of the same kind* (Duhem, 1974, p.110; emphasis added).

Markedly, it is essential that the quantities are 'of the same kind.' This idea supports previous discussion, notably that cost values from different time periods are not elements that are of like kind, hence not to be added. Earlier, Campbell (1921/1952, p.117) deliberated:

> If a property is to be measurable it must be such that (1) two objects which are the same in respect of that property as some third object are the same as each other; (2) by adding objects successively we must be able to make a standard series one member of which will be the same in respect of the property as any object we want to measure; (3) equals added to equals produce equal sums. In order to make a property measurable we must find some method of judging equality and of adding objects, such that these rules are true.

The fundamental notion is that of sameness, that each object to be measured has a like and distinguishable property. Davidson and Moore (1938/1958, p.13) noted, 'A *unit* or a *unit quantity* (from the Latin word *unus,* one) is the name given to a quantity when we use it for the purpose of comparing the magnitudes of other quantities of the *same kind as itself.*' More recently, Chambers (1998, p.41) stated, '[t]he operation of measuring, in the simplest of cases, entails the establishment, by observation, of correspondence between the magnitude of a property of an object and a particular point on a calibrated scale which is designed to represent various magnitudes of that property.' The task then of measuring properties of objects, ensuring they are of like kind, is no less crucial when dealing with financial affairs.

Notably, there has been much debate in the literature about measurement, value and valuation.[23] Some of these ideas directly relate to the current accounting practice that seeks to put a financial amount on something that is perceived to be of a future economic benefit "value" to a business entity. Arguably the result will more than likely be misleading, especially if one is to assume that the amount represents a measure. As Margenau (1950, p.374) asserted, 'never do we say that we are measuring the value of a quantity at a future time, even though it may be possible to predict that value [in some sense] on the basis of a measurement made at present.'

Hence, monetary amounts attributed to expectations of the future may well be misinterpreted. The amounts inappropriately may be given significance as facts by some, whereas 'Measurement is the discovery of an extant condition and requires a present act. One cannot measure a magnitude that lies in the future. Instead, one predicts such magnitudes and *verifies* them by a measurement operation when the future becomes the present' (Sterling, 1968, p.498). The point is that we live in the present, the past has been and gone, but the future has not happened, and as such we cannot know the facts of the future until we live them. Pointedly for accounting, Vickrey (1970, p.738) proclaimed that, '[u]ltimately, the logic and usefulness of measurements depend on the additivity of extensive properties . . . [and] *all* accounting calculations depend ultimately on addition . . . the additivity of extensive properties is the key to accounting measurement'.[24] This must surely apply in the particular circumstance of deciding the financial ability of a business entity to pay its debts and its financial capacity to continue trading activities into the future.

What Story Do Accounting Numbers Tell?

'Accounting data are reasonably expected to reflect financial reality in its legal, social and economic contexts' (Clarke *et al.*, 2003, p.266). In business, entities seek finance (money and/or access to money) from time to time in order to continue activities, expand operations and/or pursue other economic opportunities as they arise. These developments in the life cycle of a business can cause unprecedented financial distress. As such, it is evident that all debt incurred in the process of conducting business must be identified, supervised and continually managed to ensure that the entity's ability to pay its debts, whenever they become due and payable, is maintained.

There are a number of financial instruments available to business to ensure easier access to finance and to encourage creditor support. These include the uniquely Australian regulatory approved deed of cross guarantee between companies in a group structure and floating or specific charges over particular assets. Such facilities may serve to increase an entity's line of credit and so its capacity to conduct business. They may also, however, result in misleading financial information in the group accounts. This is especially of concern when separate entities in a group of entities guarantee each others' debt, as examined in what follows.

GROUP ACCOUNTS AND CONSOLIDATED DATA—IN THE CONTEXT OF A REPORTING ENTITY

Well-known to academics and practitioners is that a "group" comprises 'a parent [entity] and all its subsidiaries' (AASB127, para.4)[25] and that '[c]onsolidated financial statements shall include all subsidiaries of the parent' (para.12). Hence, '*Consolidated financial statements* are the financial statements of a group presented as those of a single economic entity' (para.4). Furthermore, '[a] *subsidiary* is an entity, including an unincorporated entity such as a partnership, that is controlled by another entity (known as the parent)' (para.4, emphasis in original). As the parent entity reports on the group's performance, '[i]ntragroup balances, transactions, income and expenses shall be eliminated in full' (para.20), and the '[c]onsolidated financial statements shall be prepared using uniform accounting policies for like transactions and other events in similar circumstances' (para.24).

Purportedly, this convoluted "fine-tuning" of various separate entities' periodic financial results into the reported financial results of a single economic entity is meant to provide users, dependent on general-purpose financial statements, with details that inform them on the overall business and its financial state. Further, those details are meant to assist them to evaluate the group's performance and make economic decisions about the allocation of scarce resources.

In Australia, the Corporations' Law requires that directors shall prepare group accounts in accord with the accounting standards (s.295(2)). In this context, professional prescriptions dictate that group accounts are consolidated for financial reporting purposes.[26] This means that no company, or separate entity, within the economic unit should be seen to profit from another entity in the group. If those entities have participated in business transactions between themselves during a particular accounting period, any inter-company profit or loss (and related items like deferred tax debits and credits), for instance on the purchase and sale of assets, would be eliminated on consolidation. In addition, any inter-group company loans would be eliminated and further adjustments made as changes in organizational structure occurred. [27]

Such factors provide the rationale for implementing accounting procedures that promote the consolidation of accounts and supposedly increase the level of information to users. Of course the parent entity, under particular circumstances, is exempted from consolidating accounts (AASB127, para.10). Prior to the release of AASB127,[28] Clarke *et al.* (2002, p.62) argued, '[a]ccounting is being asked to do what it is not geared to do-account for the wealth and progress of different legal entities and commercial alliances as if they were neither separate entities nor individually subject to the vagaries of different commercial settings.' The release of the AASB127, its implementation that incorporates the international accounting standard requirements of IAS 27, has arguably changed little.[29] As Dean *et al.* (2008, p.71) asserted, 'The serviceability of consolidated (economic entity or closed group) accounting data is demonstrated . . . to be equally problematic for those officers making those assessments in respect of an economic group and any related closed group.'

Evidently, in the process of consolidating the financial data of each entity within the economic entity, pertinent details regarding each entity are lost; hence, details on the financial state of the business structure in its entirety are lost.[30] Further, the parent entity and each subsidiary or controlled entities within the consolidated group forgo their unique identity to a mythical construction—the economic entity.

Individual entities in the group structure are generally accepted, in accounting, to be separate divisions of the one company. Noted is that the 'type of group settings in Australia differs from those in other jurisdictions. Thus, . . . [certain arguments] are setting-specific and may not be generalisable to those other jurisdictions' (Dean *et al.*, 2008, p.73). Nonetheless, it is applicable generally that:

> [I]f the desire is to report the activities of the separate (especially wholly-owned subsidiary) companies as if, from the group point of view, they were mere branches of the controlling company to be operated as branches, why have them as separate companies in the first place? . . . whereas the defects of historical cost accounting would remain, the aggregation of the branches' data would not require the fabrication of accounting artifacts as occurs in the professionally and legally prescribed consolidation process (Clarke *et al.*, 2003, p.272).

The conventional consolidation process actually enhances opportunities for those preparing the statement to engage in inventive financial procedures. Inventive or creative accounting, given the choices available within the accounting standards (international or country specific), may be *par for the course* under GAAP, but inventive to the point of *feral* accounting is quite a different concern.[31]

In 2003, the Parmalat saga in Italy reinforced concerns of the potential obfuscatory nature of corporate group structures and their related consolidated accounting. Consolidation procedures further detract from the financial information available in conventionally-prepared accounting reports, from the believability of results when such accounting numbers are used in financial analysis. They make contestable claims that *quality information* can be derived from the financial details provided in such accounts. Scheutze (2001a, p.12) appositely noted:

> Only by requiring that assets and liabilities have a reference point in the marketplace and that the amounts representing those assets and liabilities be verifiable by reference to sources, competent sources, outside the enterprise, will we be able to produce financial statements that include reliable numbers . . . and, only if such change is made will the financial statements be of high quality.

During the past decade, nothing has changed to constrain that point of view of Scheutze (2001a). Such concerns would appear to be exacerbated with the use of financial instruments such as debt guarantees like the ASIC Class Order Deed of Cross Guarantee. The *quid-pro-quo* of using the Class Order Deed is the need *only* to provide consolidated accounting data—the subsidiaries (who execute the Deed) do not need to have audited accounts filed with ASIC.

ASIC CLASS ORDER DEED OF CROSS GUARANTEE: AN ILLUSTRATION

In Australia, the all-inclusive ASIC Deed became operative in late 1991 when it supplanted the NCSC Deed of Indemnity that had been introduced in 1986.[32] A class order deed of cross guarantee essentially means that each entity in a group that participates in the deed is liable for the debt of the others.[33] As noted, the cross guarantee reduces the financial reporting requirements for corporate groups, thereby purportedly reducing their costs of disclosure.[34] Such entities are referred to as a *closed-group* within the economic group.[35] Even with such an arrangement, directors of each company are required by law to know the current financial state of the entity under their direction, but what entity? For instance, each company in the closed-group is a separate legal entity, in its own right, but the compensating covenants of the ASIC Deed allow financial reporting relief to each subsidiary company in the closed-group.

So, those published financial reports relate to the group of companies as one notional entity—the group enterprise—effectively for reporting purposes one company. Hence, an abstract entity, the group, becomes the only reporting entity. The financial results of business transacted by each separate entity in the group are not lodged with ASIC, and potentially information is lost to the public. For the closed-group, however, increased investing and financing opportunities due to the cross guarantee of debt may arise, and the off-shoot stakeholder confidence might increase. Nonetheless, there is another dimension. There is a decrease in the already questionable degree of the quality of the financial information contained in conventional accounting reports.

Now with regard to solvency, 'What is it that we want for investors when we say "high quality financial statements" or "high quality information?" . . . financial statement amounts (numbers) that are relevant and reliable' (Scheutze, 2001a, p.13). As Lewis (2010, p.400) with reference to *Hall v. Poolman* (2007) and *Sheahan v. Hertz Australia Pty Ltd* (1995) asserted:

> It is not appropriate to base an expectation of solvency upon the prospect that the company might trade profitably in the future, thereby restoring its financial position. The question is not whether the company might be able to pay its debts in the future if given time to trade profitably, but whether at the *relevant* time it is able to pay its debts as they become due (emphasis added).

Earlier, with regard to accounting "rules" and procedures, Wolnizer (1987, p.148) remarked:

> [T]he reliability of accounts is directly determined by the quality of their design, and accounting rules are the expression of that design. *Reliability* entails fitness for use over a specified period of time. To build into accounts that quality necessitates that accounting rules have the character of specifications; and this *presupposes contemplation of the function to be served by accounts and the nature of the environment in which accounts are to perform that function* (emphasis added).

Apparently without such focus, on the function—hence, the quality of financial reports—the ASIC Class Order Deeds of Cross Guarantee formed part of the 1998 Australian Corporation Law amendments. And the 'confusion generated by the regulatory imposition of the *avant-garde* ASIC Class Order Deed of Cross Guarantee and CASAC's proposed "opting-in" arrangements'[36] continues. In 2008, Dean *et al.* examined perceptions of corporate officers on solvency and noted:

> A pervading focus exists. Corporate officers' perceptions of the nature of a corporate group are often at odds with the legal reality. Notions such as "group solvency" and the means of assessing it invite an appeal to a legal nonsense. . . . Particularly significant is access to a voluntary, regulatory-approved ASIC deed of cross-guarantee (deed) by which group companies guarantee the debts of one another, thereby simultaneously retaining but by-passing the corporate veil. [Including] proposed regulatory attempts to lift the veil, such as the *ex ante* "opting-in" and "opting-out" arrangements and *ex-post* judicial pooling facilities (p.72; emphasis in original).

The ASIC Deed supersedes the ASIC Class-Order Deed of Cross Guarantee that extended the previous NCSC[37] indemnity provision where the subsidiary companies in the closed group were not required to guarantee the debt of all other subsidiary companies.

> The ASIC stated that the rationale for extending the [previous NCSC] cross-claim indemnity to a cross-guarantee by all companies in the "closed-group", was to ensure that by entering into a "Deed of Cross Guarantee, a wholly owned subsidiary (effectively) pools its assets and liabilities with its holding company" (Clarke *et al.*, 1995, p.52).

For further insight into the pooling of funds, closed-groups and the corporate veil, refer to Dean *et al.*, (2008) and Dean and Clarke (2003). Debt guarantees across related entities can be a positive business strategy for the corporate group but only when the financial state of each entity within the closed-group is able to be, and is, substantiated (externally verified) from time to time. Without this knowledge, the situation for closed-groups may be particularly precarious. For instance, 'the grouping and pooling issues that Justice Owen observed at HIH . . . stresses the importance of understanding the separate legal entity principle enunciated in *Salomon v Salomon*. And while Justice Owen's observations were specific to insurance companies they resonate for all companies. . . . Consider the particulars of the [later] Sons of Gwalia case' (Dean *et al.*, 2008, p.77).[38]

Earlier, Clarke *et al.* (2003, p.249) revealed:

> Despite the image of size and solidarity and perpetuity generated by large corporate groups, history shows that once one of the related companies

> topples, the rest may fall like a line of dominoes. Westmex in the 1980s and HIH and One.Tel in the 1990s were seminal Australian examples. But, it is also possible for any solvent company within a group to walk away from the obligations of the insolvent if they *legally* can, as occurred with the MLC at H.G. Palmer in the 1960s and Air New Zealand with Ansett in 2001. Corporate solidarity is a financial and legal myth. Sentiment does not get in the way of corporate business. That is a major reason why corporate cross guarantees generally, and the ASIC Deed of Cross Guarantee specifically, came into existence, and CASAC's proposals *opting-in* selected subsidiaries were developed.

Similarly, without the use of instruments such as deeds of cross guarantee, Enron, prior to its collapse, hedged risky tech stock with a number of specific investment vehicles (funded by Enron and New Power)[39] to protect a likely $1 billion in income. An unanticipated 'fall in the New Power stock threatened to topple one of the . . . structures, triggering a domino effect that would knock over the others.'[40] Apparently, within a matter of weeks, the various entities were insolvent or heading that way. Following this, the Italian-based international (and perceived by many as impregnable) dairy products Parmalat group was duly placed under Italian bankruptcy administration with the likelihood of a sell-off of its overseas subsidiaries. This occurred without Parmalat's published financial reports indicating such an impending financial demise.

Fundamentally, the use of debt cross guarantee instruments may create a financial façade between trading entities in a group—unless each separate entity in that group is financially sound. This is partly because once the deed is implemented the deed confuses the boundaries of the reporting entity. Ultimately, a deed of cross guarantee cannot be reliably functional without directors and other corporate officers having access to the facts of each separate entity's financial state within the group. And if directors and other corporate officers have access to such financial facts, then why should not all its stakeholders?

This is particularly so when considering the number of possible separate entities in any one closed-group. For 'despite the rhetoric, a "group" of companies [including a closed group] is neither a single entity under the present general interpretation of the law, nor (usually) reasonably identifiable as a separate economic unit' (Clarke *et al.*, 2003, pp.266–267). Arguably, events with Air New Zealand scuttling its wholly-owned subsidiary, Ansett, provide an apt illustration.

It is worth considering the following limited extracts of results from an unpublished work (Clarke, Dean and Houghton, 2003), where questions were asked of preparers of closed group consolidated reports and related solvency assessments.[41] In response to the question "When preparing your solvency statement in respect of closed group companies do you draw on information contained in the closed group financial statements?", 29 respondents (out of 80 companies surveyed that have an ASIC Deed of Cross Guarantee) answered as shown in Table 4.1

Table 4.1 Brief Summary of Responses

Number of Respondents	*Financial Reports Employed*
18	(i) Financial statements of individual companies in the group of companies
15	(ii) Financial statements of the relevant company's closed-group reports prepared in accord with Accounting Standards
10	(iii) Each of these companies sought information from other sources than their closed-group financial reports
6	Combined (i) and (ii) above
4	Utilised (i), (ii) and (iii) above
3	Employed (i) and (iii)
1	Made use of (ii) and (iii)

Source. Clarke, Dean and Houghton (2003).

Subsequently, Dean *et al.* (2008, p.75) elaborated, and interviewees were asked the following:

> *If you answered b)* . . . [the equivalent to (ii) in Table 4.1] *then do you consider your company's closed-group financial statements, prepared in accordance with accounting standards, alone provide a sufficient basis for your solvency statement* (emphasis in original)?
>
> Of the 15 respondents who answered 'b)' [ii as above] (either exclusively or in combination with 'a)' or 'c)' . . . [equivalent to (i) and (iii) as above] 10 agreed their company's closed-group financial statements (prepared in accordance with accounting standards) *did not provide a sufficient basis for their solvency statement.* It is unclear however, from the [question] 17.1 b) responses how many of those particular respondents sought information from other sources (Dean *et al.*, 2008, pp.75, 76; emphasis added).

Of concern, 'it appears that company officers hold equivocal perceptions regarding solvency and entertain multiple factors in their determination of it' (Dean *et al.*, 2008, p.76). A reasonable inference to draw from these data are that there is contestable information contained in the closed-group consolidated reports (now prescribed by regulation to be included in the 'Notes to the Consolidated Accounts') of a parent company executing an ASIC Deed of Cross Guarantee and that any solvency assessments would not have recourse to data contained therein. Directors would not use the data as starting points to undertake their assessments.

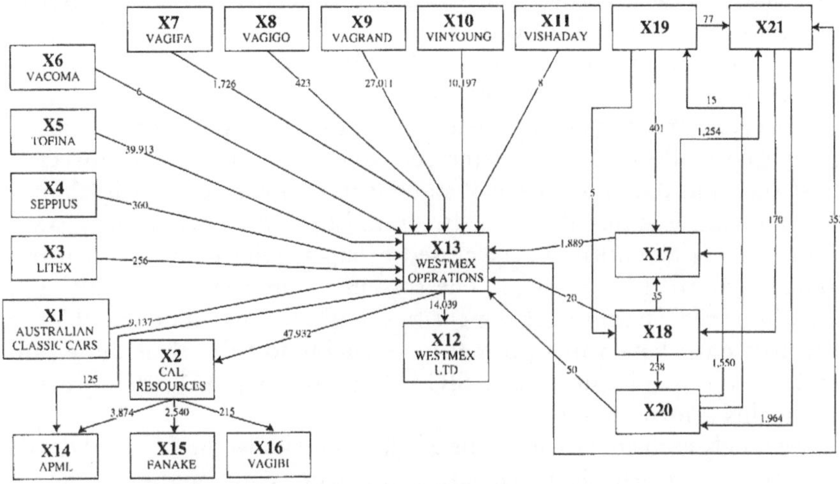

Figure 4.1 'Intercompany commercial dealings between Westmex "closed-group" companies ($000s).'

The incongruity of reporting on an abstract entity is further illustrated in Figure 4.1, which shows a closed-group of separate entities within Westmex, an economic group that collectively forms an economic entity for reporting purposes. Details in the figure highlight inter-company financial transactions between the entities that are not given in consolidated accounts of the economic entity. This is likely to further exacerbate the 'idiosyncratic consolidating mechanisms [that] make those *aggregations* [of accounting numbers] even less capable of meaningful interpretation' (Clarke *et al.*, 2003, p.269), especially when arbitrary risk factors are incorporated into the financial statements of institutions, such as general insurers in an attempt to compensate for the particularly stochastic nature of general insurance business.[42]

ASIC Deed of Cross-Guarantee: An Australian Example

ASIC explain the functions and features of the deed. Interestingly, although all entities in the closed-group are included in the deed, a wholly-owned entity may be excluded from the deed if 'relief' is not required.[43] For example, if a partially-owned entity in the group seeks relief, then all other entities in the group that form part of that ownership must be included in the deed. In contrast, 'a stand-alone, [but] wholly-owned entity that has no ownership interest in that partially owned entity, does not have to be included in the deed.'[44] The key point is that all entities that seek relief are to be included in the deed as well as all entities that, directly or indirectly, hold shares in those entities that seek relief. An entity planning to expand may consider it convenient to be a party to the deed and so be included, although it is not required to do so. In short, the boundaries of the economic entity are further confused.

It is necessary, however, for each entity that forms part of the closed-group to provide a solvency statement. To do this, at least two directors must sign and date the solvency statement.[45] This statement is qualitative. Further, it is possible that directors issue only one solvency statement to cover all entities in the closed-group as long as the directors are common to all those entities. The solvency statement apparently is to contain or reflect details of the entities' ability to pay its debts. Hence, directors must have this information arguably to fulfil their duties and abide by the requirements of ASIC.[46] But from where do the directors access this information?

Seemingly each entity within the group would know the financial details of its ability to pay its debts. Hence, each separate entity within the closed-group would be able to report and publish details of their financial position, if required. Each entity then would be able to elaborate on those debts that may adversely affect the group. So, why not publish this information? Given that deed guarantee covenants are not readily available to the public, it will be interesting to see how a court would interpret the ASIC Deed. This has not yet been established. To further convolute the situation, CASAC (2000, p.39) under Recommendation 2 stipulated that:

> The Corporations Law should provide that a wholly-owned corporate group can "opt-in" to be a consolidated corporate group for all or some of the group companies . . . [and that] . . . companies in a consolidated corporate group should be governed by single enterprise principles.

Were this proposed reform to be adopted, the original corporate concept of limited liability and the separate entity approach to corporate law as practiced in common law countries would be changed substantially. The single enterprise approach, contrary to the separate entity ideal, 'recognises and attaches considerable legal significance to economic integration within a corporate group . . . it treats the corporate group as a unitary economic enterprise functioning to further the interests of the group as a whole, or those of its dominant corporate body' (CASAC, 2000, p.23).

Fundamentally, it seems there is little difference, if any, between the availability of corporate deeds of cross guarantee, within the separate entity concept and the "opting-in" approach provided for under CASAC's proposed single enterprise scheme. Such moves appear to increase the issues surrounding corporate governance in the twenty-first century.

The ASX requirements for corporate governance, for instance, advocate an increase in compliance reports for publicly listed corporations. This is of concern as professional bodies and other regulators have yet to produce convincing evidence 'to support the idea that the quality of accounting data and financial reporting can be guaranteed through mandating compliance with prescribed practices' (Clarke *et al.*, 2003, p.328). And that includes the current hype in the business community concerning corporate governance practice and corporate governance reports to stakeholders.

Continuing earlier discussion, the following sub-section elaborates on the intricacies of dealing with an abstract economic entity in contrast to an observable legal entity.

The Concept of an Abstract Entity

A group of companies, where each company is a separate legal entity, is an abstract entity. For accounting purposes, this abstract entity is a reporting entity, and reports are compiled as consolidated financial statements.[47] It is arguable whether this process of consolidating financial data succeeds in providing meaningful information on the financial state of a group of companies. It has been argued by some academic and financial commentators that it is more likely to result in increased confusion for users of financial reports not least because the entity being reported is a technical creation. It is an abstract and imaginative organization (in the minds of accountants) of separate legal entities. Yet, the main purpose seems to be to summarize the financial results of the group of related companies and report those results as though the collective set were actually one company. Whether this can be accomplished meaningfully, in essence, is debatable.[48]

Conflicting ideas on the serviceability of consolidated financial data permeate academic literature. More than thirty years ago, the Accounting Standards Committee (UK) (ASC) stated:

> It is generally accepted that consolidated financial statements are usually the best means of achieving the objective of group accounts which is to give a true and fair view of the profit and loss and of the state of affairs of the group . . . the same principles apply to consolidated financial statements as would apply to the financial statements of a single entity (ASC, 1978, SSAP14).

The ideas implied that the general standard of financial reporting would not diminish with consolidated statements, but in that same year Walker (1978, p.386) remarked, 'By 1940 consolidated reports had become an accepted vehicle for corporate reporting . . . [yet] uncertainty was reflected in an array of inconsistent and confused practices and rules.' Nearly twenty-five years later, Clarke *et al.* (2003, p.269) argued that consolidated statements 'contradict the legal, social and financial essence which their constituent corporations enjoy.' Precisely:

> Consolidated statements report on a fictitious structure, the group, which lacks legal capacity generally to exercise property rights, to sue or be sued, to incur physical or financial damage or impose it on others. . . . By virtue of legal incapacity, *group* assets and *group* liabilities are an impossibility unless the legislature intervenes, for example, by introducing covenants such as apply under a Class Order Deed of Cross Guarantee (Clarke *et al.*, 2003, p.269).

Nevertheless, and as seems to be the case in consolidating group accounts, once an accounting procedure becomes part of general practice, the idea is likely to become entrenched in society. The practical application of the procedure is then more than likely to become habitual rather than thoughtful.[49] In reporting financial information to users, it is evident that 'artifactual data only generated by the consolidation process are inserted in the consolidated statements, whereas genuine transaction data are excluded. Consolidation processes manage to nurture the worst of both sides of creative accounting' (Clarke *et al.*, 2003, p.271).

More than twenty-five years before, Metcalf (1977, pp.188, 189) stated:

> The term creative accounting is widely used to describe accepted accounting techniques which permit corporations to report financial results that may not accurately portray the substance of their business activities . . . creative accounting is recognized as a synonym for deceptive accounting. . . . Creative accounting methods are noteworthy because they remain in use as generally accepted accounting principles, even though they have been shown to be deceptive in many cases.

Consider recent examples of Enron and WorldCom in the US and HIH and One.Tel in Australia—yet creative accounting is arguably permissible within the constructs of accounting standards; it is preferable to talk of feral accounting. The aforementioned cases and others discussed in following chapters reflect a number of similarities that may be related to the case of Westmex Ltd.,[50] where each entity's published financial statements apparently masked the *true* dated financial position of the business.

Deeds of Cross Guarantee and the Group Structure—Westmex Ltd

This sub-section draws on Clarke *et al.* (2003, p.198), who explained that Westmex Ltd. began operations in 1969 in Western Australia. It was a publicly listed Australian company. During the late 1970s to mid 1980s, Westmex's business activities diversified from mineral exploration to real estate, option and share trading and earthmoving contracts, until finally by 1985 the group's investment focus was on equity trading and gold.[51] Then, from the mid 1980s, Westmex's operations underwent further change under the direction of its new CEO, Russell Goward. The group continued to develop and expand as its organisational structure altered. It moved quickly into overseas entrepreneurial business ventures and was soon trading in specialized investments across industries throughout the world.

At that time, Westmex consisted of more than 50 companies, 36 forming a closed-group under the protection of an NCSC deed of indemnity. Figure 4.1 depicts the final position (at the time of the Westmex group liquidation) of transactions within the closed-group and illustrates the extent of relationships between entities within Westmex. The figure[52] shows the separate entities, the expected inflow of funds to and the repayment of debt due to Westmex Operations and, in turn, its debt obligations to Westmex Ltd.

The companies on the perimeter of the figure, with arrows pointing inwards to Westmex Operations, owed that entity the amount shown in $000s. Hence, each entity's separate inter-company debt arrangement with Westmex Operations is evident.

If the debt of each separate entity in the group were tabulated, the overall information content as depicted in Figure 4.1 would remain intact. However, when such financials are aggregated in eliminating within group transactions, information on the liability of each separate entity in the group is lost.

Consolidating the financial details of separate entities within a group of entities that form an *economic entity* for reporting purposes, such as in Figure 4.1 of Westmex, creates an illusory financial picture. The consolidated financials of the abstract entity, as in the case of Westmex Ltd., are more likely to confuse and mislead an unsuspecting public, as 'data so contrived, so removed from real world referents [are unlikely to] inform of the wealth and progress of the constituent companies, either individually or collectively' (Clarke *et al.*, 2003, p.273).

With regard to Westmex, for instance, prior to the end of the 1980s, the financial press seemed unconcerned about its financial condition. However, a deed of cross guarantee that secured the financial state of companies within the closed-group was soon revealed as a façade in terms of the group's financial stability.[53] 'Westmex was placed in liquidation in early 1990 [notwithstanding that] the list of creditors in the Statement of Affairs included major Australian banks, some overseas banks and many of the other major Australian financial houses' (Clarke *et al.*, 2003, p.200).[54]

Furthermore and as legally required, directors had attested the solvency of the group, particularly the relieved companies within the closed-group. Nonetheless, the reported trend in the prior years of increasing Westmex profits, asset growth and expanding corporate realm were eventually shown to be questionable with particular regard to the entity's state of solvency. This situation is evidenced in Table 4.2 but is more extensively documented in Clarke *et al.* (2003, pp.202, 203).[55]

Table 4.2 Westmex Ltd.—Some Reported Financials: 1983–1989

Variable	*1983 $000*	*1984 $000*	*1985 $000*	*1986 $000*	*1987 $000*	*1988 $000*	*1989 $000*
Total current assets	1,769	2,145	2,986	3,268	5,998	74,656	172,775
Current liabilities	161	187	399	1,852	21,230	71,586	198,377
Net working capital	1,607	1,958	2,587	1,417	-15,233	3,070	-25,602
Total invested capital	2,171	2,391	2,782	5,295	78,903	102,144	144,493
Long-term debt	0	0	0	0	0	49,244	224,082
Other deferred liabilities	0	0	0	0	0	834	2,893
Ordinary equity	2,171	2,391	2,782	5,295	78,903	36,829	-152,483
Intangibles	50	50	0	0	0	18,307	239,497
Total assets	2,383	2,628	3,181	7,146	100,133	192,037	582,367
Profit (after tax) Westmex A/Cs	126	45	163	355	7,294	17,645	27,015

Source. Clarke *et al.* (2003, pp.202, 203).

Although reported profits were increasing in the accounting records of Westmex, by 1990, the Group was in liquidation. Its reported total asset figure meant little, if anything, in the way of security for creditors.[56] The financial emphasis given to intangibles during 1988 and 1989 meant little with regard to Westmex's financial capacity to cover its accumulated debt. Its fluctuating working capital figure also demanded attention in line with its increasing long-term debt during the 1988–1989 period.[57] Such circumstances diminished its creditor's comfort zone and emphasised the 'Security façade of Cross Guarantees.'[58]

Clarke *et al.* (2003, p.210) suggested, '[a] characteristic of those deeds . . . [was] to limit investors' and creditors' access to public sources of the financial data relating to subsidiaries comprising a "closed-group."' Although stakeholders could access the consolidated accounts of Westmex, the financial data of each subsidiary in the created group would effectively be lost. This meant the reported financial state of the Group during the late 1980s was more likely to be fiction than fact. Notwithstanding the favourable press reports the Group received, Henry Bosch was one who questioned the *quality* and extent of *truth and fairness* in the Group's reported financial

Table 4.3 Commonalities of Corporate Collapse

Company Name	*Meaning/ Definition of Words: disclosure*	*Concern about GAAP*	*Measure-ment Issues*	*Rules, Regs. & Related Concerns*	*Unexpected Collapse or Business Failure*
Westmex Ltd.	*	*	*	*	*
Budget Corp. Ltd.	*	*	*	*	*
Duke Group Ltd.	*	*	*	*	*
Burns Philp Pty. Ltd.	*	*	*	*	*
HIH Insurance Ltd.	*	*	*	*	*
One.Tel Ltd.	*	*	*	*	*

Source. Adapted from Clarke *et al.* (2003, pp.198–211).

accounts.[59] The fall of Westmex and other corporate entities throughout the 1980s (Clarke *et al.*, 2003) are similar in circumstance to corporate collapses and other financial sagas discussed in Chapters 5, 6 and 7. Table 4.3 provides a brief summary of issues similar to Westmex Ltd., and the cases are explored in later chapters herein.

Preamble to Case Study Critique

Drawing on the 'observational order' of events, the case analyses in Chapters 5, 6 and 7 examine practical aspects of being in business and accounting for an entity's business activities. Difficulties of quantifying a business' financial state from conventionally prepared accounting reports are investigated. The method used is deductive and interpretive and empirical—based on observable data. The sources of data include mainly publicly available financial reports, printed judgements, media reports and company prospectus.

Such case analyses provide instances of what Chambers (1973b) described as 'observation—a method of enquiry' here, drawing on detailed illustrations from several different cases across time, definitive of an empirical form of research. The actual revealed performance of each company becomes the control against which the reported financial numbers are compared. Each of the cases embodies *unexpected financial failure or corporate collapse after its financial statements had been published that depict the entity as solvent.*

Hence, Chapters 5, 6 and 7 elaborate the critical inquiry of previous chapters. The investigations demonstrate further accounting defects formerly identified, examined and evaluated by Chambers (1973b/1986) using national and international case studies and by Clarke *et al.* (1997/2003) in their primarily Australian case analyses. These investigations, as previously explained, indicate that certain accounting deficiencies have existed from the 1960s throughout the 1990s and continue into the new millennium.

5 Circumstances of One.Tel and HIH

> *Flavius:* 'Call me before the exactest auditors [a]nd set me on the proof' (Shakespeare, *Timon of Athens*, II:ii).

ON BUSINESS CONTINUITY

Business failure, corporate collapse, *unexpected* corporate collapse; of course, little is new. Historically, different words were evident—concern was with ensuring entities reported "truthfully," and that there was "sunlight" with respect to entities' financial affairs—truth for quality, sunlight for transparency. One.Tel, along with HIH, Enron, WorldCom, Ansett, Water Wheel and others, illustrate (among other things) the likelihood that unexpected corporate collapse will continue, as the circumstances of each demise adds to the previous collection of unanticipated financial catastrophes during the twentieth century that now creep into the new millennium. Consider:

> [The] evidence before [the HIHRC] and the ASIC investigation into One.Tel [that] has revealed the flimsy foundation of many accounting practices. More importantly, they have revealed the ease with which the myriad Standards and rules of accounting practice are circumvented . . . primarily because they are divorced from the financial (and legal) reality of the transactions to which they relate (Clarke *et al.*, 2003, p.327).

With this in mind, the following explores events surrounding business failure and the collapse of several corporate entities. This chapter examines certain circumstances of One.Tel Limited (One.Tel) and HIH Insurance Limited (HIH). Chapter 6 then explores situations of the Duke Group Limited, Budget Corporation Limited and Burns Philp & Company Limited. Such cases elaborate indicators of financial distress and illustrate the essentiality for business to have ready access to current, relevant financial details to inform and to enable ongoing business operations in a dynamic economic environment.

The case of HIH is significant in that it illustrates numerous facets of business failure. But more than that, it is the epitome of what went before—the failed conglomerates of the 1960s, increased pressure on regulators throughout the 1970s, entrepreneurial flair—the role of the dominant Chairman and CEO—of the 1980s and the complex administrative arrangements that surfaced in the 1990s between subsidiaries and parent entities—focussing on related party transactions. HIH is a vibrant prototype in the analysis of how best to define quality financial information with a view to quantifying an entity's state of solvency and establishing its financial position. Clarke *et al.* (2003, p.222) explained HIH's features as follows:

> HIH may prove to be the exemplar corporate collapse—lashings of hubris, *groupthink,* creative and alleged feral accounting, alleged insider trading, lengthy regulatory inquiries, press concentration on the individuals, a judicial scalp or two and a flurry of proposed reforms. But the financial reporting system remains relatively untouched. Whither the lessons from history?

Collectively, the cases herein provide insight into accounting issues that continue to pervade generally accepted financial accounting practice and seemingly contribute to frequently unforeseen financial calamities. The following elaborates One.Tel.

ONE.TEL LIMITED

One.Tel, a new-age telecommunications business, commenced operations in the mid 1990s. Its founders, Jodee Rich and Brad Keeling, worked quickly and effectively to enable One.Tel to join the fast-growing and lucrative mobile phone market in Australia, but not as a primary carrier, as a reseller of network access to the public.[1] The new telco was soon to be an international telecommunications conglomerate with a wide-ranging suite of products.[2] In 1997, its second year of business, One.Tel's sales more than doubled—the same year that the telecommunications industry was deregulated in Australia. As it failed within four years of its birth, One.Tel is an archetype Argenti—*Type 1* failure.[3]

By November 1997, One.Tel was floated on the Australian Securities Exchange (ASX) at $2 per share, a market capitalization of $208 million.[4] The pace of the One.Tel start-up was reminiscent of another beginning sixteen years earlier with the birth of Imagineering, also led by Rich.[5] Its story provides a backdrop for the state of affairs that were soon to unfold for One.Tel (refer to Appendix 5.1).

On May 1, 1995, Rodney Adler officially launched the new company, and by June of that year, One.Tel allegedly had 1,000 customers from a population of around 2 million.[6] Three months later, One.Tel's customer base reportedly had reached 10,000 new clients; the explosion in numbers seemingly linked to the $120 incentive "loyalty" payments from Optus to One.Tel for signing each new customer.[7]

The lucrative cash agreement with Optus, however, eventually added to the telco's trauma. The agreement gave One.Tel (as a reseller) a jump on its competitors, with the somewhat generous $120 per client cash inducement to sign new customers. The strategy proved little more than a marketing tactic that provided One.Tel with the opportunity to record sales and revenues prematurely. The short-term benefits included guaranteed cash payments from Optus as One.Tel could distribute SIM cards and count them as new mobile numbers without necessarily selling handsets or signing "customers" to contracts in order to receive its money. So, One.Tel was virtually guaranteed a cash flow before it actually conducted any long-term business. In spite of this, its business failure had much to do with its cash flow problems.

In March 1996, with the arrival of Andrew Bailey at Optus' new wholesale division, One.Tel was asked to re-negotiate the loyalty cash payments deal, and by October an agreement to cancel the initiative was reached. Optus paid One.Tel $19.75 million for agreeing to end the loyalty payments, in addition to selling its shares back to the company for $4 million. But this meant the lucrative and regular cash payments from Optus to One.Tel ceased, and One.Tel was soon in financial crises. It quickly suffered from a lack of money—even though its sales reportedly escalated to $148 million by June 1997. This aptly illustrates that sales do not equate necessarily to cash in the bank.

Barry (2002, p.357) explained, One.Tel's recorded profit was mainly 'because money from the $19.7 million Optus settlement [was] still being fed into the company.' Apparently, One.Tel's revenues did not liken with its cash inflows, and maintaining the level of its cash outflows could not be sustained.

In addition to its cash flow problems, other linked accounting issues for One.Tel included revenue recognition, inflated sales and recorded asset values. The concept of a financial "value" needs to be well-considered in business and well-defined. Arguably One.Tel, regardless of book entries, showed it could not adapt to changing business conditions and changing financial demands of business quickly enough to continue to conduct its operations. And so, at that time, the larger, more powerful telco conglomerates were able to disrupt One.Tel's operations, thereby causing it continuing financial distress.

This was particularly evident with regard to the telco's cash flow position. For instance, a major cash flow problem surfaced when European wholesalers began to demand earlier payments than previously agreed for their services to the One.Tel business activities. This move was in response to a change in global operations when 'the major line wholesalers in Europe were [apparently] short of cash because they paid too much for 3G [third generation] licences.'[8] The result for One.Tel was a liquidity crisis as its working capital (mainly cash) began to diminish rapidly, and without its required cash surplus, the business faltered.[9]

One.Tel's funds, its *financial resources*, were completely depleted. Yet to many, including it seems non-executive directors, the financial state of One.Tel was a nasty surprise and its collapse unexpected. As Barry (2002, p.157) asserted:

> Having been floated in November 1997 for $208million (at which price no one wanted to buy), in late 1999 its shares were selling like hot cakes at prices that valued the company at more than $5 billion. This was around 700 times One.Tel's annual earnings and 15 times its sales revenue. . . . As with the dot-coms, there was no way One.Tel could ever make enough profit to justify this price. It only made sense because there [were those] . . . prepared to pay more . . . until there wasn't . . . and the price came tumbling down.

Similarly to HIH, One.Tel's cash flow position appeared to diminish at least three years prior to its collapse. Its focus on cash management and credit control apparently floundered as the entity's cash supplies rapidly decreased. Its reported sales and the expected future cash receipts from those sales were ostensibly *mismatched*. As sales of its products are central to the viability of any business, more so are its cash receipts. For One.Tel, interestingly recorded asset "values" (book amounts) soon came into question. After its demise (yet during 2001), Rich challenged the administrators for not acquiring reasonable prices for assets sold and for writing-off pre-paid advertising costs (a recorded asset) at $90 million.[10]

One ponders what Rich might have considered reasonable prices for One.Tel's assets. If, for example, a comparison were made between what the administrators were receiving for assets, sold under duress, and the recorded amount for those assets in the balance sheet, it could be argued, and is argued here, that they are not comparable numbers. The recorded book amount for any or all of the assets may in fact not resemble a *reasonable* amount in terms of an ongoing business, especially when compared to the current market monetary equivalent for those assets.

Alternatively, the prices attained at sale *under duress* by the administrators could well be reasonable or fair prices under those circumstances. So a better comparison to ascertain a level of reasonableness, in terms of money value, would be to compare the amounts recorded in the balance sheet to current market equivalents of those assets if sold under *normal* (everyday) business conditions. This idea was first mentioned by Chambers (1966), Sterling (1979) and many authors since.[11]

One.Tel's administrators' chose to write-off pre-paid advertising of $90 million and by so doing indicated they considered there was no likely monetary equivalent for the pre-payment in the market. Pre-paid advertising after all represents a payment for a service in the hope or expectation of receiving some revenue or increase in revenue because of the amount spent on the advertising. By August 2000, ASIC, however, 'insisted that One.

Tel deduct millions of dollars worth of advertising and customer acquisition costs it had previously been deferring . . . the company was forced to declare an extra $173 million of costs that it had previously been burying in its balance sheet' (Barry, 2002, pp.208, 209). And that balance sheet, not surprisingly, had displayed a solvent financial state for the entity.

Recall that the balance sheet test of [in]solvency (Chapter 2) requires that an entity's total assets be greater than its total liabilities, and such was the case for One.Tel as shown in Table 5.1. But what are the entity's assets—in terms of money or access to money? One.Tel included in its non-current assets a massive $559.8 million of intangibles in 2000, compared with $28 million in 1999 mainly due to spectrum licenses reported at a cost of $532.6 million, amortised by $1.1 million to net $531.5 million. Receivables had spiralled from $72 million in 1999 to $218.4 million the following year, but the provision for doubtful debts figure had not risen in proportion to the receivables due; it had escalated from $7.9 million in 1999 to $46.4 million in 2000.

These numbers indicated (at least) a potential problem with the management of the telco's debtors and its billing system. Barry (2002, p.250) later revealed, 'in the second half of 2000, bills were going out six to eight weeks late, and often going out wrong, so the figures were two months out of date. The accounts for October had to be prepared in November with figures for August.'[12] Nonetheless, the balance sheet reported an ostensibly healthy growth in total assets of 173% from $526 million in 1999 to $1,435.5 million in 2000. To add to this apparent comfort zone, One.Tel's liabilities only changed slightly from 31% of its assets in 1999 to 34% of its assets in 2000.

Table 5.1 One.Tel's Consolidated Balance Sheet as of June 30, 2000

	2000 *$m*	*1999* *$m*
Total Current Assets	628.1	296.2
Total Non-Current Assets*	807.4*	229.8
Total Assets	**1,435.5**	**526.0**
Total Current Liabilities	375.2	84.9
Total Non-Current Liabilities	115.5	78.1
Total Liabilities	**490.7**	**163.0**
Net Assets	**944.8**	**363.0**

* Notably, intangibles accounted for $559.8 million of this $807.4 million. See One.Tel's Annual Report (2000) for further details.

Source. One.Tel's Annual Report 2000.

Additionally, shareholder's equity revealed an accumulated loss of $282.1 million in 2000 from a previously recorded retained profit of $9.1 million in 1999.[13] Reserves had increased from a negative $5.4 million in 1999 to a positive $1.2 million in 2000, the difference reportedly due to a move in the foreign currency translation reserve from a negative $2.1 million up to $4.5 million the following year. At that point, technically, the entity was solvent as total assets were greater that total liabilities, which equates with the basic requirements of the current balance sheet test of [in]solvency—again! And the market was seemingly unaware that the company was losing money.[14] But why was this amazing?

In 1999, One.Tel had allegedly avoided showing a $25 million loss.[15] Apparently it deferred—not counted—costs in new ventures totalling more than $32 million, which later were revealed in accounts filed with ASIC to be in excess of $48 million.

Thus, it would seem reasonable that debate continues on what signifies adequate financial information (yet still indicates quality financial information) in conjunction with transparency of information for legal, professional and government regulatory authorities—as per Companies & Securities Advisory Committee's (2000) Final Report. Essentially it appears that those interested continue to focus on elements of audited financial statements and the extent of the director's duties in reporting quality financial information to stakeholders.[16] Of course, little is new.

Table 5.2 provides a summary of events for One.Tel from 1997 to its demise in 2001—its type 1 trajectory.

Table 5.2 One.Tel's Type 1 Trajectory

Date	*Events*	*Effect*
1997	July: Australia's telecommunications market is de-regulated. Aug: One.Tel has approx. 300 staff. Offers long distance and international call facility. Nov: Floated on ASX @ $2 per share.	Economic change Organisational growth and business expansion
1998	Jan: Global strategy to expand into Europe. Aug: One.Tel records $8.8m profit; spends $10.7m on investments & $8m on operating activities. Issues new shares to Coldstream Partners. Sept: One.Tel buys mobile spectrum for $9.5m. Proposes to build a network. Nov: Cannot pay $9.5m for spectrum. Packer and Lowry contribute $5m each. Dec: CPH buys One.Tel shares for $43m.[1]	Effect of $19.7m Optus payment in accounts. One.Tel further expands its operations to Europe and Asia.

(continued)

Table 5.2 (continued)

Date	*Events*	*Effect*
1999	Feb: News Ltd. and PBL inject $430m into One.Tel and promise $280m in future for 40% of shares. March: Massive share price increase since Dec.98 reported. April: Deal with Lucent to build mobile network $438m. May: 100,000 overseas customers; Los Angeles office closed. June: Insufficient spectrum purchased for planned mobile network. Aug: One.Tel reported a $9.8m profit but had deferred $32.4m set-up costs for business in Europe and Hong Kong. Sept: $1.15b deal with Lucent to build national network. Nov: One.Tel releases plans to bid for 3G mobile licences, and Lucent agrees to build and finance the network in Europe at $20b. News Ltd adds $200m to fund licence bids. One.Tel shares soar, market capitalization $5.3b.	Continued injection of funds to support current operations. Increased overseas operations planned. GAAP issues: $9.8m reported profit becomes more than a $20m loss with removal of conventional accounting anomalies like deferred costs.
2000	Jan: One.Tel reported a $22m pre-tax loss for six month period to Dec 1999. March: Cost of spectrum for Aust. mobile network at $523m. April: One.Tel withdraws from the UK spectrum market. May: Next generation mobile network launched in Australia. Aug: One.Tel's revenues doubled during 1999–2000, but it reported a $291m loss. Sept: $6.9m in bonuses paid to Rich and Keeling. Share price falls to $1. Dec: One.Tel's books reportedly examined by James Packer's finance team.	Plans to increase business operations continue as costs escalate. Cash flow problems seemingly unheeded. GAAP issues: Increasing revenues, reported losses: revenue recognition.
2001	Feb: $132m loss in six month period to Dec. 2000. March: Cash reserves reduced to $35m. April: UK carriers cut credit terms from 120 to 30 days. Cash reserves reduced to $25m. May: Reportedly Ernst & Young concluded $240m to $370m required for One.Tel to continue for another six months. It was reminiscent of Imagineering more than a decade before.	'One.Tel is insolvent' (Barry, 2002, p.371). The actual date that it became insolvent seems to be contestable.

[1] 'The Packers' family flagship, Consolidated Press Holdings, buys 16 million of FAI's One.Tel shares for $43 million and another 1.3 million shares from One.Tel chairman John Greaves for $3.8 million' (Barry, 2002, p.359).

Source. Barry (2002, pp.349–374).

THE STATE OF PLAY

On May 16, 2001, Rich and Keeling agreed to resign, and the following day at an emergency board meeting they left the company. At that time non-executive directors, James Packer and Lachlan Murdoch, pulled together a team to investigate One.Tel's financial position while still publicly professing their faith in the company's future. By May 28, the prospect that One.Tel would continue in business looked more than grim. Packer's team reportedly found that without an immediate injection of more cash, One. Tel would 'have *minus* $11 million in the bank by the end of the month' (Barry, 2002, p.370). Additionally, overdue payments to creditors totalled $80 million, and One.Tel was (at that time) consuming between $15 million and $35 million in cash each month. It also appeared One.Tel would write-off around $50 million in bad debts.

On Wednesday, May 30, 2001, ASIC commenced its investigations into the financial circumstances of One.Tel. By July, it was reported that One.Tel directors 'could be liable for between $20 million and $80 million for insolvent trading claims, depending on the date the group became insolvent,'[17] but determining that state and when it was reached was to be no easy task for the administrators. Controversy surrounded the most likely time the company became insolvent, from somewhere between March and the beginning of May 2001, or, alternatively, it could have been earlier than December 2000.[18] This is disconcerting to most users of accounts, not least because, by law, directors must attest to the solvent state of the entity they direct,[19] in particular they must not allow a company to trade whilst insolvent. But was the company insolvent?

This aspect became even hazier by virtue of the significance of possible loans from the then existing financiers—for instance, 'the $132 million rights issue that was to have been underwritten by News Ltd and . . . PBL, but which was pulled shortly before the company collapsed [reportedly] in May 2001.'[20] Apparently, the funds were withheld because the 'board did so after advice that $130m (sic) would no longer be enough to avert insolvency and the amount needed was more like $300m.'[21] The matter was and remains controversial. At the time, the 'ASIC's investigations led it to conclude One.Tel needed at least $270m to remain solvent . . . [yet] Austin [Justice Robert Austin] leaned towards the view that [$132m] may have been enough to enable the telco to survive.'[22]

Since its demise, 'One.Tel's major backers, PBL and News Ltd, . . . claim they were "profoundly misled" over the telco's true financial position.'[23]

> In December 2001, ASIC commenced civil penalty proceedings in the Supreme Court of New South Wales [NSW, Australia] against Mr Rich, Mr Silbermann and two other former directors of One.Tel, seeking orders that each of the defendents be disqualified from managing or being a director of any company for such period as the court sees fit.[24]

In 2009, after a protracted case, the Supreme Court of NSW 'dismissed ASIC's civil proceedings against One.Tel's former joint Managing Director, Mr Jodee Rich and the company's Finance Director, Mr Mark Silbermann.'[25] Five years earlier, ASIC and John Greaves (a former chairman and non-executive director of One.Tel) reached agreement in terms of Supreme Court proceedings against Greaves.

> Under the agreement with ASIC, Mr Greaves has admitted to contraventions of the Corporations Law between January 2001 and 30 March 2001 in relation to the discharge of his duties as a non-executive director, and the chairman, of One.Tel. Pursuant to the agreement. . . . As a result of the [subsequent] hearings and submissions, Mr Justice White made orders that Mr Greaves: * be prohibited from managing a corporation for a perod of 4 years; * be found liable for the compensation of $20 million to One.Tel; and * be ordered to pay ASIC's costs of $350,000.[26]

Significantly:

> As part of the terms of the agreement, Mr Greaves admits that during the period January 2001 to 30 March 2001, he failed to take the steps that he should have in order to ensure that he and the board of One.Tel properly monitored management and were aware of the true financial position of the company. [Notably] It has never been part of ASIC's case that Mr. Greaves acted in any way dishonestly in relation to the performance of his roles at One.Tel.[27]

Herein belies a dilemma. Seemingly the distinction between executive director and non-executive director and their respective roles in business lack clarity. Why? Greaves was a non-executive director and chairman. The proceedings against Greaves resulted in a 'Landmark decision on chairman's duties' that examined legal responsibilities with regard to (among other things) the flow of financial information, cash reserves and group solvency.[28] Further, consider how James Packer (former non-executive director of One.Tel) allegedly 'admitted . . . that he never saw or asked for One.Tel management accounts in his time as director . . . he accepted information presented to him by One.Tel executives as "true and accurate" and believed he adequately discharged his duties as a non-executive director' (*AFR*, May 3, 2002).

Regardless of the adjective, a director is a director; no hair-splitting on responsibilities. Nonetheless, a pervading issue for business exists in how best to define and disseminate quality (serviceable) financial information to the board and all its directors. Arguably the board requires specific details relevant to the situation at hand to enable it to make well informed decisions. Consider another concurrent financial dilemma, the Water Wheel saga, where John Elliott, non-executive director of Water Wheel,[29] was ultimately charged and convicted of insolvent trading.

Notably—for executive directors—the warnings seem clear. On Friday, March 21, 2003, for instance, the chairman of ASIC announced through media release 03–099 that a former director of One.Tel, Bradley Keeling, was liable to pay $92 million compensation to One.Tel, in addition to ASIC's costs of $750,000, and was banned from being a director for ten years. In that case, ASIC claimed 'that all four defendants [Rich, Silbermann, Greaves and Keeling] were jointly and severally liable for the compensation.'[30] By 2009, however, circumstances altered substantially, with the case against Rich and Silbermann dismissed.[31]

There are systemic faults in the process of accounting for the financial state of business and in the regulation that provides legal support for the outcome that continue to be ignored. With regard to One.Tel, McCrann (2009) asserted:

> This case shows again that our corporate law and consequent regulation is the catastrophe. . . . The process and its outcome suggests something is seriously, fundamentally wrong. This was a civil penalties case against Rich. It started eight years ago [2001]—dealing with an issue from the dot com boom and bust that all happened back in the 20th century. . . . And as for simplify and streamline . . . 16,000-plus pages of transcripts, three years of hearings, two further years to get a judgment and a 3000-page one at that! . . . and $40 million. . . . We need real corporate law reform; and not just of the law but the process.[32]

Still, the One.Tel chronicle continues. A statement of claim issued in 2010 by the "special purpose" liquidator Paul Weston of Pitcher Partners (Australia) ensures the narrative will proceed for some time yet. Reportedly Weston is 'suing Consolidated Media Holdings, Consolidated Press Holdings, News Limited, publisher of *The Australian*, James Packer, Lachlan Murdoch, Peter Macourt and Peter Yates' with regard to the $132 million aborted rights issue.[33] So, no one is quite sure where the One.Tel saga will yet end.

Although there may be individuals (not necessarily in cases mentioned here) who are ready to deceive others for their own personal gain, *this is not always so*. In the midst of controversy and grief at financial loss, whether at a personal, local community, national or international level, it remains that much of the financial suffering is due to endemic problems in our economic system internationally—*inter alia* our generally accepted methods of accounting for business activities. Clarke *et al.* (2003, p.32) proclaimed, '[c]ontrary to the popular view, . . . compliance with the so-called *spirit* of many conventional practices and endorsed Standards produces grossly misleading data, without necessarily any intention to deceive on anybody's part.'

There are many other similarly perplexing stories to that of One.Tel, such as that of HIH Limited, which briefly follows.

HIH LIMITED

> The criminal investigation into the $5 billion collapse of HIH . . . turned into an $82 million crusade. . . . Both the Commonwealth DPP and ASIC . . . received more than $42 million to pursue criminal charges for the [then] next three years against those responsible for the HIH collapse. The year-long royal commission by Neville Owen cost $40 million (Koutsoukis and Main, 2003, p.1).

THE AUDACIOUS

At the time of its collapse, HIH was second only in size to NRMA general insurance in Australia's insurance industry. Its responsibilities covered business interests in five of the world's continents, with companies incorporated in the United Kingdom, the US, New Zealand, Hong Kong, Argentina, Malaysia, Sweden, Greece, Russia, Fiji, Papua New Guinea and the Philippines as well as Australia.[34] The Group developed from a smallish company set up in 1968 by entrepreneur Ray Williams that was subsequently taken over in 1971 by British listed C. E. Heath Insurance.

In 1992 the entity was listed on the ASX with a stock (securities) market value of $240 million, and in 1995 operations expanded with the purchase of CIC Insurance and a partnership agreement made during the same year with Swiss insurer Winterthur. Around this time a program of further overseas expansion was introduced, although Williams was reportedly warned of trouble brewing in the UK.[35] Main (2003) provides colourful insight to the role Williams played in the HIH saga (particularly leading to his resignation in October 2000) and the apparently unheeded contributions of several "whistleblowers" over such concerns as reinsurance arrangements and under-reserving.

Nonetheless, Justice Owen asserted in his Report on the HIH Royal Commission's inquiries that the 'ambitious growth strategy adopted by HIH had a serious impact on the company's failure' (HIH *Final Report*, 2003, Pt.2, s.3.5). Yet expanding business operations by merger, acquisition, increasing products and services or other *bona fide* corporate activities is not necessarily of concern. Problems for HIH mainly emerged from poor management and arguably the lack of relevant quality information.

For HIH there were real-time issues, reportedly with regard to reinsurance arrangements recognised as assets that more appropriately were liabilities, related-party transactions that allegedly inflated HIH's share price (hence market capitalisation) and the subsequent effect of conventional accounting methods such as capitalising expenses and deferring acquisition costs, including FITB's and goodwill—the result, inflated profit figures and a distorted view of the entity's dated financial position.[36]

Regardless of its published financial statements, however, that to most portrayed the business as a going-concern, by March 2001, HIH had collapsed, with losses estimated at around $5.3 billion.[37] This occurred after the Group had reported the apparently successful purchase of FAI insurance for $300 million in 1999 followed by a 112% rise in profits by the first half of 2000 when HIH auditors signed off financial accounts in June of that year showing net assets of $939 million.[38] An extract from the Profit and Loss Statements (2000)[39] of HIH (Table 5.3) shows the variance in operating profit figures for 1999 and 2000 dependent on adjustments for abnormal items, extraordinary items and income tax.

The final profit figure reveals a considerable increase in operating result for the year ended June 2000, but the main point of interest rests with how the figure was derived. In May 2001, a Brisbane newspaper reported 'a significant disaster has been HIH's acquisition of FAI Insurance for $300 million in January 1999. It is now accepted HIH paid considerably too much . . . possibly three times FAI's worth, or $200 million, too much.'[40] The point being that the rise in profits to June 2000 was, as poignantly explained in the same article, 'a sham. The company had only . . . [reported] a profit [ostensibly] because it had effectively made up, through an accepted accounting practice, a $163 million increase for goodwill relating to FAI.'[41] Goodwill was reported at note 18 of the HIH Annual Report (2000) at a cost of $555.9 million as at June 30, 2000, and $392.1 million as at June 20, 1999. The cause of the increased amount is a dilemma as indicated below.

Table 5.3 Profit and Loss Consolidated Statement for the Year Ended June 30, 2000

	July 1, 1999 to June 30, 2000 ($m)	*January 1, 1998 to June 30, 1999 ($m)*
Operating profit before abnormal item & income tax	61.9	102.0
Operating profit after abnormal item	55.9	52.0
Operating profit after abnormal item and income tax	19.2	37.3
Operating profit/loss after extraordinary items and income tax attributable to members of the parent entity	**18.4**	**(21.2)**

Source. HIH Annual Report (2000).

Abnormal items for 2000 included a $6.0 million provision for goods and services tax (GST), along with a restatement of deferred tax balances of $18.8 million. In 1999, a $50.0 million provision for GST was recorded. Then, after accounting for an accumulated loss of $26.5 million at the beginning of the 2000 period, there remained a loss of $8.1 million compared to a profit of $68.7 million available for appropriation in 1999.[42] Yet dividends (April and October) and other distributions (from convertible and converting notes) were provided for and paid, $95.2 million in 1999 and $49.4 million in 2000. Subsequently, the reported results were not profits, for 2000 or for 1999, but accumulated losses in the financial statements at the end of each period, $26.5 million in 1999 and $57.5 million at the end of 2000.[43] Further, the Group reported an operating profit for 2000 of $18.4 million.[44] Notably, a major problem for stakeholders in publicly listed corporations is to interpret "profit" and other published financials. In the case of HIH, the use by the auditors of an "emphasis of matter" unqualified opinion arguably added to the problem.

The Misinformed

Justice Owen remarked, 'misinterpretation of the [accounting] standards and of the requirement of the Corporations Law to present financial statements that were "true and fair" allowed HIH to publish financial statements that *did not truly or fairly represent the financial position or performance of the HIH group*' (HIH *Final Report*, 2003, p.4, s.7; emphasis added). Yet, under the *Corporations Act 2001*, s296 financial reports must comply with legislated accounting standards, and under s297 financial reports and notes to accounts must comply with the *true and fair* override, with emphasis on the latter—s.295(3)(c).

Nonetheless, HIH's hazardous financial state was a surprise, apparently, to many stakeholders and not evident from the usual media remarks on business affairs.[45] The eroded financials of HIH were indicative of earlier failures,[46] take, for instance, Westmex (1989), where 'accounts gave their usual impression of truth and fairness, undoubtedly masking the higher level of financial risk involved' (Clarke *et al.*, 2003, p.200). But risk comes in many forms; consider how:

> WorldCom's capitalisation of [its] operating expenditures, Waste Management's lengthening of its truck fleet's assets' lives to decrease amortisation charges, Enron's and Xerox's front-end loading of revenues hit the headlines, [but] few noted them repeat performances . . . [also notably] accounting conventions that WorldCom, Waste Management, Enron and Xerox stretched almost certainly have induced errors in the accounts of every company that complies with them (Clarke *et al.*, 2003, p.329).

For HIH, on the face of its net assets for 1999 and 2000(Table 5.4), the Group looked solvent.

Table 5.4 Balance Sheet Extract as of June 30, 2000

	2000 ($m)	*1999 ($m)*
Total Assets	8,327.1	8,051.1
Total Liabilities	7,388.0	7,104.1
Total Net Assets	**939.1**	**947.0**

Source. HIH Annual Report (2000).

In fact, HIH had published increasing asset amounts from $3.9 billion in 1997 to $8.3 billion in 2000. During this period, the Group's reported assets were in excess of its reported liabilities that had ranged from $3.4 billion in 1997 to $7.3 billion in 2000. Thus, if one applied the basic balance sheet test of insolvency,[47] these figures indicated the Group was solvent.[48] Yet, with the benefit of hindsight—especially from the HIH Royal Commission revelations—it is known that this was not likely to have truly depicted the position.

THE BLAMED

History shows that public incredulity follows an unexpected corporate collapse. People want to administer blame; they want someone to blame and they want to know: Who or what is responsible? The collapse of HIH Insurance Limited was no different.[49] Sarre (2001, p.292) recounted:

> The official regulator . . . (APRA), claimed a lack of resources contributed to its alleged neglect. The auditors, Arthur Andersen, claimed that they had been given incorrect information. The company directors blamed economic and other forces beyond their control. The Australian Securities and Investments Commission (ASIC) claimed that it was APRA who bore the responsibility of regulatory oversight. . . . The Howard government's response was a suggestion that there ought to be a tightening of the law and rigorous enforcement of its criminal sanctions. Finally, the actuaries noted that they had provided warnings 12 months earlier but that these had gone unheeded.

Justice Owen's Final Report implied mismanagement as the primary reason for the collapse of HIH.[50] The implication was not new—again the individual(s) were to be blamed. The system went unscathed.

Owen did, however, counter with the comment, '[b]y and large the people who were involved were not inherently bad or in some way set upon being part of a corporate disaster' (Pt.6, s.6). This was an insightful comment as in the 1960s it was '[p]rimarily, managers [who] were blamed for those . . . failures' (Clarke *et al.*, 2003, p.295). It seems a trend could develop, if it hasn't already—to focus on the corporate individual, or team of company officials, who may prove to be easy targets in like circumstances but who, in many cases, may not be deserving of the *generous proportion of the blame* attributed to them. In HIH, Justice Owen asserted:

> [A]n important factor contributing to the failure of HIH was inaccurate reporting of financial information . . . caused partly by HIH officers and auditors misinterpreting the requirements and application of the existing accounting standards. *But it was also caused by deficiencies in those standards* (*HIH Final Report*, 2003, s.7, pp.7, 8; emphasis added).

For decades, many scholars—nationally and internationally—have questioned the content and requirements of legislatively backed accounting standards. They have questioned accounting procedures and have proffered alternatives to conventional accounting practice, and they have argued the need for a fundamental change to the accounting system that produces anomalies in dated financial statements.[51] Yet there has been little, if any, change to the concepts that underpin conventional accounting practice. Instead, we continue to ignore evidence of the past and present, that '*unexpected* corporate collapses . . . have exposed [and continue to expose] gross anomalies and continuing generic defects of existing accounting practice' (Clarke *et al.*, 2003, p.331).

A MESSY CONDITION

Revelations of the HIH saga indicate repeatedly that balance sheet constructs, without any real-world referents, continue to plague the efficiency of business. HIH included around $1 billion of intangibles in its balance sheet as of June 30, 2000—a balance sheet that depicted the entity as technically solvent—yet shortly afterward it collapsed. The intangibles recorded in the financial statements did little to assist any of HIH's stakeholders to determine the entity's factual financial state. Such intangibles, not readily marketable items, diminished the quality of the financial information therein. Specifically, they did not help demonstrate HIH's ability to pay its debts. Rather they served to obscure the financial details of HIH and inflate its reported financial position. Enron, One.Tel and FAI, for instance, are other timely examples of this.

In July 2002, APRA[52] released new prudential standards for general insurers in Australia that required (among other changes) intangibles to be removed when determining the insurer's capital adequacy, otherwise referred to as its solvency. The argument developed above is that for all entities in all industries, society would be better served were corporations not to include intangibles in statements of financial position and were required to report up-to-date market related financial details of its assets. This is not to suggest that they be ignored. One alternative, as Chambers (e.g. 1966, pp.209–212; 1973, pp.56, 57) noted many decades ago, is that such data could be appropriately dealt with and appear as part of a Double Account System of reporting in the 'Capital Account' section of that system.

This is especially so, as historical cost-based data and the continued use of GAAP in recording questionable amounts for intangibles such as goodwill, capitalizing expenses such as start-up costs and physical assets at cost, and implementing somewhat ad-hoc asset write-downs will inevitably produce misleading financial statements, which are aimed at informing business stakeholders of solvency and related financial matters.

Consider briefly some particulars and similarities at Enron. Free fall in Enron's share price occurred as the market became—albeit perhaps too late—increasingly aware of the accounting artistry used to deal with its complex investment arrangements (in special purpose vehicles) and off-balance sheet partnerships.[53] Additionally, how capitalised expenses and premature revenue recognition (among other things) served to inflate its reported financial position. Nothing, however, could compensate for its lack of cash, and ultimately 'cash *was* draining out of Enron, undercutting the energy-trading operation that had been its crown jewel. . . . Nearly all of Enron's revenue was coming from its energy-trading operations' (Behr and Witt, 2002, p.A01).

Reportedly, 'energy trading generated most of its record $101 billion in revenue in 2000. . . . [and] In 2000, the company's cash flow from operations had actually declined by $2.5 billion. . . . By mid-November . . . energy traders were insisting on burdensome upfront cash deposits, accelerating the company's cash drain' (Behr and Witt, 2002, p.A01). Such circumstances are reminiscent of the tragic lack of cash that coincided with other traders' early demands for payment, suffered by One.Tel.

For Enron, the extent of its debt was a major and crippling factor in its financial structure. The total amount of debt it had incurred was largely unknown, but it was alleged to be relevant to its catastrophic financial state. For instance, '[i]n September, Enron had said its debts totalled $12.5 billion. But it had billions more in off-balance-sheet obligations.'[54] Funds received from banks were treated as trading transactions (revenue) by Enron, its *true* market-related cash position and debt position unknown by most if not all stakeholders; the funds were in effect loans and had to be repaid.

The reported risk indicators at Enron were not too dissimilar to the reported position at HIH due to the reporting of its reinsurance agreements with Credit Suisse that were really not reinsurance but funds deposited in a bank account to be available for re-draw at a later time. In that situation, all the risk was taken by HIH, the reinsurer for all intents and purposes acting as a bank, not an insurer. The funds that Enron received from the banks alleviated its cash problems (short-term) and improved its reported financial state but increased its risk of operations because the trading transactions were in reality loans, and, as such, they increased Enron's debt obligations. Enron was sinking fast, deprived of cash and drowning in debt, its share price at $8.41 on November 8 'a 90 percent plunge from its peak the year before.'[55] By November 28, Enron had been reduced to junk-bond status, its share price bottoming at 0.61 cents.

But this was after Dynergy Inc., a much smaller and relatively unknown corporation in the energy-marketing industry, surfaced to consider a takeover of Enron. The idea was fraught with danger. The reported financials of Enron could well be accused as a major contributing factor to its demise and the failure of the takeover bid. Watson, the chief executive of Dynergy, later 'complained that no one could tell him what Enron was really worth [and] the deal was dead.'[56] Similarly, the Duke affair (discussed in Chapter 6) illustrates varied valuations of a target company. Therein, Western United, in an event filled attempted takeover and reverse takeover, that finally ended in a lengthy and expensive court-room battle between numerous stakeholders, the actual valuation of the target disputed—perhaps to this day—by many.

Back to HIH. Table 5.5 details HIH's financial performance from its published financials over a five year period from 1996 to 2000 inclusive. The table is an extract taken from the financial performance schedule in HIH's annual report for 2000.

Fundamentally, what can be determined from these figures? At the time of the HIH collapse under AASB1023: *Financial Reporting of General Insurance Activities*,[57] premium revenues were recognised on an earned/unearned basis, and so reported revenue figures could be over or under-stated. At that time, the concept of premiums liabilities were not recognised under AASB1023 possibly as they are contingent liabilities, likely to arise at some time due to premium business written. Yet, liabilities as outstanding claims provisions were recognised and measured in accord with GAAP and AASB1023 as 'the present value of the expected future payments' (para.5.1), although the measurement is purportedly not risk based.[58] So, recorded liabilities and the claims incurred figures were, at that time, likely to be under-stated. The underwriting loss figures indicated poor performance, yet without precise market details, the actual performance could be considerably different, perhaps much worse. The operating profit/(loss) figures presented a brighter scenario, but as earlier shown, their quality with regard financial information is questionable.

Subsequent to the HIH calamity, several regulatory changes were inevitable. Currently under the renamed AASB1023: *General Insurance Contracts*;[59] premium revenues are 'recognised from the *attachment*

Table 5.5 HIH's Financial Performance Summary from 1996 to 2000

Financial Performance Summary	*12 mths June 1996 ($m)*	*12 mths June 1997 ($m)*	*12 mths June 1998 ($m)*	*12 mths June 1999 ($m)*	*12 mths June 2000 ($m)*
Premium revenue earned: net figure	888.5	1,067.0	1,300.5	1,662.2	1,995.4
Claims incurred & expenses	905.4	1,094.5	1,344.8	1,808.4	2,098.9
Underwriting profit/(loss)	(16.9)	(27.5)	(44.3)	(146.3)	(103.5)
Return on policyholders' funds	88.7	105.6	109.6	174.8	175.0
Return on shareholders' funds	26.1	95.8	31.4	71.1	60.4
Insurance result	71.0	33.5	38.1	42.8	72.8
Goodwill amortisation	(4.7)	(5.2)	(7.3)	(17.2)	(35.3)
Operating profit/ (loss) after income tax, attributable to shareholders	59.2	78.3	37.5	(39.8)	18.4
Dividends per share (cents)	***13.0***	***15.0***	***16.0***	***12.0***	***6.0***
Earnings per share (cents)	***20.5***	***25.6***	***9.9***	***(0.4)***	***(0.6)***
Net tangible asset backing per share	***1.23***	***1.38***	***1.66***	***1.02***	***0.67***
Return on equity	***15.4%***	***16.3%***	***6.5%***	***-5.0%***	***2.0%***

Source. HIH Annual Report (2000).

date as soon as there is a basis on which it can be reliably estimated' (AASB1023, para.4.2). The attachment date relates to the degree of risk accepted by the insurer. Whereas:

> The amount of premium is determined by a general insurer or reinsurer so as to cover anticipated *claims*, reinsurance premiums, administrative, acquisition and other costs, and a profit component (having regard

> to expected income from the investment of premiums). The amounts collected in respect of these components are income of an insurer on the basis that they are collected in consideration for the insurer rendering services by indemnifying those insured against specified losses (AASB1023, para.4.2.1).

However, any unearned premium is not recognised in the insurer's comprehensive income statement; it is 'recognised in the statement of financial position as an unearned premium liability' (AASB1023, para.7.1). The amount relates to future costs of claims under the general insurer's contracts and includes deferred acquisition costs to be later 'recognised as an expense in the statement of comprehensive income in future reporting periods' (AASB1023, para.7.1.1). So, the amounts attributed to general insurers' premium revenues and liabilities currently are cognisant of underlying risk factors of the insurance industry, where '*insurance risk* means risk, other than financial risk, transferred from the holder of a contract to the issuer' (AASB1023, para. 19.1). While:

> *Financial risk* means the risk of a possible future change in one or more of a specified interest rate, financial instrument price, commodity price, foreign exchange rate, index of prices or rates, a credit rating or credit index or other variable, provided in the case of a non-financial variable that the variable is not specific to a party to the contract (AASB1023, para.19.1).

At this time, emphasis in the industry is placed on current market situations and likely future circumstances. Following the HIH debacle, this inherently risk-based industry is now, more than ever, focused on alleviating difficulties of measurement and recognition with regard to risk assessment, risk attachment, risk margins and patterns of incidence of risk. Measurement of premium revenues, for instance, are recognised 'in accordance with the pattern of the incidence of risk expected under the general insurance contract' (AASB1023, para.4.3). The actuarial difficulties in calculating expected revenues, expenses and liabilities are noted. Notwithstanding the complexities of the industry emphasis in recording and reporting on general insurers' performance and outcomes focus on determining fair values, capital adequacy, truth and fairness and risk management skills.[60]

Returning to HIH and Table 5.5, the ratio results are simply a product of the anomalous characteristics in the accounting numbers. Although they indicate a declining financial state of affairs for the general insurer, the extent of the financial dilemma is unknown. The collapse of HIH and others (some examined here) highlight 'the inadequacy of the outcomes of complying with the conventional Accounting Standards for assessing whether an enterprise is solvent' (Clarke *et al.*, 2001, pp.94,

95). Moreover, the Royal Commission into the demise of HIH mandates that the *Corporations Act 2001* "true and fair" override, which seeks to ensure corporate entities state their actual financial position, must be complied with and that the accounting standards do not take precedence over this corporate responsibility.[61] In 2011, the true and fair override remains in the *Corporations Act 2001*—at s.297 and s.295A(2)(c).

Since July 2002 under APRA's revised guidelines for general insurers, the Australian prudential standards have focussed on the stochastic nature of insurance, and they have done so partly because AASB1023 (at that time) did *not emphasise risk margins* in insurers' financial reports. This was a major issue in the fall of HIH and is now a primary concern of stakeholders with regard to prudential regulation requirements in Australia for general insurance companies.

'It may be that superimposing the problems of conventional accounting upon the inherent difficulties of assessing liabilities of insurance companies created a fatal mix' (Clarke *et al.*, 2003, p.237). It may also be that a like situation is created for all companies under the influence of professional accounting standards, who are forced to utilise the inherent anomalies in those standards, under the weight of the law. As in the Enron saga, it was largely '[a] multitude of technical truths added up to a false portrait of [financial] success. . . . Of Enron's $1.5 billion in earnings in the 15 months leading up to September 2001, more than $1 billion came from financial and accounting gimmicks' (Behr and Witt, 2002, p.A01).

As Clarke *et al.* (2003, p.222) stated, 'Whither the lessons from history?'

APPENDIX A5.1

Before One.Tel: Imagineering

Briefly, in 1981, Imagineering began business as a retailer of Apple products but soon changed to wholesale dealings in software applications for Apple, Commodore and IBM. By 1983, Imagineering's sales soared mainly due to the launch of IBM's personal computer in Australia. The following year it had moved operations to New Zealand, and by 1985 it had grown with offices opened in Hong Kong, Singapore and Los Angeles. That year Imagineering was floated on the ASX at $12 million. The float reportedly raised $4.8 million cash at an offer price of 50 cents per share. With hindsight, a crucial factor at that time with regard to the offer price was its 'net tangible assets [at] only 3 cents; the rest [was] "goodwill"' (Barry, 2002, p.350). Arguably, there was not much substance there. Table A5.1.1 provides a synopsis of Imagineering's path to ultimate failure.

Table A5.1.1 Imagineering's Business

Date	*Details*	*Crucial Factors*
1985	Employs 100 people. Sales at $26 million and reported profit at $1 million.	Focus: Marketing
1986	International and national expansion continues.[1] Sales increase to $48 million.	Rapid Growth
1987	New product—Imagineering's Ultra PC. Orders accumulate. Rights issue raises $8.6m.	Continued expansion
1988	Sales at $196 million. Rights issue raises $17m. Overseas and domestic expansion continues. Debt increases as interest rates rise. $6 million from Bankers Trust.	Non-loan & loan financing increases
1989	March: Imagineering's share price drops from around $2 to 65 cents.	Market focus: rising debt
	May: Financial (half-year) results in $2m profit. Sept: Increasing debt and interest rates. Oct: First Pacific provides $18m cash. Imagineering announces $1m profit. Nov: Loss of $4m.	GAAP: Deferred expenditure questioned.
1990	Sixteen month results reveal a $52m loss and a 'Going Concern' qualification. July: ANZ calls in $38m loan. Re-financing arrangement with First Pacific approved by shareholders. Sept: Jodee and Steven Rich depart.	Write-offs: $10m—bad debts and stock; $14m goodwill.
1991	Feb: Imagineering reports a $41m loss.Staff reduced to 150 from 390, international & national operations downsized. May: Imagineering privatised at 10 cents a share. 'An expert report values the shares at minus 93 cents, and warns that more losses are on the way' (Barry, 2002, p.354).	Write-offs: obsolete stock; Valuation issues.

[1] 'The company opens offices in Wellington, Brisbane and Taipei, and expands in Sydney, Melbourne, Hong Kong and Los Angeles' (Barry, 2002, p.351).

Source. Barry (2002, pp.350–353).

A major problem with the development of Imagineering's business activities seemed to be its inability to service its ever-increasing debt, partially due to rocketing interest rates, possibly, a sign of the times![62] The business eventually faltered under its accumulated debt, the cost of which was likely exacerbated by management's continued expansion strategies and diminished cash reserves. Within a few short years, One.Tel would emulate the predicaments of Imagineering. It would prove to be difficult, nigh impossible, to determine the actual dated financial state of One.Tel.

When Imagineering's shares were listed at 50 cents, the entity was apparently under-capitalised with inflated goodwill. To aggravate the situation, there was also deferred expenditure, an item soon questioned by First Pacific[63] and eliminated from the accounts, along with massive write-offs of obsolete stock and bad debts. Apparently the definition of, and the monetary equivalent of, Imagineering's assets were questionable, particularly with regard to its financial capacity to pay its debts when due and payable and its ability to continue to conduct its business in a dynamic environment.

In September 1990, 'Jodee and Steven Rich [were] tossed off the board [of Imagineering]' (Barry, 2002, p.353). Nonetheless, in 1994, Jodee, this time with Brad Keeling (former head of Marketing at Imagineering), was back in business with a focus on high-tech mobile telecommunications.[64] Financial support for the new venture was soon forthcoming and reportedly included Optus ($1.5 million for a 28.5% shareholding), FAI ($950,000 for 18%) and James Packer (around $250,000 for 5%). Herald the beginning of One.Tel, a reseller of mobile services in Australia.

Abnormal items for the year 2000 included a *loss* of $1.5 million for software modification costs, receipt of a non-performance payment of $7.9 million and a prior year deferred expenditure write-off of $39.9 million. As depicted in Table A5.1.2 below, the non-performance payment was not explained. The cost of $1.4 million in 1999 related to software modification. Of course the abnormal expense in 2000 reportedly gave rise to a tax benefit, but significantly One.Tel did not recognise that future benefit due to its uncertainty.

During 2001, perhaps to regain some market confidence and recapitalise, One.Tel proceeded with a massive two billion new share issue.[65] This, at a time when the telco suffered a further decreasing cash position:

Table A5.1.2 Profit and Loss Consolidated Statement for the Year Ended June 30, 2000

	2000 ($m)	*1999 ($m)*
Operating Profit (loss) before abnormal items	(262.4)	11.3
Abnormal Items	(33.5)	(1.4)
Operating Profit (loss) before income tax	(295.9)	9.9
Operating Profit (loss) after income tax	(291.1)	7.0

Source. Annual report (2000).

'it had consumed almost $800 million . . . it had eaten up all the money it had raised from PBL, News Ltd and the other investors during the year' (Barry, 2002, p.209).[66] At that time, the restructure included changes on the Board, with both co-founders Jodee Rich and Bradley Keeling exiting the company. Yet, with bold optimism, 'News Limited chief executive John Hartigan, in a joint statement with PBL's Peter Yates, said . . . the board changes and recapitalisation would "set the framework" for One.Tel to become a fully fledged telecommunications provider.'[67]

The move was to provide One.Tel with $132 million that would increase its shares by around 45% to 5.3 billion shares on offer. Consequently, this did little to impress analysts or the market—as reflected in its share price that dropped to 23 cents on the day.[68] Peter Struk of Reynolds Stockbrokers was reported to say, 'I have never seen that many shares in anything. . . . It does not matter which way you look at it. . . . News Corp and PBL are bailing One.Tel out again.'[69] But ultimately there was no further bail out, and the administrators moved in amidst controversy over One.Tel's actual financial state as opposed to its booked financials.[70] Controversy still reigns over the $132 million (Moran, 2010).

REVISITING THE 1990S AT ONE.TEL

Rich and Keeling moved swiftly to develop One.Tel. First conceived in August 1994, it was blessed by good timing as the founders of the new telco were able to strike a lucrative business deal with Optus, which provided cash incentives for signing new customers.[71] This was a bonus for One.Tel, but considering the billions it cost Optus to lay its network, the major carrier 'sorely needed to get some calls . . . [therefore, Optus] could sell spare capacity to Rich at almost any price and still do better than before' (Barry, 2002, p.57). Or, so it seemed.

Caught in a rush of new ideas—apparently one of those times right for a new idea—One.Tel aimed its business at young people, sports clubs, tradespeople, companies, or any clientele that Optus might otherwise have missed,[72] mainly to identify and establish a market niche. During the evolving foray, Rich and Keeling snared the interest and backing of Rodney Adler at FAI and, despite somewhat loosely written objectives,[73] continued to surge forward at an ever-increasing rate. Before long the financial backers also included Optus. The final structure was as follows:

> Kalara would control One.Tel, with just over 50 percent of the shares, most of which belonged to Jodee. Keeling would have five percent, although this was not made public. Optus would have 28 percent and Rodney Adler around 17 percent. All up, the company would have around $4 million to play with (Barry, 2002, p.63).

But One.Tel soon found its business path scattered with obstacles, some *financially* impassable, to the extent that eventually all progress ceased. Initially, however, One.Tel's product was marketable, evidenced by its accumulated sales (particularly in the early years), and readily found financial backing for its business plans—witness the involvement of the Packers, Murdochs and Rodney Adler.

So what went wrong?

Prior to its demise and in Australia, One.Tel was listed third in the placements for fixed-wire national and international calls after Telstra and Telecom New Zealand/AAPT, with Optus fourth. One of the entity's major business advantages was that it operated on a high spectrum band (1800) compared to most other mobile networks (900). This meant that One.Tel's customers received clearer reception than those of its competitors, but the disadvantage was that their mobile range was limited.[74] Nonetheless, the product as reported was sound and initially able to compete in a tough market.[75]

Business Beginnings

When One.Tel officially began business on May 1, 1995, it focussed on simple and convenient operating plans for its customers. Its founders drew on their marketing skills to create One.Tel's public image, to get the business started and to generate enthusiasm in stakeholders. Unfortunately, the early anticipation of an ever-growing clientele, enjoying swift and efficient services, soon gave way to ever-increasing complaints from customers. The result was growing tension and stress levels of and between One.Tel employees, as well as its customers. Staff turnover was reportedly quite remarkable[76] as were the lack of internal operating systems and control strategies. Barry (2002, p.82) reported that at one time, 'a staggering 60 to 70 percent of customers either paid late or did not pay at all, because so few checks were made when they signed on.' Effective internal operating systems apparently came second to flamboyant sales and marketing practices.[77]

Table A5.1.3 provides a glimpse of One.Tel's reported cash flows for 1999 and 2000.

Among other activities, in 2000, One.Tel's financing operations included a share issue, the main contributor to its positive cash flow at year end. Increased operating costs diminished its cash flows and likely signalled an operating systems problem. This was virtually confirmed by the weakened bank balances in April, 2001, when seemingly:

> One.Tel was not collecting nearly as much as . . . [assumed] . . . the company [reportedly] would have $75 million in the bank at the end of June. The very next day, the company's bank balance was $34 million below that target. Two weeks later, it was $50 million short (Barry, 2002, pp.261–262).

Table A5.1.3 Statement of Consolidated Cash Flows for the Year Ended June 30, 2000

	2000 ($m)	*1999 ($m)*
Cash Flow from Operating Activities		
Receipts from customers	510.9	300.1
Payments to suppliers and employees	(684.8)	(328.1)
Interest received	16.9	1.9
Interest and other borrowing costs paid	(11.9)	(3.5)
Income tax refunded	—	0.7
Net cash used by operating activities	**(168.9)**	**(28.9)**
Cash Flow from Investing Activities		
Proceeds from sale of investments	—	1.6
Proceeds from sale of plant and equipment	—	19.2
Payment for plant and equipment	(87.5)	(34.0)
Purchase of licences	(525.6)	(9.5)
Purchase of controlled entities	—	(6.9)
Payment of deferred consideration	(1.8)	—
Loans provided to other parties	—	(2.6)
Net cash used by investing activities	**(614.9)**	**(32.2)**
Cash Flow from Financing Activities		
Proceeds from issue of shares	818.5	280.3
Proceeds from borrowings	139.8	59.0
Finance lease principal repayments	(11.2)	(4.2)
Dividends paid	(1.8)	(2.5)
Share buy-back	—	(106.4)
Net cash provided by financing activities	**945.3**	**226.2**
Net increase in cash held	161.5	165.1
Cash and cash equivalents at beginning of year	172.6	8.4
Exchange rate adjustment	1.6	(0.9)
Cash and cash equivalents at end of year	**335.7**	**172.6**
Reconciliation of cash at end of year:		
Cash at bank	11.9	4.8
At call deposits with financial institutions	323.8	167.8
Total:	**335.7**	**172.6**

Source. One.Tel Annual Report (2000, note 25).

Reported losses that accumulated over a three year period totalled $586 million—'a lot for a relatively recent startup to bear' (Jay, 2001, pp.35, 36). Nonetheless, by April 2001, the 'Foster Stockbroking report value[d] One.Tel at $2 billion—78 cents a share—and rate[d] the company a "Buy"' (Barry, 2002, p.366).

APPENDIX A5.2

Background—The HIH Group

HIH began in 1968, when Ray Williams and Michael Payne started an underwriting insurance business—MW Payne Liability Agencies Pty. Ltd. By 1970, a business expansion program had commenced, with activities moving first to Tasmania and then other Australian States. By 1971, CE Heath plc, listed in the United Kingdom (UK), acquired the company and afterwards operated under the name CE Heath Underwriting Agencies Pty. Ltd., which by 1989 had changed to CE Heath International Holdings Limited.

In June 1992, CE Heath listed on the ASX as a general insurer, with around 45% of the issued capital held by the public.[78] By August 1993, the company had expanded into the UK establishing the subsidiary Heath International Holdings (UK) Limited. In June 1995, CE Heath acquired the CIC Insurance group. The acquisition involved (i) CIC Holdings subsequently changing its name to Winterthur Holdings Australia Limited,[79] (ii) CE Heath issuing shares to Winterthur Australia to fund the acquisition, and (iii) CE Heath plc (parent of CE Heath) selling its shareholding in the subsidiary to Winterthur Australia, which later became the largest shareholder of CE Heath.

In May 1996, Winterthur Australia changed its name to HIH Winterthur International Holdings Limited, and one year later it acquired the operations of Colonial Mutual General Insurance in Australia and New Zealand. By August of the same year, Winterthur proposed a merger with Credit Suisse that was finalised by early 1998; the company became a major global enterprise. Within months Credit Suisse had sold its shareholding in HIH Winterthur with a $2.58 public offer that was fully subscribed, and by October 1998, the name HIH Winterthur had changed to HIH Insurance Ltd. Then early in 1999, HIH acquired FAI Insurance, a company it had regarded with some interest since 1995, for the (later to be discovered) inflated amount of $300 million. The purpose was reportedly 'to secure a major share of the Australian general insurance market.'[80]

By August 2000, HIH sold a controlling share of its Australian general insurance business in order to meet changes in APRA's prudential guidelines. Then in September 2000, HIH announced that its chief executive Williams intended to resign, and by February 2001, HIH shares stopped trading.[81] During March 2001, the Board of HIH was apparently warned of problems associated with the company's accounting practices but it was too late; approximately one week later, the Group was placed into liquidation with reportedly around $800 million in losses.[82]

Reminiscent of other corporate collapses, by July 2001, the press were suggesting '[c]riminal charges may be laid against three former HIH directors over claims that $10 million was improperly removed from the insurance giant.'[83] Moreover, Geoffrey Carmichael, chair of APRA, was reported by AAP General News (Australia) to say that 'a royal commission would determine where responsibility for the HIH failure should rest. "But [as in the 1970s, 1980s, 1990s, and now the 2000s] certainly the first port of call would be the board and management of HIH." '[84] Once again, it appears that the regulatory system of reporting the financial affairs of business entities to stakeholders is likely to remain virtually unscathed (see Table A5.2.1).

Table A5.2.1 HIH's Journey

1968	With Michael Payne, Ray Williams started HIH Insurance— previously named CE Heath Insurance
1988	Rodney Adler takes over FAI on the death of his father, Larry
1992	CE Heath lists on the ASX
1995	CIC Insurance purchased by CE Heath from Swiss insurer—Winterthur (the latter takes 48% in the company)
1996	CE Heath changes its name to HIH Winterthur and begins overseas expansion
1997	HIH shares at $3.50 but commence to slide
1998	Winterthur sells its stake in the merged entity and its name is dropped
	FAI executives involved in signing side letters to a reinsurance contract (allegedly to hide losses in published accounts)
Jan. 1999	HIH completes takeover of FAI at a cost of $300 million
Dec. 1999	Reportedly, HIH spends $735,759 on Christmas party
March 2000	APRA consults HIH; there are concerns that the insurer does not have enough funds to meet future claims. HIH shares continue to slide.
June 2000	Managed by Adler, the Pacific Eagle Equities deal begins Reportedly, the trust received $10 million from HIH & uses $4 million to buy HIH shares
Aug. 2000	HIH sells Australian general insurance operations to Allianz
Mid 2000	Williams apparently authorised $4.6 million on executive bonuses
Sept. 2000	Williams announced intention to resign

(continued)

Table A5.2.1 (continued)

Oct. 2000	Geoffrey Cohen (HIH chairman) proffered HIH as financially strong—profitable
Dec. 2000	Williams leaves HIH
Feb. 2001	HIH shares stop trading and Adler resigns as director
Mar. 2001	Liquidator appointed
May 2001	ASIC launches civil proceedings against Adler, Williams and Dominic Fodera (HIH Finance Director). Federal government announces a $500 million rescue package, and Royal Commission to investigate the fall of HIH.
Sept. 2001	HIHRC starts to hear evidence
May 2002	Adler banned from being company director for 20 years, Williams for 10 years, both and Fodera fined
Dec. 2002	ASIC starts criminal proceedings against Adler (over PEE)
Jan. 2003	Closing submissions by counsel—HIHRC
April 2003	RC Justice Neville Owen hands down his Final Report

Source. Details from "Road to Disaster" (*Australian*, April 17, 2003).

APRA's Solution

In July 2002, APRA released new prudential standards, part of a revised framework for general insurers focusing on the fundamental risk-based nature of insurance business. HIH's annual report for 1999–2000 revealed that its published financial statements basically complied with GAAP and the mandates of AASB1023, but the clarity of HIH's *actual financial state* was, as in previous unexpected corporate collapses, somewhat masked.

While the report mentioned some negative aspects of the HIH business, the financial results of those (and other) business activities were not accounted for in current financial terms. For instance, HIH's financial operations in the United Kingdom were reported to be diminishing rapidly, whilst its workers compensation business in the US was becoming increasingly volatile and difficult. Both situations added to the problems the general insurer was experiencing in its Asian markets. Additionally, APRA was in the process of introducing its reforms, mentioned above, that would 'make Australia one of the world's most capital intensive insurance jurisdictions'[85] and rapidly alter the *status quo* of prudential reporting.

Nonetheless, prior to its collapse, HIH was operating apparently within the bounds of the old regime, one that was reportedly less rigorous than the revised regulations intended by APRA. Table A5.2.2 details the outcome under the prudential regulator's then "new" solvency rulings that show 'the "triggers," according to APRA, that would have pushed the HIH group [at that time] below the new regulatory [financial] requirements' (APRA, 2002, p.74).[86]

Prudential Standards—Vs—AASB1023

The insurance business is fundamentally risk-based, with liabilities virtually unknown until they occur. Following the collapse of HIH, prudential standards for general insurance companies in Australia were amended in July 2002 to focus more on the stochastic nature of insurance. This change is partly because AASB1023 did not apparently emphasise adequately that risk margins were to be accounted for in the insurer's published periodic financial results. Instead the financial statements of insurers, like all corporate entities, were mainly expected to accord with generally accepted accounting convention. In effect, a widening gap emerged among the mandates of Australian corporation's law, the professional accounting standards and prudential standards with specific regard to the insurance sector of the Australian financial industry, in this case general insurance.

The accounting standards, unlike prudential standards, have legislative backing that (given a range of choice) prescribes the content of external financial reports. As APRA requires periodic prudential reports from general insurers that comply with its standards, and not necessarily the accounting standards, it seems the *quality* of the outcome of applying accounting standards was (perhaps still is) of concern to the prudential regulator. At the time of HIH, prudential requirements were not included in the published annual reports of general insurance entities, and so those details were not publicly available information.

In light of events investigated by the Royal Commission, Justice Neville Owen recommended six changes (see below) be made to AASB1023, and he advocated that the changes be adopted prior to the introduction of the international accounting standard for general insurance. He emphasised issues, as previously examined in Chapters 2 through 5, be catered for, such as thoughtfully *defining* that of which we speak, providing stakeholders with *relevant* and *reliable* financial information on the financial state of the business, and that includes the immediate recognition of expenses rather than deferring and capitalising such costs as an asset—further explained in Table 5.2.2.

Firstly, consider the following recommendations of Justice Owen (2003, s.7, p.20):

- a definition of insurance that includes the requirement for a material transfer of insurance risk
- a requirement that insurance liabilities be valued at a level of sufficiency of at least 75%, as required by APRA's prudential standards. Companies should be explicitly permitted to set prudential margins in excess of 75% if the company's board considers that appropriately reflects a true and fair view of the financial position of the insurer
- a requirement that entities disclose in their financial statements—the valuation of their insurance liabilities at a central estimate—a 75% level of sufficiency—the margin ultimately adopted by the [particular insurance reporting] entity

- a requirement that premium revenue and insurance liabilities be recognised on the commencement of a contract of insurance. This will require the recognition of premium liabilities
- a requirement that, in estimating the present value of liabilities, future cash flows be discounted using a risk-free rate similar to that required by the prudential standards
- a requirement that companies subject to the standard disclose a ten year claims-development table that includes past estimates of claims on an undiscounted basis as well as the actual costs of settling claims. This information should be provided both net and gross of reinsurance.[87]

Previously, APRA's work on new prudential standards for general insurance companies in Australia began in 1998, and four new standards were released in July 2002. They emphasised the recognition of revenue and expenses as at the date of transacted business. And as Table A5.2.2 shows, "appropriate" risk margins in the financials of the insurer are to help assess its state of solvency, but, one might add, only with the additional support of a current market-based focus on financials included in its accounting reports.

APRA supported by the Institute of Actuaries of Australia (IA Aust) asserted that different measurements basis to those advocated by AASB1023 are essential for prudential reporting purposes. It is noted that the insurance industry, inherently risk based, covers complexities of asset definition not necessarily found elsewhere. Table A5.2.2 provides a brief comparison of the requirements of APRA's revised prudential standards as opposed to those of the AASB1023—relevant to HIH. A major difference is evident in the prudential regulator's then requirement for expenses to be recognised fully when paid instead of deferred into the future and amortised across time.

Table A5.2.2 An Illustration of the Differences Between APRA and AASB1023 Requirements

	APRA	*AASB1023*
Premium income	Recognise fully from date of acceptance of risk	Defer and amortise
Reinsurance expense	Recognise reinsurance premiums paid fully as a reinsurance expense	Defer and amortise
Deferred acquisition costs	Recognise fully as an acquisition cost	Defer and amortise
Insurance liabilities—Outstanding Claims Provisions (OCP)	Risk based—to be measured under GPS210 Liability Valuation for General Insurers	Measured in accordance with GAAP under AASB1023 and is not risk based

(continued)

Table A5.2.2 (continued)

	APRA	*AASB1023*
Premium Liabilities[1]	Recognised and measured under a prospective basis, as a component of claims exp.	The concept of premiums liabilities is not recognised under AASB1023
Unearned premiums provision	Not recognised as a liability. Premiums written are recognised as premium revenue fully at date of acceptance	Premiums written are recognised as premium revenue on an earned/unearned basis; component unearned is recognised as a liability
Deferred reinsurance expense	Not recognised as an asset, as reinsurance premiums paid are recognised fully as an expense at date of acceptance	Recognised as an asset
Deferred a cquisition costs	Not recognised as an asset, it is expensed as an acquisition cost fully when paid/payable	Recognised as an asset

[1] Liabilities that 'are likely to arise from premium business written . . . a more effective means of recognizing potential risk over the term of the policy written, compared to the accounting concepts of premium earned/unearned' (APRA, 2002, p.76).

Source. Derived from APRA's Prudential Standards GPS110: *Capital Adequacy for General Insurers*; GPS210: *Liability Valuation* and the legislatively backed Australian Professional Accounting Standard AASB1023: *Financial Reporting of General Insurance Activities.*

6 Dilemma in Diversity

Continuing Issues in Quantifying Solvency

'Once in a frivolous moment I calculated that there were 2,971,332,000 different book values that could be reported for inventory' (Sterling, 1968a, p.592).

AMIDST THE MAYHEM

Prior to the new millennium, amidst numerous corporate collapses, three major cases commanded public attention with regard to issues of valuation, communication and diverse business activities. They were the Duke Group Limited, Budget Corporation Limited and Burns Philp Company Limited, respectively. This chapter examines certain circumstances of each case.

The Duke affair, for instance, emphasised what Canning (1929, p.319) had appositely raised over sixty years earlier—that 'diverse valuations of diverse things . . . cannot possibly have a common significance' and cannot possibly contribute quality to the calculation of an entity's financial worth. Similarly as indicated below in the revelations on Budget Corporation, to determine the substance of an entity's assets over its reported liabilities requires additional quantitative and qualitative details to generally accepted accounting practice (GAAP); to establish, for instance, the extent to which those assets may assist in paying an entity's debts when they are due and payable.

Moreover, the Duke affair and Budget recall issues investigated earlier with regard to governance concerns including the knowledge of, and reporting on, the actual financial position of a business entity. Chapter 2, for instance, examined legal and moral duties of directors in clearly defining elements used in accounting reports on an entity's financial state. Further, the Duke case illustrates two major accounting, legal and social issues: first, how to determine the financial state of more than one corporate entity,[1] and second, that corporations, company directors and professional accounting firms can and will likely be held accountable for their actions.

In contrast, the Burns Philp case illustrates the criticality for directors and all senior managers to be well-informed continually about the current state, financial and otherwise, of their business. Although the circumstances of Burns Philp's financial distress were different than those of other failures because the entity did not ultimately collapse—a central part of its business operations failed. And the diminishing financial state of the business at that stage seemed, to many, unexpected. The main difference between the cases herein is that Burns Philp was able to then re-structure and survive as a going concern. Firstly, the Duke Group and—what may be deemed a reasonable valuation!

THE DUKE GROUP LIMITED

Troilus: 'What is aught, but as 'tis valued?' (Shakespeare, 1602, p.ii).

The Value of an Acquisition

Valuation—in particular valuation of the Target Company—was a major issue in the *Duke Group Ltd. (in Liq) v. Pilmer & Ors*,[2] or what became known as the "Duke affair."[3] It began in 1987 when Kia Ora Gold Corporation NL (the Acquirer) initiated a takeover of Western United Limited (The Target), a Perth based financial services and merchant banking Group. Table A6.1.1 (in Appendix A6.1) details events up to 1989, surrounding the 'history of the development of [the] two companies and ownership of issued capital of both of them [that] are relevant to issues in [these] proceedings' (Mullighan, 1998, p.9).

The acquisition centred on what was to become a most controversial valuation, prepared by the accounting firm Nelson Wheeler Perth. Initially, the "discounted cash flow" method of valuation was proposed by Nelson Wheeler, but following discussions with Kia Ora, the "capitalisation of future maintainable earnings" approach was finally used.[4] Subsequently, Nelson Wheeler valued Western United at $82.6 million apparently based on financial details extracted from financial statements prepared as of March 31, 1987, plus forecasts made by the directors with regard to possible future trading results and the company's up-to-date performance for 1987–1988. The valuation was reportedly equal to $3.22 per share.[5]

Kia Ora proposed an offer of $1.20 in cash for each share in Western United plus five Kia Ora shares for two shares in Western United. There was an alternative offer of four shares in the capital of Kia Ora for each share held in Western United. The market share price at that time for Kia Ora was $1.10 per share, and for Western United it was $2.45 per share. Nelson Wheeler suggested that the offer valued Western United at between $3.95 and $4.40 per share. They subsequently conveyed to Kia Ora that, 'In our opinion it is reasonable for Kia Ora to pay a premium to acquire all of the shares in Western United. Further, we are of the opinion that, from the point of view of Kia Ora, the price proposed to be offered is *fair and reasonable* in all of the circumstances'[6] (emphasis added).

However:

> At a price of \$3.95 if existing options for Western United shares had been exercised at 30th September 1987, the price to be paid by Kia Ora was \$101,400,675. At a price of \$4.40 that price is \$112,952,651 . . . it [was] the plaintiff's case that the value was nothing like either of these amounts, or even the \$82.6m mentioned in the report and whatever basis is adopted, *the true value of Western United was less than \$21m* (Mullighan, 1998, p.72; emphasis added).

Apparently the true and fair (reasonable) financial worth of Western United at that time was disputed. Noted is that the issue here is the valuation of the whole firm with focus on share price, which is not the same as the aggregation of the sum of the firm's assets for financial reporting purposes.

Initially, the accounting firm of Arthur Young had been retained to report on the price for the whole company, and they concluded that it was "fair." This was later contested. Nevertheless, the Target's shareholders had been advised that the takeover price was fair and reasonable, and at a general meeting on October 26 they approved the takeover. Recall, however that inherent in those details was a range of intangible assets—including goodwill. For the purpose of determining the entity's financial state, this posed a particular problem.[7]

Goodwill and the Issued Capital of Western United

Usually, goodwill is calculated as the difference between the price paid for the business (in this case for the issued capital of Western United) and the fair value of the net tangible assets of the business.[8] The concept of fair value is defined as 'the amount for which an asset could be exchanged between knowledgeable, willing parties in an arm length's transaction' and is so used throughout a number of accounting standards.[9] Such was the case in the takeover of Western United.[10] Apparently, it was determined that the existence of goodwill would be due to such intangibles as management strength, distribution networks and location.[11] J. Mullighan remarked that one may 'expect finance related companies to trade at or about net tangible assets with, possibly, a small amount of intangibles' (p.342).

Interestingly, the Nelson Wheeler report made no mention of goodwill. Seemingly the accounting firm 'did not address the level of net tangible assets or the goodwill implicit in their valuation' (p.342). In the takeover price of \$4.40 per share, however, an amount of \$103.5 million worth of goodwill was implied. This is a curious situation, because the Nelson Wheeler report identified management and the connections and influence of controlling shareholders as two assets that might contribute to future cash flows.[12] Conversely, J. Mullighan was of the opinion that it was 'questionable whether any of these managers, with the possible exception of Harold Abbott had any skills or capacities which attracted significant goodwill' (p.342).

More precisely, Easton from Easton and Hall, independent valuation experts, stated, 'the implied goodwill in the Nelson Wheeler Perth valuation could not be justified on any ground and was plainly erroneous' (p.342). Then Newman, a chartered accountant with Nelson Wheeler, 'acknowledged that the goodwill implied in the takeover offer was within the range of about \$86m to \$100m' (p.343). Simultaneously:

> An independent expert's report by Nelson Wheeler valued Western United at between \$100 million and \$113 million. Justice Mullighan found the valuation to be "incompetent" and the takeover price to be "grossly inflated"... [reportedly] Justice Mullighan found *the actual value of the company was \$6.5 million* (Financial Review, January 31–February 1, 1998, p.3; emphasis added).

By early 1988, shortly after all issued shares of the Target had been acquired, it became apparent that the involved companies were in financial distress. Presently, the valuation of the Target became a contestable issue. Clearly, how the foundation and the quality of the source on which the many different valuations of the Target were based was and arguably remains questionable. The dated financial state of both Kia Ora and that of Western United must be considered where a dated *valuation* of both entities is to be reasonably determined. Whether this occurred is doubtful.

Pre-Takeover Financial Condition

Details of Kia Ora's financial circumstances during the period leading to the takeover of Western United are summarised in Table 6.1. According to the reported figures, the total net assets of Kia Ora increased by more than \$22 million from 1980 to 1986. But exactly what assets were considered essential to the report and why? At that time, GAAP emphasised an intangible based view of assets, and it still does. Hence, the reported net asset figure of any entity may well be inflated. If so, a substantial increase in the reported net asset figure of a business entity (without further explication) is somewhat meaningless.

As indicated in revelations on Budget Corporation, to determine the substance of an entity's assets over its reported liabilities requires additional quantitative and qualitative details to GAAP, to establish the extent to which those assets may for instance, assist in paying an entity's debts when due.

Table 6.1 Financial Summary of Kia Ora Leading to the Takeover of Western United

	1980 ($m)	*1981 ($m)*	*1982 ($m)*	*1983 ($m)*	*1984 ($m)*	*1985 ($m)*	*1986 ($m)*
Operating Loss	0.83	1.4	1.9	2.44			
Total Loss	1.03						
Accumulated Losses	3.0		11.2	13.9			
Total Net Assets	2.4	2.1	2.9	4.7	14.4	14.4	25.0
Operating Profit					0.47	0.5	2.7

Source. Financial details have been taken from the Court transcript of *Duke Group Ltd.* (*in Liq*) v. *Pilmer & Ors.*

Table 6.1 shows that escalating operating losses from 1980 became operating profits from 1984. Interestingly in that year, Kia Ora changed its accounting policies and reported its sales of assets. Whether asset sales were a normal operating procedure of the business is speculative, but the reported sales certainly increased the reported profit figure. It is notable that this technique was not uncommon in the mid 1980s. Clarke *et al.* (2003, pp.187–190) describe how, for example, Bond Corporation relied extensively on such a practice. The financial picture of Kia Ora as portrayed by the accounting numbers in 1986 could have indicated to stakeholders either an improved business performance as reflected in 1987 when the takeover of Western United was initiated or the effect of a change in accounting policy and accounting procedures. One is reminded of the dilemma later outlined in Budget as to what really is business and/or financial "success."

Accounting policy choice may be influenced by directors where, for example, they have, or are seen to have, an advantage related to their shareholdings. This issue relates to corporate governance matters particularly, as directors' responsibilities to stakeholders might be swayed if they have conflicting interests.

Directors' Shareholdings

In the Duke affair, the shareholdings of directors were a major concern when assessing control strategies initiated by a number of them in the first takeover bid.[13] For instance, executive decisions that resulted in the reverse takeover were shown in court to be in effect, a plan to secure personal financial gain for some of the directors. Shareholdings of those directors from 1980 to 1986 are detailed in Table 6.2.

Table 6.2 Total Ordinary Shares Held by Directors of Kia Ora

	1980 ($m)	*1981 ($m)*	*1982 ($m)*	*1983 ($m)*	*1984 ($m)*	*1985 ($m)*	*1986 ($m)*
Harold Abbott		.14	.19	73	N/A		4.75
Alfred Schneider-Paas		18.0	24.0	24.0	N/A		47.0
Lee-Steere		.20	.50	.19	N/A	.14	.14

Source. Details from the court transcript, judgement of J. Mullighan, pp.10, 11.

Although specific numbers are not available from the court transcript, in 1984 the shares held by Abbott and Lee-Steere reportedly decreased slightly. The shareholding of Schneider-Paas, however, remained much the same as it did in 1985.[14] In 1986, Harold Abbott reportedly held 4,750,259 shares through companies he controlled or with whom he was associated. Moreover, 1,350,000 options were in his name and 200,000 were held through affiliations with other companies. Schneider-Paas, in conjunction with associated companies, held approximately 47 million shares and 300,000 options. That year Somes accepted 300,000 options. On June 27, 1986, the company issued 2.5 million options, and 300,000 options were issued to each director. This left the total number of shareholders at 20,490 with issued capital of 261 million ordinary shares at .25 cents per share for a total of $65.25 million. In 1987, Kia Ora made its successful takeover bid for Western United.

Although Schneider-Paas appeared the heavy-weight in terms of number of shares held, it was Harold Abbott, in conjunction with others, that was later shown to be at the helm in orchestrating the takeover strategies.[15]

Post-Takeover and Reverse Takeover Proceedings

Following the takeover, during 1988, Harold Abbott, Gary Abbott and Milligan owned or controlled 38 million shares of Kia Ora. Schneider-Paas controlled 16 million shares. Collectively, this group owned or controlled 41% of the issued capital of 133.5 million shares. Various institutions and nominees held 16 million shares, and another party named Newton controlled 5 million shares. By this time, Western United was a wholly-owned subsidiary of Kia Ora and was delisted from the stock exchange. It was apparently suffering financial distress.[16]

The environment was unstable, and at a meeting of directors of Kia Ora, it was resolved to lend Western United $5 million to strengthen the merchant bank's position.[17] Then on March 18, 1988, at a meeting of directors,

'Harold Abbott advised that he and Gary Abbott "had been holding" discussions with several parties who were interested in taking a financial interest in Kia Ora' (1998, p.126).

The idea was that Kia Ora would acquire the assets of the Duke Group and then the Duke Group would acquire the issued capital of Kia Ora and so control its assets; *a reverse takeover would be in progress.* Primarily it seems that an asset stripping exercise would occur. This involved a proposed cash outlay of $16 million to gain a controlling shareholding equal to 20% of the company's issued capital. On April 11, 1988, Harold Abbott signed an agreement on behalf of Kia Ora with representatives of the Duke Group that Kia Ora would purchase assets of the Duke Group for $67 million on or before June 30, 1988.

Payment would be made by $12.25 million in cash, with $28 million of the Duke Group's liabilities to be accepted by Kia Ora and an allotment of 59,444,444 shares at 45 cents per share in Kia Ora to the Duke Group. This amounted to approximately $26,750,000.[18] It is important to note that all those transactions involved money. Critically, therefore, one would presume any *valuation* underpinning them should have recourse to money or money equivalents in its derivation.

On May 6, 1988, Harold Abbott told the directors of Kia Ora about the agreement and that he and others had sold their shares in Kia Ora to the Duke Group that amounted to 19.9% of the issued capital of Kia Ora. The directors involved in the transaction received in excess of $11.9 million.

In 1988, although Kia Ora had acquired all the issued shares of Western United, the future had begun to look bleak. By July 11, 1989, the Acquirer was deemed insolvent and placed in liquidation by order of the Supreme Court of South Australia. On August 19, 1992, legal action commenced and damages were claimed for losses allegedly sustained as a consequence of the acquisition in 1987–1988. The trial commenced on June 15, 1994, and nearly four years later on January 30, 1998, the Honourable Justice Mullighan handed down his judgement. The lengthy trial followed an involved takeover, one that included a reverse takeover and ultimately the collapse of the corporate Group.

The Duke Group creditors finally received a 70 cent on the dollar payment after a $35 million out of court settlement in 1992 between the Duke Group and accountants Arthur Young. This settlement was over the valuation calculated by the accountants, submitted in the expert valuation report, for Kia Ora's reverse takeover of the Duke Group. Justice Mullighan (1998, p.130) stated it was 'not possible to say from the evidence adduced at the trial when the plaintiff became insolvent and it is unsafe to use the Arthur Young report as evidence of the financial state of Kia Ora prior to the reverse takeover.'[19] This would seem to indict GAAP and other valuation bases put in evidence.

Following, the case of Budget Corporation Limited (Budget) illustrates some similarities to the Duke Group. In particular, governance issues that stress directors' knowledge of, and reporting on, the financial state of a business entity is crucial to enable ongoing communication of financially sound business outcomes. Such ideas align with corporate governance principles asserted by the Australian Securities Exchange (ASX)—in particular, Principle 3: *Promote ethical and responsible decision making* and Principle 4: *Safeguard integrity in financial reporting.*

BUDGET CORPORATION LIMITED

> '[I]f we are to avoid confusion we must be sure that the recipient of our ideas can understand what we say' (Werntz, 1941/1968, p.51).

The Initial Public Offer (IPO)

Budget Corporation Limited (BCL), a subsidiary of Budget Transport Industries (BTI), was originally incorporated in New South Wales, Australia, as Kizjuly Limited on April 29, 1988. The company name changed to BCL in September of that year. At that time, BCL directors Robert (Bob) Ansett and Stuart Hamley had a significant amount of controlling interest and influence in the corporate group (Appendix A6.2). BCL's 1988 prospectus indicated that its investors would benefit from the Budget Group's recognised past commercial success that included profiting from the marketing ability of Bob Ansett.

Predominantly, the concept of "success" in its many guises—financial and otherwise—seemed to be the core of the Budget case. The prospectus included promises of success. However, the meaning attributed to the word (success) was problematic. Whether the intention was to project *marketing* as opposed to *financial* success was debatable. Ultimately, the contents of the prospectus were contested in court in Australia. BCL's directors were charged, due to statements made in the prospectus, with an alleged breach of section 108 of the Companies (NSW) Code. They pleaded not guilty,[20] and after a lengthy and expensive trial the outcome was a hung jury. The Department of Public Prosecutions (DPP) did not pursue the defendants with a retrial.

The purpose of examining details of the BCL float herein is to add to our understanding of the difficulties confronting directors in cases of [in] solvency. Evidently business communication, like all attempts at communication, requires clarity—clearly defined language. Further events that unfolded at BCL illustrate this—that is, the necessity to define carefully that of which we speak or proclaim in written form; and in business that is with particular regard for the legal and social duties and responsibilities of directors. This is especially pertinent given the requirement in financial matters for accounting to provide exact financial details to directors and managers of a business about its financial state.[21]

Convictions were *not recorded* against the directors in the BCL case, and hence court transcripts and other related data did not become publicly available. The primary source of information relied on below are the company's prospectus issued to the public in 1988, articles reported in the financial press at and around that time and the Krasnoff and Ansett (1999) book, *The meaning of success*. The method, descriptive and interpretive, is based on a set of observations of the events regarding the BCL float and BCL's subsequent demise. Briefly, the circumstances of the case follow.

Circumstances of the Case

BCL was promoted as an organisation with no operating business activities; its '*only* responsibility . . . was to market the Budget name' (Krasnoff and Ansett, 1999, p.143). It was to own the intellectual property of and contractual rights to the Budget car rental business. Reportedly, the purpose of the BCL issue was:

> To provide the necessary funds to pay part of the consideration for the acquisition of certain industrial, property and contractual rights to the conduct of the motor vehicle renting business using the "Budget System" in Australia, Japan, Papua New Guinea and the South Pacific (including rights to the receipt of income from franchising of the System) (BCL Prospectus, 1988, p.23).

Directors Ansett and Hamley beneficially owned Budget Rent-A-Car Systems (BRACS) and another car rental business named Thrifty.[22] This meant the financial statements and details of operations of BRACS were not necessarily available to the public. This is important because BRACS effectively would control and manage the Budget car rental operations, with twenty-nine outlets in its own right. It was also the lessee of the majority of Budget's 11,000 cars as most of the licensees sub-leased their vehicles from BRACS.

The sole income of BCL comprised royalties received from BRACS and other Australian licensees that formed the group association of the Budget car rental business at that time. BCL would derive its income from payments of 3% of BRACS's turnover and 5% of franchise turnover. BRACS was to be responsible for running the fleet cars, secretarial duties including reservations and credit card management, general administration and accounting functions.[23] Hence, BRACS was to provide the operating support services for the franchisees. In the event of anything happening to BRACS, the franchisees would need to find another operator to provide such services.[24]

On that basis, the structure of the Budget Group seems *prima facie* straightforward, but the relationships between the entities involved in the group were apparently a little more complex.[25] Consider Figure 6.1 showing a public holding of 58.1% of BCL and 41.9% by Budget Investments (BI), a wholly-owned subsidiary of BTI. BTI is given as the holding company of BCL in addition to BRACS and other unnamed BTI subsidiaries. The flow of funds to BCL includes service fees from BRACS and other BTI subsidiaries. BRACS, in turn, receives management fees from BCL. Further, BCL receives service fee income from international licensees and domestic licensees. Such details support the idea that BCL would be heavily, if not totally, reliant on service fee income for its existence.

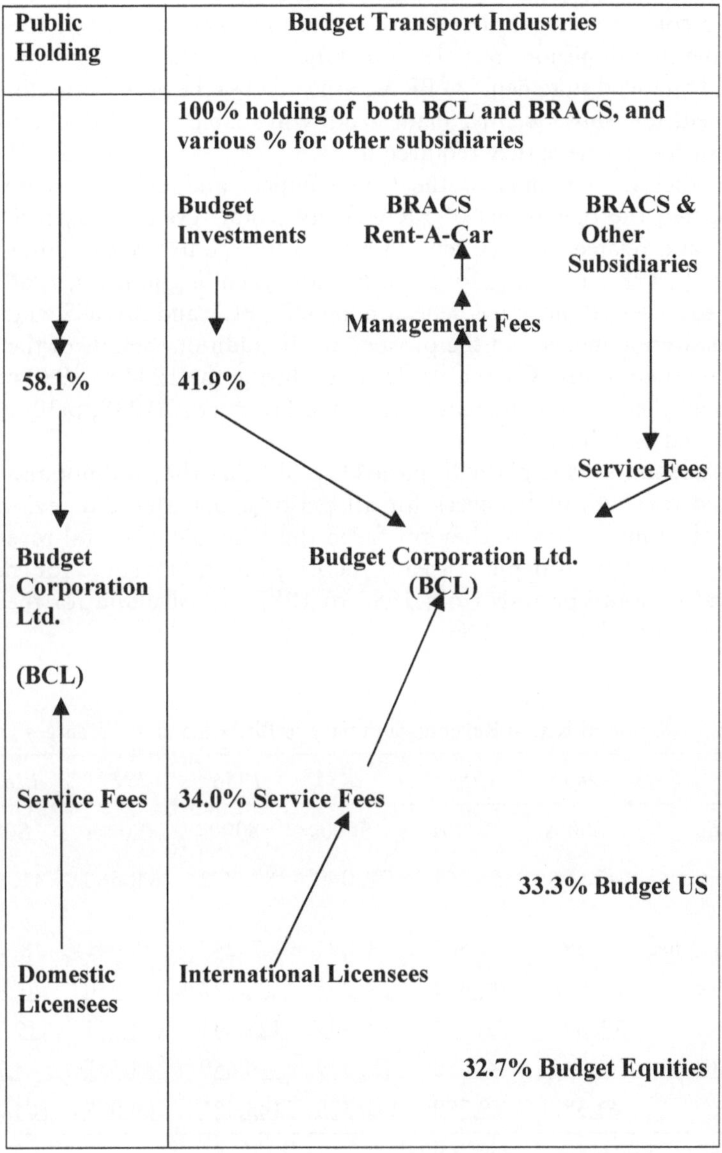

Figure 6.1 Corporate structure of the Budget Group as of September 1988.
Source. BCL Prospectus (1988, p.9).

Appendix A6.2 examines further the likelihood of financial inter-dependencies among BCL, BTI and BRACS. BCL's apparent dependence on service fee income implies that the financial state of BRACS and, perhaps to a lesser extent, other BTI subsidiaries were somewhat crucial to the ongoing operations of BCL. Briefly, the following explores reported financial circumstances of BRACS as of September 1988.

Although the publicly available financial details of BRACS are minimal, the vendor consideration report included in the BCL Prospectus (1988) contained a concise review of the financial circumstances of BRACS for a five year nine month period from 1983 to June 1988 inclusive. There were no detailed financial statements of BRACS included in the prospectus nor were they then, nor subsequently, made readily available to the public in any other form—nor were they required to be.

Nonetheless, members of the firm Coopers and Lybrand reportedly investigated the operations of BRACS, its rental revenue, its service fee income and related licensee rental revenues for the five years ending September 30, 1987, as well as for the nine months ending June 30, 1988. The firm also reviewed the agreements among BTI, BCL and BRACS, and their findings were published in the prospectus. In addition, details of the total rental revenue of BRACS and its licensees during the 1983 to 1988 period were published in table format in the BCL Prospectus (1988, p.30) and is reproduced as Table 6.3.

The accountants explained (para.11, p.30) that they did not audit the reported revenues of licensees for all periods, but they did review the source documents before they prepared the schedule of rental revenues. The reported figures depict a steady increase in total revenues for each of the twelve month periods from 1983 to 1987 inclusive and for the nine months ending June 30, 1988.

Table 6.3 Reported Rental Revenue Summary of BRACS and its Licensees

	*1983**	*1984**	*1985**	*1986**	*1987**	*1988***
Domestic	$000s	$000s	$000s	$000s	$000s	$000s
BRACS Cars & Trucks	42,556	53,761	71, 060	80, 872	64, 560	41, 111
BRACS Other	392	1, 507	3, 394	7, 247	9, 041	8, 221
Licensees	16, 692	20, 469	25, 395	34, 722	64, 950	70, 465
	59, 640	**75, 737**	**99, 849**	**122,841**	**138,551**	**119,797**
International	1, 742	4, 052	12, 529	20,650	48,357	44,731
TOTAL	61,382	79,789	112,378	143,491	186,908	164,528

* Years ending September 30, 1983–1987.
** Nine Months ending June 30, 1988.
Source. BCL Prospectus (1988, p.30).

In addition to those revenues, the vendor consideration report included *projected* revenues and expenses based on what could have been expected from the (BTI, BCL and BRACS) agreements if those agreements had been in place during the 1983 to 1988 period. Moreover, Coopers and Lybrand calculated a future maintainable earnings pattern for the company, also derived from details in the agreements. They asserted the figures were an "opinion" only and not meant to be a forecast of the earnings potential of BCL (BCL Prospectus, 1988, para.10, p.30).

To this end, a schedule of implied historical earnings for BCL was included, reproduced here as Table 6.4, in which the figures were based on a number of assumptions. For instance, advertising and promotional expenses were restricted to an amount not exceeding 32.5% of the service fees, net of the management fee, for each year during the five years and nine months ending June 30, 1988. There was an assumption made that a $250,000 administration expense had been incurred in each year for the same period, with no allowance for inflation during that time.

Table 6.4 Implied Historical Earnings (Before Tax) of BCL from 1983 to 1988 Inclusive

	*1983**	*1984**	*1985**	*1986**	*1987**	*1988***
Implied Service Fee Income Net of Management Fees						
Domestic	$000s	$000s	$000s	$000s	$000s	$000s
BRACS Cars & Trucks	1, 277	1, 613	2, 132	2, 426	1, 937	1, 233
BRACS Other	4	15	34	73	91	82
Licensees	835	1, 023	1, 270	1, 736	3, 248	3, 523
	2, 116	**2, 651**	**3, 436**	**4, 235**	**5, 276**	**4, 838**
International	17	41	125	207	484	447
Total Income	**2, 133**	**2, 692**	**3, 561**	**4, 442**	**5, 760**	**5, 285**
Expenditure						
Advertising & Marketing	693	875	1, 157	1, 444	1, 872	1, 718
Administration	250	250	250	250	250	187
Total Expenditure	**943**	**1, 125**	**1, 407**	**1, 694**	**2, 122**	**1, 905**
Implied Earnings Before Taxation	1, 190	1, 567	2, 154	2, 748	3, 638	3, 380

* Years ending September 30, 1983–1987.
** Nine Months ending June 30, 1988.

Source. BCL Prospectus (1988, p.31).

As previous chapters noted, accounting numbers such as those contained in Table 6.4 may be of concern to some, not least because of the assumptions that underpin conventional accounting procedures used to compile financial reports. If the assumptions are incorrect, unrealistic, infeasible or in any substantive way questionable, then results of analysis are problematic. Nonetheless, with regard to Budget:

> Smithers who was in fact the investigating accountant said: In my opinion based upon my examination of the accounts of Budget at 30th of June 1988 and from my review of the post balance date transactions, the financial information set out in this report presents a true and fair view of the state of affairs at 30th of June 1988 and . . . in accordance with the Australian accounting standards and the provisions of the companies (New South Wales) Code. "What more could the principal of the issuing company rely upon, than that statement?" (Krasnoff and Ansett, 1999, p.34).

What more indeed, the "true and fair" override with regard to accounting standards was clearly evident in the investigating accountant's statement. So arguably Krasnoff and Ansett were perhaps vindicated in their assumptions.

However, Justice Owen later investigating the HIH demise provided more than a caution. He was scathing in his remark that the preparers of financial accounts had over time, regardless of the rhetoric, effectively forgotten the "true and fair" override.[26] He considered:

> [T]he accounting standard setters, the AASB and the International Accounting Standards Board need to pay close attention to *clarity and ease of interpretation* of standards. . . . The preparation of accounting standards is too important to be left solely to accountants, just as the preparation of legislation is too important to be left solely to lawyers (Owen, 2003, s.7, p.3; emphasis added).

Nevertheless, according to the implied earnings figures for BCL in Table 6.4, historically it would have reported steady growth in earnings to 1987, and that result would have positively contributed to the growth of the Budget Group. After all, as Krasnoff and Ansett (1999) explained, one reason for the float was to increase the capital of Budget, and at that time BRACS:

> [H]ad a turnover in excess of $250 million . . . its monthly cash flow was over $20 million. . . . No matter what the borrowings were, assets always exceeded liabilities. The concept of a float was seen by me [Ansett] to be a very secure investment . . . because it wasn't dependent upon the profitability of BTI or BRACS. Budget Corporation Limited's (BCL) source of income was on turnover, not profitability (p.33).

Decisively cash flow, income and assets were vital considerations. Crucial was that the entity would report its assets, as listed in the financial statements, in excess of its liabilities. The latter is fundamentally in accord with the balance sheet test of insolvency, as discussed in Chapter 2. So, what went wrong?

Assets—What Assets?

Ansett and Krasnoff (1999) emphasised that if assets exceeded liabilities, the financial state of the entity would be secure. But that would depend upon what denotes an asset.

Furthermore, the weight Ansett placed on BCL's income from turnover, not profitability, suggests a leaning toward the balance sheet—that is, using the balance sheet as a means to determine the entity's change in financial worth as the difference between its assets and liabilities at the beginning of a period and against the difference between its assets and liabilities at the end of the period. Hence, this is a balance sheet approach to ascertain income and change in financial state, and arguably there is nothing wrong with that. It is a similar approach to the balance sheet test of [in]solvency as discussed in Chapter 2. In addition, if turnover were used as an indicator of long-term stability, as with the asset turnover ratio, both revenues and the entity's assets are significant. Hence, the definition of assets is again of consequence—in the case of Budget, as it is in the following story of Burns Philp.

BURNS PHILP & COMPANY LIMITED

> 'When cash inflows diminish . . . a company's second line of defence against insolvency is its assets' (Chambers, 1986, p.33).

Diverse Things

Burns Philp, established around 130 years ago by Sir James Burns, continues to operate today as a multi-national organisation. The business is widely known as a leading producer of yeast products and manufacturer of other bakery ingredients. During recent years, the Group increased its 'portfolio of food businesses . . . [including, in 2003] the integration of the Fleischmann yeast and bakery ingredients business in Latin America.'[27] Additionally, in 2003, the Group reduced its investments in non-core bulk liquid storage in Australia and industrial vinegar businesses in North America.[28] The ASIC Report on Burns Philp[29] and the Group's annual reports from 1992 to 2003 inclusive are the primary sources of financial data that are used in this review.

The timeline is important because this period informs about the entity's then diverse business operations and outcomes attributed to same. Also it is instructive that, following the late 1990s restructure, Burns Philp continued to adapt to changing business circumstances; an example, the acquisition of Goodman Fielder in 2003.[30]

It began that during 1988, Burns Philp expanded its business activities by buying into the herbs and spices industry. Seemingly the company reacted to a growing consumer demand for herbs and spices as public tastes changed to, what was perceived to be, a healthier style of cooking away from products heavily laden with salt and saturated fats.

Hence, Burns Philp entered a market that complemented its existing and successful, long-standing involvement in other food products and services like yeast and bakery, arguably "sticking to their knitting." Subsequently, the company moved to establish a niche in the foods industry as a single source supplier for food ingredient products,[31] and well-respected brand names were apparently an important consideration in the Burns Philp marketing and growth strategy. The Group expanded as it acquired existing herbs and spices businesses in North America and Europe. It focussed on the acquisition of quality trade names and its ability to further increase business in the long-term; to take advantage of economies of scale.

At that time, the Group concentrated on the consumer sector of the herbs and spices business, leaving the industrial sector to others. This occurred as consumer preferences again altered and individuals, social groups and families more frequently visited restaurants and take-away food outlets. As previously noted, altering consumer preferences are quintessential features of a market economy. So, as could be expected, the change in customer tastes did not adversely affect the industrial sector as much as it did the retail market, and that, for Burns Philp, was a problem. In reality, the Group had to contend with increasing capital costs, escalating operating expenses and rising competition. Eventually its business activities in herbs and spices were not financially sustainable.

Arguably the problem was exacerbated by conventional accounting procedures that showed reduced reported costs at a time when the Group's business expenses were actually rising—for instance, by way of restructuring and rationalization costs that were capitalized as assets, in addition to slotting fees expenses, whereas they were monetary outlays associated with the Group's operating activities. As a result of such accepted accounting practices, the Group's assets and reported profits, for some time, were inflated.[32]

Exacerbating this were the questionable amounts attributed to its intangibles viz, trade names.[33] In 1996, three independent parties were commissioned to assess the Burns Philp trade name values that were later determined generally to be over-valued in the accounts.[34] The total reported for 1994, 1995 and 1996 for trade names, trademarks and brand names fluctuated from $792.7 million, $1,121.4 million to $1,014.6 million, respectively.[35] This occurred when total assets were reportedly $3,062.1 million, $3,380.9 million and $2,978.5 million, respectively, and reported operating profits/

(loss) ranged from $123.0 million in 1994, $115.1 million in 1995 to a loss of $61.8 million in 1996.[36]

In 1997, the Group decided to sell its investments in herbs and spices. As a result of that decision, the Group further decided that as of June 30, 1997, 'all herb and spice intangible assets [were to be] . . . written off as an abnormal item.'[37] In addition, the Group reduced other reported intangibles related to its continuing businesses. Nonetheless, the accounts remained in accord with [at that time] the requirements in Australia of AASB1040: *Statement of Financial Position* and the requirements of SAC4, para.14, essentially being based on capitalised costs. Currently such requirements have not altered much and have International backing in the requirements of AASB101: *Presentation of Financial Statements* that has support of IAS1 its international equivalent. Moving into the new millennium, Loftus and Miller (2000, p.41) explained:

> Traditionally financial reporting has not reported explicitly the risks and uncertainties associated with an entity's activities and financial position. In addition, there has been little emphasis on communicating financial flexibility [adaptive behaviour].[38] These omissions are major weaknesses [especially] if one of the purposes of financial reports is to flag entities that are so exposed that they could easily suffer a major financial reversal and, lacking financial flexibility, collapse into insolvency.[39]

Accounting For Diversified Business Interests

For Burns Philp, a major problem was how best to record slotting fees and other intangible costs; recall slotting fees were an operating cost to the business. Initially, the fees were paid to ensure shelf space in supermarkets for the Groups' herbs and spices. In accounting for the costs, they were capitalized as "Other Assets" and amortized over time. Additionally, at each acquisition, the Group created a provision for rationalization and restructuring costs. Such provisions resulted in an increase in intangible assets like goodwill and trade names. The expenditures subsequently related to those accounts were written off against the provision. Alternatively, the expenses might have been recognised as such immediately and charged against profit, thereby not inflating the Group's recorded assets.

Similar stories on provision accounts, capitalised expenses and deferred costs pervade the past annals of finance in Australia (refer to Clarke *et al.*, 2003). There were, for instance, Reid Murray and H. G. Palmer in the 1960s; Associated Securities, Minsec and Cambridge Credit in the 1970s; Bond Corporation, Westmex and Adsteam in the 1980s; and then more recently Enron, WorldCom, HIH and One.Tel in the 1990s and into the new millennium. Technically creative accounting procedures, as mentioned above, in accord with generally accepted accounting practice (GAAP) have erred. For Burns Philp (and many others), the outcome leaned unintentionally perhaps towards an inflated financial result.

Arguably it was not until around 1996 that the full financial effect of the accounting methods became evident for Burns Philp when the provision accounts expired and restructuring and rationalization costs were actually charged against annual profit.

Table 6.5 provides a twelve year financial summary of Burns Philp's assets, debts and capacity to cover its interest expense. But what useful financial information can actually be derived from the summary?

> [T]he only kind of calculation that can determine the financial outcome of a business venture over its entire life—[is] a comparison between the sum of money with which it commenced and (in like terms) the sum of money or its equivalent with which it finishes—for that is all that periodic financial statements can reasonably achieve (Clarke *et al.*, 2003, p.279).

The details in the financial summary in Table 6.5 are unlikely to provide such a comparison, due partly to the elements therein and their recorded book values. Nevertheless, data in Table 6.5 indicate a fluctuating financial state for Burns Philp during the period under review. The Group's assets show a relatively steady increase up to and including 1995 and then a decline to 2002, with slight fluctuations between the years. Liabilities are shown to continually vary during the period, with net debt reportedly peaking for the Group in 1998 at $1,364.8 million. Concern remains with assets that are likely to be intangible with no true marketability. This is significant partly because accumulated debt with its contracted monetary obligation must be paid if not forgiven. Hence, an entity requires sound assets with monetary equivalents that may be turned into cash or assist the entity to access cash.

If assets are not represented in active current markets, they are unlikely to have an observable monetary equivalent. Thus, the entity's reported figures (book values) would only by chance indicate its capacity to access cash in a timely manner to cover its debt payments in any factual, up-to-date monetary sense.

The *times interest-covered ratio* shown above indicates that the financial state of the Group with regard to its financial capacity to pay for, and so cover, its incurred debt slides from 1992 to 1998. Recall discussion in Chapter 4 that such ratio results are derived from an arithmetic procedure of dividing calculated operating profits before interest and taxes by interest expense. So here the ratio result is primarily dependent on what anomalies are included in the Group's calculation of its operating profits. Thus, to explore the actual financial circumstances of the Group requires more details. Although the diminishing value in this reported ratio result may coincide with the adverse circumstances the Group suffered after it

Table 6.5 Burns Philp—Twelve-Year Financial Summary

Year	*Net Debt ($m)*	*Total Liabilities ($m)*	*Total Assets ($m)*	*Times Interest Covered*
1991	256.9	978.8	2,084.4	2.4
1992	319.1	1,041.7	2,275.3	4.5
1993	707.5	1,479.2	2,778.6	4.2
1994	996.6	1,736.6	3,062.1	3.4
1995	1,108.8	2,018.7	3,380.9	3.2
1996	964.6	1,737.3	2,978.5	2.9
1997	1,124.6	1,894.0	2,200.4	1.4
1998	1,364.8	2,209.0	2,238.2	1.3
1999	1,073.2	1,384.3	1,417.9	1.7
2000	1,031.4	1,467.1	1,596.7	2.2
2001	1,093.5	1,582.9	1,860.8	2.2
2002	731.9	1,885.0	2,364.5	2.8

Source. Financial data sourced from the Historical Financial Summaries in Burns Philp & Company Limited's Annual Reports of 1995, 2000 and 2002.

diversified into the herbs and spices industry, this may be only one of a number of factors leading to that result.

Diversified business interests might reduce risk and promote growth opportunities that in turn create the potential for increased financial wealth for the business and its stakeholders. But this is not always so. 'Acquisition brings growth, but it does not necessarily generate property, increase wealth or ensure ongoing profits' (Clarke *et al.*, 2003, p.173).

Loftus and Miller (2000) examined a number of previous studies that compared accrual-based measures against cash flow data to investigate that which would most likely benefit the economic decision-maker. A few of these ideas are pursued in the following section.

Accounting Numbers and Cash Flows

Following the lead of Sharma's (1996) case analysis of the failed Brash Holdings Ltd., the current ratio plus, return on assets (in this case, net operating profit/total assets) and leverage as long-term debt/total assets are briefly reviewed. In Sharma's case:

> The accrual-based measures indicated that the company was profitable, albeit declining, and liquid until 1992 with signs of declining

> financial strength appearing in 1993. The cash flow ratios calculated by Sharma provided additional insights into, and *earlier warning of, the financial difficulties* faced by Brash (Loftus and Miller, 2000, p.282; emphasis added).

Not surprisingly, the cash flow data were apparently more informative than the available accrual-based details. In Burns Philp's case, financial data taken in the context of the twelve year period from 1991 to 2002 show that the current ratio, although fluctuating and with a noticeable drop in 1998, was likely not of much concern to stakeholders. Whereas the times interest covered ratio shown in Table 6.5 details a steady decline from 1993 to 1999—possibly reflecting the move into herbs and spices. Nonetheless, the two results send conflicting messages. At that time, the current ratio might have indicated a reasonable liquidity situation, but there could be concern over the Group's capacity to cover its interest charges on its debt. And if so, this might lead to a liquidity crisis.

More recently, the new millennium years up to 2003 indicated a financially stronger presence for the Group than exhibited in the latter 1990s, with an apparently substantial decrease in net debt. For instance, the Group's consolidated cash position, seemingly from its operating activities, advanced considerably from $118.4 million in 2001 to $213.1 million in 2002, although there was a slight dip in 2003 to $201.5 million. From a ratio perspective, Table 6.6 provides some useful insight.

Table 6.6. Ratios of Liquidity, Return on Assets and Leverage for Burns Philp

Year	*CA/CL*	*NPAT/TA*	*LTD/TA*
1991	2.02	0.08	0.23
1992	1.93	0.04	0.24
1993	1.76	0.04	0.31
1994	1.32	0.04	0.27
1995	1.68	0.03	0.39
1996	1.98	–0.02	0.40
1997	1.25	–0.40	0.55
1998	0.97	–0.13	0.53
1999	1.46	0.05	0.79
2000	2.16	0.05	0.77
2001	1.20	0.047	0.58
2002	3.10	0.06	0.63

CA/CL represents Current Assets/Current Liabilities; NPAT/TA represents Net Profit After Tax/Total Assets; LTD/TA signifies Long-Term Debt/Total Assets.

Source. Financial data from Burns Philp & Company Limited's Annual Reports (1991–2002).

Certainly the current ratio should be adjusted for inventories, and any prepayments to provide a more precise measure but the unknown element of doubtful, or bad debts, in accounts receivable would remain. Moreover, the ratio still concentrates only on the probability of liquidity—the entity's capacity to pay its "immediate" debt obligations. This emphasises the problem of what debt should be taken into consideration when assessing an entity's financial state, in the short-term and in the long-term, in conjunction with its financial capacity to continue to operate as a going concern.[40]

Hence, the result, in financial terms, is contestable. The major point here is that financial ratios based on conventional accounting numbers provide limited information, the quality of which is disputable, because the constituent parts are not of like kind—particularly in terms of money and its worth. Essentially the worth of money in a monetary economy has regard for and to its purchasing and debt paying power—in accord with time.

Returning to the above analyses, the return on assets indicator points to struggles in or before 1995—as the negative return for the following three years implies. Moreover, the profitability ratio might provide some confirmation of a downturn in economic events, but with the benefit of hindsight, changes in accounting procedures likely contributed to a sizable and negative influence on the calculation of profit. Recollect that when the provision accounts for restructuring costs were no longer available and the capitalization of slotting fees ceased, expenses were then charged against profits. If these were to be expensed in the years 1995–1998, for instance, then the reported profits for those years would have been reduced, at least, by the reportedly prepaid slotting fees (refer to Table 6.7).

With regard to the reported 'Nil' slotting fee prepayment in 1997, Burns Philp's Annual Report explained that 'total prepaid slotting *allowances* at 30 June 1996 of $119.3m comprised gross expenditure of $248.0m and accumulated amortisation of $128.7m' (1997, note 14 (a)). After 'the decision to sell the herb and spice businesses, the unamortized balance of slotting allowances at 30 June 1997 of $136.4m has been *written off as an abnormal item*' (1997, note 4; emphasis added).

Finally, the leverage of the Group shows an increasing reliance on debt over the years except mainly for two slight downward movements in 1994 and 1998, until 2001 and 2002. This could imply that management strategies were risk oriented, but the degree of that risk is unknown. Other

Table 6.7 Slotting Fee Prepayments: 1995–1998

Slotting Fees	*1995 $000*	*1996 $000*	*1997 $000*	*1998 $000*
Current	54,200	35,300	Nil	6,800
Non-current	131,700	84,000	Nil	12,300

Source. Burns Philp Annual Reports: 1995–1998.

factors like changing levels of competition in the food industry, expansion policies, increased operating and capital costs, improved technology and operating capacity, changing business plans and strategies of management all combine to increase an entity's financial risk and business risk position. But this is not necessarily bad—business takes risks as the dynamics of an ever-changing economic environment demand. What management and all stakeholders surely are entitled to are factual financial results that stem from the financial and business risks taken—so that eventual returns can be matched against the known risks (high or low) as taken. That is how companies and investors in an efficient market operate.

Burns Philp's cash flows during the 1991 to 2002 period tend to reveal some negative influences, especially in cash flows from financing activities for 1999. Notably the depressed cash flows from investment activity partly reflect the Group's move into herbs and spices and the subsequent drain on business resources during the 1993 to 1997 period. For Burns Philp, its unfortunate foray into herbs and spices illustrated a dilemma in diversity.

In 1994, the Group reported a consolidated loss on sale of non-current assets and businesses of $33.4 million, an increased loss from 1993 when $25.7 million was reported (Annual Report, 1994, note 38b). The latter partially explains the effect on the accounts of the Group's restructuring and expansion activities through its takeovers and mergers.[41] But as previously discussed, particularly in Chapter 4, to more clearly determine the financial circumstances of the loss would require a de-consolidation of the figures. As Clarke *et al.* (2003, p.272) remarked:

> Consolidation techniques entail recourse to the counterfactual: notions of group profits and losses, group rate of return, group gearing and the like, imply that the profits and losses of the separate entities will filter ultimately . . . into the ultimate parent entity; notions of group solvency implies that the assets of the entities comprising the group are separately and collectively available for the discharge of the liabilities of one another.

A number of conglomerates, however, especially in their recent and not-so-recent activities illustrate that the assets of separate entities in a Group of entities are not usually available to bail the other group companies out of a sticky situation. For instance, Air New Zealand abandoned Ansett in the 1990s and Ansett Transport Industries walked from Associated Securities Limited (ASL) in the 1970s. 'It is now well known that a portion of the reported growth in ASL's assets was the product of capitalising period costs of holding and developing real estate—a variation on the historical cost theme that money spent on acquiring and holding physical assets necessarily adds wealth' (Clarke *et al.*, 2003, p.137). Arguably such a variation is not a universally accepted idea.

In Table 6.8, the figures show a decline in cash from operating activities from 1995 to 1996, and an improvement in 1997 that was quickly followed by a sharp drop from 1997 to 1998. The last change reflects subsequent financial results from the Group's move into herbs and spices, as revealed by

Table 6.8 Burns Philp's Cash Flows: 1991–2002

Year	*Cash (Op)*	*Cash (Inv)*	*Cash (Fin)*	*CashYD*
1991	100,265	196,027	-9,257	422,756
1992	115,430	-105,513	-50,371	397,744
1993	119,500	-451,200	250,800	311,000
1994	101,100	-432,800	186,600	154,900
1995	113,900	-200,300	188,200	254,300
1996	80,100	-75,900	75,500	319,100
1997	126,500	-193,000	-27,300	235,100
1998	-154,800	267,500	119,300	455,400
1999	122,400	120,500	-640,300	71,600
2000	152,100	-32,900	-21,400	187,500
2001	118,400	-89,800	-17,500	216,000
2002	213,100	-105,800	607,400	922,700

Source. Financial data from Burns Philp & Company Limited's Annual Reports (1991–2002).

the current ratio results previously shown in Table 6.6, although to a lesser extent. There, the Group's liquidity position also appeared to improve, and its profitability seemed to increase and stabilise in 1999 and 2000, a time when cash received from its operating activities was apparently enhanced.

The more recent years (2001 and 2002) update the Group's financial details as it moved into the new millennium and away from its mid-1990s financial crisis. Notably cash used in investing activities substantially increased from 1999 to 2002, reportedly due to payments for property, plant and equipment as well as payments for businesses. Although cash receipts, from operations, in 2002 somewhat outweighs the negative effects of borrowing costs and cash payments for operating activities, the main cash contributors to financial activities as reported in the 2002 annual report were a draw-down of borrowings and an issue of senior subordinated notes, 'with the balance maturing in 2012.'[42]

Although still operating in the herbs and spices industry in 2002, the Group increased rationalisation and improvements in herbs and spices to reduce costs and 'invested approximately $82 million on capital expenditure . . . [mainly] in profit enhancement programs' (Manager's review, Annual Report, 2002). Increased profits, however, may result from changed accounting policies and business strategies, rather than actual financial results from business operations, such as when 'Adsteam acquired major shareholdings in numerous companies throughout the 1980s. [And] Coincidentally, . . . disclose[d] a similar pattern of increases in reported profits over that period' (Clarke *et al.*, 2003, p.155).

Across time, cash, access to cash and cash management issues crucial to the ongoing financial success of business, although included in rhetoric, are seemingly second to that habitual key to reported financial success—accounting profit. Previously, Chambers (1973) and Clarke *et al.* (1997/2003) explored cash-crisis cases, for example, the circumstances of H. G. Palmer, Minsec, Cambridge Credit, Westmex, Adsteam and then, more recently Ansett, One. Tel, HIH, Enron and WorldCom. All were experienced businesses that failed partly due to insufficient cash flows and the outcome of applied accounting procedures that among other things had capitalised costs.

Burns Philp, however, re-focussed its operations and, by the early 2000s, split its activities among Yeast/Bakery (69%), Herbs and Spices (16%), Vinegar (6%), Technical and Corporate (5%) and Terminals and Bulk Storage (4%) (Annual Report, 2002, 'Managing Director's Review'). Although the Group managed to survive its 1990s venture into herbs and spices, it was not without comment and rejoinders, not least of all from the Australian Investments and Securities Commission (ASIC).

ASIC AND BURNS PHILP—CONCLUDING REMARKS

In 1998, ASIC revealed that Burns Philp planned to obtain the necessary funds for its advance into herbs and spices from two main sources: the sale of non-core business assets and debt. Consequently, two main issues arose. First, ASIC questioned the accounting treatment of assets in the Group's reported financial statements. Second, ASIC expressed concerns with regard to corporate governance issues and the activities of the Burns Philp executive. Although corporate governance is not a new idea, it has recently gathered momentum—and the perceived lack of governance has won public notoriety for some—during the past two decades, likely due to the continued spate of unexpected corporate collapses throughout the world.

Critical for Burns Philp was a solvency crisis that adversely affected its business operations and its market value in terms of a diminishing share price. Eventually the ASIC report (1998) on the Group's financial crisis included several questions concerning the responsibilities and duties of the Group's corporate officers. ASIC was particularly concerned with corporate governance areas such as:

- Directors are responsible to ensure that the board functions effectively;
- Directors are responsible to ensure that they are appropriately informed about business performance;
- Directors must question and evaluate key features of intangible asset valuation reports;
- Directors are responsible to ensure that shareholders are appropriately informed.

Each point entailed governance issues that had, and still do have, regard for financial information and the quality of financial information provided to directors. Yet to fulfil corporate governance responsibilities as described above, in addition to their legal and social duties, entail directors to know whether the entity they direct is solvent—at a specified point in time—and whether it has the financial capacity to continue to conduct its business operations after it has paid its accumulated debts. It seems incontestable then that directors need continual, factual financial details about the ever-changing financial structure of the business they direct as well as up-to-date financial results of its operating activities. Cases such as BCL, the Duke Group, Burns Philp, HIH, One.Tel and others illustrate that directors require, but do not necessarily have, access to such quality (serviceable) financial information.

Chapter 7 examines issues of solvency from an insolvency perspective. It includes data and cases on insolvency issues that further explore the evident: solvency is a critical commercial financial attribute that is dealt with inconsistently at law and in accounting, and its quantification in financial accounting is lacking.

APPENDIX: A6.1

Background to the "Duke" affair

Kia Ora was incorporated in South Australia on September 13, 1954. The company was principally involved in gold mining activities in Western Australia but later developed interests in other areas such as mineral, oil and gas exploration. From 1979 to 1989, certain shareholders accumulated enough shares to result in a takeover of Western United.

By way of explanation, on March 28, 1972, a wealthy industrialist named Schneider-Paas became a director of Kia Ora, and by 1979 he had accrued substantial interests in four associated companies: Kia Ora, Uranium & Nickel, United Nickel NL and Inter Copper NL. At that time the first three companies were publicly listed on the Australian stock exchange, and the last had been delisted. This company was, however, relisted on April 26, 1985, as Kia Pacific Gold Limited.

Of the companies named, Kia Ora and Uranium & Nickel were essentially speculative mining companies until mid 1979. Uranium & Nickel, so named on March 26, 1968, was originally known as Weaber's Rising Sun NL.[43] On June 30, 1982, the company's name was again changed, this time to Western United Holdings Limited, and so it became a public limited liability business. Following suit, Inter Copper NL became Kia Pacific Gold Limited early in 1985. Its principal activities were mineral exploration and investments in subsidiaries.

On August 23, 1985, Kia Ora moved to acquire all issued capital of Kia Pacific that it did not already own. The offer was accepted, and Kia Pacific became a fully owned subsidiary of Kia Ora in October 1985. Somes and Lee-Steere as directors of Kia Ora supported the takeover initiated by Harold Abbott and Schneider-Paas. Harold Abbott had been a director of Kia

Pacific since May 1983, yet the company recommenced its activities early in 1985. When Kia Ora issued forty-one million shares in the takeover of Kia Pacific, the company had virtually no assets, but it did have some debt. The convoluted strategy forms the background to the takeover of Western United and a reverse takeover between Kia Ora and the Duke Group that eventually led to the collapse of the Duke Group (refer to Table A6.1.1).

Table A6.1.1 Events Leading to the Takeover of Western United: 1979–1989

1979	Kia Ora and Uranium & Nickel re-activated.[1] In September 1979, Abbott approached Milligan to assist in the re-establishment of the companies. Milligan became a director of Kia Pacific in September 1987 along with Abbott, Schneider-Paas and Gardiner.
1980	On August 24, the Marvel Loch mine officially re-opened and became a major business activity of the company. Kia Ora then purchased the interest of Uranium & Nickel in Marvel Loch by issuing shares and options in Kia Ora and allocating them to shareholders in Uranium & Nickel. Kia Ora issued employee incentive options including 200,000 to Harold Abbott.[2]
1981	Kia Ora acquired a 40% interest in Western Drilling Services Pty. Ltd., a 20% interest in Kalgoorlie Assay Laboratory Pty. Ltd., a 20% interest in Palmerston Corporation Ltd. and a 20% interest in Dingup Bricks Ltd.
1982	Kia Ora acquired the balance of issued capital in Western Drilling that then became a wholly-owned subsidiary and sold its interest in Palmerston Corporation and Kalgoorlie Assay Laboratory to Uranium & Nickel. Then Uranium & Nickel changed its name to Western United Holdings Ltd., and its principal operation was the Marvel Loch Mine with net assets of $2.9 million, operating loss of $1.9 million and accumulated losses of $11.2 million.
1983	In 1983, Kia Ora acquired all the issued capital in Central Victorian Gold Mines NL for $625,000. Then the company was floated as a separate public company to raise $5 million. Consequently, Kia Ora owned 30% of issued capital. Kia Ora then sold all its shares in Dingup Bricks for $160,000 to Western United Holdings with net assets of $4.7 million, operating loss at $2.44 million (excluding extraordinary items) and total accumulated losses of $13.9 million but issued capital increased to 144 million shares.
1984	During this year, there were changes to accounting policies and sale of assets such that Kia Ora reported a small profit of approximately $474,000. This was the first reported profit since the Marvel Loch Mine was re-opened. At this time, net assets were reported at around $14.4 million in the case transcript.
1985	In April, open pit mining commenced at Marvel Loch and a new Mill was brought into production to expand the milling capacity. Kia Ora paid its first dividend of .25 cents per share.

(continued)

Table A.6.1.1 (continued)

1986	During this year, the processed ore reportedly almost trebled, gold produced and revenue earnings doubled. This was about 1% of the total Australian gold production measured at that time. A substantial increase in profit from 1984 was calculated at approximately $2.7 million and net assets had increased to around $25 million. Furthermore, issued capital was now in the vicinity of 261 million ordinary shares @ 25 cents per share.

[1] Harold Abbott became involved, and as Mullighan (1998, p.9) remarked, '[Milligan] had a background in merchant banking and business and developed proposals for the reactivation of the companies, including development of the Marvel Loch mine.'

[2] At the same time, the company reportedly had operating losses of $833,079 and a total loss of $1,028,736 in addition to accumulated losses of approximately $3 million.

Source. Details from the court transcript *of Duke Group Ltd. (in Liq) v. Pilmer & Ors*, Judgement of the Honourable Justice Mullighan, January 30, 1998

The Trial and the Judgment

The Duke Group case commenced in June 1994 and took 471 days to complete, with total legal costs estimated at $35 million. The statement of claim alleged that Kia Ora had actually acquired Western United for $80 million more than it was worth. Similarly the acquisition of FAI by HIH at around $300 million was reportedly much more than it was worth. Of course problems of "valuation" are not new; recall the plight of Adsteam and Bond Corporation, for instance, in the 1980s with their complicated acquisition forays—that also stressed the 'crucial issue in this regard is how to determine an asset and its worth' (Clarke *et al.*, 2003, p.163).

In Duke, the judgement was found for the plaintiff to the amount of $93,863,796.81 (including interest). In addition the plaintiff was entitled to be indemnified for any amount of Capital Gains Tax that the Commissioner of Taxation may demand due to this judgement, as well as costs incurred on a solicitor and client basis. Judgement was against five company directors of the Duke Group and around fifty accountants, in partnership, with the firm Nelson Wheeler (see Table A6.1.2).

The Accountants

With regard to the accounting firm of Nelson Wheeler, the defendants denied liability and alleged that if they were in breach of duty to Kia Ora causing financial loss, then Kia Ora caused or contributed to that loss. Consequently, Nelson Wheeler defendants sought indemnity or an apportionment of responsibility, hence contribution from the directors. That apportionment was advocated to be Harold Abbott at 50% whilst Lee-Steere, Somes, Quilty and Singleton were assessed at 5%. This responsibility was to be met by payment on third party proceedings brought by Nelson Wheeler Perth, the first defendants, against the above named directors of the plaintiff, the Duke Group.[44]

Table A6.1.2 The Defendants from the Duke Group and Nelson Wheeler

First	Second	Fifth
Angus Claymore Pilmer Alan Robert Crawford Dominic Vincent Martino Peter John Messer Peter Lawson Munachen	Francis Anthony Quilty Keith David Singleton	Members of other firms throughout the mainland States of Austalia
Geoffrey James Stokes Robert John Grey		that practised in partnership under the style or firm name of Nelson Wheeler. A total of 45 members.
All practising accountants in Partnership with others, under the style or firm name of Nelson Wheeler in Perth.		
Asserted by first defendants:	**Third:** ***Harold Abbott***	
That Munachen and Stokes were not partners at material times as they had earlier retired from partnership.		
	Fourth	
J. Mullighan stated that there was 'compelling evidence that Stokes and Munachen were partners until 30th June 1989' (p.220).	Sir Ernest Henry Lee-Steere Kevin Clarence Somes & one alternative Gary Ross Abbott [not a party to these proceedings]	

NOTE: All of the above were also directors of Western United. Alfred Carl Schneider-Paas died in May 1988 before legal action commenced on August 19, 1992

Source. Details from the court transcript of Duke Group Ltd. (in Liq) v. Pilmer & Ors, Judgement of the Honourable Justice Mullighan, January 30, 1998.

APPENDIX: A6.2

Details of the Budget Public Issue

The Budget issue included an offer for subscription of 12,500,000 ordinary shares of 50 cents each at a premium of 50 cents per share. Effectively, the total issue price was $1.00 per share. The full amount was to be paid on application, with the minimum subscription set at $12,500,000, and this amount was to be received by the company before any shares were to be allotted. The minimum application was set at 500 shares, in multiples of 500 thereafter. Subscription lists were to open on December 12, 1988, and to remain open until December 23, 1988. The directors reserved the right to close or extend the issue at their discretion. Underwriters Dicksons Limited and Oakminster Limited agreed to underwrite the shares offered for a commission of $562,500. Further to this, there were three companies who agreed to sub-underwrite the issue of particular shares, as detailed in Table A6.2.1.

Robert Ansett and Stanley Hamley were, at the time of offer, directors of Budget Investments Pty. Limited, and, as reported in the BCL Prospectus, they controlled the company. Furthermore, Hamley was a director of Quadrax Corporation and Oakminster Limited as well as being the controlling shareholder of Quadrax. In addition to the shares on offer, there were a number of options and convertible note entitlements given to the directors and other corporations as shown in Table A6.2.2.

Table A6.2.1 Shares Underwritten by Commission

Company Name	*Shares Underwritten*	*Commission*
Budget Investments Pty. Ltd	2,500,000	$75,000
Quadrax Corporation Pty. Ltd	4,000,000	$120,000
Oakminster Limited	6,000,000	$180,000

Source. BCL Prospectus (1988, p.23).

Table A6.2.2 Details of Options and Notes on Issue

No. of Options to Be Issued	*No. of Convertible Notes on Issue*	*Option or Convertible Note Holder*
2,375,000	2,000,000	Budget Investments Pty. Ltd., 3rd Floor, 4-10 Bay Street, Double Bay, N.S.W. 2028.
2,000,000	NIL	Robert Graham Ansett, 53 Wilson Street, North Carlton, Vic., 3054.
1,400,000	NIL	Stanley Albert Hamley, 2 Notts Avenue, Bondi, N.S.W. 2026.
1,000,000	3,500,000	Tricontinental Corp. Ltd., 385 Bourke Street, Melbourne, Vic., 3000.
400,000	1,500,000	Quadrax Investments Ltd., 3rd Floor, 4-10 Bay Street, Double Bay, N.S.W. 2028.
1,825,000	NIL	Various executives of BTI and licensees of Budget Group.

Source. BCL Prospectus (1988, p.38).

From the circumstances of the issue, the directors controlled the structure of the company. Ansett appeared to be influential in the management of its business affairs, as evidenced in the structure of the Group.

Relationships among BTI, BCL and BRACS

On September 30, 1988, BCL entered into agreements with BRACS effective from that date primarily 'to assign from BRACS the agreements to use and license the Budget Rent-A-Car name, logo and system ("the Agreements") in Australia and Papua New Guinea, and South-East Asia and the South Pacific. In addition, BRACS assigned all existing sub-licence agreements entered into by BRACS as at that date' (BCL Prospectus, 1988, p.29).

In 1988, it was intended that BRACS continue its business operations as a licensee of BCL. A management agreement was entered into among BTI, BCL and BRACS, that BRACS would conduct its own administrative and commercial activities for a management fee. Under the agreement, BRACS would receive from BCL any amounts initially received as service fees,[45] and BRACS was also to retain any initial license fees negotiated in the process of obtaining new licensees for BCL. Additionally, BTI and BCL established a five year service agreement with Ansett that required him to spend at least 50% of his time engaged in the businesses of BCL and BTI and to also agree not to compete in any business venture with BCL, BTI and BRACS.

Furthermore, a marketing services agreement was set up between BTI and BCL under which BCL would receive a $200,000 fee payment, indexed in accord with the Consumer Price Index, for a five year period to 1993 inclusive. BCL was also 'to assume the liability of a prior assignment, to Budget Equities Pty. Limited, of 49% of the service fee income payable to BRACS in respect of the international licensees' (BCL Prospectus, 1988, p.29).

Based on these agreements, a total amount of $23 million, payable in cash, was required to fund the payment to BRACS. In order to raise this figure, BCL intended to issue 8,999,990 shares of 50 cents each to Budget Investments Pty. Limited, in addition to the 2,000,000 ($1.00) non-interest bearing, unsecured, subordinated and non-redeemable convertible notes. The shares would be entitled to a dividend, 50% of that payable to the public, for a period of two years from September 1988. The 5,000,000 ($1.00) convertible notes split between Quadrax Investments Limited and Tricontinental Corporation Limited were to be issued at 12%, unsecured and subordinated.

These issues would augment the cash monies to be received from the public issue of BCL and enable changes to the corporate structure of the Budget Group to be completed. The amount to be received by BRACS was subsequently reviewed by the chartered accounting firm of Coopers and Lybrand. They were commissioned as the investigating accountants into the business affairs and financial position of BRACS and reported on the firm's financial state, in view of its rental revenue, at the time of the BCL float. However the actual financial state of the organisation seemed difficult to determine.

Financial Inter-dependencies among BTI, BCL and BRACS

The Companies and Securities Advisory Committee (CASAC) released a discussion paper on corporate groups in December 1998.[46] (A final report appeared in May 2000.) The aim of the 1998 paper was to specify a series of possible law reform options with regard to Corporate Groups. Specific issues covered regulation of the groups, directors, minority shareholders, tort liability, corporate group reconstruction and liquidation of group companies. Some of the ideas expressed in that document are drawn on here—the time period relevant to the case.

CASAC stated (para.1.7, p.2) that, '[t]he degree of economic and organisational integration of different corporate groups can be compared according to various organizational, market and public image criteria.' They then specified several questions within each category that might assist such an inquiry. This section investigates the possible degree of financial inter-dependencies among BTI, BCL and BRACS using questions from each category as proposed by CASAC in that December 1998 "Discussion Paper."

The following categories and questions are used:

(1) *Economic organisation*

Do the subsidiaries have an administrative infrastructure that will enable them to operate independently, or do they depend on a central group organisation for essential administrative support services?

Do the subsidiaries depend on the group for financing or loan guarantees?

(2)*Market*

What is the extent of horizontal or vertical integration of the businesses being conducted?

(3) *Public image*

To what extent is the group held out to the public as a single integrated enterprise, with the constituent companies described as components of the group?

Economic Organisation

Do the subsidiaries have an administrative infrastructure that will enable them to operate independently, or do they depend on a central group organisation for essential administrative support services?

BTI as the Holding Company of Budget Investments, BRACS and various other BTI subsidiaries was a company equipped with its own administrative infrastructure. It did, however, enter into a management agreement with BCL and BRACS in relation to the administrative and commercial aspects of the rent-a-car business. This entailed that BRACS would continue to supply the administrative services associated with the rent-a-car business after the float of BCL. BCL and BTI, as mentioned earlier, entered a five year service agreement with one director (Ansett) that he was to divide his time equally between each of the businesses, BCL and BTI, and to refrain from conducting any business in competition with BTI, BCL or BRACS. BCL was receiving income derived from administrative support (and other) services BRACS provided to the franchisees of the rent-a-car business. For Budget franchisees, the administrative infrastructure of BRACS was the central body that supplied and was to continue to supply essential business administration. In that vein, the franchisees were dependent on the continuity of BRACS's business operations; otherwise the franchisees would need to locate another operator to supply administrative (and other) services.

Do The Subsidiaries Depend On The Group For Financing Or Loan Guarantees?

Group financing or loan guarantees were not evident. It may be that a strategy of the Group was to ensure financial support through financial interdependency among the companies. This was not stipulated as the direct provision of finance from one company to another in the group, and there was no obvious statement that the companies have entered into any loan guarantees. Nonetheless, financial support by way of an agreed fee income was apparent:

> In return for its services, BCL will receive a licence fee (a predetermined percentage of turnover) from all operators of the "Budget System" in Australia and the Asian Pacific Region. In addition to these service fees, BCL will also receive a management service fee for marketing services performed on behalf of Budget Transport and Budget Orient Leasing Limited (BCL Prospectus, 1988, p.7).

There was no indication that BCL was to market its services or compete with other companies for its revenue. It was effectively guaranteed its revenue from companies within the Group. Further, there were a number of inter-related financial agreements among many of those companies. Briefly, under the management agreement, BCL was to pay BRACS a specified fee. In addition, BCL entered a marketing services agreement with BTI whereby BTI was to pay BCL $200,000 for the year ending June 30, 1989, and for each of the years to September 30, 1993, an annual amount indexed to the Consumer Price Index.[47] Other arrangements among companies in the Group extended to BCL assuming the obligation of a prior assignment to Budget Equities Pty.—limited again in relation to service fee income but this time from international licensees, payable to BRACS. To finance the total payment due to BRACS, BCL issued shares and convertible notes to another subsidiary, Budget Investments Pty. Limited, and convertible notes to other related entities, as well as the issue to the public.

It would seem that if the financial state of one of these entities cracked and then crumbled, the others would most likely follow suit—the domino effect of Clarke *et al.* (2003, p.247).

Market

What is the extent of horizontal or vertical integration of the businesses being conducted?

Primarily, the business was the rent-a-car service of Budget. BCL was incorporated to acquire 'certain industrial property and contractual rights relevant to the conduct of the business of renting motor vehicles and to permit the Company to engage in the management, marketing and promotion of other activities in the transportation, hospitality and recreational industries in Australia and elsewhere' (BCL Prospectus, 1988, p.3). Due to the organizational structure of the group, an extensive support system for each of the companies with regard to both business activities and finance was indicated. The public could interpret the Budget group as financially sound, with involvement in diversified business operations, known or considered to be successful. In that sense, the prospectus indicated both horizontal and vertical integration of business interests.

The following quotes show that an assertive, yet emotional attitude was used to promote the strength, substance and business potential of all the companies that formed the Budget group:

> 'The Budget Group in Australia has shown dynamic growth in revenue since its inception in 1965 to occupy the number one position in the Australian car and truck rental market.'
>
> 'Unlike its major competitors in Australia, the company is entirely Australian owned.'
>
> 'The Budget Group's growth has been experienced locally and overseas. . . . Additional growth has been achieved through both the Budget Group's own locations or through licensees using the Budget name

in the provision of car and truck rental services, chauffeur driven services and leisure vehicles.'

'The selective use of the Budget name in the leisure and tourism industry shall continue to provide a new avenue of growth.'

'The Budget Group has also diversified into companies providing fully maintained fleet leasing, financial services, motor vehicle retailing and advertising services.'

'The Budget Group's strong record of growth can be substantially attributed to the commitment of its management team. Mr. Bob Ansett has maintained a high profile commitment by way of successful marketing and promotion in Australia and overseas of the Budget Group's activities.'

'The opportunity now exists for investors to participate in Budget's acknowledged success via subscription for shares in the company.'

Source. The BCL Prospectus (1988, p.7).

Public Image

To what extent is the group held out to the public as a single integrated enterprise, with the constituent companies described as components of the group?

The organizational structure of the group in 1988 indicated that business activities of each company, although in part different, were nonetheless fully integrated. The BCL Prospectus provided details of this structure briefly, in a corporate flowchart (p.9), information summary (p.4) and with specific parts of the structure further explained throughout the text. The image given to the public was that the activities of the various entities in the group of companies were part of the operations of the group as a whole.

A summary of the group's composition highlights that two of the directors of BCL, Ansett and Hamley, controlled BTI and its subsidiaries. Through that group of companies, they retained an interest in BCL to the extent of nine million shares and two million convertible notes. BTI promoted the listing of BCL and in return received nine million free options that were subsequently nominated as per details set out above. Hamley had other related interests. He was a director of Quadrax Investments Limited, which held one and a half million convertible notes in BCL, and a director and controlling shareholder of Quadrax Corporation Pty. Limited. That company was also a sub-underwriter of the issue offered through the BCL Prospectus. Oakminster Limited, of which

Hamley was a director, was another sub-underwriter for part of the BCL issue. In addition, a subsidiary of BTI, Budget Investments Pty. Limited, agreed to underwrite part of the issue. Both Ansett and Hamley were directors and controlling shareholders of Budget Equities Pty. Limited, another subsidiary of BTI. Under the agreements for the development of BCL, Budget Equities would continue to be entitled to its royalties of 49% received from International Franchisees with regard to the hiring of vehicles. Furthermore, both BCL and BTI employed Ansett under an agreement that stipulated his non-competitive business activities for a five year period.

Degree of Integration in the Group

The nature of this corporate group according to the economic, market and public image criteria used in this section may be explained in the following context. Inter-relationships between the above companies and at least two of the directors in the group appear self-evident. The organizational structure and type of business activities undertaken by the companies indicate integrated operations with the constituent companies discussed as components of the group. These circumstances allude to possible operating problems for any company, mainly due to the likelihood of conflicting interests.

Chapter 4 explained that corporate groups (theoretically) might be viewed as a separate entity or a single enterprise:

> Australian corporate law, like UK company law, has traditionally applied the separate entity approach to corporate groups. It does not permit the controllers of a corporate group to treat the group as a single enterprise for the purpose of their entrepreneurial activities. Instead, the separate legal personality of each company must be maintained' (CASAC, 1998, para.1.60, p.23). Also refer CASAC's Final Report (2000, para.1.72, p.26).

If the Budget group were approached as a separate entity, then, in common law, the company directors would owe a duty to their company. Each company in the group would be considered a separate legal entity in its own right. As such, '[t]he orthodox common law position is that directors of a company in a corporate group owe fiduciary duties to that company and not to other entities in that corporate group' (CASAC, 1998, p.19).

Yet in this case, Ansett and Hamley were directors of a number of related companies in the group, and Ansett was directly employed by two of those companies. CASAC (1998, p.19) continued, '[t]he interests of other group companies may be taken into account only to the extent that this furthers the interests of the directors' own companies.' This point would be difficult to determine for Ansett and Hamley, given the interrelationships built among the companies, especially for the BCL issue and the agreement between BTI and BCL that Ansett devote 50% of his time to each company.[48] The quandary remains of how to define the legal entity and for what purpose is the entity defined.

7 Insolvency Stats and Stories
2004 to 2011

'Accounting is nothing but sublimated common sense applied to finding and telling the truth about business' (Cole, 1915, p.vi).

AN ONGOING CONCERN

Previous chapters reveal that solvency is an ongoing concern in financial accounting. In this chapter, solvency is examined from an insolvency perspective. Although solvency is a critical commercial financial attribute, the legal and accounting domains reveal inconsistent ways of determining solvency at law and in accounting (refer to Chapter 1). Arguably it is essential for a business entity to quantify its state of solvency to better enable it to trade into the future as a going concern. Currently conventional financial reports do not include a quantified solvency statement, although directors are, in some countries, required to sign a declaration of solvency with regard to the entity they direct. In Australia, for instance, under the Australian *Corporations Act 2001* (Act), directors include a signed declaration (solvency statement) in the published annual reports of their company. Quantifying the entity's solvency would support and add further credibility to that solvency statement.

In its current form, the directors' solvency statement articulates 'whether, in the directors' opinion, there are reasonable grounds to believe that the company, registered scheme or disclosing entity will be able to pay its debts as and when they become due and payable' (s.295(4)(c)). Moreover, the directors are of the opinion that 'the financial statement and notes are in accordance with the Act, including (1) section 296 (compliance with accounting standards); and (2) section 297 (true and fair view)' (s.295(4)(d)). The "true and fair" override is important—to comply with the professional accounting standards and also to comply with the true and fair override is somewhat problematic. Various issues on "true and fair" have been debated at some length throughout the literature.[1] And the debate continues.

Presently in Australia, accounting for financial assets of insurers (and other financial institutions) are measured at fair value and are at times marked-to-market[2] (different than being marked-to-model), whereas operating assets for other corporate entities are not.[3] The reasons for such differences still remain unclear. Clarke *et al.* (2003, p.310), when referring to HIH's June 2000 published financials, noted the entity:

> [B]rought to account nearly $1 billion dollars of Future Income Tax Benefits, goodwill and various capitalised expenditure [assets] all potentially in accord with the prevailing [accounting] Standards. Those balances [were, and] are of highly contestable relevance to any assessment of the company's solvency at the time or of its overall financial position.

It is not just the balances of accounts that are frequently of concern, but, as discussed in previous chapters, some elements therein referred to as assets are also highly contestable.

In 2003, the Corporations and Markets Advisory Committee (CAMAC) highlighted the importance of solvency in a group setting; its discussion paper then focussed on rehabilitating large, complex enterprises in financial difficulties.[4] CAMAC (2003, s.1.1) emphasised that directors should know the level of solvency of the business they direct to enable it to continue 'in business as a going concern' and to assist directors to fulfil their legal obligations in preventing insolvent trading (s.1.35). Additionally, under the concept of a financial stress test, CAMAC indicated that directors should determine the extent of the entity's 'actual or likely insolvency' prior to initiating any rehabilitation process.[5]

Duns (2007) explored the likelihood of discouraging "insolvency misconduct" by considering 'the impact of the proposed corporate insolvency reforms on directors and other company officers' (p.173).[6] Therein Duns examined two particulars. Firstly with regard to reform proposals concerning directors and other corporate officers, and secondly on the reforms subsequently settled. The former included concerns that were originally stipulated in *Corporate Insolvency Laws: A Stocktake* (2004), a report of the Parliamentary Joint Committee on Corporations and Financial Services (PJC), such as:

(a) whether directors should be liable for the costs of restructuring the financial records of failed companies and issues surrounding proof of insolvency generally;
(b) whether deterrence of phoenix activity requires further duties to be imposed on officers; and,
(c) whether existing provisions should be strengthened in certain areas, notably in relation to voluntary winding up, uncommercial transactions and liability for avoiding obligations to employees (Duns, 2007, p.173).

On insolvent trading, the courts seek to determine the date that the business was insolvent. This is not easy. 'It is generally accepted that, from the plaintiff's point of view, proving the company's insolvency will commonly be the most difficult part of such proceedings. The company's financial records will often be a critical component in establishing the company's insolvency' (Duns, 2007, p.174). Crucially, financial accounting could, but arguably does not, enable solvency to be readily determined.

Recall discussion in Chapter 4 that investigated difficulties of quantifying solvency from conventional accounting reports. Argument emphasised the unlikely relationship among various elements in those reports and the financial amounts attributed to those elements. Further, it discussed how the problem was exacerbated when dealing with corporate groups. In the context of corporate groups, Harris (2007, p.78) asserted:

> The James Hardie example has brought home to the public the difficulties in shifting liability within groups of related but legally separate companies. The problem of shifting liability between members of corporate groups is exacerbated where the group companies are insolvent, because (unlike with James Hardie) the total assets within the group are insufficient to meet the liabilities of each individual company within the group. This issue has been raised in several high profile corporate collapses including Qintex, Ansett, HIH, Westpoint and most recently Fincorp.[7]

Fincorp is discussed later in this chapter. Returning to the notion of phoenix activity and insolvent trading, Harris (2007, p.8) stated, 'in many cases phoenix activities will be used where a company is nearing insolvency or is insolvent and the directors are allowing it to incur debts to creditors with the intention of winding up the company before repayment is made.' Although as Duns (2007, p.175) remarked, 'Phoenix company activity is not readily susceptible to precise definition . . . but has been described [with reference to the Cole Royal Commission] as an "activity where an incorporated entity fails and is unable to pay its debts or acts with the intention to deny unsecured creditors equal access to the entity's assets in order to meet unpaid debts." '[8] Harris (2007, p.2) further explained:

> Phoenix activity is typically associated with directors who transfer the assets of an indebted company into a new company of which they are also directors. The director then places the initial company into administration or liquidation with no assets to pay creditors, meanwhile continuing the business using the new company structure.

Historically, the effect of phoenix activity on the Australian economy is widespread and costly. However, 'the literature confirms that the phoenixing (sic) syndrome is not unique to Australia' (Roach, 2010, p.91). Hence, it is likely that the costs attributed to phoenix activity for the global community is ever-increasing. With regard to Australia, in July 1996, the Australian Securities Commission (forerunner to the ASIC) released a research paper on *Phoenix Companies and Insolvent Trading*,[9] in which an 'estimate of annual losses to the Australian economy as a result of phoenix activities was [at that time] $1.3 billion, representing 0.28% of GDP' (Martin, 2007, p.3). By 2010 phoenix activity was reportedly 'estimated to cost the [Australian] economy [at least] $2.4 billion a year.'[10] The industry sector mostly affected by phoenix activity is the small to medium sized business sector. Even so, Ferguson (2010, p.3) reported:

> Research for Weekend Business by Dun & Bradstreet reveals that of the 10,200 companies that went belly-up in the past year 29 per cent involved companies that had one or more directors previously involved with a wound-up entity. This compares to just 10 per cent in 2004–05. [Moreover]
>
> The analysis, which examined the 2.8 million Australian companies on Dunn and Bradstreet's database, also shows a 4 per cent increase in the number of companies entering external administration in the 2009–10 financial year with at least one director who had been involved with a wound-up entity. This follows a 38 per cent increase in 2008–09 and a 56 per cent increase in 2007–08—when the global financial crisis began.[11]

With increasing pressure on government and regulators to stem the growth of phoenix activity, '[o]n 14 November 2009 the Assistant Treasurer announced the release of a proposals paper canvassing options to address fraudulent phoenix activity.'[12] Lobbying included demands for law reform—for instance, to oust recalcitrant and/or inept directors and increase the severity of fines and other punishment, including the length of possible custodial sentences. Ferguson (2010, p.3) also asserted:

> [T]here are 170 directors in corporate Australia who have been associated with more than 15 company collapses and that the number of directors associated with two incidents of business failure has increased from less than 8 per cent of business failures in the 2004–05 financial year to almost 20 per cent in the most recent financial year [2010].
>
> The significance of these findings is that directors involved in a business that has gone into external administration are 250 per cent more likely to be involved in an insolvent wind-up at some stage in the next 12 months.[13]

Of course not all directors act with the intent to mislead. And sometimes directors complain of being misled themselves on the financial state of the business they direct.[14] Arguably, the reference above to (possible) fraudulent phoenix activity is crucial here, because not all defined phoenix actions are illicit. As Roach (2010, p.91) asserted: 'The acquisition of business nous is . . . an iterative process, with each business failure informing future business endeavours.' He explained further 'in terms of "*innocent phoenixing*", "*occupational hazard*" and "*careerist offenders*" ' (p.93).

Apparently it is the latter group that are of the most concern—and perhaps so within the international community.[15] The situation evolved because 'these operators intentionally structure their businesses to engage in cyclical phoenix activity, exploiting loopholes in insolvency laws and fractures in communication between government agencies and the insolvency profession' (Roach, 2010, p.93). Furthermore, 'Phoenixing . . . is ultimately an abuse of the limited liability concept and any analysis of phoenixing must necessarily consider the purpose of the corporate form and the theory underpinning company law' (Roach, 2010, p.92).

Given the array of corporate collapses globally and continuing business failures across countries, across time, societal *tolerance* of *unexpected* financial catastrophes and their outcomes has waned. Society wants answers and action. The impetus of insolvencies and insolvent trading is sickening to most. The disastrous financial and non-financial consequences for, and to, national and international communities is evident. Some have included this heightened concern under the umbrella of governance or corporate governance.

In April 2010, CAMAC published its 'Guidance for Directors' report, which that details continuing challenges for directors with regard to governance. From a financial perspective, '[i]n order to carry out their role, directors need to . . . keep informed about the company's activities and financial position' (CAMAC, 2010, s.2.1.3, p.9). In such a context, Roach (2010) stated, '[m]ost corporate governance systems across the international arena require directors to minimise the impact of insolvency by ceasing to trade as soon as it becomes clear that a business cannot be saved.' As discussed previously, however, the clarity of the date of when a business is insolvent is difficult to identify and for many likely remains contestable.[16]

In November 2009, ASIC released its consultation paper 124, 'Duty to prevent insolvent trading: Guide for directors,' in which it proposed four principles of which the first two stated:

(1) Directors must keep themselves informed about the company's financial affairs, and regularly assess the company's solvency; and
(2) Directors should investigate financial difficulties immediately they identify concerns about the company's financial viability.

Both of the above valid proposals are essential, in accord with the requirements of the *Corporations ACT 2001*, s.588G—director's duty to prevent insolvent trading.

Interestingly during the period 2004–2010 since the CAMAC (2003) exposé on solvency and insolvent trading, 640 companies in Australia have been listed under insolvency, of which 107 identified under voluntary administration and 97 identified with a receiver appointed (DatAnalysis, 2011). In 2010, the ASIC National Insolvent Trading Program (NITP) Report 213 stated, '[t]he objective of the voluntary administration is to maximise the chances of a company, or as much as possible of its business, continuing in existence or, if that is not possible, to provide a better return to creditors than would result from an immediate winding-up' (ASIC, 2010, p.20). However, if the company does liquidate, a creditor's voluntary liquidation (winding-up) is most common. Table 7.1 shows the percentage distribution of external administration appointments in Australia for one year, as detailed by ASIC (2010, p.21).

Table 7.1 External Administration Appointments in Australia: 2009–2010

Creditor Winding-up	46%
Court winding-up (including provisional liquidators)	21%
Voluntary administration, DOCAs and schemes	16%
Receiver/Receiver and manager	9%
Controller/ Managing controller	8%

Source. ASIC's National Insolvent Trading Program report (2010, Appendix 1: Insolvency landscape pp.20, 21).

Recall the earlier reference to 'a 4 per cent increase in the number of companies entering external administration in the 2009–10 financial year' (Ferguson, 2010, p.3).

Notably ASIC (2010, p.21) reported that 'statistical data collected from statutory reports lodged by insolvency practitioners, [revealed that] most external administrations relate to small to medium proprietary companies.' The ASIC, by means of the NITP, visited in excess of 1,530 companies deemed in financial distress from 2005 to 2010 and 'observed that 15% of companies reviewed . . . were subsequently placed into external administration—mostly by the directors' (ASIC, 2010, p.4).

> In Australia, company insolvencies fall under the Corporations Act and are monitored by ASIC, [whereas] personal bankruptcies have a dedicated Bankruptcy Act and a separate regulator, ITSA [Insolvency and Trustee Service Australia], and failed co-operatives fall under the Department of Fair Trading and a separate piece of legislation.[17]

Nonetheless, the data collected on insolvent companies and/or companies in financial distress are not always easily available and are possibly incomplete. To help with this and for their review, the NITP utilised a variety of ways to distinguish between companies including:

- complaints received from the public, such as complaints from employees, unpaid creditors or other stakeholders;
- credit agencies, such as Dun & Bradstreet and the ABR Credit Gazette;

- auditor notifications under s311 of the Corporations Act relating to insolvency concerns;
- financial accounts lodged with ASIC;
- referrals from other stakeholder teams within ASIC; and
- other sources (e.g. media, insolvency practitioners, credit managers, accountants and lawyers) (ASIC, 2010, p.6).

It is wise to be cautious, however, on categorizing evidence with regard to the size of companies such as small, medium, large and multi-national. For instance, one of the NITP's main objectives was to 'ensure that directors took steps to remain properly and fully informed about the financial affairs of the company [they direct] at all times' (ASIC, 2010, p.6). Given the aforementioned legal requirements of directors, that objective is likely to include all types and sizes of companies. Another major aim of the NITP was reportedly to 'make directors of potentially insolvent companies aware of their responsibilities and the implications of continued trading if they knew that their company was insolvent' (ASIC, 2010, p.6). Although the NITP revealed that, in Australia, most external administrations involve 'small to medium proprietary companies,' report 213 emphasised the legal duties imposed on directors generally was 'to prevent insolvent trading' (p.5).

It is clear that directors need to know the financial state of their company. It follows, then, that directors require timely reports of current financial details on the business they direct to enable them to do their job. Given the continued surge of unexpected corporate collapses and other unexpected business failures, from the twentieth century into the twenty-first century, it is contestable that they do have access to such reports. It is incontestable that they should.

Further, the *Corporations Act 2001* mandates directors exercise their duties and power with diligence and care (s.180) and that they do not act improperly (s.182, s.183). As directors are expected to be fully informed about the financial details of the company they direct, that includes its state of solvency. They are to prevent insolvent trading (s.588G). Remember directors must, under s.295A(2)(c), declare 'the financial statements and notes for the financial year give a true and fair view (see section 297)' and under s.295 (4)(c) declare as to the entity's solvency. At s.297, the true and fair override stipulates compliance with regard to '(a) the financial position and performance of the company, registered scheme or disclosing entity; and (2) if consolidated financial statements are required—the financial position and performance of the consolidated entity.' Recall discussion in Chapter 4.

Similarly, Kirk (2006) reported on three studies with a focus on "true and fair" in the context of the quality of financial reporting and highlighted the dilemma that:[18]

> All three studies found that true and fair view was not associated with the user perspective of financial reporting. No group saw "true

> and fair view", or any of the phrases containing "fair", or complying with GAAP and regulations, as similar to "understandable and comprehensible" or "relevant and useful." . . . [However] The findings of this study confirm that respondents distinguish between "true and fair view" and other potential qualitative terms. . . . The finding also suggests that "true", as one of the elements separating "true and fair view" from terms that include only "fair", may be an important element in participants' perceptions of factors required for financial reporting quality (Kirk, 2006, pp.224, 225).

Furthermore:

> The results also show that "true and fair view" is not seen as equivalent to "fairly reflect" or "fair presentation". The general similarity of auditors', financial directors' and shareholders' responses and that of other empirical research also suggests that the globalization of financial reporting may be leading to a lessening of between-country differences in perceptions of terms such as "true and fair view" in financial reporting (Kirk, 2006, p.225).[19]

Arguably the concept of true and fair and its meaning, in the context of financial report information, are important to users of financial reports. Also, the truth about the elements (in definition and monetary equivalent) used to determine an entity's solvent state is vital to its quantification. Informatively and with regard to earlier discussion on phoenix activity and [in]solvency, Switzer (2010, p.12) reported, 'Mendelson, [chief executive of Prushka Fast Debt Recovery] unlike politicians and public servants, has a practical solution to the problem. He thinks all companies should be compelled to provide a "solvency statement" to any intending or current creditor on request.'[20] This seems a good idea. But, why to creditors only? The notion requires agreement on what denotes the solvency statement. A quantified solvency statement, for instance, advances the idea and might be included in the suite of financial statements published in companies' annual reports or (at least) made available to the board of directors to assist them in their decision-making.

Arguably to enable directors to decide on their entity's state of solvency necessitates access to timely and relevant financial facts. Stakeholders' confidence in the directors' current declaration on solvency would likely be enhanced knowing their directors are given these details. This may already occur in some companies, but, given the continued assortment of astonishing corporate collapses, it is not widely perceived that it does. In this context, the current solvency statement (declaration) required of directors in Australia under the *Corporations Act 2001* is arguably inadequate, if not erroneous.

The outcomes of financial accounting practice in terms of quality financial accounting reports remain topical and of concern to all business stakeholders, particularly as many elements within those financial reports are newsworthy and used, by some, to analyse an entity's financial capacity for business continuity. The following elaborates with focus on common indicators of financial distress.

SIGNIFICANT FINANCIAL INDICATORS OF PENDING DISASTER

The NITP (2010) identified a number of indicators, internal and external, of insolvency concerns for business entities. It was noted (p.9) that its lists were not exhaustive. It is also "noticeable" that the points of concern do not really indicate anything new. Nonetheless, they do highlight issues that may be linked to financial accounting and management concerns. Hence, the NITP common indicators with particular regard to [in]solvency included:

- The company is experiencing cash flow difficulties.
- The company is experiencing difficulties in selling its stock or collecting debts owed to it.
- Creditors are not being paid on agreed trading terms and/or are placing the company on cash-on-delivery terms, before they will supply further goods and services.
- The company is not paying its Commonwealth and state taxes when due.
- The company is unable to produce accurate financial information on a timely basis that shows the company's trading performance and financial position or that can be used to prepare reliable financial forecasts.
- It is not certain that there are assets that can be sold in a relatively short period of time to provide funds to help meet debts owed without affecting the company's ongoing ability to continue to trade profitably.
- The company has reached the limits of its funding facilities and is unable to obtain appropriate further finance to fund operations.
- The company auditor has qualified their audit opinion on the grounds that there is uncertainty about whether the company can continue as a going concern.

Although nothing really new, some emphasise the possibility of increased circumstances of insolvent trading. Given that the NITP reviewed around 1,533 companies and decided where 'significant insolvency indicators [were identified] . . . the objective of the NITP was to encourage directors to seek advice from an insolvency professional about the appointment of an external administrator' (ASIC, 2010, p.14) it seems the notion of *putting the cart before the horse* prevailed. For if directors, at all times, were cognisant of the actual financial state of the business they direct, they would not be in need of such encouragement. Moreover, the business would be unlikely to trade if insolvent, unless of course the directors were recalcitrant, corrupt or otherwise acting with intent to err.

On solvency and the role of directors, CAMAC (2010) was specific. These issues have regard to societal demands and expectations of directors, directors' relationship with management, directors' accountability to shareholders and other stakeholders and include:

- In order to carry out their role, directors need . . . to keep informed about the company's activities and financial position.
- The directors are reliant to a considerable degree on the capacity of management . . . to keep the board informed about matters material to the performance and direction of the company.
- The extent to which a director can rely on the advice of management and other advisers continues to be a live issue.
- A major focus of legislative and judicial guidance, as well as much of the guidance by regulators, is on legal duties and compliance matters.
- The Corporations Act and other legislation relevant to the operation of companies (as well as common law principles) provide a legal framework within which directors operate.

Again, such guidance is not really new. Directors, for instance, must operate within the framework of the law.[21] Judicial decisions across time illustrate the legal structure within which corporations and directors are expected to conduct business. Specifically, in *Hall v. Poolman* (2007)[22] with regard to insolvent trading, for instance, the court provided guidance to directors on circumstances that might apply to a reasonable expectation of solvency.

The following illustrate circumstances of companies that have unexpectedly collapsed or suffered financial distress throughout the period 2004–2010. Ferguson (2010), for example, with regard to phoenix activity and issues on insolvency, reported, 'the collapses of Sonray, Great Southern, Timbercorp, Babcock & Brown, Westpoint, Fincorp, Opes Prime, ABC Learning and Allco [are] still fresh.'[23]

CASES AND COMPANIES

Of the companies mentioned by Ferguson (2010), the following were clearly evident on the insolvency DatAnalysis 640 companies listing (2004–2010). The delisted date of each company is in brackets and sourced from "Morningstar DatAnalysis" online. Hence, ABC Learning Centres Limited (1/8/2009), Allco Finance Group Limited (1/9/2009), Great Southern Limited (30/8/2010), Babcock and Brown Limited (18/6/2009), Babcock and Brown

Environmental (25/6/2008), Timbercorp Primary Infrastructure (30/8/2010), Allco Hit Limited (1/9/2009), Allco Hybrid Investment Trust (14/1/2009) and Great Southern Plantations Limited (5/3/2007). The DatAnalysis list totalled 640 companies because some companies were listed a number of times for a variety of reasons, which indicated financial dilemma.

Of those companies, Great Southern Limited, Allco Hybrid Investment Trust, Babcock and Brown Limited and Timbercorp Primary Infrastructure were included on the DatAnalysis listing of 107 companies under voluntary administration. Data then provided that Great Southern Limited, Allco Hybrid Investment Trust, Babcock and Brown Limited and Timbercorp Primary Infrastructure were of the ninety-seven companies with a receiver appointed. Further explanatory details of these companies and others are included on the relevant DatAnalysis listings.

The following covers circumstances of Great Southern and Timbercorp, the Fincorp Group and Allco Finance Group Limited. These cases serve to illustrate further those recurring events (some apparent in Chapters 5 and 6) that reveal continued challenges for financial accounting in determining [in]solvency.

Great Southern Limited

For Great Southern, a major issue focussed on assets, their "value" and its escalating debt. Briefly, in 1987, the Great Southern Group of companies was formed. In May 1999, the Group was publicly listed and 'changed its name from Templegate Services Ltd to Great Southern Plantation Limited' (Directors' Report, Annual Report, 1999, p.8). In 2007, the Group changed its name to Great Southern Limited. Until the 2000s, the mainstay of its business remained managed investment schemes (MIS), after which the group diversified its product and business activities to include cattle, olives, viticulture and almonds.[24] Ultimately, its principal activities were reported as the 'development, marketing and management of agribusiness based projects,' whereas initially it was established 'to package, promote and manage investment in timber plantations.'[25]

Although Great Southern continued to sell mainly MIS, by 2007, it expanded into funds management with the acquisition of Rural Funds Management Ltd. At the same time, 'retaining its diversified agricultural assets fund and offering a new share fund and a blended property fund.'[26] Notably:

> The Great Southern Group in 2008 formed Australia's largest agribusiness managed investment scheme operation. The company comprised a parent entity, Great Southern Plantations Limited (renamed Great Southern Limited from 2007), and over forty subsidiaries, almost all wholly owned. Those subsidiaries held or operated Great Southern's businesses, including providing management services.[27]

In addition, it provided investor finance, and reportedly '[b]y 2009 its loan book comprised 14,500 loans with an average value of approximately A$50,000.'[28] However, investor returns were somewhat diverse and risky due partly to the time delay before yields could be expected. For instance:

> Investors in Great Southern generally purchased lots (typically of 1 hectare) on land owned or leased by Great Southern. Thus investors owned the plantations, but the land assets belonged to the company. While investors owned individual woodlots, risks and returns were distributed across all investors in individual projects, with growers sharing "the average yield at harvest for the entire Project . . . rather than the return from their individual woodlot". These were not high rates of return for the length of investment involved.[29]

Due to its falling share price and other dilemmas including drought, Great Southern decided 'to subsidise returns to its early investors [which] was a looming problem: [because] its forestry plantations were not performing to expectations.'[30] So, although sales and profit figures in 2006 were reportedly alright, 'with over A$450 million in sales, and a net profit after tax of A$133 million,'[31] the harvest for the same period was substantially down on expected yield. At that time, Great Southern reacted by inflating 'the returns to A$4100 [to investors] using its own funds.'[32]

Recall, by 2008, the company had increased its activities and diversified its interests across forestry, almonds, beef cattle, wine grapes and poultry production. However, the Group's debt also increased and did so at a seemingly disproportionate rate. In 2008, after years of reported profits, the Group tabled a loss of around A$64 million—more on this later. Then the global financial crisis hit, and by 2009 regulatory authorities were looking with increased interest at schemes such as MIS. Hence, pressure, particularly financial pressure, increased. Reactions included trying to increase asset sales (to recoup money) and to refinance debt. Unfortunately, the banks did not agree.

> Great Southern's banks refused a request in 2009 for a further $35 million loan . . . and by May 2009, when a trading halt was called, the company's shares were trading for just 12 cents. On 16 may 2009 administrators were appointed under the [Australian] *Corporations Act 2001*, with the companies' assets passing into control of receivers McGrathNicol on 18 May 2009. The assets of the group were primarily its land holdings. By the time it went into administration, they were worth [apparently] A$1.8 billion, however, despite company expansion plans, its net assets had not grown for four years.[33]

Across the years, the Group's financials fluctuated with its net assets story problematic. Table 7.2 shows an extract of the reported financials of the Group for the period 1999 to 2008, although information is limited and, as inherent to conventional financial statements, comparisons can be difficult. It is noted that in 2007 the Group changed its reporting period from a June base to a financial year end at September 30. The Chairman reported, '[t]his change is seen as more appropriate to the company to reflect the seasonal nature of its agricultural operations and business model, and enables us to provide more meaningful information to shareholders and the broader market' (Annual Report, 2007, p.5).

However, the circumstances changed. To elucidate, in 1999, the Group's consolidated net assets were A$82,218,000, with an increase to A$706,375,000 by 2008. Whereas the parent entity's net assets in 1999 were A$68,083,000 that by 2008 totalled A$297,194,000. There was a markedly different increase between the two entities across those years (7.6 times to 3.4 rounded), but otherwise the numbers alone don't tell much of a story. Noticeably, the consolidated losses for the Group in 2008 were A$(63,804,000), whereas the parent entity's losses were *somewhat larger* at A$(219,039,000). The major difference was seemingly an "allowance for related party loans" of A$(213,732,000), which translated into 'impairment losses recognised on receivables' (Annual Report, 2008, notes 4, 13).

Critically, some informative details may have been shelved in the consolidation process (refer to Chapter 4). Still the figures reveal little other than a notable difference between the consolidated group results and those of the parent entity, including a somewhat spectacular move from profit to losses during the ten year span. Nonetheless, the Group's reported net assets were positive and in accord with the balance sheet test of insolvency, indicating a solvent state. The cash flow test of insolvency, however, would delve further to examine monetary equivalents of some assets. Table 7.2 elaborates, with net assets highlighted.

Conspicuously, the loss of A$63.8 million begs the question: What happened? There were a number of surprises in rising expenses and write-offs. For example, from 2001, the Group reported "Agriculture and MIS related expenses" that revealed a steady climb from A$(16,668,000) in 2002 to A$(26,326,000) in 2004. The following year, 2005 marked a hike to A$(63,746,000), with a substantial jump in 2006 to A$(166,952,000). For 2007 and 2008, the expense rapidly increased to strike A$(199,988,000) and A$(223,833,000), respectively. And from 2005, there were adjustments to the comparative figures in succeeding years' accounts that likely indicated changes to accounting policies.

In 2006, change was evident. Finance costs reportedly climbed by some A$(18,201,000), and a fair value adjustment to investment property was made at A$(3,282,000); the marketing—selling—promotion costs were up A$(19,109,000) also. There was a further increase in fair value adjustment to recognise decrement to investment property by A$(3,628,000) to the three months from June 2006 to September 30, 2006. This reflected one of

Table 7.2 Great Southern's Consolidated Numbers: 1999–2008

	1999 $000	*2000 $000*	*2001 $000*	*2002 $000*	*2003 $000*	*2004 $000*	*2005 $000*	*2006 $000*	*2007 $000*	*2008 $000*
Total Revenue	49,756	96,868	63,052	54,571	99,449	208,344	318,849	499,511	525,184	444,368
Operating Profit/ (Loss) after tax	22,129	38,295	21,921	17,215	41,397	93,226	124,307	132,859	71,508	(63,804)
Total Assets	154,324	235,985	205,898	214,601	297,146	646,564	1,180,776	1,607,869	1,720,351	1,790,121
Total Liabilities	72,106	75,122	34,157	26,052	70,308	197,648	418,933	851,629	954,389	1,083,746
Net Assets	**82,218**	**160,863**	**171,741**	**188,549**	**226,838**	**448,916**	**761,843**	**756,240**	**765,962**	**706,375**

Source. Details sourced from the Annual Reports (by year) of Great Southern available online at DatAnalysis company annual reports. For instance: http://0-datanalysis.morningstar.com.au.alpha2.latrobe.edu.au/af/company/annualreport?ASXCode=GTP&daterange=all&subtype=03001&subtype=03017&subtype=03011&anntypes=0,1,2,3&xtm-licensee=dat

the adjustments to accounts due to a change in the Group's reported financial year from ending June to ending September.

Further changes occurred as an impairment of horticultural assets was recorded at A$(40,072,000) at September 30, 2007. By 2008, the story emphasised *grim* with an increase to the allowance for doubtful debts by A$(51,304,000), recognition of a non-MIS managed fund of A$(14,045,000) and impairment of Goodwill at a somewhat massive A$(30,000,000). During this time, the directors' declaration was duly published as required by corporations' legislation, and the auditor's report provided an unqualified opinion.

Business continuity for Great Southern may have been deemed challenging (by some), with a focus on its diminishing share prices. Nonetheless, there were those who missed the "apparent" warnings that may be attributed to fluctuating financials, a rapid increase in business activities and diversified business interests—but such change can be reminiscent of good business practice, and the auditors' report was fine and the directors' declaration indicated solvency. However, there were increased capitalisation of expenses and continued funding of shortfalls on sales.[34] The latter was not a good look. Finally, there was the huge impairment to goodwill (a suspect asset) and:

> In 2009, as a result of worsening economic conditions and regulatory issues, the company [Great Southern] was placed in administration. The collapse of Great Southern group, in conjunction with the failure of another high-profile agribusiness company, Timbercorp, led to two separate Australian parliamentary committee inquiries into the MIS industry.[35]

In July 2009, the receivers determined the company was insolvent. 'By April 2010, timber company Gunns had taken over as the responsible entity running most of Great Southern's pulpwood schemes, but the land on which they were being grown [the assets] . . . were yet to be sold.'[36] By August 30, 2010, Great Southern Limited was delisted.

Notably, Timbercorp Primary Infrastructure Fund (another MIS company) went into receivership around a month earlier, although both entities were delisted on the same day, August 30, 2010.

Timbercorp, like Great Southern, was established in 1987.[37] Its principal activities were '[t]o acquire, develop and manage agricultural investment properties for lease to Timbercorp Limited.'[38] It was also 'established to . . . [include] associated infrastructure and permanent water rights, for use in agribusiness projects.'[39] In 2009, Timbercorp held '120,000 megalitres in water assets' and managed around 120,000 hectares of horticulture and forestry assets that included eucalypts, almond and citrus orchards, olives and other fruit, such as table grapes, glasshouse tomatoes, avocadoes and mangoes.[40]

On Friday, April 24, 2009 LaFrenz (AFR) reported that 'Timbercorp . . . suspended its forestry and horticulture operations . . . leaving its 18,500 investors in the managed investment schemes (MIS) it runs in the dark as to their position as creditors.'[41] In its 2009 online "Business Summary" for the Timbercorp Primary Infrastructure Fund, DatAnalysis listed the responsible entity as 'Orchid Investments Management Limited.'

Major issues around the collapse of Great Southern and Timbercorp included the apparent "social injustice" of MIS investments. Recall the Parliamentary Committee inquiries as mentioned earlier:

> [T]hat some MIS investments resembled Ponzi schemes, where securing financial returns for existing investors relied on attracting new investors rather than on successful economic activity . . . [and] rapid expansion had been underpinned by high levels of debt, and in difficult economic circumstances in which new investment was diminishing and new borrowings were hard to obtain, that debt could not successfully be serviced.[42]

Topical issues continue in determining an entity's accumulated debt against its net asset worth. Argument with regard to the concept of book amounts versus current market equivalents of assets remains a newsworthy topic. The case of the Allco Finance Group is a particular example, but first circumstances of the Fincorp Group elaborate an area of growing anxiety for many stakeholders—liabilities in excess of assets.

Fincorp Group

Twenty-one separate entities formed the Fincorp Group of companies.[43] Primarily, Fincorp was a fixed-interest investment provider, and fixed-interest investments are considered generally to be relatively safe. However, fixed-interest investment returns are not always what they may seem to be—low risk and reliable. The circumstances of Fincorp, Westpoint and Estate Mortgage serve to illustrate the riskiness associated with fixed-interest investments, at least for the unwary. The ASIC had warned investors about the incompatibility between high returns for seemingly low risk investments—put another way, the inherent 'risks of [innocently believing in] high-yielding fixed-interest investments' (Francis, 2007, p.3).[44] A major accounting issue in this case was determining the financial worth of the entity's assets.

Similarities among 'Fincorp, Westpoint and Estate Mortgage—[included, that they] relied on property assets for the success of their fund, had high fee structures and relied on aggressive marketing to get investors involved.'[45] Fincorp utilised direct advertising while Estate Mortgage and Westpoint cultivated 'high commission payments to financial planners.'[46] It was—business as usual—however, amidst all the hype, prior to and after its demise:

> Many Fincorp investors—who poured a total of $201 million into the failed property group—held unsecured notes and . . . [were likely to]

> receive nothing. The "first-ranking" note holders who invested $178 million . . . [could] expect to receive 30c for each dollar invested. . . . [and] Rubbing salt in the wounds of investors, banks and financial institutions who had $95 million of "first-ranking mortgages" over the ten properties in the Fincorp group . . . [would] likely recoup all of that money.[47]

No social justice there! In later years, the circumstances for some investors improved slightly as they recouped half their investment.[48] Nonetheless, Fincorp was to some a twofold financial disaster that diminished the wealth of unsuspecting investors and drained the financial circumstances of many others in the wider community. On March 23, 2007, Fincorp was placed in receivership.[49] At that time, reportedly, it owed $200 million to a suite of investors and a further $95 million to a number of financial institutions, including banks.[50] The group's debt levels were apparently exorbitant against its reported assets, yet previously:

> The Australian Securities and Investments Commission [ASIC] insisted an independent expert scrutinise Fincorp's loans when it made its final attempt to raise tens of millions of dollars from unsuspecting individuals a year before its collapse. But the examination concluded that all of the $200 million in loans made from the main Fincorp company to its property development and investment subsidiaries could be recovered in full.

Now, how could that be so? Especially if the Fincorp debt levels were diagnosed in excess of its assets, in which case Fincorp would be technically insolvent using the balance sheet test of insolvency (see Chapter 2). It remained, however, that:

> [A] team of investigating accountants . . . appointed by Sandhurst Trustees, whose job it was to oversee Fincorp's investments on behalf of investors . . . [and ASIC Chairman D'Aloisio had] insisted on the report before allowing the last fund-raising exercise to proceed . . . [and when] The report . . . came back, it gave Fincorp a clean bill of health.
>
> [Hence] 'This report confirmed "no impairment" which, in effect, meant that the loans were (in the independent expert's opinion) recoverable by Fincorp in full,' Mr D'Aloisio [reportedly] said in a nine-page statement to the committee. Indeed, the Fincorp audited accounts filed on October 9, 2006 for the year ending June 30, 2006 were not qualified in relation to "no impairment."[51]

Primarily that report was to gauge the likelihood of full recovery of the loans made by Fincorp to its subsidiaries. This was important because ASIC (based on the outcome of the report) permitted Fincorp 'to raise a further $72 million between June [2006] and February [2007] . . . its fourth such fund raising since 2002.' Recall the receivers moved into Fincorp in March

2007, when the ill-fated company owed around $300 million. Apparently, it was a travesty of errors!

In May 2007, ASIC released a "Statement on Fincorp" 'to provide an update to the Senate Standing Committee on Economics of ASIC's involvement with the Fincorp group of companies' (ASIC, 2007, p.2). The statement of some nine pages was necessary partly in response to the public outcry of: Where was ASIC? As Khan (2007) reported:

> Federal senator and Opposition superannuation spokesman Nick Sherry has accused the Australian Securities and Investments Commission of a soft-touch approach, saying the regulator should be "proactive" in determining whether there were any breaches of law by Fincorp directors leading up to its collapse. [Furthermore:]
>
> "At the moment [2007] we don't even know what the problems were leading into the collapse—let alone what remedies are required to prevent it happening again. ASIC needs to provide a detailed response as to why no issues have been identified to date."[52]

So ASIC responded. The Commission identified key areas of concern as the 'current [financial] status of Fincorp' and that included amounts owing to secured and unsecured noteholders (around $200 million); the first ranked notes secured over its floating assets. The major asset of Fincorp was its loans receivables.[53] Khan (2007) also referred to problems associated with accumulated losses, increasing debt and payments to related parties. Subsequently, on July 26, 2007, the Administrators KordaMentha released a "Summary Report to Noteholders" to further explain the situation.[54] The administrators were concerned, among other things, about the possibility of a breach of directors' duties.

Eventually they were found to be correct in their concern as Thomson (2011) reported:

> Fincorp founder Eric Krecichwost was found guilty yesterday in the NSW District Court of dishonestly using his position as a director to pay himself and family members more than $3 million in fees to which he had no claim. [Reportedly] . . . Krecichwost orchestrated the payment of three cheques to himself and members of his family for "spotter's fees" for setting up property transactions. . . . The jury found Krecichwost guilty on all three charges. Each offence carries a maximum jail sentence of five years and a fine up to $220,000.[55]

In May 2011, the 'finance director of the Fincorp group, Jacob Quigley . . . [went] on trial in the NSW District Court, charged with dishonestly using his position as a director to pay himself and others $1.98 million in a sham "spotter's fee." '[56] In Australia, directors are increasingly under the microscope with regard to directors' duties, governance and adherence to legal statutes. Arguably such concerns include directors' ethical and moral responsibilities with regard to stakeholders in the businesses they direct and more broadly related to issues of social justice.

On April 8, 2011, the ASIC media release 11–78AD reported that Eric Krecicichwost was sentenced to jail (for three years and six months) with regard to the three offences to which he was initially charged. Furthermore, 'Mr Krecichwost will also be disqualified from managing a corporation in Australia, including acting as a director of a company, for five years from the date of his release from prison, pursuant to section 206B of the Corporations Act.'[57]

Similarly to Fincorp, accounting issues with regard to the Allco Group were focussed on assets and determining the financial substance of same. Sensibly, business entities require a balance between their accumulated debt and their assets to maintain a positive level of residual equity. To determine an entity's net asset worth, one might use the recorded book amounts of its assets and alternatively ascertain the monetary market equivalent of same, with the market being an *active general market* not a buying and selling frenzy of items under duress. For financial assets, an example of the latter would be the securities markets following events from the sub-prime mortgage collapse in the US. Evidently, securities markets under duress were one element of the distress of the global financial crises (GFC).

The use of book amounts as opposed to monetary market equivalents to represent assets in a financial statement, if applicable, will be applicable under different circumstances. Specifically, assets with regard to determining an entity's level of solvency relate to a monetary equivalent of same or denote access to a monetary equivalent. If there is no active market for trading such assets, they are arguably of questionable financial worth in terms of solvency.

Further, the book amount is a number derived from a variety of accounting procedures (refer to Chapter 4 and sources therein) whereas the monetary market equivalent has regard for the purchasing power of money and its changing financial worth as time passes. Thus, the latter relates to the exchangeability of an entity's assets for another asset. For example, operating assets such as plant, machinery, stock on hand, land, cars or office furniture if exchangeable for cash—in current monetary terms in an active general trading market—would help indicate an entity's financial ability to pay its debts when due and payable.

Nonetheless, the basic concept of the exchangeability of assets with regard to ascertaining an entity's state of solvency remains, whether the assets are financial assets or other operating assets. Following, the case of the Allco Group further highlights the essentiality of being able to manage and maintain a balance between an entity's accumulated debt and its current asset worth.

Allco Finance Group Limited

The Allco Group was founded in 1979 'to originate and arrange structured financial transactions for aircraft, ships and rolling stock. Over the years

. . . [it grew] to provide funding for other services, including infrastructure and commercial finance.'[58] Allco merged with Record Investments, originally established in 2001 as Allco's listed investment vehicle and after the merger became the Allco Finance Group. By 2006, the Group listed on the ASX.[59] At that time, the merged entity was reportedly valued at A$3 billion.[60] Five years later it was under external administration (ASIC, 2011) with its 'next review date [noted as] March 11, 2012.'[61]

Briefly, on November 4, 2008, approximately two years after the group listed on the ASX, receivers were appointed to the merged Allco Finance Group.[62] 'The banks were forced to appoint their own receivers, Ferrier Hodgson, once the Allco directors took the decision to appoint voluntary administrators in McGrathNicol.'[63] By May 2009, stakeholders were advised the Group would be 'placed in liquidation with debts of more than $1 billion, opening the way for potential legal action against former directors of the collapsed investment firm.'[64] Fifty of the fifty-two business entities of the Allco Group were to be liquidated and McGrathNicol would be the liquidators. The remaining 'two Allco entities related to the aviation leasing business . . . [would be] put in a deed of company arrangement at the request of bank creditors ahead of an attempt to sell the assets.'[65]

Drawing on the Lending Central Team's (2009) review (2009), the following points elaborate:

> 'Allco, . . . [owing] creditors about $1.145 billion, is one of the highest profile Australian corporate collapses in the wake of the global financial crisis, alongside Babcock & Brown and ABC Learning Centres.'
>
> 'Allco's banks are looking to recover about $640 million in secured loans.'
>
> 'The remaining creditors, including former employees of Allco, are seeking the repayment of $505 million of unsecured and subordinated loans.'
>
> 'In its investigations, the liquidator will be paying particular attention to $400 million of director-related transactions, particularly Allco's $327 million acquisition of Rubicon Holdings Ltd in December 2007.'
>
> 'Mr Hayes and Mr McGrath will also examine the secured lender status of the bank creditors . . . [because] The banks achieved secured lender status, giving them priority over other creditors, as a result of deals done in the six months before the administrators took over.'

Furthermore:

> 'Former employees of Allco are also in court against the receivers, which brought an action in the Federal Court to establish which entity employed the workers.'

> 'The receivers argue[d] the employees were contracted to a subsidiary of Allco known as AFG Pty Ltd, and so have no claim on certain assets.'
>
> 'The employees argue that while there may have been a line in their contracts saying that AFG was the employing entity, it had no bank account and no assets, and so they were employees of Allco.'[66]

Due to such conflict, Ferrier Hodgson sought a declaration from the Federal Court 'regarding the entity of which the employees are priority creditors.'[67] On November 2, 2010, Ferrier Hodgson provided a letter to the employees of the Allco Group to advise them that they (Ferrier Hodgson) were reviewing the Court judgement, issued on October 28, 2010, on evidence related to the Group's employment structures. Employees were to be contacted shortly thereafter to advise them further on the matter. Intricacies of this story are yet to unfold.

Meanwhile, back to availability of money:- In the case of Allco, *the apparent lack of money and access to money* were increasingly of concern. Specifically, there was a difference between the book values of assets and their likely market value—for example, with regard to certain investments, there was a gap of some $300 million. That is, the book value was inflated, and that portrayed an inappropriate financial position to stakeholders. Johnson (February, 2008) explained:

> At 31 December [2007], the accountants estimated Allco's book value at $2.4bn, or $6.52 per share . . . but [there were] . . . dubious components of that book value. The ones we know about include: $1.3bn of goodwill relating to the Record merger, which is probably worth zero; "management rights" valued at $176m that are probably worth zero; an $89m loan to one of its mortgage subsidiaries . . . and $605m worth of listed investments with a current market value [at that time] of $235m.[68]

None of these were apparently obvious to all stakeholders. Hence, Allco's accumulated debts, its reported assets financial worth and its perceived inability (at least by some) to pay its ongoing debt obligations were of concern. Allco suffered from a lack of a fundamental need in business to have, and to have access to, actual money. Those circumstances exacerbated Allco's reported '[c]onflicts of interest caused by myriad related party transactions and complicated internal systems . . . [and the entity's complex structure] Allco is believed to have had 700 subsidiaries, with individual ownership, crossover management and the web of relations [inevitably] causing tensions and conflicts.'[69] Recall a web of intrigue and similar circumstances related to much earlier cases as discussed in Chapter 4.

'Essentially, Allco borrowed too much to fund its expansion, which included assets like trains, planes and property' (Lannin, 2010, p.2).[70]

Furthermore, as Singleton (2009) reported, "The directors didn't [even] have the funding available to continue paying the ongoing costs of compliance [with ASX requirements]."[71] So, how many stakeholders were at that time "in the dark" about the financial debacle unfolding and about to unfold? According to Boyd (2008):

> The writing has been on the wall for Allco since March when the share price collapsed from $3 to below $1 and then later to a trading range of between 10 cents and 20 cents.
>
> Actually, the writing was on the wall long before March this year [2008]. Legendary financial commentator Trevor Sykes under his better known pseudonym Pierpont raked over various conflicts of interest and uncertain mathematics that underpinned the Allco Max business model, a clone of Allco, in August 2005. He gave a clear warning signal to steer clear.[72]

Yet Boyd's comments (as above) pre-suppose many stakeholders would take note of what Pierpont proffered—some would probably, some may not even read his articles. Argument suggests many stakeholders might rely on their own assessment of the situation in conjunction with media reports, directors' statements, auditors' opinions, financial analysts' assertions and other publicly available information. Furthermore, stakeholders are a diverse group with diverse talents and diverse interests, and some are more equipped than others to make economic decisions.

For all stakeholders, however, the crunch came when Allco collapsed—unpredictably to some but to the chagrin of many. During its climb, Allco reportedly reached 'a market value of $5 billion at its peak.'[73] It was, however, delisted from the ASX on September 1, 2009.

Boyd (2008) asserted the losses hit four "broad" categories: 'Firstly . . . the shareholders and subordinated note holders . . . the Allco founders and management . . . the financiers . . . [and] finally . . . the directors.'[74] Arguably, all of them should have been well-informed of the pending disaster but possibly were not. And considering the extensive array of corporate collapses across time, the public may well ask, Why not? Let's not focus solely on the obvious—shareholder stakeholders. Arguably there is an extensive range of stakeholders, all important, that includes the entity's employees, its creditors, the consumers, the economic community generally—local, national, international—and other businesses, as well as public interest groups, regulators and more.

Conventional financial statements available in the public domain are not likely to inform all stakeholders about the financial worth of listed corporations. This deficiency may be attributed in part to the conventional focus on general-purpose statements. With regard to certain elements of business, for instance, solvency, stakeholders might rightly demand specific financial details to support the declarations of those who direct and govern.

CONCLUDING REMARKS

Notably, the majority of stakeholders in listed corporations have access to financial details that are publicly available only. So the quality of those financial details published to inform interested parties of the business' financial circumstances are constantly of concern. In addition to the suite of financial statements included in companies' annual reports is the Directors' declaration of solvency—at least in some jurisdictions. It is this declaration that has the potential to add further credence to the audited financial statements. At present this is not the case necessarily. This is mainly because corporations have collapsed, surprisingly to many, after they have published unqualified audited financial statements and published directors' declarations of solvency.

Previous chapters have argued the necessity for clear definition of elements used and precision of financial details included in determining an entity's solvency. Solvency is, and has been, a critical commercial financial attribute for aeons. Financial accounting could, but currently does not, provide a major input in assessment of an entity's solvency mainly because its quantification has not been considered in continuum. Moreover, in financial accounting, there is no apparent progress on how to quantify solvency. This is particularly evident as there is no appreciable change to the financial accounting definition of an asset, and the definition of an asset is crucial in determining its use in quantifying an entity's solvency.

Chapter 8 evaluates the role of financial accounting in business and in quantifying solvency. It elaborates the integral role of market-based accounting data, quality financial information and directors' governance responsibilities to report on the authenticated financial state of the business they direct.

8 The Quantification of Solvency

> 'In matters of consequence to ourselves that entail dealing or interaction with others, we must . . . be constantly on guard against confusing facts with figments or fictions' (Chambers, 2000, p.327).

Drawing on previous analyses, this chapter evaluates the role of accounting in business in how financial accounting might contribute serviceable details to inform business on an entity's state of solvency. Further, it evaluates quality financial information in the context of business continuity and elaborates major financial accounting issues that link between many cases across time. Thus, it demonstrates the quantification of solvency.

SOLVENCY AND THE ROLE OF ACCOUNTING

This study focused on the concept of solvency and the necessity to quantify solvency in business. Given directors' increasing responsibilities within the Australian *Corporation's Act 2001* (Act) and in similar legislation across other Western countries, it is incontestable that dated financial facts pertaining to a business entity's operating activities be periodically made available to directors and arguably to other stakeholders.[1]

Yet as shown here, business entities continue to publish financial details that portray corporate entities as profitable and financially sound shortly before they collapse unexpectedly.[2] The repercussions for society resound.

Consider previous discussion and the enforcement results announced by ASIC (2002) that nineteen individuals were convicted of corporate crimes and jailed for a total of 74 years.[3] Further, twenty directors were fined or banned from holding directorates and thirty-five were completely banned from financial services. ASIC at that time reported a 15% increase in corporate investigations, including "successful" court proceedings against 'HIH, Harris Scarfe, the British Marine Bank scam, Yandal' to name a few.[4] Table 8.1 outlines the ASIC enforcement results for subsequent years to 2010.

Interestingly, in 2010, the 'ASIC banned 70 [of the 90] directors from managing companies for insolvency-related offences, which was an increase of 43% over 2008–09' (ASIC, annual report, p.17, under *Phoenix trading*). The quality of publicly available information on corporate activity and its financial results continue to be under scrutiny by our regulators. If only that were to be so systematically!

For in spite of the attention apparent, accounting processes, its output and its outcomes have been shown to be lacking. Nonetheless, during the twentieth

Table 8.1 ASIC Enforcement Results: 2003–2010

	2003	*2004*	*2005*	*2006*	*2007*	*2008*	*2009*	*2010*
Convictions	43	67	49	27	42	49	34	22
Jailed	29	28	27	17	21	23	19	12
Recoveries ($)	121m	101m	119m	144m	102m	>50m	>14.5m	>287m
Directors fined/banned	16	22	33	44	110*	Unclear**	49	90

* '81 bannings involved directors in failed and assetless companies, the balance of 29 disqualified for breaches of the law' (ASIC, annual report, p.16 under Key Results—Enforcing the law).

** In consultation with the CDPP, we commenced criminal proceedings against 13 company directors and officers for a range of offences including dishonesty, making false representations, fraud and managing companies while disqualified. We obtained court orders banning 7 directors for periods of 3–16 years, and banned another 7 directors through administrative proceedings. We also obtained the extradition of four defendants to face charges in relation to their conduct as company directors and officers' (Under *Corporations and Insolvency*, ASIC Annual Report, 2007–08, p.17).

Source. Details from enforcement section of the ASIC Annual Reports from 2003 to 2010 inclusive.

century at least—from the 1960s through the 1970s—the regulators, more to the point, society tended to blame "bad management" for the financial and social misery that inevitably followed unexpected business failures. The 1980s focussed more on the entrepreneurial flair of management—those "corporate cowboys"[5] and their lavish spending, media charm and high profile antics that (at that time) made good press, sold newspapers and seemingly encouraged ever-increasing public investments. But, the spate of unexpected corporate collapses continued into the 1990s and beyond, exacerbating ethical dilemmas for, and between, internal and external stakeholders. Moving into the twenty-first century, local and world communities firmly embraced yet another rhetoric to apply to these unexpected financial disasters—the lack of corporate governance and, supposedly, as though the concept of governance in business was new.[6] Poignantly ASIC's Annual Report (2002) was titled "Ethics and Governance."

What society has failed to do, however, is concentrate on the understated role of the output of accounting systems—the *quality* of the content of financial reports—especially with regard to the effect thereof on the fortunes or misfortunes of business and its stakeholders. Those reports provide an inbuilt "check"—an "independent" accountability mechanism. In that context, regulators and society alike have somewhat shunned the notion that therein exists systemic problems in reporting on the financial state of business entities internationally.

This book concentrated on one problem, inherent, of conventional financial accounting—its inattention to quantify an entity's state of solvency. And it examined the lack of definition of solvency in conventional financial accounting with special regard to determining that financial state of an entity. Throughout, the underlying theme of this study remained how best to determine *quality* financial information for business and its stakeholders—namely, that the reported financial data are serviceable and, hence, fit for the uses normally made of them.

Chapter 4, in particular, demonstrated that conventional financial statements lacked substance in ascertaining an entity's dated financial capacity to pay its debts when due and payable and still be able to continue to conduct its business activities. Then, using case analyses, Chapters 5 through 7 further examined the book's main premise—that conventional financial statements are deficient in quantifying an entity's solvency and equally lacking in establishing its dated financial state. And that is an integral aspect of financial accounting. It is argued that facilitating the mandates of corporations' law and to enable the professional status of accounting[7] to continue into the future requires up-to-date financial information to be readily available for all stakeholders in business.

In this context, five case studies of major Australian business demise (prior to 2004) were examined in Chapters 5 and 6. In addition, data available on insolvencies post 2004 to 2011 were elaborated in Chapter 7 and a further three cases analysed therein. With specific links highlighted between the cases, this diagnostic part confirmed earlier findings—that financial data prepared under GAAP, using a plethora of accounting conventions, are grossly inadequate in providing stakeholders with quality financial information on an entity's dated financial state.

The analysis detailed a number of factors yet to be addressed by financial accounting to better enable the quantification of solvency. In sum, and building on the work of previous scholars, mainly Chambers (1966, 1973a, 1973b), Briloff (1972, 1976, 1981), Sterling (1979), Wolnizer (1987) and Clarke, Dean and Oliver (1997, 2003), this story highlighted deficiencies in accounting methods that, although not new, continue (repeatedly) to thwart financial accounting practice in the matter of quantifying solvency; hence reporting clearly on an entity's financial state to its stakeholders. *The emphasis on solvency and its explicit link with the statement of financial position was a major extension of this study to those earlier works.*

And, why is this so?

After all, the dynamics of business and its environment can be observed. The operating results of transacting business in a market-based economy can be observed. The financial results of conducting ever-changing business operations in a dynamic market environment can be factually documented and reported in the context of up-to-date financial details. Further, such is the case for all substantive markets regardless of the commodities produced and/or exchanged. Yet, up-to-date financial details are frequently not contained in conventional financial statements of an entity's worth.

And, why is this so? Is it due perhaps to a complacent attitude and/or habitual behaviour? That is, a continued focus in accounting on compliance with rules? As West (2003, p.175) asserted:

Forced into an almost exclusive reliance on formally stated rules to justify particular accounting procedures, accounting practitioners are left without significant authority in connection with matters not subject to an accounting standard. To rely upon regulatory fiat to justify particular technical practices is to concede a lack of authority regarding matters that cannot be similarly substantiated. Practitioner response to this dilemma appears to involve simply forsaking concern with matters not expressly covered by accounting standards.

QUALITY INFORMATION IN DETERMINING SOLVENCY

The problem addressed herein, crucial for business and its stakeholders, is particularly significant from a public policy perspective given the many unanticipated corporate collapses of the twentieth and now into the twenty-first century. The difficulty of precise communication in conventional accounting was dealt with as the study explored terminological deficiencies—the sloppy use of words—especially those relating to the process of accounting for an entity's financial position and determining its solvent state *á propos* the elements of financial accounting reports.

Both legal and accounting notions of solvency were appraised.[8] The legal view of solvency mandates that an entity be able to pay all its debts when due and payable.[9] Accounting makes no such demands. In accounting, the AASB Framework[10] (para.16) provides guidance as: 'Liquidity refers to the availability of cash in the near future after taking account of financial commitments over this period. Solvency refers to the availability of cash over the longer term to meet financial commitments as they fall due.' But the definitions of relevant components to quantifying solvency remain, by and large, intangible. In this way accounting emphasis rests with defining the elements of general-purpose financial statements.

On solvency, national and international courts have relied historically on one (at times, both) of two tests of insolvency, viz the "Balance Sheet" test and the "Cash Flow" test.[11] Both tests are based on the content of conventional financial accounting reports. Notably the balance sheet is sometimes referred to as a statement of financial position. Arguably it is not a statement of financial position. By definition the AASB SAC 2 provides: ' "financial position" means the economic condition of a reporting entity, having regard to its control over resources, financial structure, capacity for adaptation and solvency' (para.5). The balance sheet does not provide such details. The balance sheet is a statement of ledger balances compiled at a certain point in time—after the profit and loss statement, also referred to as a statement of performance or income statement or such like,[12] has been compiled.

This study demonstrated that such tests, *vis-a-vis* conventional financial statements, are deficient in terms of establishing the financial position of an entity and equally lacking with regard to quantifying its state of solvency.[13] Financial reports based on GAAP were shown to be of limited use in establishing a business's financial capacity to pay its accumulated debts when due and payable—hence, defective in terms of quality.

Here, *quality* information—especially that relating to current market-based financial referents—is proffered as a fundamental criterion for the quantification of solvency and equally essential to determine an entity's financial position. Accumulated evidence[14] shows that such financial details are not *readily available* in published financial reports.

The following synthesizes the material of earlier chapters, detailing specific elements relating to financial accounting and its output that are commonly used in reporting the financial state of corporate entities. It is demonstrated that these variables consistently appear in the published dated financials of business entities (audited financial reports) prior to the unexpected demise of central business operations or the entity's unexpected complete corporate collapse.

THE OBSERVATIONAL ORDER

Using multiple methods of analysis based on observation of published data, this study endorsed the view that to ascertain the dated financial state of a business demands dated financial facts. Additionally, stating factually an entity's financial worth necessitates relating the rudiments of the financial statement to their actual monetary equivalents in an active general market—in other words, observable, changeable and tangible realities.

Gaffikin (2000, p.287) stated, '[c]onstant allusions to "facts" and conforming to "reality" indicate a realist ontology.' But, whether "reality" is derived from what is or from an assumption of *what should be* both concepts ultimately follow an observational order of the state of the world—albeit from a different premise of that world. If accounting is a practical affair relating to business activities,[15] then accounting procedures should surely be expected to produce output directly relatable to the observable, factual financial results of those activities. Or, put another way, financial output from contemporary accounting systems could be expected to produce dated financial results of doing business in a constantly changing environment. Conventional accounting practice, however, is based on a static, unchanging view of enterprise. Yet, in a constantly changing market-driven economy, an adaptive (flexible) approach to recording and reporting the events of business would seem to be more logical—more correct!

It follows that components of conventional financial statements without *bona fide* monetary equivalents in available markets cannot assist in determining the dated financial state of a business and should not be included in quantifying solvency. Figure 8.1 details such elements, variables from published data of case studies in Chapters 5 and 6.

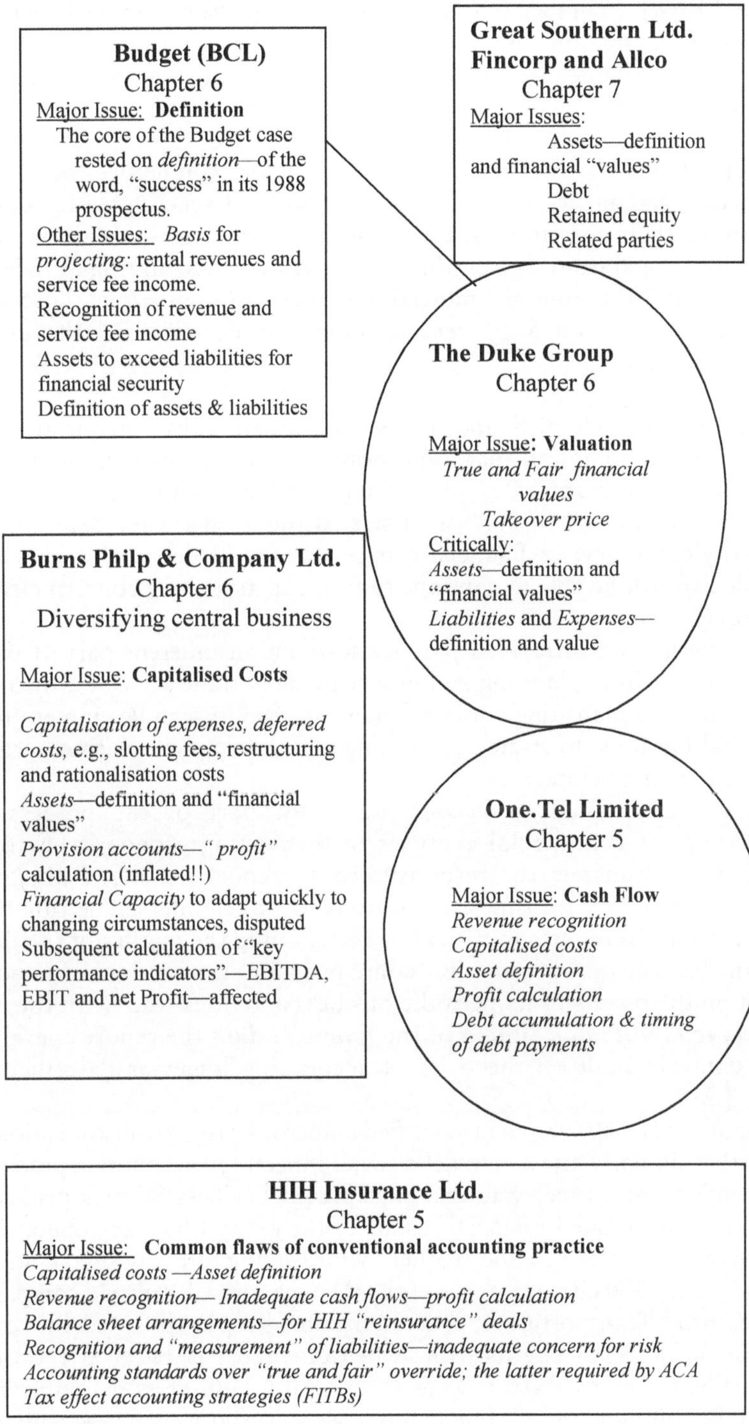

Figure 8.1 The ignominy of GAAP in corporate collapse—some examples.

Figure 8.1 lists a number of financial accounting issues, similarly evident between the cases, and likewise easily linked to previous case studies of failed business ventures across time (see also Table 8.2). In effect, such associations perpetuate:

> [T]he truth . . . that the present contents of companies' published income statements and balance sheets are not serviceable for determining their current financial positions or for discovering how they arose . . . [is] ironic, given that the Australian Accounting Standards now label the annual financial statements *Statement of Financial Performance* and *Statement of Financial Position* (Clarke *et al.* (2003, p.299).

The current mode of financial reporting on an entity's financial state, based on the *assumption* that a business is a "going-concern," in a business world that is *static*—devoid of change, and one that promotes (among other things) *capitalised costs* as assets, without regard for determining the entity's solvency; its financial capacity to pay its debts when due and payable *and* still be able to continue to function as a going concern clearly requires change.

Accounting is a diversified practice forming an inherent part of business systems—from planning and observing daily trade activities, through supervising and managing various production facilities and/or larger areas of central business, to strategic planning and development with regard to the entire conglomerate.

Additionally, financial accounting forms part of the process of accounting for commercial ventures in a changing economic environment, with ultimately the responsibility to report the dated financial results of the entity's business operations to stakeholders. The function of such financial reports is critical in determining the quality of the data therein. Hence, the information content of an entity's dated financial report on the results of its periodic business activities rests with the *relevance, reliability and timing* of the *financial data* the report contains. That data are built on the basis of accounting issues as described in Table 8.2.

Chambers (1973/1986) had identified numerous cases to those mentioned above that similarly attested to deficiencies inherent in accounting practice. The result (across time) was that unexpected business failures occurred as the published dated financial results of the entity's business operations were shown to be flawed and frequently misleading to many stakeholders. Consider the 1970 circumstances of the then massive US railroad company, Penn Central Transportation, ordered into bankruptcy by a federal court because it could not pay its debts when due and payable.[16] At the time reportedly, the entity's assets were around $4.6 billion, its debt approximately $22 million, yet its liquid funds were in short supply—*seemingly very short supply.*

Table 8.2 Accounting Issues Cross-Linked between Some Cases of Corporate Collapse: 1960s–2000s

Issues	*2000s*	*1980s, 1990s*	*1960s, 1970s*
Capitalising Costs—general problems for *all* entities that use HCA methods	Enron, HIH, Harris Scarfe, WorldCom, One.Tel	Westmex, Bond Corp., Adsteam, Compass	ASL, Cambridge Credit, Minsec
Provisions: e.g., Rationalisation and Restructuring; Goodwill; trade-names; D. Debts; Depreciation; FITB	HIH, Waste Mgt, One.Tel, Enron	Westmex, Burns Philp	HG Palmer, Cambridge Credit, Reid Murray
Asset Values	HIH, Enron, One.Tel, Harris Scarfe, WorldCom	Duke Group, Adsteam, Compass, Westmex	Minsec, Latec Investments, Reid Murray, HG Palmer, ASL, AlliedCrude
Asset Write-Offs/ Write-Downs	One.Tel, Ansett, NAB, News Corp	Bond Corp, Compass, Westpac, ANZ	Minsec, New Investments, Reid Murray
Revenue/Income Recognition "earned/unearned"	Enron, HIH, Xerox, One.Tel	BCL, Adsteam	Cambridge Credit, ASL, Latec Invments, Reid Murray
Profit Calculation	HIH, Harris Scarfe, Enron, One.Tel	Adsteam, Inter West, Rothwells, Ariadne, Bond Corp	Minsec, Reid Murray, Cambridge Credit, Gollins Holdings, HG Palmer
Cash Flow	HIH, Enron, One.Tel	Adsteam, Bond Corp, Burns Philp	Minsec, HG Palmer, ASL
Debt Recognition/ Gearing Bad Debts	HIH, Enron, One.Tel, HarrisScarfe	Adsteam, Bond Corp, Qintex	Mainline Corp., Cambridge Credit, Reid Murray, HG Palmer, ASL, Atlantic Acc. Corp.
Related-Party Transactions	HIH, One.Tel, Enron, WorldCom	Lintner, Westmex, Adsteam, Bond Corp Maxwell Com.	Minsec, Cambridge Credit, Stanhill Dev., Reid Murray
Valuation	One.Tel, HIH, Enron	Duke Group, Westmex, BCL, Burns Philp	Cambridge Credit, ASL, Allied Crude, Stanhill Dev.
Consolidated Data/ Practices	Enron, HIH, One.Tel, World Com, Ansett	Westmex, Bond Corp., Adsteam, Duke Group	Minsec, Cambridge Credit, Stanhill Dev., Reid Murray

Source. Details from Chambers (1973/1986) and Clarke *et al.* (2003) in addition to the investigations of this work.

Earlier the Australian finance conglomerate, Latec Investments, failed to recognise its bad debt problem. For around seven years, it apparently under-provided for bad and doubtful debts and miscalculated its reported profit figures. In 1961, Australia's Latec wrote-off 1.9 million pounds of bad debts—its reported net profits for the previous seven years were around half that amount.[17] Beforehand, Liberator Permanent Benefit Building Society capriciously designed its dated financial position for many years by (among other things) crediting, in advance, interest payable to it by its debtors and 'arbitrarily writing up the values of assets . . . [until] Twenty years of dissipation of the company's assets ended in failure in 1892' (Chambers, 1986, p.182). All of this is permitted by prevailing professional accounting standards and companies' legislation.

Alternatively and as earlier discussed, an entity's periodic accounting reports have sometimes resulted in damages claims being lodged against its directors, auditors and other corporate officials. Historically—in the early 1960s, for instance—auditors, directors and other officers of the trucking company, Yale Express System, were held responsible for reporting misleading income earned/unearned figures over three sets of financial statements. The reporting methods were correct, permitted within conventional accounting practice guidelines, but to stakeholders they caused worry, and those stakeholders implemented court action claiming damages against the officers of the company for material omissions in the financial statements—the major problem lay apparently in its method of calculating periodic profit.[18] A similar circumstance in accounting practice has nonetheless generally prevailed. We still have an essentially capitalisation-of-expenses based model, augmented by fair values, market prices on occasions (Clarke *et al.*, 2003). And now in the 2000s, there are the catastrophic unexpected financial flops of Enron, Worldcom, HIH, One.Tel, Water Wheel and others to keep interested observers occupied.

For aeons, financial tragedy—for many—from repeated and *unexpected* corporate collapse and/or unexpected central business failure has tampered with the world's societal business framework. And it has done so in the midst of increased regulatory controls that—surprisingly to some—continue to rely essentially on conventional accounting practices. Ultimately, under the auspices of habitually using GAAP, the reputation, nationally and internationally, of professional accounting bodies and its members has suffered. West (2003, p.189) admonished, 'Professionalism in accounting, it seems, has moved to an uncertain and disputatious stage. Standards of performance have been deemed unsatisfactory and only an equivocal acceptance of responsibility for those standards demonstrated.' Further, with some verve, Clarke *et al.* (2003, p.328) asserted:

> Accountants would do much better for themselves were they to adopt the current vogue and have mission statements and the like prescribed by their professional bodies with the view towards producing serviceable data in financial statements. As it is, they have "mission impossible" forced upon them.

In quantifying solvency and determining insolvent trading, such is of concern to directors and others. Directors must be confident to declare that the entity they direct is solvent (s.295(4)(c)); further, it is illegal to trade when insolvent (refer to previous case discussion—for instance, Water Wheel). Executive and non-executive directors, chief executive officers and other corporate officials presently work under the ever-increasing weight of ostensibly endless professional and legal rules and regulations. This continued move towards a more strictly controlled corporate environment has arguably diminished the opportunity for the world's business communities to access specificity of dated financial information on conglomerates. To quantify an entity's level of solvency requires precise and current financial details—true *to the issue of solvency.*

The meaning of truth has been bandied around the business community and courts of law for decades,[19] as though its meaning is too old-fashioned to recognise. Yet, the true and fair override remains in corporations' legislation, as arguably it should. The truth (perhaps except for post-modernists) has regard for what is commercially useful and the common concept of what is true has regard for what is factual.

> [I]n the verification of facts, we need the help of others . . . we must be able to rely on other people . . . to trust their word . . . [thus] there is a principle which binds society together, because without it the individual would be helpless to tell the true from the false. This principle is truthfulness (Bronowski, 1959/1965, p.57).

Chambers (1986, pp.21–26), focusing on accounting and its output, illustrated the concept of truth—relating it to the 'function of accounts'—with examples from the eighteenth century through to the twentieth century. He demonstrated that from the earliest time, the general style of accounts were expected to reflect financial details based on the notion of *exactness* and *truth.* The concept of what is true and fair remains part of corporations' legislation (Act, s.297). And its prominence was reinforced in the CLERP 9 bill[20] *and in the US's (2002) Sarbanes–Oxley Act.*[21] Further, Tables 8.3 and 8.4 exemplify that accounting processes and the notion of *truth* in accounting practice have been linked for ages. Truth is shown as a general principle, at least one of the principles 'held as the reasons for, or as guides to, the keeping of accounts' (Chambers, 1986, p.21).

Table 8.3 True and Fair: From the Eighteenth Century to the Twentieth Century

YEAR	EXAMPLE (*emphasis as referenced*)	REFERENCES *also in Chambers (1986, 1995)*
1777	'[W]e can . . . at any time . . . know the exact state of our affairs'	Wardhaugh Thompson *The Accomptant's Oracle*
1788	'It is much more proper to value the goods on hand in conformity to current prices, than at prime cost'	Robert Hamilton *An Introduction to Merchandise*
1800	'The end aimed at in book-keeping is to represent distinctly the *true state of one's affairs*;'	John Mair *Book-Keeping Moderniz'd*
1801	'A merchant's books should exhibit the *true state of his affairs*'	P. Kelly *The Elements of Book-Keeping*
1887	'It was the duty of the auditor . . . to see that it was a *true and accurate* representation of the company's affairs'	J. Stirling *Leeds Estate Building and Investment Society Ltd.* v. *Shepherd* [1887] 36 Ch.D.787
1889	'The balance sheet . . . if properly drawn . . . shows the *exact financial position* of the company'	F. W. Pixley *Auditors: Their Duties and Responsibilities*
1894	'*[T]he accounts must show the truth* and not be misleading or fraudulent'	L. J. Lindley *Verner v General and Commercial Investment Trust Ltd.* [1894] 2 Ch. 239.
1915	'Accounting is . . . sublimated common sense applied to finding and *telling the truth* about business . . . and truth telling consists of using language which will make the listener know the *facts*'	W. M. Cole (professor, Harvard) *Accounts, Their Construction and Interpretation*

Source. Details from Chambers (1973/1986, 1995).

Table 8.4 True and Fair: From the Twentieth Century to the Twenty-First Century

1926	'An auditor [is] also responsible for ascertaining the true position of the business, whether disclosed properly by the books or not'	J. Astbury *Trustees of the Property of Apfel (a bankrupt) v. Annan, Dexter & Co.* 70
1931	'Technical rules of accountancy . . . are the letter and not the spirit. It is no good observing merely the letter; the fundamental object of the profession is to ensure . . . a true and accurate account of the affairs of the company is given'	The Attorney General, closing speech for the Prosecution, *Rex v. Lord Kylsant and another*
1941	'No part of the function of accounting can be useful unless it is truthful'	E. B. Wilcox and R H. Hassler (practitioners, Illinois) *A Foundation for Accounting Principles*
1953	'Accounting language must be consistent with the facts and realities of commercial life'	H. G. Avery *The Accounting Review*, January
1967	'If true and fair were to be judged purely on its dictionary meaning there would be one unique balance sheet only at any one time, and there would be no room for misunderstanding and misinterpretation'	J. Horrocks *The Australian Accountant,* October
1970	'The investment community is being made expensively aware that "true and fair" means no more than "that's one way of looking at it" '	C. Marley *Journal of Business Finance,* Winter
1983	'Accounts will not be true and fair unless the information they contain is sufficient in quantity and quality to satisfy the reasonable expectations of the readers to whom they are addressed'	L. Hoffmann & M. H. Arden *Accountancy* (UK), November

(continued)

Table 8.4 (continued)

1994	'The process of negotiating the truth in financial statements is a disturbing element of auditing and financial reporting'	Michael Wright "Accounting, Truth and Communication: The Case of a Bank Failure" *Critical Perspectives on Accounting*
2003	'Under s.297 of the Corporations Act, annual financial statements and notes must give a true and fair view of the financial position and performance of an entity . . . If the financial statements and notes prepared in accordance with accounting standards would not give a true and fair view, additional information must be included in the notes to the financial statements under s.295(3) (c) of the Act'	Justice Neville Owen *HIH Royal Commissioners' Report* s.7 Financial reporting and assurance (at s.7.1.2)

Source. Details from Chambers (1973/1986, 1995) and Clarke et al. (2003), in addition to the investigations of this work.

Findings and Conclusion

Fundamentally, on quantifying solvency, this study supports the theory of accounting espoused by Chambers (1966) and later sustained by Sterling (1979) and others, like Wolnizer (1987), Clarke *et al.* (1997/2003) and Scheutze (2001), who have persistently argued for a rational market-based approach to accounting and a common-sense method of reporting the financial results of conducting business. This principle complements the demands of the *true and fair* override in corporations' law, a matter advocated throughout this work; one that promoted the incontestable nature of, and need for, *quality financial information* for stakeholders in business.

This work incorporated a case study approach to examine published output of conventional accounting practice and as such sought to add to the case study based work of Chambers (1973/1986) and Clarke *et al.* (1997/2003). This type of analysis—described by Chambers (1973b) as 'Observation—A Method of Inquiry'—provides a practical means by which to explore central business operations of specific corporate collapses, of varying size and circumstance, over time. It is the archetype empirical study.[22] The cases themselves become the control for the analyses undertaken (see Chambers,

1973b). Hence, this work investigated the likely relevance and reliability of financial information contained in a variety of published conventional financial reports.

Basically, financial reports are the output of accounting systems set up to serve the functions of business. Financial accounting, in particular, provides reports to a variety of stakeholders on the financial results of periodic business activities. This is a practical affair. It closely relates the changing situations of doing business in a dynamic market environment to the details proffered to stakeholders on dated statements of an entity's financial worth. Unfortunately, conventional financial statements portray economic markets as static, unchanging environments. Yet, they are the opposite. Regrettably, such accounting reports comprise a mix of data that relate to various time periods and that may or may not (frequently do not) have anything much to do with the date on the statement.

However, to enable accounting practice and *accounting as a profession* (see West, 2003) to proceed further into the twenty-first century, with a serviceable product for business and its stakeholders, requires a common-sense approach to reporting on the changing circumstances of doing business in a dynamic market environment. Nonetheless such a move necessitates an intellectually rigorous theory. Chambers (1966) developed such a theory for accounting,[23] one that was steeped in logic, common-sense and truth with regard to recording and reporting the dated financial results of business operations. For, 'like all the standard-setters to that time, [Chambers] was [his work still is] concerned with the usefulness of general-purpose financial statements' (Gaffikin, 2000, p.292).

Given the facts of "sudden" corporate collapse and business failures throughout the twentieth century and now into the new millennium, the *usefulness* (specifically in terms of money and money's worth) of conventional financial statements remains undeniably questionable. 'It is not difficult [however] to imagine that . . . an alert judge will question the serviceability of conventional accounting data . . . [especially] Against financial commonsense' (Clarke *et al.*, 2003, p.330). Historically, numerous cases, some mentioned in Chapters 2, 3 and 5 through 7 support this view, as do the reported findings of Justice Neville Owen on the investigations of the HIH Royal Commission (2001–2003) in Australia. The demise of Enron, WorldCom, Global Crossing and Adelphia in the US during 2002–2003 and more recently Great Southern, Timbercorp, Fincorp, Allco and others through to 2011 in Australia also add fuel to the same old fire.

By comparison, the relatively low-keyed Australian business collapse of Water Wheel (2002) with subsequent charges and conviction against its non-executive director for insolvent trading, and the Special Liquidator's inquiries into determining when One.Tel became insolvent, further support the premise—that conventional financial statements are deficient in establishing the dated financial position of an entity and equally lacking with regard to the quantification of an entity's state of solvency. The

Water Wheel case provided another instance of the legislative justification for this analysis.

The current system of accounting for the financial state of business activities in a dynamic commercial environment is lacking in its capacity to *quantify solvency* and produce *quality financial information* for all stakeholders.

Business requires and stakeholders *should demand* radical change to conventional accounting systems. This is long over-due. The ever-changing nature of a dynamic business world necessitates a recording and reporting system that produces (contemporaneously) dated financial facts of the results of national and international business transactions. As active economic markets facilitate business, markets change to suit the needs and wants of consumers. Assisting an orderly commercial environment and the continuity of trade in such a vibrant setting calls for financial accounting reports that comprise data that rightly reflect the adaptive nature of business and rigorously align elements in the report with authentic market referents pertaining to the date on, and the title of, the report. To quantify solvency necessitates this rationale.

Notes

NOTES TO CHAPTER 1

1. For example, SAC2, para.5 refers to solvency in the definition of financial position. Following, para.32 re-emphasises the definition only, hence the link between an entity's financial position and its state of solvency. The AASB Framework for the Preparation and Presentation of Financial Statements (that replaced SAC3 and SAC4), in effect since 2005, elaborates the objective of financial reports 'to provide information about the financial position, financial performance and cash flows of an entity' (para.12); and that assets, liabilities and equity are 'elements directly related to the measurement of financial position' (para.49). Yet measurement is referred to as a 'process of determining the monetary amounts at which the elements of the financial statements are to be recognised and carried in the balance sheet and income statement' (para.99). Not all elements in the balance sheet, however, have regard to a "monetary amount." Depreciation for instance is a calculated number determined by application of a formula. It is an allocated number (to decrease the recorded amount of a fixed asset) across time. Further, para.100 states: 'A number of different measurement bases are employed to different degrees and in varying combinations in financial reports'; those bases include: historical cost, current cost, realisable value and present value. The latter is determined by formula—a present discounted amount attributed to "future" net cash flows.
2. Refer to Owen (2003, s.19, p.20). In accounting many authors, historically, for instance, Fisher (1906/1965, p.82), Carter (1923/1956, p.43), Fitzgerald (1956, p.62), Mathews (1962, p.279), emphasised the importance of working capital and the necessity for an entity's assets to exceed its liabilities. Hawkins (1971, p.38), Ma *et al.* (1987, p.426) and others focussed specifically on current assets and current liabilities and the relationship apparent between liquidity and solvency. In all cases the definition of an asset was of import. More recently, Loftus and Miller (2000, p.9) stressed that liquidity refers to the entity's *'nearness to cash'* whereas solvency is 'the entity's capacity to pay its obligations as they fall due in the foreseeable future.' AASB107 (2009, para.4) proclaimed: 'A cash flow statement, when used in conjunction with the rest of the financial report, provides information that enables users to evaluate the changes in net assets of an entity, its financial structure (including its liquidity and solvency)' but does not elaborate on how to quantify solvency.
3. The balance sheet (asset) test and the cash flow (commercial) test of [in]solvency are examined extensively in Chapter 2.
4. At the time of HIH's demise, s.30(1) of the Insurance Act cautioned that not all *assets* could be included in determining an entity's minimum solvency. Since

that time prudential standards released on July 1, 2002, for instance, increased the requirements for general insurers to establish minimum solvency. Refer GPS110—*Capital Adequacy for General Insurer* and GPS210—*Liability Valuation*. Subsequently, standards updated and effective from July 1, 2008, included GPS110—*Capital Adequacy*, GPS112—*Capital Adequacy: Measurement of Capital* and GPS120—*Assets in Australia* and others.

5. For further details on the Cotesworth letters of credit, see Owen (2003, s.19.1, p.20).
6. The Australian Prudential Regulatory Authority (APRA) was created in 1998 and in 2002 released new and revised prudential standards and proposed amendments (2003) focused specifically on quantifying the financial state (financial position) of general insurance companies in Australia.
7. 'Generally accepted accounting principles are conventional—that is, they become generally accepted by agreement (*often tacit agreement*) rather than by formal derivation from a set of postulates or basic concepts' (AICPA, 1970, APBS4). See Chambers (1995, s.720, pp.670–676) for many additional references on defining GAAP.
8. The standard was initially issued by the Accounting Standards Review Board (ASRB, 1990) re-issued as AASB 1023 in 1996 with amendments to claims development disclosures. Refer *CA Financial Accounting Handbook* 2005, the Institute of Chartered Accountants in Australia.
9. Refer to AASB 139: *Financial Instruments Recognition and Measurement* from para.43—IAS 139 is the International equivalent—and AASB 1023: *General Insurance Contracts* (para.15).
10. Refer to AASB Framework (paras.99–101).
11. Refer to the *Oxford English Dictionary* for further details and definition and discussion throughout this book relating to quality financial information—for instance, in Chapter 4 (regarding solvency and financial reports).
12. As explained by Clarke *et al.* (1997/2003).
13. See note 10.
14. See also Chambers (1976), the article that responded to Demski's "Normative impossibility."
15. CAMAC (2003, s.1.1).
16. For example, refer to Corporations and Markets Advisory Committee (2003, s.1.35) under "Personal liability of directors for insolvent trading.' Also refer to the proceedings of Waterwheel (2003), further details at www.millsoakley.com.au/pdf/Waterwheel.pdf and the case: ASICvPlymin (2003) 46 ACSR 126.
17. Refer to Corporations and Markets Advisory Committee (2003, ss.1.7, 1.8, 1.12) under 'Principles for effective corporate rehabilitation.'
18. Refer to International Bar Association (1994) and Honsberger (1980).
19. Authors, for decades, have noted such deficiencies in commerce; see for example the works of Paton (1922/1962), Canning (1929), Sweeney (1936/1964), MacNeal (1939), Alexander (1950), Edwards and Bell (1961), Moonitz (1961), Sprouse and Moonitz (1962), Chambers (1966), Sterling (1979), Wolnizer (1987), Clarke *et al.* (1997/2003, and 2007) and Dean *et al.* (2008).
20. See Wolnizer (1987) for a definition and analysis of what would determine "quality" in accounting reports, which includes reference to quality assurance, quality control and quality design. Many official investigations into alleged 'accounting irregularities' have referred to the need to seek quality in accounting information in, for example, the NYSE Blue Ribbon Committee's Report (1999), O'Malley (2000) and SEC Studies (2003, 2005, 2008, 2009).
21. A point later discussed at length, predominantly in Chapter 4.

22. More recently, refer to the O'Malley (chairperson) report on the US inquiry into the effectiveness of Auditing (2000) and the US Blue Ribbon Committee report on 'Improving the Effectiveness of Corporate Audit Committees' (1999) details available at www.sec.gov and www.nyse.com.
23. Refer to the many recent press releases (some included later in this book) that illustrate government, professional and public interest currently in insolvency matters. A major motivating aspect of (for) this book is the increasing level of that interest as reported by the media, particularly by the press, and not only the financial press.
24. Three particular risk areas identified 'in the failures of Enron and other high profile companies in the United States' were capitalized and deferred expenses, recognition of revenue and recognition of controlled entities and assets (ASIC, media release 02/460, 2002, p.1, available at www.asic.gov.au).
25. Refer to ASIC media release 02/460 (December 2002) and media release 03/125 (April 2003).
26. Refer to ASIC media release 02/460 (December 2002).
27. Further details in media release 03/125 (April 2003). Also note: The concept of a financial value and its use in accounting are contestable. Herein the concept of value in the context of "fair value" is considered in terms of financial worth—a serviceable financial amount.
28. The following argument draws heavily on the ideas of Chambers.
29. For instance, Paton (1943), Schumpeter (1947), McCracken (1948), Trunbull (1958), Pfiffner and Sherwood (1960), Cyert and March (1963) and Vickers (1981). Additionally, myriad references are contained in Chambers' (1995) *Thesaurus*, particularly under 'Organizations' (s.271) and 'The firm as an adaptive concern' (s.274).
30. In the case of HIH Insurance Ltd., for instance, the treatment of capitalized costs and intangible assets in the group accounts (for example, FITB) formed part of detailed inquiry '[b]ecause of the appearance of solvency which the inclusion of those assets in the group balance sheet provided' (HIH Royal Commission, court transcript, December 3, 2001, p.10). Similar circumstances applied in other cases such as Water Wheel, One.Tel, Enron and WorldCom.
31. The case of Burns Philp is an exemplar and is discussed in Chapter 5.
32. As later shown in case analyses, it is an obligation of corporate officers to ensure they have access to certain (here considered relevant and reliable) financial information. Consider that 'the primary obligation imposed upon each of the [HIH] company's and its directors was to ensure that the accounts gave a true and fair view of the company at the snapshot in time in respect of which those accounts were prepared' (HIH Royal Commission, court transcript, December 3, 2001, p.20). The definition of the term "true and fair" is crucial in determining the outcome of such an obligation—and the need to carefully define that of which we speak—a theme perpetuated throughout this book. Refer also to Chambers and Wolnizer (1990), which elaborates on a "true and fair view' with regard to financial position.
33. Refer to past opinions such as American Institute of Accountants (1939), Stempf (1943), Potter (1951), AICPA, SAP33 (1963), Field (1969) and Solomons (1989). This is relevant today.
34. 'There is evidence that perceived poor quality financial reporting is a major factor in the continued criticism of accounting and auditing practices following *large*, more often than not, *unexpected*, corporate collapses' (Dean and Clarke, 2003, p.286).
35. Further details in Clarke *et al.* (2003, p.338, note 14).

36. See Haberler (1937/1941), for instance, 'the work which money must and does perform rises and falls with the ups and downs of the business cycle' (p.14).
37. In the case of HIH, 'specific obligation [was] imposed on the directors in respect of finding out whether the value of non-current assets [was] appropriate' and 'the law as it was prior to 1 July 1998, imposed a particular obligation on directors to add whatever information was necessary to ensure that the accounts give a true and fair view of the position of the company' (HIH Royal Commission, court transcript, December 3, 2001, pp.20, 21). Again the emphasis on the *true and fair* override in Corporations Law signals the need for a clear definition of elements contained in financial reports and the monetary equivalent so recorded.
38. Novam Orgamum (Bacon, 1620/1891). Quoted in Chambers (1995).
39. See also Keynes (1917, p.159), Flew (1953, p.5) and Hospers (1967, particularly p.2 for words and meaning and p.18 for definition). A specific point of concern with regard to accounting procedures and questionable definitions may be related to Ackoff (1953, p.59), which asserted 'one particularly harmful form of arbitrary defining arises when a test is developed to measure a poorly defined property. Then the property is defined as that which the test measures. Aside from the circularity of such a procedure, it prevents us from improving our methods of measuring the property.'
40. In 2001, Walter Scheutze (former chief accountant, SEC, US) presented the R. J. Chambers Research Lecture at the University of Sydney (November 27). The lecture contained precise and practical illustration and reference to what likely denotes quality financial information for the purpose of managing and reporting a business entity's operations. Scheutze advocated change and change of a specific nature in order to achieve high quality financial statements. He remarked, 'I have been talking about, making speeches about, and generally advocating and promoting, market value accounting since the late 1950s. By "market value accounting," I mean estimated selling price for assets and estimated settlement price for liabilities' (Scheutze, 2001a, p.1).
41. ACA (2010, s.95A (1) and (2)) and other references related to overseas countries as included in Chapter 3.
42. Detailed in Behr and Witt (*Washington Post*, July 28, 2002, from p.A01), the first of five articles on the fall of Enron. Then available at www.washingtonpost.com, with full details in the bibliography under 'newspaper articles.'
43. Ibid., Article 5.
44. Available at Australian corporate news (2003, p.111) under "insolvency"; also available at www.cch.com.au.
45. Wolnizer (1987, p.64) explained, 'concern is with those technical properties of accounts which render them fit [or unfit] to function as an informative guide to future action in the market economy. To be useful within this setting, accounting information must relate to observable market phenomena possessing financial characteristics, namely the monetary equivalents of assets and liabilities. It must have "real-world" referents.'
46. Extracts of a survey conducted by Dean, Clarke and Houghton (2003) from some of the top 200 publicly listed companies on the Australian Securities Exchange (ASX).
47. There are two approaches to regulating corporate groups, as a separate entity or a single enterprise. In Australia the separate entity approach is commonly used to administer and regulate corporate entities. ASIC deeds of cross guarantee include the concept of a "closed group." This refers to a holding entity and its wholly-owned subsidiaries, basically regulated under the separate entity approach. It is also possible to have an extended closed group that includes entities that are controlled but not wholly owned. Alternatively, an "opting-in"

arrangement was proposed by the Companies and Securities Advisory Committee in their final report on corporate groups (May 2000) to merge the operations (ex ante) of wholly-owned group companies with each other and their parent company. The entities so consolidated would be governed for all purposes as a single enterprise. The analogous position of "closed groups" versus an "opting-in" arrangement and subsequent pursuits are discussed in Chapter 4.

48. Accounting has often been referred to as the language of business. On the one hand, Stone (1971, p.149) referred to accounting as 'the language not of business but of accountants.' On the other hand, Avery (1953) examined the concept of accounting as a language and asserted, 'it [accounting] must develop a . . . [clear] system of communicating ideas and a sound means of expressing its symbolic doctrine' (p.83). Mason *et al.* (1959, p.1) proffered accounting as the language in which to express business events, and Jameson (1988, p.8) described accounting as the language that 'communicates aspects of business to its owners and other interested parties.' Previous authors, for instance, Montgomery (1938), MacNeal (1939, p.1) and Foulke (1945, p.29), described the language of accounting linked to finance and financial concerns rather than business *per se*.
49. For aeons, in accounting and cognate disciplines, much has been written on the various components of financial reports; their definition or lack thereof, ambiguity and questionable use of words and phrases. Fitzgerald (1936, p.133) remarked on these and other matters and empathised the misuse of words, terms and lack of precision generally. Moonitz and Staehling (1952, p.121) proclaimed the need for improved terminology, not just different terminology. Walters (1967, p.198) advocated the need for precision in defining words and terms in accounting. Wolk *et al.* (1984, p.266) disparaged the move from a precise focus to a broader economic concept of terms that resulted in the meaning of an asset, for instance, becoming 'hazy and ambiguous.' Wolnizer (1987, p.165) elaborated with regard to accounting records of financial data that 'does not presuppose a knowledge of the character, meaning, interpretability or functional fitness of those data.' Chambers (1995, pp.882–885) provided an array of examples decrying inexact terminology in accounting communications.
50. Refer to Laverty (2003) for a well developed comparison of phenomenology and hermeneutic phenomenology, with reference to Husserl, Heidegger and Gadamer (pp.22–25).
51. See, for instance, Korzybski (1933/1958, p.412), Whatmough (1957, p.22), Chambers (1966, pp.166–183) and Feyerabend (1975/1982, p.223).
52. This was a point of discussion of the Joint Committee on Corporations and Financial Services reported in the Official Committee Hansard (March 11, 2004) "Joint Committee on Corporations and Financial services." For instance, Professor Dean argued that 'the unexpected nature of those [corporate] crashes and the quality of the data that appear to the market participants . . . lead to the general lack of market confidence' (CFS.51, 52).
53. For instance, CLERP3, 'Directors' Duties and Corporate Governance,' Proposals for Reform (1997). Available at http://www.treasury.gov.au.

NOTES TO CHAPTER 2

1. As '[f]inancial statements are not objective statements of reality' (Wright, 1994, p.373). Much earlier, Canning (1929, pp.199, 319) reiterated.
2. A situation evidenced by increases in penalties for company directors for insolvent trading included in ACA, s588. Further, directors of Australian companies must provide a solvency statement s301(5) as part of the company's published

financial reports. Reference to particular case law with regard to the fiduciary duties of directors is provided, for instance, by Duns (2000).

3. For an entity to adapt to changing business circumstances requires that the entity has money and access to money on a continual basis. Also, 'It is relevant to note that the courts have clearly decided that in determining solvency, the money of the company which is taken to be available to pay debts which are due not only includes cash resources, but can include money which is able to be procured by realising (by sale or by mortgage) its assets within a relatively short time. This is indicative of commercial realism' (Keay, 1995, p.320).This follows the views of others, like Shackle (1970), who defines an entity's wherewithal as its existing capital plus what additional borrowing that capital would facilitate. Precisely that a 'firm's fortune at any moment comprises the market value at that moment of all material objects and legal rights which it then possesses, plus the money it has, plus the debts owed to it less those it owes to others' (Shackle, 1970, p.28).
4. What follows provided the main threads of what appeared in Margret (2002).
5. See, for example, R. M. Goode (1990, pp.26, 27). Also see the International Bar Association (IBA) survey of 1994.
6. See, for example, Duns (2000).
7. Later discussion elaborates this point, for instance, when the court's view on debt and future liabilities is discussed with regard to *Re European Life Assurance Co.* (1869) L.R. 9Eq. 122.
8. Refer to Duns (2000, pp.22–34). Also see Honsberger (1980, pp.153, 154).
9. For further discussion on this point, refer to Keay (1995, pp.312–322); and Duns (2000, p.27).
10. See Duns (2000, p.29) for comment on the importance of applying 'an appropriate insolvency concept' especially with regard to employing a net asset test of insolvency.
11. Accounting academics and practitioners have argued over the definition and concept of an asset (and debt) for a long time. See, for example, Lisle (1899, p.67), Sprague (1907/1972, p.36), Esquerre (1914, p.135), Couchman (1924/1982, p.28), MacNeal (1939, p.200), Paton (1949, p.15), Goldberg and Hill (1958, p.17), Chambers (1966, p.56), Hinton (1972, p.56), Wolnizer (1987, p.58), Scheutze (1991, p.116) and Scheutze (1993, p.68), particularly Chambers (1995, p.1005). Many such references were also mentioned in Potter (1999, pp.55, 56).
12. Currently, the AASB Framework (para.49(a)) states, 'An asset is a resource controlled by the entity as a result of past events and from which *future economic benefits* are *expected* to flow to the entity' (emphasis added). This conventional accounting view of an asset as to opposed alternative ideas of marketable, tangible elements as expressed throughout the accounting literature is revisited later in this chapter. Note, AASB framework is equivalent to the *International Framework for the Preparation and Prensentation of Financial Statements* issued by the IASB except for paragraphs prefixed with "Aus." Further details are available in the Australian Accounting Handbook (2010, p.21).
13. Such a view implies that 'an economic resource . . . [be] defined as an element of wealth that possesses . . . utility, scarcity and exchangeability . . . [and] exchangeability means that an economic resource is separable from a business as a whole and that it has value in and of itself—that it is not solely dependent on the fortunes of the particular business enterprise to which the resource is attached' (Hinton, 1972, p.56).
14. Notwithstanding this view, it has been contestable as to what is the current monetary equivalent of a liability (see article by Bradbury, 2000).
15. Refer to Keay (1995, pp.319–321).

16. The conceptual definition of liabilities in AASB Framework (2010, para.49(b)) [IASB equivalent] asserted, 'A liability is a present obligation of the entity arising from past events, the settlement of which is expected to result in an outflow from the entity of resources embodying economic benefits.' Hence, emphasised is the expectation of future sacrifices of economic benefits rather than recognition of contractual obligation. Further, 'A liability is recognised in the balance sheet [only] when it is probable that an outflow of resources embodying economic benefits will result from the settlement of a present obligation and the amount at which the settlement will take place can be measured reliably.'.Arguably, this is all too problematic.
17. The NZ Companies Act 1993 Part 1 states as part of the meaning of the solvency test that 'the value of the company's assets [must be] greater than the value of its liabilities, including contingent liabilities' s4(1)(b).'
18. Refer to Walker *et al.* (2000) and especially the monograph by Lennard and Thompson (1995) cited in Walker *et al.* (2000, p.137). Also refer to AASB137 para.36, which elaborates the measurement [best estimate] of provisions
19. For further details of the committee's view on implications for valuation of provisions and contingencies, refer to AAA (1998, pp.192–200).
20. As indicated earlier, the AASB Framework (2010, para.49) stated, 'An asset is a resource controlled by the entity as a result of past events and from which future economic benefits are expected to flow to the entity.' Emphasis is on control not ownership of the asset and on the probability that future economic benefits will eventuate. Such benefits of course may not eventuate. Furthermore, the entity's assets (the same as for its liabilities) must be able to be reliably measured, and that is frequently problematic. Also the entity's assets may be tangible or intangible. Hence, the definition is ambiguous, and as the monetary amounts attributed to assets in conventionally prepared financial statements are usually based on historical costs, they do not indicate current values of money, the current financial worth of that money or possible access to money to pay debts when due.
21. For instance, in *Re Newark Pty. Ltd. (in liq)* (1993) 1 Qd R 409, Justice Thomas stated, 'A debt does not necessarily become "due" within the meaning of the section upon the date originally stipulated for its payment.' Also see Keay (1995, p.317) and Duns (2000, pp.31, 32) for an insightful discussion of this point.
22. See Goode (1990, p.27) and Keay (1995, p.308).
23. For instance, 'if the time for payment of a debt is extended then the debt is not payable and cannot be taken into account in assessing solvency' (Keay, 1995, p.321).
24. In *Expo International Pty.Ltd (in liq) v. Chant* (1979) 2 N.S.W.L.R. 820; (1979–80) C.L.C. *40–608*, the court looked to future debt as well as the debt then due and payable. It was held that debts due in the immediate future as well as debts payable at the relevant date were to be taken into account in ascertaining insolvency. The use of the phrase "immediate future," however, emphasised a potential problem with regard to the use of the word *immediate* in terms of the entity's future debt. Immediate, according to the *Oxford English Dictionary*, means 'at once,' which would denote a very short look into the future. In relation to calculating an entity's debt paying ability, this seems to be a short-term approach that may prove to be inadequate in the future.
25. Support for this idea can be found in *Bank of Australasia v. Hall* (1907) 4 C.L.R. 1514, where the court held that all liabilities, otherwise provable in insolvency, were to be considered debt. C. J. Griffith stated that '[t]he words "as they become due" require . . . that some consideration shall be given to

the immediate future; and, if it appears that the debtor will not be able to pay a debt which will certainly become due in say, a month . . . by reason of an obligation already existing, and which may before that day exhaust all his available resources, how can it be said that he is able to pay his debts "as they become due" out of his own moneys.'

26. A famous case of this was the action in 1970 of a smallish US bank that was owed around US$10 million by the US Railway conglomerate, Penn Central—ultimately the bank was instrumental in forcing the reportedly $7 billion asset rich railway into bankruptcy (see Salsbury, 1982).
27. See Keay (1995, pp.316–319).
28. 'At present, the primary source of information about financial position is the balance sheet, which can reveal much about the reporting entity's liquidity if the assets, liabilities and equity are appropriately identified and categorised [and arguably reported at their monetary equivalent]' (Loftus and Miller, 2000, p.105).
29. Under AASB101 (IAS 1 equivalent) in 'preparing financial statements, management shall make an assessment of an entity's ability to continue as a going concern' (para.25) and in 'assessing whether the going concern assumption is appropriate, management takes into account all available information about the future' (para.26). The emphasis clearly is on assessing future occurrences; the future, however, is an unknown.

    Previously under 'Going concern basis' paras.7.1–7.1.3 and as defined under AASB1001, para 9.1(b), a going concern similarly was *'expected to* . . . continue in operation without any intention or necessity to liquidate or otherwise wind up its operations' (emphasis added). The point of concern for some is that the going concern basis of accounting is premised on an assumption (an expectation) of the entity's future financial viability, as opposed, for instance, to an analysis of the current marketability of its assets and their financial worth contrasted with the entity's accumulated financial debt obligations.
30. Furthermore, '[w]hile some references to this dynamic view of a firm as a going concern may be found in the accounting literature [e.g. Paton, 1917, p.25; Pixley, 1926, Vol.1, p.520; Canning, 1931, p.163; Edwards and Bell, 1961, p.38], the implications of it for accounting practice have been substantially ignored except by Chambers [in several works, e.g. 1986, chapter six, but especially and systematically in his principal exposition of CoCoA, 1966] and Sterling [e.g., 1979]' (Tabart-Gay and Wolnizer, 1997, p.194).
31. AASB Framework '*for the Preparation and Presentation of* Financial Statements was introduced for annual reporting periods beginning on or after 1 January 2005' (CPA Handbook, 2010, p.19). For earlier reference, see, for example, Australia's then SAC4, para.129 (now replaced by the AASB Framework) and the FASB's, SFAC1, para.2.
32. Refer to AASB 116: *Property, Plant and Equipment* (particularly paras.43–62). AASB116 incorporates IAS 16, issued by the IASB, and supersedes the previously applicable AASB1021: *Depreciation of Non-Current Assets.*
33. '*Depreciation* is the systematic allocation of the depreciable amount of an asset over its useful life,' and the '*Depreciable amount* is the cost of an asset, or other amount substituted for cost, less its residual value' (AASB116, para.6). Both definitions are problematic.
34. The concept is further explained in AASB136 (IAS136) paras.59–64.
35. Refer to AASB101 (IAS1-equivalent) paras.54–76. For previous reference, see, for instance, AASB1010: *Accounting for the Revaluation of Non-Current Assets*, para.3.1, and AASB1040: *Statement of Financial Position*, para.8.1(b), arguably still relevant.
36. In addition to the extended arguments provided by Chambers (1966) and Sterling (1979), see, for example, Canning (1929, p.199), Boulding

(1950/1962, p.187), Sterling (1970, p.101), Wolnizer (1987, p.76), Chambers (1995, pp.886, 887), Clarke *et al.* (1997, pp.220–225), Margret (2002) and Clarke *et al.* (2003, pp.268–274).

37. Succinctly, Canning (1929, p.45) stated, '[m]any an economist and statistician, in reading the accounting texts, must have been aware of a great mass of unsupported assertion, inconsequential argument, apparent statistical inconsistency, and lack of homogeneity and completeness.'
38. Also see Chambers (1973/1986, pp.32, 33).
39. This part draws on the International Bar Association (IBA) survey of 1994.
40. The work of Keay (1995) was particularly helpful when selecting relevant legal cases.
41. Relevant sections of the *Corporations Act 2001* used in this case were s95A(1),(2) and ss459A, 459C, 459C, 459D, 459G(2), 459P, 459S, 465C.
42. Court transcript is available at http://www.austlii.edu.au.
43. J. Lindgren observed in *Melbase Corporation Pty.Ltd.* (1995) 17 ACSR 187 at 198, s95A(1) of the *Corporations Act* states a "cash flow test" rather than a "balance sheet test" of insolvency.
44. Other recent cases referenced include *David Grant & Co Pty.Ltd. v. Westpac Banking Corporation* (1995) 184 CLR 265; *Howship Holdings Pty.Ltd.* (1996) 14 ACLC 1549; *Melbase Corporation Pty.Ltd. v. Legenhoe Pty. Ltd.* (1995) 17 ACSR 187; *The Roy Morgan Research Centre v. Wilson Market Research Pty.Ltd.* (1996) 39 NSWLR 311; *Re Bond Corporation Holdings Ltd.* (1990) 1 ACSR 350; and *Trade Practices Commission v. Arnotts Ltd* (No.5) (1990) 21 FCR 324.
45. 'Each company's circumstances are going to be different. It is an area where one cannot be technical. Rather, a court must assess each company's overall trading and financial position and ascertain whether the company is able to meet its debts' (Keay, 1995, p.316).
46. See also Kehl (1941/1976, pp.3–13).
47. Refer also to *Parker v. Gossage* (1835) 2 C.M. & R. 617; 150 E.R. 262, 263.
48. (1966) 115 C.L.R. 666, 670.
49. Nonetheless, it may be determined in this type of case that money borrowed has the characteristics of trading stock.
50. Not least because 'the concept of capital maintenance provides a benchmark that can be used to establish whether or not income has been earned' (Carsberg, 1982, p.60) and '[t]he concept of maintaining capital intact is important because it is used as the benchmark for the definition and measurement of income' (Barton, 1975/1984, p.90).
51. Refer to cases discussed in Clarke *et al.* (2003, pp.87–203) and to the cases in Chambers (1973).
52. Refer to Chambers' (1979) review of Canning's work that questioned what Canning meant by "purchasing power accounting."
53. FASB (1984) defines financial flexibility as 'the ability of an entity to take effective actions to alter amounts and timing of cash flows so it can respond to unexpected needs and opportunities.' Loftus and Miller (2000, pp.25, 26) give a detailed and technical exposè on the term *financial flexibility.* Chambers (1966) referred to the adaptive behaviour of business entities.

NOTES TO CHAPTER 3

1. For example the introduction of a "closed-group" reporting entity with the implementation of ASIC Class Order Deeds of Cross Guarantee in Australia. More recently the recommendation that Corporations Law provide 'that a

wholly-owned corporate group can "opt-in" to be a consolidated corporate group for all or some of the group companies, by resolution of the directors of each relevant group company' (CASAC, *Corporate Groups: Final Report,* May 2000, Appendix 2).

2. CLERP Bill (2003): Audit Reform and Corporate Disclosure; it followed CLERP9: *Proposals for Reform: Corporate Disclosure,* released September 18, 2002.
3. The IASB emphasised *truth and fairness* in reporting the financial state of an entity (ASX , 2003, para.16).
4. 'Although incorporation with limited liability became available in the nineteenth century [1844 in the UK], the term "corporate governance" does not appear in either the professional or academic literature before 1980' (CIMA, Corporate Governance: history, practice and future, p.2). Nonetheless the notion of corporate governance in business is not new, but it is in danger of becoming an over-used substitute to *take the heat off* system defects in conventional accounting practice. See Clarke *et al.* (2003, pp.266–332).
5. Consider that Longo (1999, p.20) reported '[i]n the latest financial year, ASIC took action against dishonest directors, bankrupts managing companies, insolvent trading, "phoenix company" activity, and failure to cooperate with external administrators. Ten of the 22 people jailed in 1998/99 were company directors who [allegedly] cheated investors or creditors of small to medium-sized companies or who were involved in managing companies while disqualified.' Chapters five, six and seven delve further into such issues and the role directors' play in business through the lens of eight different case studies on financial dilemma.
6. Probably '[w]e all agree about the role of a board: to agree strategy, to monitor performance, to approve major investments, to ensure major risks are managed, to appoint the CEO and approve succession plans and top management compensation, to ensure compliance on all fronts and to establish ethical standards for the company's operations and people' (Wallis, 2000, p.15). Previously Hawkins (1977, pp.46, 47) remarked, '[o]wners entrust funds to management and management is expected to use these funds wisely. Periodically, management must report to the owners the results of management's actions. Financial statements are one of the principal means whereby management fulfils this reporting responsibility'.
7. In the Duke case; the directors were apportioned responsibility for the financial condition of the business, although not all directors were reportedly knowledgeable of the entity's actual financial state. More recently, One.Tel illustrated the plight of directors—particularly non executive directors—when apparently unaware of the factual financial state of the entity they govern. It is arguable however that all directors ought to know the financial state of the entity they direct. More recently John Elliott, a non-executive director of Water Wheel was more than admonished, he was convicted of allowing the company to trade while insolvent.
8. Refer s.7—*Financial reporting and assurance* of the HIH Royal Commissioner's Report. For instance 'because the accounting standards have the force of law those who are responsible for the preparation of accounts [may] have . . . forgotten about the "true and fair view" requirement . . . they ought to be reminded' (Owen, 2003, s.7, p.20) at www.hihroyalcom.gov.au
9. As required under the *Corporations Act 2001,* s297 'True and Fair view'. Although s296 stipulates that s297 does not affect the entity's obligation to comply with accounting standards, which constitutes a real dilemma for directors. This is discussed in the JCPAA *391 Report,* section 3, ss.3.53–3.82.
10. Earlier (pre 2005) the *Corporations Act 2001,* s60(1)(a) stated that a director may be 'a person occupying or acting in the position of director of the body,

by whatever name called and whether or not validly appointed to occupy, or duly authorised to act in, the position'. Now it does not—it speaks instead of relevant relationships.

11. Under the *Corporations Act 2001*, Pt.1.2, s.9 an 'Officer' is defined as '(a) a director or secretary of the corporation; or (b) a person (i) who makes or participates in making decisions that affect the whole, or a substantial part, of the business of the corporation; or (ii) who has the capacity to affect significantly the corporation's financial standing . . .'.
12. Hogan (1997, p.40) explained that '[a] major issue in corporate governance relates to the role of shareholders in monitoring and rendering accountable the directors and management of any one company'.
13. Consider case discussion in Chambers (1973/1986, particularly pp.162–180) and Clarke *et al.* (2003, pp.55–245 but also pp.290–312) the latter on issues of 'Accounting's Diminished Serviceability'.
14. 'The focus on corporate governance has grown in the last 10–15 years for a variety of reasons. As major corporations expanded in the 1970s and 1980s on a global basis, there was a growing separation of ownership and control. The professional manager was accumulating too much power; a constraint on this concentration of power was needed' (Wallis, op.cit., p.15).
15. Refer to Clarke *et.al.* (2003) for relevant case analyses.
16. 'The fundamental purpose of a business judgement rule is to protect the authority of directors in the exercise of their duties, not to insulate directors from liability . . . While it is accepted that directors should be subject to a high level of accountability, a failure to expressly acknowledge that directors should not be liable for decisions made in good faith and with due care can have the effect of encouraging business behaviour which is risk-averse' (CLERP 3, 'Proposals for Reform—Directors Duties and Corporate Governance', 1997, p.23).
17. See Chambers (1973) for detailed explication.
18. 'The complexity of business and the speed of change generally in the global business world also requires a rethink of the traditional board models' (Wallis, op.cit., p.17). The conventional role of a director and a board of directors will most likely continue to change into the future as the demands of business become more time-consuming and increasingly complex.
19. '*Corporate governance,* the 1990s new-age buzz-phrase within commerce generally has gradually gained the ascendancy . . .' (Clarke *et al.*,2003, pp.298).
20. In s236(2)(a) auditors are required to state 'whether in the auditor's opinion the balance sheet and profit and loss account . . . have been properly prepared in accordance with this Act . . .' and 'whether in their opinion a true and fair view is given . . . (i) in the balance sheet, of the company's affairs . . . (ii) in the profit and loss account . . . of the company's profit or loss . . . (iii) in the case of group accounts, of the state of affairs and profit or loss . . .' s236(2)(b). The section stipulates that auditors are to comment on whether the balance sheet provides a true and fair view of the company's state of affairs.
21. For example, s16.20 states that '[a] corporation shall furnish its shareholders annual financial statements, which may be consolidated or combined statements of the corporation and one or more of its subsidiaries . . . If financial statements are prepared for the corporation on the basis of generally accepted accounting principles, the annual financial statements must also be prepared on that basis'.
22. For instance, as under s.401(b).
23. See NCSC (1984), ASA & ICAA (1985) and JCPAA (2002).
24. '[T]o provide information about the financial position, financial performance and cash flows of an entity that is useful to a wide range of users in making economic decisions' (AARB Framework, para.12) IASB equivalent.

25. In July 2002 the Sarbanes-Oxley Act was signed into law by the US President, an Act considered by some to be a significant step forward since 1934 and the forming of the SEC. Broad-ranging reforms included '[a]n additional benefit [that] is the facilitation of greater convergence between U.S. GAAP and international standards' (SEC, 2003, Executive Summary pursuant to s.108(d)) available then at www.sec.gov/news/studies/principlesbasedstand.html
26. 'Developments towards the measurement of quality suggest that its requisite properties have been defined with precision, are measurable and capable of objective valuation' (Wolnizer, 1987, p.5).
27. Appendix 1 includes further details on this topic including areas of possible defence for directors.
28. Refer AASB112 (IAS 12) *Income Taxes* CPA Accounting Handbook 2010. Importantly, the definition of liabilities and the definition of assets are crucial in quantifying an entity's financial position and thus, its financial capacity to pay its debts (its liabilities) when due and payable. In the case of HIH the Australian Shareholders Association reportedly stated '[w]e believe, as far as HIH is concerned, the market was not adequately informed by the board (of liabilities)' (Dunn and Ferguson, *Herald Sun*, May 21, 2001, p.5) Further, the quality of the financial information (depicted by its assets and its liabilities) in the HIH published financial statements was reportedly such that 'HIH's financial position was worse by a considerable margin that what was stated in the balance sheet' (Baskett, *The Press*, May 21, 2001, p.20).
29. Arguably: 'Corporate managers are placed in a no-man's-land, between a rock and a hard place—between the sword and the wall' (Clarke *et al.*,2003, p.300).
30. 'In the past decade there has been increasing pressure from the investment community, in particular, on directors to give greater attention to issues including stewardship, accountability, risk management, codes of conduct and ethical behaviour. At the same time, regulators—including the Australian Securities and Investments Commission—have been actively driving the demand for disclosure with an increased emphasis on board composition, its membership and independence' (Longo, 1999, p.19). In contrast Wallis (2000, p.17) stated '[t]he trend to measure governance performance by listing the structures and processes in the annual report is trivialising the really important issue of board performance . . .'.
31. For instance, in *Turquand v. Marshall* L.R. 6 Eq. 112 (1868); 20 L.T. 766 (1869) the official liquidator of Herefordshire Banking Company.
32. *AWA Ltd v Daniels* (1992) 7 ACSR 759 at 865.
33. Later, in the case of One.Tel (2001) internal accounting and management systems were also an issue with regard to the corporates collapse and the role of the entity's corporate officers. See Paul Barry (2002) for a colourful discussion on the story of One.Tel.
34. See also Mescher (1996, p.839).
35. L.R. 6 Eq. 112 (1868); 20 L.T. 766 (1869)
36. 'The first ground of complaint was that from 1846, down to the termination of the business of the company the directors annually presented to the shareholders false reports of the progress and proceedings of the company, and false balance sheets, and recommended the declaration of dividends upon repeated false statements that profits had been earned' (at p.58). Furthermore '[i]n addition to the false representations made by the balance sheets, it appeared that the directors had at the annual meetings and at other times, down to 1863, held out the bank to be a flourishing and prosperous institution' (at p.60).
37. Judgement included the following: 'The charges against the directors are distinct, and must be separately considered. I shall first notice the complaints

made of misconduct of the directors in rendering false accounts, and in representing the concern to be in a very different position from that which it really held; and proof is given which, in my opinion, is very conclusive and distinct, that the accounts furnished and published to the shareholders were grossly inaccurate. Convincing proof is also given that the managing directors were well aware of this fact. I am also of the opinion that the other directors, who may not have examined the books, must be taken to be liable for all the consequences which would properly flow from the fact if they had been acquainted with the contents of them. It was their duty to be so acquainted, and it was a duty which they had undertaken to perform by becoming directors; and therefore I am of opinion that they are also responsible for the falsity of the accounts' (at p.62).

38. This idea was supported at an earlier time in Turquand, where the directors' defence also centred around the fact 'that they did not know the *[financial] state* of the company, or the contents of the books'. This was not accepted and the directors were found 'liable to make good such losses as may have been sustained by the shareholders by reason of the directors not having summoned a special meeting of the company when, subsequently to 1846, the losses of the company had exhausted the whole of the surplus fund, and also one-fourth part of the paid-up capital of the shareholders . . .' (at p.63, emphasis added).
39. Refer Couper (1879/1984).
40. Mackinnon who was '[t]he respondent became a director of the bank in July 1858; and the first overt act of mis-feasance charged against him is, that he, as a director, signed the balance-sheet of 1859, to be submitted to the shareholders at the annual meeting of that year' (at p.115).
41. 'The result . . . of the operation was to increase to that extent the balance of profit for the year appearing in the balance-sheet' (at p.115).
42. Lord Mure held: 'I am of opinion that it is not, in any just sense, a payment of dividend out of capital, but an investment of the interest in America as part of the capital of the bank' (at p.122). Furthermore he added that 'a sum corresponding in amount to that carried to profit and loss as interest, was invested in America in substitution, and as a *surrogatum* for the money taken from the bank in this country when the dividend was paid. This was substantially, therefore, an investment of capital in America, and if done in the *bona fide* belief that the security was sufficient, constitutes a good defence to the present demand . . .' (at p.122).
43. Manley (1973) provides a detailed analysis of the events in *re City Equitable Fire Insurance Company Limited*.
44. For instance it was noted that, 'a person acting as a director of a large insurance company is bound to exercise the skill that a reasonable person, competent to act in that way, would exercise, and he is not entitled to say that he knew nothing about business; that he was not a business man at all, and that he was there for some subsidiary purpose' (at p.416).
45. 'While the courts have been reluctant to review judgements of directors exercised in good faith, they have also, on occasion, refused to exercise their discretion to excuse directors from liability where they have acted fairly and honestly' (CLERP No.3, *Proposals for Reform—Directors' Duties and Corporate Governance*',1997, p.22). See also, *Knightswood Nominees Pty Ltd v Sherwin Pastoral Co Ltd* (1989) 7 ACLC 536; *Chew v R* (1991) 4 WAR 21; *Commonwealth Bank of Australia v Friedrich* (1991) 9 ACLC 946;*Standard Chartered Bank of Australia Ltd, v Antico & Ors* (1995) 38 NSWLR 290; *Daniels v Anderson* (1995) 37 NSWLR 438.
46. 'The larger the business carried on by the company the more numerous and the more important the matters that must of necessity be left to the managers,

the accountants, and the rest of the staff' and '[a] director must of necessity trust to the officials of the company to perform properly and honestly the duties allocated to them' (at p.408).

47. It is also stated in the case that '[w]here directors take so little part in management of the business of the company as to make it perfectly easy, without inquiry, for one of their number to dissipate the funds of the company then they ought to be liable for the consequences' (at p.416). Topham K.C. also remarked '[i]f directors do not take as much care in looking after the funds of the company as a reasonable and prudent man would in like circumstances take in his own affairs, they are liable for the consequences' (at p.423).
48. In *Dunn v Shapowloff* [1978] 2 NSWLR 235 a case concerning the circumstances of insolvent trading and what may constitute the actions of a reasonable man, deliberation centred on a charge against an officer of the company pursuant to s303 (3) of the *Companies Act 1961* (NSW) that stated: If in the course of the winding up of a company it appears that an officer of the company who was knowingly a party to the contracting of a debt provable in the winding up had, at the time the debt was contracted, no reasonable or probable ground of expectation, after taking into consideration the other liabilities, if any, of the company at the time, of the company being able to pay the debt, the officer shall be guilty of an offence against this Act.
49. Reynolds J.A. remarked that 'with only $81,000 in the bank, a current liability of over $1m. to brokers, assets (current and fixed) which could reasonably be regarded as insufficient to meet that current debt, and no apparent prospect of borrowing money, a further debt of $131,000 was incurred, in circumstances where it could be regarded as an act of desperate speculation . . . [and] . . . The figures in the balance sheet were not a compelling guide to realisable figures' (at p.241).
50. Circumstances associated with the notion of the "corporate veil" are discussed further in chapter four.
51. Also, in certain situations the holding company may become liable for the ongoing debts of an insolvent subsidiary. See the *Corporations Act 2001*, Pt. 5.7B, Div.5, s588V-s588X and CASAC, *Corporate Groups Final Report,* May 2000, particularly para.6.44, p.163.
52. Perhaps it is true that 'too much attention to corporate governance can cloud a board's judgement. When you are surrounded by due diligence committees and numerous advisers in the boardroom . . . The process becomes an end in itself and obscures the real issues . . .' (Wallis, 2000, p.16).
53. As opposed a cook-book approach to governance duties (compliance) by simply fulfilling regulatory requirements.
54. 'There can be no doubt . . . that we need appropriate standards of corporate governance and that they play a key role in protecting . . . both the "old" economy companies and . . . "new" economy companies. So what is the issue? What is the problem?' (Wallis, 2000, p.16).
55. See for instance, chapter six of the HIH Royal Commission Report.
56. 'Whether boards are effective depends more on whether the directors have good judgement, are hard-working and smart, and also able to contribute constructively to the working of a wider team' (Wallis, 2000, p.17).
57. On the other hand, some have argued "corporate governance" is one of the distracting phrases of the 1990s. For instance Clarke *et al.,*(2003, p.299) remarked '[o]ne early product of the "better corporate governance" movement was the 1992 wisdom of the Cadbury Committee in the United Kingdom, in particular its "Code of Best Practice". Ultimately, however, the code amounted to little more than a series of motherhood statements regarding the virtues directors must display and be seen to display, plus the recommendation

for audit committees to be mandatory for all public companies'. HIH reportedly had an audit committee—certainly it had non-executive directors.

58. This has been evidenced by the chronological changes relating to corporate governance from 1986 to 1999 and beyond, that are detailed in Appendix 3.2 to this chapter. Also the Cadbury Committee of 1991 'was to report on the financial aspects of corporate governance (particularly in relation to financial reporting and accountability), to consider the responsibilities of executive and non-executive directors . . .' (CIMA, Executive Summary, pp.2,4). Wallis (2000, p.17) further stated that '[i]n future, directors will have to spend more time, often in informal discussion, with management and employees, customers, suppliers and investors to gain a greater understanding of the business.'
59. 'This need to provide information for efficient resource utilization and performance evaluation underlies both seminal works in CVA, that is, Edwards and Bell (1961) on CCA and Chambers (1966) on CCE' (Barton, 2000, p.300).
60. Further details available at www.sec.gov/news/press/2002-154
61. Refer Senate Report No.107–205, 107 Cong. 2d Session at 29, 2002. Also, at www.sec.gov/rules/proposed/33-8145.htm
62. See Release No.33/5337 March 15, 1973. Also in text at www.sec.gov/rules/proposed/33-8145.htm
63. See Release No.33–8039 December 4, 2001 [66 FR 63731]. Also, details at SEC website as above.
64. Further details contained under "Conditions for Use of NON-GAAP Financial Measures" at www.sec.gov/rules/proposed/33-8145
65. "The Sarbanes-Oxley Act of 2002: Goals, Content, and Status of Implementation" *International Financial Law review,* March 2003, available at www.sec.gov/rules/proposed
66. Both the Canada Act and the Canada Regulations are available online at http://laws.justice.gc.ca/en/c-44/9507.html
67. Refer to the Chairman's Foreword of the JCPAA, Report 391, p.iv.
68. Refer to the Chairman's Foreword of the JCPAA, Report 391, p.v.
69. Ibid.
70. Refer to the *Corporations Act 2001,* s.297.

NOTES TO CHAPTER 4

1. In addition to the *Corporations Act 2001*, s95A(1) refer to Honsberger (1980, pp.153, 154) and the International Bar Association (1994). Further, Loftus and Miller (2000, in particular Chapter 6).
2. Historically, see Canning (1929, pp.199, 319). More recently, Wright (1994, p.373) stated, '[f]inancial statements are not objective statements of reality, as there are clearly many alternatives, assumptions and estimates that are involved in producing financial statements.' Then Scheutze (2001, p.6) reported, '[i]n the spring of 1998, a national business magazine in the USA—*Forbes*—had the following banner on its cover: "Pick a Number, Any Number." That was followed by articles in the national press, such as *USA Today*, about "Abracadabra Accounting," "Hocus Pocus Accounting," and the like. The gist of these articles was that the accounting numbers were being managed or manipulated by corporations and certified as being OK by their external auditors.' The SEC issued three SABS in 1999 to specifically address aggressive earnings management (Previts *et al.*, 2003, p.153).
3. Goode (1990) discussed the point with regard to the balance sheet test and the cash flow test of insolvency; also refer to the work of Keay (1995, pp.307, 308)

and Duns (2000). Furthermore the Australian *Corporations Act 2001*, s295 (4) provides: Directors' declaration (c) regarding the company's ability to pay its debts and, N. Z. Companies Act 1993, Part 1 as part of the meaning of a solvency test 'the value of the company's assets [must be] greater than the value of its liabilities, including contingent liabilities' (s4 (1)(b)). FASB–Statement of Accounting Concepts No.5: *Recognition and Measurement in Financial Statements of Business Enterprises* emphasises an entity's liquidity.

4. Scheutze (2001, p.3) suggested that the 'preparation of financial statements and reports, their use, and their regulation should be based on intuition, not inculcation.'
5. For instance, Edwards and Bell (1961) wrote of the exit price system as that of an 'orderly liquidation,' but as Chambers (1982, p.26) explained, Edwards and Bell 'did not notice the context of . . . the orderly liquidation of assets, not of the firm. . . . [and] Failing to notice this, they depicted the system's valuation basis as that of a "liquidation fire-sale" basis." '
6. See the Report of the International Bar Association (1994).
7. Ibid.
8. However, as Sweeney (1936/1964, p.24) remarked, 'accounting procedure combines figures that are not expressed in the same kind of measuring unit, thus violating the basic mathematical axiom that "[l]ike added to like gives like." '
9. Canning (1929, p.319) proffered some thought provoking ideas, such as, '[m]any economists are grieved to find that the balance sheet valuations of accounting are of mongrel origin. . . . They find that cash has been counted (a present valuation); that accounts, bills and notes receivable have been valued at the number of dollars expected to come in (a future valuation); . . . that inventories are valued at cost or market (a purely arbitrary index); that items like organization expense, purchased goodwill, etc. having no attributes in common with the assets grouped with them are included (valuation account balances); that fixed assets are valued at an approximation to the cost of the future services expected to become available provided that cost does not exceed the cost of available substitute services (a division of costs into past and future charges). They find, moreover, that these diverse valuations of diverse things are added to find an asset total that, dollar for dollar, cannot possibly have a common significance.' Current reference (2010) to fair values for financial assets (AASB139; IAS 39) and consideration of impairment for operational assets (AASB136; IAS 36) has arguably done little to change the situation.
10. Ibid. Additionally, refer to Chambers (1966), Wolnizer (1987) and Clarke *et al.* (1997/2003). Further, as Scheutze (2001, p.12) remarked '[t]he reported numbers for assets and liabilities must be such that they can be verified by external auditors (and by regulators and courts) by reference to sources outside the enterprise. By reference to competent evidence.'
11. For example, refer to AASB Framework, para.49; IASB Framework equivalent; in addition, a critique of the Fisherian asset definition was provided by Scheutze (2001, pp.1–14).
12. Particularly as 'under our current accounting rules [internationally] there are dozens of ways to manage earnings' (Scheutze, 2001, p.6) as well as the structure of the balance sheet, and so the ongoing "appearance" of the entity's financial state.
13. See, for instance, Williams (2003) for an in-depth study on assets and changes to the concept of assets across time.
14. See, for instance, Chambers' (1995, pp.231–247) *Thesaurus* for an array of related ideas.

15. Ibid., s.500 pp.486–497.
16. Refer, for instance, to note 13 and also: AASB102: *Inventories* (IAS 2 equivalent), AASB5: *Non-Current Assets Held for Sale and Discontinued Operations* (IFRS 5 equivalent), AASB138: *Intangible Assets* (IAS 38 equivalent) and AASB101: *Presentation of Financial Statements* (IAS 1 equivalent).
17. For a rich source of ideas on measurement and measuring throughout the accounting and cognate literatures, refer to the work of Chambers (1966), but also Chambers' (1995, especially pp.222–249) *Thesaurus*.
18. AASB102 is equivalent to the International Standard IAS 2.
19. AASB102 was applicable from January 1, 2005. Differences between the current professional accounting requirements and the previous standard AASB1019 are given as an addendum to AASB102. The intricate nature of dealing with inventories, however, remains.
20. More candidly, it may well be that when applying such methods, 'accountants are doing accounting for accountants' sake, not for use by investors, creditors, underwriters, analysts, boards of directors, and regulators who are the people that we accountants should aim to please' (Scheutze, 2001, p.19).
21. Ibid.
22. Consider that '[t]here is no relevance to a datum called cost or cost minus amortization—it is just a number, a number having no information content. The "quality" of the datum called cost or cost minus amortization for assets . . . is indisputably awful: worse, it can be and often is misleading' (Scheutze, 2001, pp.3, 4).
23. The *Oxford English Dictionary* (2008) explained value as 'the amount of money that something is worth,' whereas the *Pocket Oxford* (1970) defined value in terms of a money amount or a commodity for which something may be exchanged—its determined equivalent. Valuation is subjective and involves a relationship with something; an estimate of worth. Measurement has regard for property, substance and combining things of like kind. Dohr (1950, p.116) explained, '[t]he most elementary rule of mathematics, requires that in any financial statement of computation, *every element of the computation must be stated in dollars of like purchasing power.*' More than twenty years later, Ma and Mathews (1971/1979, p.469) differentiated values and measure by stating that, '[a]ccounting is concerned with measurement and accounting processes must conform consistently to measurement rules, the most fundamental of which in this context is additivity. The necessary conditions for additivity are, first, that the properties of objects being measured are identical for all objects, and, second, that the measurement standard is uniform for all measurements.' Then the Institute of Chartered Accountants of Scotland (1988, p.57) explained, '[b]y additivity, we mean that all the numbers in a statement, when added together, *should have a sum which has the same meaning as each of the numbers taken on its own*' (emphasis added).
24. However, 'accounting is a measurement discipline if and only if at least one extensive economic property is identified which (1) is possessed by accounting phenomena, (2) is measurable in standard monetary units and (3) is accepted by accountants as appropriate for accounting measurement' (Vickrey, 1970, p.738).
25. AASB127 incorporates IAS 27 *Consolidated and Separate Financial Statements* as issued by the International Accounting Standards Board. The Australian standard AASB127 applied to annual reporting periods commencing on or after July 1, 2009.
26. For further information, refer to: AASB127: *Consolidated and Separate Financial Statements*.
27. Refer to AASB127 (paras.38–40). Also, see AASB128 *Investments in Associates* (IAS 28) and AASB131 *Interests in Joint Ventures* (IAS 31), which

elaborate accounting for investments in jointly controlled entities and details of proportionate consolidation, and AASB139 *Financial Instruments: Recognition and Measurement*, which incorporates IAS 39 of the same title.

28. '[I]ntroduced for annual reporting periods beginning on or after 1 January 2005 . . . [the] compiled version of AASB127 applies to annual reporting periods beginning on or after 1 January 2009' (Australian Accounting Handbook, 2010, p.511).
29. See, for instance, Dean *et al.* (2008) for relevant discussion with particular regard to solvency.
30. Refer to Clarke *et al.* (2003, pp.266–282).
31. For an explication on the concept of feral accounting, refer to Clarke *et al.* (2003).
32. After which CASAC (2000) *Corporate Groups: Final Report* updated details on regulating corporate groups and groups subject to an ASIC Deed of Cross-Guarantee.
33. Corrigan (1992, p.64) remarked that '[t]he cross-guarantee will effectively render each company in the group liable to the creditors of every other company within the group'.
34. Further Corrigan (1992, p.64) stated, 'the scheme will enable companies to take advantage of a standard form deed of cross-guarantee for their wholly owned subsidiaries. This will minimise the inconvenience of having to produce, and have audited, individual accounts for each company within a wholly owned "closed group" of companies.'
35. Previously, Clarke *et al.* (1995, pp.51, 52) explained that 'each "closed-group" company guarantees payment in full of the individual debts of every other company in the group.'
36. See Clarke *et al.* (2003, p.275).
37. 'An early variant of the deed, a deed of indemnity, was initiated in 1986 by Henry Bosch when he was chairman of the NCSC' (Dean *et al.*, 2008, p.72).
38. *Sons of Gwalia Ltd v. Margaretic ING Investment Management LLC v. Margaretic* [2007] HCA 1 31 January; S208/2006 and S209/2006.
39. New Power was a publicly traded electricity retailer created by Enron.
40. See Behr and Witt (2002, p.A01);available at www.washingtonpost.com.
41. Details of the questions appear in the later publication of Dean, Clarke and Margret (2008) based on Dean, Clarke and Houghton (2003).
42. This was illustrated by APRA in its submission to the HIHRC, using the financial statements of HIH Insurance Ltd. as an example. This point is discussed in the following section and examined further in Chapter 5.
43. For specific details and diagrammatic representation, see http://www.asic.gov.au at Deeds of Cross Guarantee.
44. Ibid.
45. Ibid., details contained under "Solvency statement not made by every entity seeking relief."
46. Ibid., under frequently asked questions.
47. Childs (1949, p.47) asserted, 'theoretically, the consolidated statements should reflect the effects of all transactions as though they were in fact those of one company,' but the abstract entity is not one company, it is a created entity.
48. Webster (1919, p.262) stated, '[t]he object of a consolidated balance sheet is to show the true financial position of a company and its subsidiary companies with regard to the outside public.' This statement focussed on presenting an entity's *true financial position* in accounting reports. Truth, in financial accounting reports, is a notion that has been disputed for a long time. For instance, refer to Chambers' (1995) *Thesaurus* for myriad examples. A further concern has been whether financial statements are meaningful. The

American Institute of Certified Public Accountants (1959/1961, ARB51) remarked, '[t]here is a presumption that consolidated statements are more meaningful than separate statements and that they are usually necessary for a fair presentation when one of the companies in the group directly or indirectly has a controlling financial interest in the other companies.' It may be argued, however, that a situation, a document or anything that may be derived is either meaningful or not meaningful, rather than by degrees more meaningful or less meaningful. Furthermore, if a particular type of statement is necessary for a fair presentation of financial worth, then it is necessary—and not *usually* necessary. Wixon (1962, 23:1) stressed, 'consolidated statements are prepared for the purpose of reporting the position and activities of a group of companies operated under a common control. They are intended to reflect the facts with respect to an economic rather than a legal unit.' Thus, it becomes necessary to differentiate between the economic unit and a legal unit.

49. Consider Chambers' (1966, p.38, note 1.61) suggestion that '[t]he fixation of beliefs and habits is a response to the strain of doubt.'
50. See Clarke *et al.* (1997/2003) for an in-depth analysis of Westmex Ltd.
51. See Clarke *et al.* (2003, pp.198–211).
52. *Original source:* Reconstructed from data provided in the Liquidators' Affidavit to the NSW Supreme Court, in *Westmex Ltd (in liq.)*. February 1992 (Clarke *et al.*, 2003, p.201).
53. Clarke *et al.* (2003, p.192) stated, '[t]he *cognoscenti* had been caught again. . . . Westmex's accounts gave their usual impression of truth and fairness, undoubtedly masking the higher level of financial risk involved.'
54. '[U]nder the covenants of the deed [NCSC Class Order Deed of Indemnity] the parent company [Westmex Ltd] and the relevant subsidiaries within the "closed-group" agreed "to severally, unconditionally and irrevocably" guarantee each other's debts' (Clarke *et al.*, 2003, p.208).
55. Additionally, refer to Clarke *et al.* (2003, p.209). Specifically, where '[t]he parlous position of the creditors of the Westmex group, especially the "closed-group" subject to cross-guarantees, is shown in Table 13.3' (at p.208).
56. Consider how goodwill, future income tax benefits, unamortised costs and capitalized expenses reported as assets serve to inflate an entity's picture of financial stability.
57. Arguably this is notable when the GAAP definition of assets includes such a variety of intangible, 'accounting artifacts' (Clarke *et al.*, 2003, pp.272, 273).
58. Clarke *et al.* (2003, p.198).
59. Detailed disclosure of the fall of Westmex is provided by Clarke *et al.* (2003, pp.198–211).

NOTES TO CHAPTER 5

1. At that time, 'in the UK, independent phone companies were already making a mint by buying network access from the big carriers and reselling it to the public with a different brand name, and several in Australia, such as Digicall and First Direct, were trying it too' (Barry, 2002, p.56).
2. 'One.Tel's product suite includes GSM Mobile, Fixed Wire, Internet and DSL (broadband) services' (One.Tel's Annual Report, 2000, p.6).
3. Similarly, Minsec in the 1960s was on a common (Argenti Type 1) failure trajectory, 'another "still born" failure (Clarke *et al.*, 2003, p.93).
4. Refer to Barry (2002, p.357).

5. Imagineering was 'part of Studio Australia, a company started by Jodee's father Steven in 1968' (Barry, 2002, p.350).
6. Barry (2002, p.355) stated that in June 1995, 'Australia-wide there [were] 2 million mobile phone users, [and that was] double the previous year.'
7. 'Every new mobile number registered brought the company an immediate cash payment of $120—the so-called loyalty bonus—which went straight into the bank. . . . As a result, One.Tel had a powerful incentive to sign up customers that no one else would touch' (Barry, 2002, p.80).
8. See Gottliebsen (2001, p.23).
9. It seems, at that time, this was a common problem for many companies in the communications industry. Refer to ASIC inquiries at www.asic.gov.au
10. Reported Stark (*Courier-Mail*, June 21, 2001, p.25).
11. For myriad references, see Chambers (1995, pp.329–333) under "Quality of Representations in Accounting."
12. In addition, by early 2001, 'the company had [apparently] stopped doing credit checks on Next Gen[eration] customers and there was a growing bad debt problem with local calls' (Barry, 2002, p.261)
13. As detailed in the 'Shareholder's Equity' section of the balance sheet (One. Tel's Annual Report, 2000).
14. Refer to Barry (2002, p.159).
15. See, for instance, Barry (2002, p.160).
16. An opinion supported by the controversy surrounding the later collapse of Enron in the US and subsequently investigation into the affairs of the major accounting firm Arthur Andersen.
17. 'One.Tel directors could be liable for up to $80 mln' (AAP General News, Australia, 2001). Author not available. Details also available at www.education.elibrary.com.au.
18. Refer to Barry (2002, pp.372, 373).
19. Refer to s95A and s588 of the ACA. Further relevant details are found in Chapters 3 and 4.
20. In 2004, 'James Packer and . . . Lachlan Murdoch . . . [were] summonsed by a Special Purpose Liquidator appointed late last year specifically to examine the $132 million rights issue' (*AFR*, 2004, p.4). Also refer to the article by Main (2004, p.16).
21. Frith (2009).
22. Ibid.
23. Reported by AAP General News, Australia (2001). Author not available. Also refer to Lampe (2005).
24. Refer to ASIC Media Release 04–119: High Court upholds appeal by Rich and Silbermann. For further details, see Thursday, April 22, 2004.
25. Further details are available on ASIC Media Release 09–229MR: ASIC proceedings against Rich and Silbermann dismissed, Wednesday, November 18, 2009.
26. Refer ASIC Media Release 04–283: ASIC reaches agreement with John Greaves in One.Tel proceedings, Monday, September 6, 2004.
27. Ibid.
28. ASIC Media Release 03–068: Landmark decision on chairman's duties, Monday, February 24, 2003.
29. Refer to Chapter 1 and also see Clarke *et al.* (2003, p.4).
30. Refer to Media Release 03–099. In 2004, Keeling 'settled with ASIC . . . in a deal where he is to repay $920,000 or 1¢ in the dollar of the total $92 million' (AFR, 2004, March 13–14, p.4).
31. Refer to Media Release 09–229MR, 'ASIC proceedings against Rich and Silbermann,' Wednesday, November 18, 2009.

32. Reported by Terry McCrann, 'ASIC's disgrace on One.Tel calls for corporate law reform,' *The Courier-Mail* newspaper, November 18, 2009.
33. Reported by Susannah Moran, 'One.Tel liquidator to sue media giants over capital raising,' *The Australian,* August 24, 2010.
34. In addition to the Royal Commission's *HIH final report* (2003) and details in *Collapse Incorporated* (2001), see, for instance, Brammall and Bissett (*Daily Telegraph,* May 21, 2001, p.4), Clarke *et al.* (2003, Chapter 15) and Appendix A5.2.
35. In October 1996, reportedly, 'Williams [was] warned about HIH's financial problems in a letter from British branch's chief' (*Herald Sun*, May 21, 2001, p.4) [author's name not evident]. Also available at www.elibrary.com.au.
36. See Clarke *et al.* (2003, pp.228, 232) as well as Owen (2003, s.7 on financial reporting).
37. Earlier details reported in the *Australian* (December 6, 2001, p.4), author's name not evident.
38. Refer to the *Herald-Sun*, Melbourne (May 21, 2001, p.4). Author's name not evident.
39. Such statements then re-named as a Statement of Financial Performance in accord with the requirements of AASB1018—operative for financial years from June 30, 2001. AASB1018 was re-issued in October 1999, operative for half-years ending on or after December 31, 2000. By 2011, however, AASB1018 was redundant, with relevant information and significant changes incorporated in AASB101—Presentation of Financial Statements. Now the Statement of Financial Performance re-named the Statement of Comprehensive Income (or similar)—refer to AASB101, para.10.
40. See Brammall (2001, p.7).
41. Also refer to Baskett (2001, p.20).
42. Details sourced from the HIH Annual Report (2000)—'Profit and Loss Statements for the year ended 30 June 2000.'
43. Ibid.
44. Ibid. As shown in the HIH consolidated Profit and Loss Statement (Table 5.3).
45. For further details, refer to the Clarke, Dean and Wolnizer (2002) submission to HIH Royal Commission, for instance, under "HIH—the tyranny of surprise."
46. See, for instance, UK studies (Jameson, 1988; Smith, 1992), investigations in the US (Briloff, 1972, 1976, 1981) and instances of failure in Australia (Clarke *et al.*, 2003, pp. 55–211) that span the three decades of the 1960s, 1970s, 1980s and beyond.
47. For instance, refer to Goode (1990), Keay (1995), Mescher (1996), Duns (2000) and Margret (2002) for details and discussion on the balance sheet (asset) test of insolvency and the cash flow (commercial) test of insolvency, as outlined in Chapter 3.
48. HIH increased its reported consolidated total asset holdings from $3,986,700 million in 1997 to $8,327,100 million in 2000 and its liabilities from $3,426,400 million in 1997 to $7,388,000 million in 2000.
49. Additionally, the Corporate Social Responsibility website of the University of South Australia (www.business.unisa.edu.au/cobar/corpresp) provides illustrations of relevant literature. Also, refer to Clarke *et al.* (1997, pp.37–203; 2003, pp.47–211) for selected case studies of unexpected corporate collapse.
50. Refer to the *HIH Final Report* (2003, Pt.3, s.6), *Directions for the Future and,* s.7, *Financial Reporting and Assurance.*
51. See in particular Chambers (1966) and Sterling (1979); later, Wolnizer (1987); Chambers' (1995) *Thesaurus* provides a link to myriad supporting

references. While Chambers (1973) and Clarke *et al.* (1997/2003) detail particular concerns that emanate from selected case studies, primarily of Australian causes cêlèbres.

52. APRA, the Australian Prudential Regulatory Authority for the financial industry.
53. See, for instance, articles on Enron available at www.washingtonpost.com.
54. Consider the dilemma that 'funds that Enron received from the banks [reportedly J.P. Morgan and Citigroup] were commingled with trading revenue on the company's financial statements. The transactions were a crucial source of cash, but investors could not tell that the funds would have to be repaid—just like loans' (Behr and Witt, 2002, p.A01).
55. Idem. Then available at www.washingtonpost.com.
56. 'Lay [presiding over Enron] had failed, and the company he had built over the past 15 years was failing with him. . . . Lay could not unload his company even at a bargain price to a smaller rival. His house of cards had tumbled' (Behr and Witt, 2002, p.A01).
57. Changed from 2004, under s.334 of the Australian *Corporations Act 2001*, to AASB1023: General Insurance Contracts equivalent to the IFRS 4.
58. Appendix A5.2 provides a brief comparison of the prudential requirements against those of AASB1023 pre 2004.
59. The amended AASB1023: *General Insurance Contracts* incorporates changes required by the IFRS 4: *Insurance Contracts*—hence, insurers that apply AASB1023 are compliant with the international standard IFRS 4. The standard applied to insurers' reporting periods on and from January 1, 2005.
60. See, for instance, APRA Prudential Standards GPS221—*Risk Management*; GPS311—*Audit and Actuarial Reporting and Valuation;* GPS111—*Capital Adequacy*. Details available at www.apra.gov.au.
61. Refer to Owen (2003, s.7.1.2 *Interpreting accounting standards*).
62. See, for instance, Barry (2002, p.352).
63. See Barry (2002, p.352).
64. Reportedly, this is when Rich and Keeling first considered starting 'a telephone company for *normal people*' (Barry, 2002, p.56; emphasis added).
65. 'One.Tel's share price hit a three year low yesterday after it revealed plans to issue more than two billion new shares and to replace its founding fathers. The fledgling telco's share register will balloon to about the same size as the combined might of its main shareholders, the media empires of News Corporation and Publishing & Broadcasting' (Charles, 2001, p. 37).
66. Additionally, business losses included $34 million to the Dutch operation, $39 million in the UK, $40 million in a French undertaking while the Australian business 'managed to lose more than all three foreign ventures put together' (Barry, 2002, p.209).
67. Ibid.
68. 'One.Tel shares, which were in a trading halt when the market opened yesterday, plunged when selling resumed following the announcement [of the share issue] to an intra-day low of 23c' (Trute and Gosnell, 2001, p.101).
69. See Charles (2001, p.37).
70. Reportedly the 'key question that will need to be answered is whether that $132 million would have been enough to keep the company going. Opinions still differ as to how big the One.Tel deficiency was' (Kohler, 2004, p.4).
71. Resellers in the mobile phone market assist the major carriers by signing up customers, tending to connection requirements and billing operations and freeing the others to 'focus on Pay TV, cabling Australia [or countries overseas], and other big ticket items' (Barry, 2002, p.61).
72. Refer to Chapter 4 of Barry (2002, particularly p.57).

73. As Barry (2002, p.58) reported, 'the key objectives [were stated] thus: Use a highly integrated voice and data processing system to customize the end user interface, maximize internal efficiency, and leverage the customer base. Use internal systems to provide the support for unique partnership. . . . But the idea was better than the language.'
74. As Barry (2002, p.228) colourfully illustrated, '[e]ven in Sydney, coverage was still patchy at best. Calls would drop out and there were buildings in the CBD where you couldn't get a signal at all. . . . It became a habit for the directors of the company to ring in and complain that they kept losing calls while driving to work.'
75. Also refer to Jay (2001, pp.29–37) in *Collapse Incorporated* for a brief review of the One.Tel story.
76. For instance, 'new employees there were by the hundred, because the attrition rate was appalling. When one new call centre manager arrived in early 1997 she found it was running at 100 per cent a year—which meant the entire staff was changing every 12 months. Later it got far worse than that' (Barry, 2002, p.104).
77. As indicated in Barry (2002).
78. The UK-based enterprise CE Heath plc held 44% while Australian based CE Heath directors held 11 %. Reportedly, of a total 167 million issued shares, three directors held 19.2 million (Williams with 12.8 million, Cassidy 3 million and Sturesteps 3 million).
79. 'Winterthur Holdings Australia Limited was a majority-owned subsidiary of a Swiss insurer, Winterthur Swiss Insurance Company' (Owen, 2003, p.4) under "The life and Times of HIH."
80. Ibid, p.5.
81. See 'Williams Warned About HIH's Financial Problems' (2001, p.4). Author's name not available.
82. Ibid. Also Baskett (2001, p.20) remarked, 'HIH's financial position was worse by a considerable margin than what was stated in the balance sheet.'
83. See MacDougall (2001, p.9).
84. Refer to *AAP General News*, Australia (2001). Also at www.education.elibrary.com.au.
85. See *HIH Annual Report* (2000, p.7) under "General Information."
86. Details from the APRA submission, *HIH Royal Commission* (2002).
87. Available at www.hihroyalcom.gov.au.

NOTES TO CHAPTER 6

1. The case illustrates, in a practical sense, the theoretical discussion in Chapter 4. Also refer to Clarke *et al.* (2003, p.247) for details on 'groups of holding, subsidiary and associated companies . . . [that] have proven to be a mechanism of financial obfuscation [the unclear; the unnecessarily complicated].'
2. In the Supreme Court of South Australia, *Duke Group Ltd. (in Liq) v. Pilmer & Ors*, Judgement of the Honourable Justice Mulligan, January 30, 1998.
3. Appendix A6 provides background details to the case.
4. Refer to Mullighan (1998, pp.66–71) for a detailed discussion of events.
5. 'During the financial year . . . ended 31st March 1987, the Western United Group made an operating profit before tax of a little over $1.67m [the previous year total profit was reportedly $631,924]. The net assets of the group . . . were about $8.3m [the previous year net assets reportedly were $10.8m]. The issue[d] capital of Western United had risen from 10,967,139 shares [1986] . . . to 16,166,184 shares at 31st March 1987' (Mullighan, 1998,

p.35). For additional details, see Mullighan (1998, p.31). Also refer to s.3.14 of the court transcript (Mullighan, 1998, pp.42–45) for further discussion on Western United's 1986–1987 annual report figures.

6. As reported in the court transcript (refer to Mullighan, 1998, p.72).
7. Refer to discussion in Chapters 2 and 4 on conventional accounting practice and its output, especially that which is used to ascertain an entity's dated financial state.
8. AASB138 (IAS38) *Intangible Assets* defines same as 'an identifiable non-monetary asset without physical substance' (para.8). Its identifiability is explained at para.12 and para.24 requires that the 'intangible asset shall be measured initially at cost.'
9. AASB140 (IAS40), para.5 defines '*Fair value* [as] the amount for which an asset could be exchanged between knowledgeable, willing parties in an arm length's transaction' the standard now allows for a choice of measurement after recognition—fair value model or the cost model at para.32A; AASB116 (IAS16) defines *fair value likewise at para.6* and AASB139 (IAS39): *Financial Instruments: Recognition and Measurement* emphasises the use of fair values—further explained at para.AG69.
10. Refer to Mullighan (1998, p.341).
11. Such intangibles have no apparent active market and, hence (in a monetary sense), no easily defined objective "value." IAS38, para.67 denotes: '[I]t is uncommon for an active market . . . to exist for an intangible asset . . . an active market may exist for freely-transferable taxi licences, fishing licences or production quotas. However, an active market cannot exist for brands, newspaper mastheads, music and film publishing rights, patents or trademarks, because each such asset is unique.' Such is the case for goodwill.
12. In the court transcript, it was reported that Nelson Wheeler stated, '[t]he skills and experience of existing management are considered critical in operating performance and this valuation is contingent upon their retention' (p.342).
13. Consider the unfolding of events as reported in the court transcript, in particular the telephone campaign that was instigated to persuade shareholders to accept Kia Ora's takeover offer. Mullighan (1998, p.116) asserted that '[t]his telephone campaign is clear evidence of those controlling Kia Ora being determined to ensure the success of the takeover from which they would benefit personally.'
14. For the same period of time, Mullighan (1998, p.11) stated that the annual reports 'do not show any shares owned by Harold Abbott or associated company.'
15. See Mullighan (1998, p.130).
16. Based on evidence before the court, Mullighan (1998, p.122) asserted 'that the stockbroking business, the merchant bank and the insurance business, acquired in the takeover, were experiencing financial difficulties and the [Kalgoorlie] assay business had suffered a downturn . . . [moreover] . . . the evidence discloses that Kia Ora and its subsidiaries were experiencing considerable financial difficulties.'
17. Mullighan (1998, p.122) where Somes reportedly stated 'it was desirable to increase the capital base of the bank to encourage depositors because of nervousness in the market after the earlier collapse of the Rothwell's Bank in Western Australia which happened after the share market crash.'
18. In addition, Mullighan (1998, p.127) stated, 'Kia Ora also gave a warranty that at the completion of the takeover it would have cash at hand of not less than $16 million.'
19. Furthermore that '[c]learly, Harold Abbott, Gary Abbott and Schneider-Paas decided to get out of Kia Ora and take what they could get for themselves.

When they made that decision is not known. Given that the reverse takeover was being undertaken soon after the takeover of Western United had been completed, it is possible that it was first considered sometime before' (Mulighan, 1998, p.130).

20. Refer, for instance, to Lampe, *Business Age* (October 22, 1994, p.31) and related articles.
21. Investigations into the 2001 collapses of One.Tel and HIH Ltd. further demonstrate this point and also show that such issues are not "industry specific." For instance, 'ASIC's investigations [re:One.Tel] . . . focused on issues of market disclosure and governance (duties of officers and directors)' (Media Release 01/343, September 24, 2001). However, the Australian Prudential Regulatory Authority's (APRA) submission to the HIH Royal Commission at www.hihroyalcom.gov.au advocated increased prudential standards—required to supplement deficiencies inherent in conventional accounting standards.
22. Refer to BCL Prospectus (1988, p.16).
23. Refer to Krasnoff and Ansett (1999, p.143).
24. Ibid, further details at p.147.
25. Refer to Appendix A6.2 for additional details on the entities interrelationships.
26. Refer to Owen (2003, s.7, p.5).
27. Further details contained in the managing director's review, see the Burns Philp Annual Report, 2003.
28. See the Burns Philp Annual Report (2003, Managing Director's review).
29. ASIC (1998, pp.1–52).
30. 'Following the integration of Goodman Fielder, Burns Philp prepared to complete its exit from the herbs and spices market. In March 2004 the company announced its intention to sell off its North American holdings, by then grouped under the Tone's name. In the meantime, the company had achieved new growth for its yeast business, buying up the Fleischmann business in South America that had been owned by Kraft Foods. The transformed Burns Philp now looked forward to smoother sailing in the new century.'Refer to http://www.fundinguniverse.com/company-histories/Burns-Philp-amp;-Company-Ltd-Company-History.html for further details—quote included in last paragraph of transcript there available. Accessed June 2011.
31. 'As the company entered the herbs and spice market it was a niche market, fragmented and open to rationalisation opportunities. As a consequence, the opportunities presented were complementary to Burns Philp's proven and successful yeast strategy. Furthermore in many instances, it enabled the company to be a single source supplier to many customers for their food ingredients products' (in Alan McGregor's speech at the Burns Philp AGM, Nov. 5, 1997). See also the ASIC Report of the Investigation into Burns Philp & Company Limited (1998, p.3).
32. Similarities to be repeated on a much grander scale in the Enron (2001) debacle.
33. Refer to the ASIC Report on Burns Philp (1998, pp.12–15) for details of its separate tradename valuation methods.
34. Ibid.
35. Refer to Burns Philp Annual Report (1996, note 13a—Independent valuations).
36. Ibid. Statements of Profit and Loss for the year ended June 30.
37. See Burns Philp Annual Report (1997, note 13).
38. Chambers (1966) spoke of adaptive behaviour in and by business; the idea of financial flexibility is in line with this concept.

39. The monograph of Loftus and Miller (2000) *Reporting on Solvency and Cash Condition* is extensively referenced in this work and acknowledged for its significant contribution to continued debate on financial reporting.
40. The deliberations of Chapters 2, 3 and 5 are relevant to the discussion in this part.
41. In 1994, the Group reported a provision for business closure and rationalisation of $15.4 million (Annual Report, 1994, note 17).
42. For instance, 'On 21 June 2002 the Group raised US $400 million of new senior subordinated debt in the US. This debt has a term of 10 years, maturing in 2012 . . . the Group's debt being restructured . . . its earliest maturity is now 2006 with the balance maturing in 2012' (Burns Philp Annual Report, 2002, Managing Director's Review of operations).
43. Incorporated in South Australia on October 4, 1953.
44. It was 'alleged that each of them was in breach of his duties as a director of Kia Ora in various ways which caused or contributed to the loss which . . . Kia Ora sustained by reason of the takeover,' and furthermore, '[t]he plaintiff, in large measure, adopted the allegations against the directors and during the course of the trial amended the statement of claim to also seek damages from them. In the end result the plaintiff claims the same damages against all of the defendants' (Mullighan, 1998, p.2).
45. For instance, from BRACS for car and truck rental operations as exceeds 3% of the related revenues; from other licensees for car and truck rental operations in Australia as exceeds 5% of the related revenues; from BRACS and other licensees in Australia for other rental and other services as exceeds 1% of the related revenues; and from licensees outside Australia as exceeds 1% of the related revenues, after deducting amounts collected on behalf of Budget Corporation Limited (US) and Budget Equities Pty. Limited (BCL Prospectus, 1988, p.31, para.14).
46. Available at http://www.asic.gov.au under "Contents" on the "What's New Page." Also refer to CASAC (2000) *Corporate Groups Final Report.*
47. BCL Prospectus (1988, p.29).
48. Furthermore, CASAC (2000, p.22) explained that 'directors would breach their fiduciary duties if they sought to put the interest of the corporate group above that of their companies. Directors of a group company may face difficulties in balancing their fiduciary duties to that company against the overall commercial and financial interests of the group. This problem may arise, for instance, where directors of a particular company consider that to advance, or preserve, the corporate group requires the financial support or sacrifice of their company by providing other group companies with loans, assets, securities or guarantees' (at paras. 1.57, 1.58).

NOTES TO CHAPTER 7

1. See, for instance, Kirk (2006), Dean and Clarke (2005), Chambers (1999) and Wolnizer and Chambers (1991).
2. Refer to the SEC's Study on Mark-to-Market accounting (2008); also, AASB 139: *Financial Instruments Recognition and Measurement* from para.43 (IAS 139—the International equivalent); and AASB 1023: *General Insurance Contracts* (para.15).
3. Refer to AASB Framework (paras.99–101).
4. Refer to www.camac.gov.au.
5. Refer to CAMAC (2003, ss.1.7, 1.8, 1.12) under 'Principles for effective corporate rehabilitation.'

6. See the *Corporations Amendment (Insolvency) Bill 2007 (Cth).*
7. Also refer to Clarke *et al.* (1997/2003).
8. See the Cole Royal Commission *Final Report*, Vol. 8, "Reform—National Issues, Part 2," Chapter 12 on Phoenix Companies, p.115. The Royal Commission at that time was into the Building and Construction Industry.
9. Martin (2007, footnote 4, p.3) quoted the publication as: 'ASC research paper, *Phoenix Companies and Insolvent Trading,* No. 95/01 (July 1996).' That publication and phoenix activity statistics on small to medium businesses were also quoted by Coburnl (2003).
10. Refer, for instance, to articles by Adele Ferguson as reported on December 11, 2010, "A free rise from the ashes of others," *The Sydney Morning Herald*, and "The phoenix dilemma," *The Age*, Melbourne.
11. Refer to Ferguson (*Sydney Morning Herald*, December 11, 2010, p.3).
12. Available at www.treasurygov.au/contentitem.asp?NavId=&ContentID=1647 accessed 22 March 2011.
13. See Ferguson (*The Age*, December 11, 2010; *Sydney Morning Herald*, December 11, 2010, p.3). Supporting details at Dun & Bradstreet, for instance, http://dnb.com.au/Header/News/News_Archive/2009/Australia_experiences_a_dramatic_spike_in_directors_associated_with_multiple_business_failures/printdl_5643.aspx?printView=true accessed April 2011.
14. Refer, for example, to the One.Tel saga.
15. Roach (2010, p.93) stated, '*Innocent phoenixing* occurs when a business comes under financial stress due to poor (as opposed to deliberately fraudulent) management decisions, inadequate record keeping and poor cash flow and financial management techniques. In some industries, such as building and construction, phoenixing is considered an *occupational hazard* in that once the business has collapsed, the operator's skill set drives them back into the same industry, where they are at high risk of failing again. They are affectively locked in to the industry by their skill set. However, it is *careerist offenders* that pose the most serious concern for tax administrators [and arguably others].'
16. Refer to Chapters 3, 4, 5 and 6 and sources therein as well as Duns (2007).
17. Ferguson (2010).
18. In Kirk's (2006, p.225) study,: 'The shareholder group was confined to the top forty shareholders of listed companies in New Zealand. As such this excluded smaller shareholders, and would be expected to include a higher proportion of institutional and sophisticated shareholders than the total population of New Zealand shareholders.'
19. 'The finding also partially counters the earlier conclusions by Higson and Blake (1993) and Parker (1994) that the "true and fair view" concept contributes to deharmonization and by Blake *et al.* (1996) that it leads to "declustering" ' (Kirk, 2006, p.225).
20. Switzer (2010).
21. Previously discussed in Chapter 1; also refer to Chapter 2 on financial tests of [in]solvency.
22. *Hall v. Poolman* [2007] NSWSC 1330 at [261]–[275]
23. Refer to Ferguson (2010).
24. 'Most of the Group's business was in plantation forestry to supply woodchips for the pulp and paper industry, but in the 2000s it diversified into high-value timbers, beef cattle, olives, viticulture, and almond production' (Wikipedia, Great Southern Group, p.1) available at http://en.wilipedia.org/wiki/Great_Southern_Group accessed April 2011.
25. DatAnalysis online at http://0-datanalysis.morningstar.com.au.alpha2.latrobe.edu.au/af/company Also, 'Since 1992 the Company's emphasis was on the establishment of Tasmanian blue gum plantations, a preferred species

which provides woodchip for the production of high quality paper (for photocopying, facsimiles, magazines, etc). With its short rotation time of approximately 10 years and a high fibre yield it provided a superior alternative to the harvesting of native forests for woodchip' (Ibid.).

26. Refer to Wikipedia "Great Southern Group" available at http://en.wikipedia.org/wiki/Great_Southern_Group accessed April 2011.
27. At Wikipedia online: Great Southern Group, under Business Activities. Further details are available in the annual reports of Great Southern (2007, 2008).
28. Ibid. Under "Business Activities."
29. Ibid. Ultimately, investor benefits were questionable: 'Returns to investors comprised a tax deduction in the year in which they bought the products, and [at] point of harvest 10–12 years later for plantations, "and up to 23 years for horticultural projects such as almonds." Great Southern would [also] deduct management fees from the final sale value' under "Business Activities" at http://en.wikipedia.org/wiki/Great_Southern_Group accessed April 2011.
30. Ibid.
31. Ibid. Further details in Great Southern's annual report (2006).
32. Ibid.
33. Ibid.
34. Ibid., under "Fall." See also Grigg (2009).
35. See Wikipedia p.1 at http://enwikipedia.org/wiki/Great_Southern_Group accessed April 2011.
36. Ibid.
37. Refer to LaFrenz (2009).
38. Refer to DatAnalysis "Morningstar" under 'Corporate Details.'
39. Ibid., under 'Business Summary.'
40. See LaFrenz (2009).
41. Ibid. Available at www.afr.com
42. Wikipedia Great Southern Group online (URL above) under "Analysing the Group's failure."
43. Refer to ASIC (2007, p.2), "Statement on Fincorp."
44. See "Fincorp a painful lesson on risk" available at www.eurekareport.com.au/iis,nsf/ak/Uv6qBt?
45. Ibid., p.1.
46. Ibid.
47. As reported by Klan (2007)available at www.theaustralian.com.au/business/property/retirees-lose-all-in-fincorp-collapse accessed April 2011.
48. Refer to 'Fincorp holders to get half back,' *The Australian*, July 27, 2007. For instance, sale of assets and creditors' approval secured noteholders would eventually recoup half their investments.
49. Reportedly, 'Fincorp, a Sydney company, went into receivership on March 23, this year owing $200 million to individuals and a further $95 million to banks and financial houses' John (2007).
50. Ibid.
51. Ibid.
52. See Khan (2007).
53. Refer to ASIC (2007, p.2) for further details.
54. Refer to KordaMentha (2007).
55. See Thomson (2011).
56. See Lamont (2011).
57. See ASIC media release 11–78AD, 'Fincorp director imprisoned for dishonesty offences', Friday 8 April, 2011, at www.asicgov.au/asic.nsf/byheadline/11-78AD accessed April 2011.

58. At http://en.wikipedia.org/wiki/Allco_Finance_Group accessed May 5, 2011.
59. Ibid., and Murray (2006) as below.
60. Refer to Murray (2006) available at http://www.theage.com.au/news/business/recordallco-decision-to-go-to-shareholders/2006/05/02/1146335732273.html
61. Details from ASIC's database available at http://www2.search.asic.gov.au/cgi-bin/gns030c?acn=077_721_129&juris=9&hdtext=ACN&srchsrc=1 accessed May 19, 2011.
62. 'Steven Sherman and Peter Gothard were appointed Receivers of the . . . Companies on 4 November, 2008.' Further details available at www.ferrierhodgson.com under "Allco Finance Group Limited (Receivers & Managers Appointed)," accessed May 5, 2011.
63. For further details, see Boyd (2008).
64. Reported by the lending central team (LC Team), Wednesday, May 27, 2009 available at http://www.lendingcentral.com/2009/05/27/allco-finance-group-placed-in-liquidation-by-creditors/
65. Ibid.
66. Ibid.
67. Letter from Ferrier Hodgson to the employees of the Allco Group November 2, 2010, available at http://www.ferrierhodgson.com/Current%20Matters/Corporate%20Recovery%20Matters/Allco%20Finance%20Group%20Limited.aspx
68. Johnson (2008).
69. John (2010).
70. "The Allco Show Comes to Town," March 25, 2010, available at http://www.abc.net.au/news/stories/2010/03/24/2854636.htm accessed June 6, 2011.
71. See John (2009).
72. Refer to Boyd (2008).
73. Refer to Lannin (2010).
74. Ibid. Also, Boyd (2008) provided a colourful description of events.

NOTES TO CHAPTER 8

1. Refer to Act, s297. Also, s.7 "Financial reporting and assurance" of Justice Neville Owen's final report on the HIH Royal Commission.
2. See, for example, Clarke *et al.* (1997/2003); Chambers (1973b) and previous chapters herein.
3. ASIC (2002) Annual Report, *Tackling ethics and governance*, s.6 "Description of ASIC directorates" under enforcement results.
4. Ibid.
5. A term used by Clarke *et al.* (1997/2003).
6. Ibid., pp.315–317.
7. West (2003) provides an in depth thesis on "Professionalism and Accounting Rules."
8. As discussed throughout this book, but particularly in Chapters 2, 3 and 4.
9. Refer, for instance, to Chapter 1 and s.95A of the Australian *Corporations Act 2001*.
10. Equivalent to IASB Framework.
11. See discussion in Chapter 2.
12. Refer to AASB101 and its international equivalent IAS101—Presentation of Financial Statements.
13. Refer to earlier analyses in Chapters 2 through 4.

14. For instance, as referenced herein and throughout earlier studies, including Chambers (1973b), Wolnizer (1987), Clarke *et al.* (2003) and West (2003).
15. For instance, Littleton (1956).
16. See Chambers (1986, p.184).
17. Ibid., p.181.
18. Ibid., p.191.
19. Refer, for instance, to the work of Chambers and Wolnizer (1990, 1991).
20. 'Where [for instance] compliance with accounting standards does not present a true and fair view the Bill extends disclosure from the financial statements to the directors' report. The directors report must discuss the reason why, and indicate where additional information can be found' (CLERP 9, *Implications for Australian Business*, available at www.pwcglobal.com/Extweb/manissue.nsf). The December version of the Bill suggested amendments to the existing Corporations Law to strengthen the position that the true and fair view criterion is an effective override were deleted from the October draft of the Bill. In the March 2004, *Proof* Committee Hansard, Professor Dean (CFS.53) remarked, 'you would expect to have found somewhere . . . reasons for why the JCPAA recommendations were not deemed appropriate. To us, it seemed a totally appropriate way to reinforce the significance of the true and fair view override.'
21. The Sarbanes–Oxley Act was passed by Congress in the US in July 2002, with particular emphasis on the concept of the 'true and fair' override.
22. See Beveridge (1950/1957, p.40).
23. Also refer to Chambers (1955, 1957, 1961, 1973b, 1991, 1999). Full details can be found in the Bibliography.

Bibliography

Ackoff, R. L. (1953) *The Design of Social Research,* University of Chicago Press, Chicago.

Adelberg, A. H. and Farrelly, G. E. (1989) 'Measuring the Meaning of Financial Statement Terminology: A psycholinguistics approach', *Accounting and Finance,* May, pp.33–59.

Aitken, M. and Czernkowski, R. (1991) 'Organizational Change within the Stockbroking Industry: A contracting perspective', *Abacus,* Vol.27, No.2, September, pp.97–116.

Alexander, S. (1966) *Space,Time and Deity: The Gifford lectures at Glasgow, 1916–1918,* Macmillan Publishing Company, London.

Alexander, S. S. (1950) 'Income Measurement in a Dynamic Economy', *Five Monographs on Business Income,* The Study Group on Business Income, The American Institute of Certified Public Accountants, New York.

American Institute of Accountants (1939) 'Extensions of Auditing Procedure', *The Journal of Accountancy,* Vol.67, No.6, June, pp.342–349.

American Institute of Accountants (1943) 'Depreciation', *The Journal of Accountancy,* Vol.76, No.6, December, pp.484–487.

Ames, J. and Lettner, M. (1990) *Ontario Business Corporations Act,* Annotated, Butterworths, Canada.

Anderson, D. S. (1961) *The Accountant's Magazine,* The Institute of Chartered Accountants of Scotland, May, in Chambers, R. J. (1995) *An Accounting Thesaurus: 500 years of accounting,* Pergamon, Elsevier Science Ltd., Oxford, UK.

Andersen and Co. (1987) *Accounting Standards for Business Enterprises Throughout the World,* Arthur Andersen and Co., Chicago.

Anthony, R.N. (2004) *Rethinking the Rules of Financial Accounting: Examining the rules for proper reporting,* McGraw-Hill, New York.

Australasian Association for Phenomenology and Social Philosophy (1990) 'Proceedings /1990 Conference of the Australian Association for Phenomenology and Social Philosophy', edited by Jocelyn Dunphy and Purusottama Bilimoria, Melbourne, Victoria.

Avery, H. G. (1953) 'Accounting as a Language', *The Accounting Review,* Vol.28, No.1, January, pp.83–87.

Bacon, F. (1620/1891) *Novum Orgamum* (1620), J. Devey ed., Bell, London, (1891) Listed in Chambers, R. J. (1995) *An Accounting Thesaurus: 500 years of accounting,* Pergamon, Elsevier Science Ltd., New York, s.854, p.805.

Bagranoff, N. A. (1990) 'The Semantic Differential: A prescription for use in accounting research', *Journal of Accounting Literature,* Vol. 9, pp.65–80.

Bagranoff, N. A., Houghton, K. A., and Hronsky, J. (1994) 'The Structure of Meaning in Accounting', *Behavioral Research in Accounting,* American Accounting Association; Item 10504753 and 9510180828, 1994 Supplement Conference Papers, Vol.6., pp.35–57.

Ball, R. and Brown, P. (1968) 'An Empirical Evaluation of Accounting Income Numbers', *Journal of Accounting Research,* Autumn.

Barry, P. (2002) *Rich Kids,* Bantam Books, Milsons Point, NSW.

Barton, A. (2000) 'Reflections of an Australian Contemporary: The complementarity of entry and exit price current value accounting systems', *Abacus,* Vol.36, No.3, pp.298–312.

Barton, A. D. (1975/1984) *The Anatomy of Accounting,* University of Queensland, St. Lucia, 3rd edition.

Beveridge, W. I. B. (1950/1957) *The Art of Scientific Investigation,* revised edition, Random House, New York.

Beer, S. (1959) *Cybernetics and Management,* London, English Universities.

Bentley, H. C. (1911) *The Science of Accounts,* Ronald Book Co., New York.

Bierman, H. and Drebin, A. R. (1978) *Financial Accounting: An introduction,* WB Saunders Company, Philadelphia, 3rd edition. Originally published 1968, Macmillan, New York.

Bochenski, J. M. (1965) *The Methods of Contemporary Thought,* D. Reidel Publishing Company, Dordrecht-Holland.

Boulding, K. E. (1950/1962) *A Reconstruction of Economics,* John Wiley and Sons Inc., Science Editions, New York.

Boulding, K. E. (1970) *Economics as a Science,* McGraw-Hill, New York.

Bradbury, M. E. (2000) 'Issues in the Drive to Measure Liabilities at Fair Value', *Australian Accounting Review,* Vol.11, No.2, pp.19–25.

Briloff, A. J. (1972) *Unaccountable Accounting,* Harper and Row, New York.

Briloff, A. J. (1976) *More Debits than Credits: The burnt investor's guide to financial statements,* Harper and Row, New York.

Briloff, A. J. (1981) *The Truth about Corporate Accounting,* Harper and Row, New York.

Bronowski, J. (1959/1965) *Science and Human Values,* Harper & Row, New York, 2nd edition. First Harper Torchbook edition published 1959, copyright by J. Bronowski 1956.

Brooks, C. (ed) (1933) *The Royal Mail Case,* William Hodge, Glasgow.

Brown, H. (1987) *The Wisdom of Science,* Cambridge University Press, Cambridge.

Brown, R. G. and Johnston, K. S. (1963) *Paciolo on Accounting,* McGraw-Hill Book Company, Inc., New York.

Budget Corporation Limited (BCL) (1988) *Prospectus* dated November 20, 1988, that expired on May 20, 1989. Lodged with and registered by the Corporate Affairs Commission, N.S.W. Australia.

Burns Philp and Company Limited, *Annual Reports* for the period 1992 to 2003 inclusive.

Burns Philp and Company Limited, 'Historical Financial Summaries', *Annual Reports,* 1995, 2000 and 2002.

Burns Philp and Company Limited (1992–2003) 'Corporate Governance Reports', in the Company's *Annual Reports.*

Burton, J. (1974–1975) 'Fair Presentation: Another view', *The Emmanuel Saxe Distinguished Lectures in Accounting,* City University of New York, February 18, 1975, available at http://newman.baruch.cuny.edu/digital/saxe/saxe_1974/burton_75.htm

Campbell, D. (1992) *International Corporate Insolvency Law,* Butterworths, London.

Campbell, N. R. (1921/1952) *What Is Science?,* reprinted Dover Publications, New York, 1952.

Cann, R. (1993) *Formal Semantics: An introduction,* Cambridge University Press, Cambridge, UK.

Canning, J. B. (1929) *The Economics of Accountancy: A critical analysis of accounting theory,* The Ronald Press Company, New York.

Canning, J. B. (1931) 'Cost of Production and Market Price', *The Accounting Review,* AAA, Vol.6, No.3, September, pp.161–164.

Carnegie, G. and Wolnizer, P. W. (1999) 'Unravelling the Rhetoric about the Financial Reporting of Public Collections as Assets', *Australian Accounting Review,* Vol.9, No.1, pp.16–21.

Carnegie, G. D. and Napier, C. J. (1996) 'Critical and Interpretive Histories: Insights into accounting's present and future through its past', *Accounting, Auditing & Accountability Journal,* Vol.9, No.3, pp.7–39.

Carroll, J. B. (ed) (1956) *Language, Thought and Reality: Selected writings of Benjamin Lee Whorf,* MIT Press, Cambridge, MA.

Carsberg, B. (1982) in Sterling R. and Lemke K. (eds) *Maintenance of Capital: Financial versus physical,* Houston Scholars Book Co., Houston, TX, pp.59–74.

Carter, E. M. (1910) 'What Is an Annual Balance Sheet?', *The Accountant,* UK, October, pp.560–566.

Carter, R. N. (1923/1956) *Advanced Accounts,* Pitman, London.

Center for Advanced Research in Phenomenology (2000) 'What Is Phenomenology? Seven Widely Accepted Features of the Phenomenological Approach', CARP, Inc., available at www.phenomenologycenter.org/phenom.htm

Chambers, R. J. (1955) 'Blueprint for a Theory of Accounting', *Accounting Research,* pp.17–25.

Chambers, R. J. (1957) 'Detail for a Blueprint', *The Accounting Review,* April, Vol.32, No.2, pp.206–215.

Chambers, R. J. (1961) *Towards a General Theory of Accounting,* Australian Society of Accountants, Sydney, Australia.

Chambers, R. J. (1965) 'Measurement in Accounting', *Journal of Accounting Research,* Vol.3, No.1, Spring, pp.32–62.

Chambers, R. J. (1966) *Accounting Evaluation and Economic Behaviour,* Prentice-Hall, Englewood Cliffs, NJ, reprinted Scholars Book Company, Houston, TX, 1974.

Chambers, R. J. (1972) 'Quo Vado?', *The Chartered Accountant in Australia,* August, pp.13–15.

Chambers, R. J. (1973a) 'Accounting Principles and the Law', *Australian Business Law Review,* June, pp.112–129.

Chambers, R. J. (1973b) *Securities and Obscurities: A case for reform of the law of company accounts,* Melbourne, Gower; reproduced 1986 as *Accounting in Disarray,* Garland Publishing Inc., New York.

Chambers, R. J. (1976) 'The Possibility of a Normative Accounting Standard', *The Accounting Review,* July, pp.646–652. Response to J. S. Demski (1973) 'The General Impossibility of Normative Accounting Standards', *The Accounting Review,* October.

Chambers, R. J. (1979a) 'Canning's the Economics of Accountancy—After 50 Years', *Accounting Review,* Vol.54, No.4, October, pp.764–775.

Chambers, R. J. (1979b) 'Usefulness—The Vanishing Premise in Accounting Standard Setting', *Abacus,* Vol.15, No.2, December, pp.71–92.

Chambers, R. J. (1982) 'Edwards and Bell on Income Measurement in Retrospect', *Abacus,* Vol.18, No.1, June, pp.3–39.

Chambers, R. J. (1986) *Accounting in Disarray: A case for reform of the law of company accounts,* Garland Publishing Inc., New York; originally published 1973 as *Securities and Obscurities,* Gower Press, Melbourne.

Chambers, R. J. (1986) *Financial Management,* Law Book Company, Sydney, Australia, 4th edition.

Chambers, R. J. (1991) *Foundations of Accounting,* Deakin University Press, Geelong, Victoria, Australia.

Chambers, R. J. (1995) *An Accounting Thesaurus: 500 years of accounting,* Pergamon, Elsevier Science Ltd., Oxford, UK.

Chambers, R. J. (1998) 'Wanted: Foundations of accounting measurement', *Abacus*, Vol. 34, No.1, March, pp.36–47.

Chambers, R. J. (1999) 'The Case for Simplicity in Accounting', *Abacus*, June, pp.121–137.

Chambers, R. J. (2000) 'Common Sense, Science and Technology', *Abacus*,Vol.36, pp.327–333.

Chambers, R. J. and Falk. H. (1985) 'Serviceability of Financial Information: A survey', *Canadian Certified Journal Accountants' Research Foundation*, Vancouver, Vancouver, Canada.

Chambers, R. J. and Wolnizer, P. W. (1990) 'A True and Fair View of Financial Position', *Company and Securities Law Journal*, December, pp.353–368.

Chambers, R. J. and Wolnizer, P. W. (1991) 'A True and Fair View of Position and Results: The historical background', *Accounting, Business and Financial History*, Vol.1, No.2, pp.197–213.

Chartered Institute of Management Accountants (The) (1998) 'Corporate Governance: History, practice and future', Executive Summary, CIMA Publishing, London, available at www.cimaglobal.com

Chase, S. (1956) Foreword, in Whorf, Benjamin Lee (1956/1962), *Language, Thought, and Reality*, edited (and introduction) by John B. Carroll, MIT Press, Cambridge, MA.

Cherry, C. (1957) *On Human Communication*, reprinted Science Edition Inc., New York, 1961. .

Childs, W. H. (1949) *Consolidated Financial Statements*, Cornell University Press, Ithaca.

Clarke, F. and Dean, G. (1993) 'Law and Accounting—The Separate Legal Entity Principle and Consolidation Accounting', *Australian Business Law Review*, Vol.21, No.4, August, pp.246–270.

Clarke, F. L. (1996) 'A Treasury of Accounting Thought—R. J. Chambers' an Accounting Thesaurus: 500 years of accounting', *Abacus*, Vol.32, No.1, March, pp.111–117.

Clarke, F. L. and Dean, G. (2001) 'Corporate Collapses Analysed', part 11, chapter 3, in *Collapse Incorporated: Tales, safeguards and responsibilities of corporate Australia*, CCH Australia Limited, North Ryde, NSW, pp.72–98.

Clarke, F. L. and Dean, G. (2001) 'Distressed Businesses—Predicting Failure', part 111, chapter 6, in *Collapse Incorporated: Tales, safeguards and responsibilities of corporate Australia*, CCH Australia, North Ryde, NSW, pp.148–183.

Clarke, F. L. and Dean, G. (2007) *Indecent Disclosure: Gilding the corporate lily*, Cambridge University Press.

Clarke, F. L., Dean, G., and Houghton, E. (1995) 'Cross Guarantees and Negative Pledges: A preliminary analysis', *Australian Accounting Review*, Vol.5, No.1, pp.48–63.

Clarke, F. L., Dean, G., Oliver, K. G. (1997/2003) *Corporate Collapse: Regulatory, accounting and ethical failure*, Cambridge University Press; revised and reprinted 2003 with a new sub-title: 'Accounting, regulatory and ethical failure'.

Clarke, F. L., Dean, G., and Wolnizer, P. W. (2002) 'HIH—the Tyranny of Surprise', submission to the HIH Royal Commission, available at www.hihroyalcom.gov.au

Coburn, N. (2003) *Coburn's Insolvent Trading: Global Investment Fraud & Corporate Investigations*, Thomson Lawbook Company, Sydney, Australia, 2nd edition.

Cohen, M. R. (1957) *A Preface to Logic*, Meridian Books, Sydney, Australia. First published September 1956, second printing December 1957. Reprinted by arrangement with Henry Holt and Company, Inc. Copyright 1944 by Henry Holt and Company, Inc.

Cole, W. M. (1908/1915) *Accounts, Their Construction and Interpretation*, Houghton Mifflin, Boston.

Colinson, R. (1683) *Idea Rationaira*, Lindsay and others, Edinburgh, in Chambers, R. J. (1995) *An Accounting Thesaurus: 500 years of accounting*, Pergamon, Elsevier Science Ltd., Oxford, UK.

Companies and Securities Advisory Committee (2000) *Corporate Groups Final Report*, Sydney, NSW, May, available at www.asic.gov.au/publications CASAC papers.

Corrigan, M. (1992) 'Accounting Relief for "Closed Group" Companies', *Australian Accountant*, April, p.64.

Couchman, C. B. (1924) 'The Balance-Sheet: Its preparation, content and interpretation', *The Journal of Accountancy Incorporated*, pp.233–235.

Couchman, C. B. (1924/1982) *The Balance Sheet*, reprinted Garland Publishing Inc., New York, 1982.

Couper, C. T. (1879/1984) *Report of the Trial of the Directors and the Manager of the City of Glasgow Bank*, originally published as *Report of the Trial before the High Court of the Justiciary, Her Majesty's Advocate against the Directors and the Manager of the City of Glasgow Bank*, Edinburgh Publishing Company, Edinburgh, 1879, reprinted Garland Publishing Inc., New York, 1984.

Crosby, A. W. (1997) *The Measure of Reality: Quantification and Western society, 1250–1600*, Cambridge University Press, New York.

Cyert, R. M. and March, J. G. (1963) *A Behavioral Theory of the Firm*, Prentice-Hall, Englewood-Cliffs, NJ.

Davidson, J. and Moore, E. T. (1938/1958) *Mathematics*, The English Universities Press Ltd., London.

Davison, E. H. (1951) 'The Accounts Organization in a Large Industrial Concern', *The Accountant*, March, UK, pp.303–310.

Dean, G. and Clarke, F. (2003) 'An Evolving Conceptual Framework?', *Abacus*, Vol.39, No.3, pp.279–297.

Dean, G., Clarke, F., and Houghton, E. (2003) 'Survey: Working paper', presented at Monash University. Data will appear in a revised Working Paper in 2004. Further details may be obtained from the authors.

Dean, G., Clarke, F., and Margret, J. (2008) 'Solvency Solecisms: Corporate officers' problematic perceptions', *Australian Accounting Review*, Vol.18, No.1, March, pp.1–10.

Dickerson, R. W. V. (1966) *Accountants and the Law of Negligence*, Canadian Institute of Chartered Accountants, Toronto.

Dickinson, A. L. (1913/1975) *Accounting Practice and Procedure*, reprinted Scholars Book Company, 1975.

Dohr, J. L. (1941) 'On the Understanding of Accounting', *The Journal of Accountancy*, Vol.71, No.3, March, pp.200–205.

Dohr, J. L. (1950a) 'Materiality—What Does It Mean in Accounting?', *The Journal of Accountancy*,Vol.90, No.1, July, pp.54–56.

Dohr, J. L. (1950b) 'The Next Step in Depreciation Accounting', *The Journal of Accountancy*, Vol.89, No.2, February, pp.114–119.

Duhem, P. (1974) *The Aim and Structure of Physical Theory*, translated by Philip P. Wierner, Atheneum, New York.

Dun and Bradstreet (2009) 'Australia experiences a dramatic spike in directors associated with multiple business failures', November 17, available at http://dnb.com.au/Header/News/News_Archive/2009

Duns, J. (2000) ' "Insolvency": Problems of concept, definition and proof', *Australian Business Law Review*, Vol.28, No.1, February, pp.22–34.

Duns, J. (2007) 'Deterring Officer Misconduct: The impact of the proposed insolvency reforms on company officers', *Insolvency Law Journal*, Vol. 15, pp.173–183.

Editorial (1895) *The Accountant*, UK, in Chambers, R. J. (1995) *An Accounting Thesaurus: 500 years of accounting*, Pergamon, Elsevier Science Ltd., Oxford, UK.

Editorial (1946) *The Accountant*, UK, in Chambers, R. J. (1995) *An Accounting Thesaurus: 500 years of accounting,* Pergamon, Elsevier Science Ltd., Oxford, UK.

Editorial (1964) *Accountancy*, UK, in Chambers, R. J. (1995) *An Accounting Thesaurus: 500 years of accounting,* Pergamon, Elsevier Science Ltd., Oxford, UK.

Edwards, E. O. and Bell, P.W. (1961) *The Theory and Measurement of Business Income,* University of California Press, Berkeley.

Edwards, J. R. (1980) *British Company Legislation and Company Accounts, 1844–1976*, Arno Press, New York.

Edwards, J. R. (1985) 'The Origins and Evolution of the Double Account System: An example of accounting innovation', *Abacus,* Vol.21, No.1, March, pp.19–43.

Edwards, J. R. (1986) *Legal Regulation of British Company Accounts, 1836–1900,* Garland Publishing, Inc., New York.

Eisenberg, M. A. (1991/1993) *Corporations and Business Associations Statutes, Rules, and Forms,* The Foundation Press Inc., Westbury, New York.

Esquerre, P. J. (1914) *The Applied Theory of Accounts,* Ronald, New York.

Fairfax, L. M. (2004) 'Spare the Rod, Spoil the Director—Revitalizing Directors' Fiduciary Duty through Legal Liability', Vol.42, Houston Law Review (2005–2006), pp.393–415, available http://www.heinonline.org/HOL/CSV.csv?index=-journals&collection=journals

Ferguson, A. (2010) 'Insolvency Report Is in, Now for Some Action', *The Age,* September 15.

Ferguson, A. (2010) 'A Free Rise from the Ashes of Others', *Sydney Morning Herald*, December 11, p.3, available at http://www.smh.com.au/business/a-free-rise-from-the-ashes-of-others-20101210-18std.html accessed March 25, 2011.

Ferguson, A. (2010) 'The Phoenix Dilemma," *The Age*, Melbourne, December 11.

Fetter, F. A. (1937) 'Reformulation of the Concepts of Capital and Income in Economics and Accounting', *The Accounting Review,* American Accounting Association, March, pp.1–11.

Feyerabend, P. K. (1975/1982) *Against Method,* Verso, London.

Field, R. E. (1969) *Financial Reporting in the Extractive Industries,* ARS 11 of AICPA, New York.

Fisher, I. (1906/1965) *The Nature of Capital and Income,* reprinted Kelley, New York, 1965.

Fitzgerald, A. A. (1936) *Proceedings of the Australasian Congress on Accounting,* Melbourne, Congress.

Fitzgerald, A. A. (1956) *Analysis and interpretation of financial and operating statements*, Butterworths, Sydney.

Flew, A. (1953) *Logic and Language,* Blackwell, Oxford, second series.

Flew, A. (1975) *Thinking about Thinking,* Fontana/Collins, Glasgow.

Flint, D. (1982) *A True and Fair View in Company Accounts,* Gee, London.

Foulke, R. A. (1945) *Practical Financial Statement Analysis,* McGraw-Hill, New York.

Foster, G. (1978) *Financial Statement Analysis*, Prentice-Hall, Englewood Cliffs, NJ.

Frank, P. G. (1955/1962) 'Foundations of Physics', in *Foundations of the Unity of Science,* edited by O. Neurath, R. Carnap, and C. Morris, University of Chicago Press, Chicago and London.

Fremgen, J. R. (1968) 'The Going Concern Assumption: A critical appraisal', *Accounting Review*, October, pp.649–656.

Gadamer, H. G. (1960/1998) *Truth and method*, 2nd ed., Continuum, New York.

Gaffikin, M. J. R. (2000) 'Chambers on Methods of Inquiry', *Abacus,* Vol.36, No.3, pp.285–297.

Gilman, S. (1939) *Accounting Concepts of Profit*, Ronald Press Company, New York.

Glautier, M. (1983) 'Searching for Accounting Paradigms', *The Accounting Historians Journal,* Vol.10, No.1, Spring, pp.51–67.

Goldberg, L. and Hill, V. R. (1958) *The Elements of Accounting,* Melbourne University Press, Melbourne.

Goode, R. M. (1990) *Principles of Corporate Insolvency Law,* Sweet & Maxwell, London; Centre for Commercial Law Studies, Law Book Company, Sydney, Australia.

Gordon, R. A. (1948) 'Short-Period Price Determination in Theory and Practice', *American Economic Review,* Vol.38, June, pp.265–289.

Great Southern Plantation Limited, Annual Reports 1999 to 2008.

Grigg, A. (2009) 'How Timber Chief Cashed in Its Chips', *Australian Financial Review,* pp.1, 60.

Haberler, G. (1937/1941) *Prosperity and Depression: A theoretical analysis of cyclical movements,* League of Nations, Geneva, 3rd edition.Hamilton, R. (1788/1982) *An Introduction to Merchandise,* Elliot, Edinburgh, reprinted Garland, New York, 1982.

Haried, A. A. (1972) 'The Semantic Dimensions of Financial Statements', *Journal of Accounting Research,* Autumn, Vol.10, Issue 2, pp. 376–391.

Haried, A. A. (1973) 'Measurement of Meaning in Financial Reports' *Journal of Accounting Research,* Spring, pp.117–145.

Harris, J. (2007) 'Corporate Group Insolvencies: Charting the past, present and future of "pooling" arrangements', *The Insolvency Law Journal,* Vol.15, No.2, pp.78–99.

Hartshone, C. (1970) *Creative Synthesis and Philosophic Method,* Open Court Publishing Company, LaSalle, IL.

Hatfield, H. R. (1927/1971) *Accounting Its Principles and Problems*, Scholars Book Co., Houston, TX.

Hatfield, H. R. (1939/1982) *Accounting Principles through the Years*, Garland, New York.

Hawkins, D. F. (1971) *Corporate financial reporting*, Irwin, Homewood.

Hawkins, D. F. (1977) *Corporate Financial Reporting: Text and cases,* Richard D. Irwin Inc., Burr Ridge, IL.

Heath, L. C. (1978) *Financial Reporting and the Evaluation of Solvency,* Accounting Research Monograph 3, American Institute of Certified Public Accountants, New York.

Heath, L. C. (1987) 'Accounting, Communication, and the Pygmalion Syndrome', *Accounting Horizons,* Vol.1, No.1, March, pp.1–8.

Heidegger, M. (1927/1962) *Being and time*, Harper, New York.

Hill, J. (1995) 'Corporate Groups, Creditor Protection and Cross Guarantees: Australian perspectives', *The Canadian Business Law Journal,* Vol.24, No.3, February, pp.321–356.

Hilmer, F. G. (1993) *Strictly Boardroom,* Business Library, Melbourne.

HIH Insurance Limited (2000) Annual Report.

Hinton, P. R. (1972) 'Objectives of Financial Statements', *Accountancy,* UK, Vol.83, No.951, November, p.56.

Hobson, J. A. (1911/1914) *The Science of Wealth,* Williams and Norgate, London.

Hoffman, L. and Arden, M. H. (1983) *Accountancy,* UK, November, in Chambers, R. J. (1995) *An Accounting Thesaurus: 500 years of accounting,* Pergamon, Elsevier Science Ltd., Oxford, UK.

Hogan, W. P. (1997) 'Corporate Governance: Lessons from Barings', *Abacus,* Vol.33, No.1, pp.26–48.

Homans, G. C. and Curtis, C. P. (1934/1970) *An Introduction to Pareto,* Howard Fertig, New York.

Honsberger, J. Q. C. (1980) 'Failure to Pay One's Debts Generally as They Become Due: The experience of France and Canada', *American Bankruptcy Law Journal,* Vol.54, pp.153–163.

Horrocks, J. (1967) 'Are Published Balance Sheets Untrue and Unfair?', *The Australian Accountant,* Vol.37, October, pp.567–576.

Hospers, J. (1967) *An Introduction to Philosophical Analysis,* Routledge, London, 2nd edition. First published in Great Britain, 1956, by Routledge and Kegan, reprinted six times. Published 1953, 1967 by Prentice-Hall, Inc., Englewood Cliffs, NJ.

Houghton, K. A. (1988) 'The Measurement of Meaning in Accounting: A critical analysis of the principal evidence', *Accounting, Organizations and Society,* February, pp.263–280.

Houghton, K. A. and Messier, W. F. (1990) 'The Wording of Audit Reports: Its impact on the meaning of the message communicated', in *Accounting Research: Improvements in communication and monitoring,* edited by S. R. Moriarity, University of Oklahoma, Norman, OK.

Husserl, E. (1970) *The idea of phenomenology,* Nijhoff, The Hague, The Netherlands.

Institute of Actuaries of Australia (2002) *Submission to the HIH Royal Commission,* available at www.hihroyalcom.gov.au

Institute of Chartered Accountants of Scotland (The) (1988) *Making Corporate Reports Valuable,* Kogan Page Limited, London.

Institute of Chartered Accountants of England and Wales (1958) 'Presentation of Balance Sheet', N18, in Chambers, R. J. (1995) *An Accounting Thesaurus: 500 years of accounting,* Pergamon, Oxford, UK.

Jameson, M. (1988) *A Practical Guide to Creative Accounting,* Kogan Page, London.

Janicki, K. (1999) *Against Essentialism: Toward language awareness,* Lincom Europa, München, Germany.

Jay, C. (2001) 'The Day of Reckoning', in *Collapse Incorporated: Tales, safeguards and responsibilities of corporate Australia,* CCH Australia Limited, North Ryde, NSW, pp.10–40.

John, D. (2007) 'ASIC Admits Fincorp Gaffe', *Business Day, Sydney Morning Herald (SMH),* June 4, available at www.smh.com.au/news/business/asic-admits-fincorp-gaffe

John, D. (2009) 'Allco Finance Property Manager Bites the Dust', August 11, statement by Neil Singleton of PPB, available at http://www.smh.com.au/business/allco-finance-property-manager-bites-the-dust-20090810-efnt.html#ixzz1OShd2esq accessed May 2011.

John, D. (2010) 'Allco Hearings Reveal Failure at Every Level', March 29, available at http://www.smh.com.au/business/allco-hearings-reveal-failure-at-every-level-20100328-r54q.html#ixzz1OSpOUjPX accessed May 2011.

Johnson, S. (2008) 'Hangover Hits Allco', *The Intelligent Investor,* February 26, No.243, available at http://www.intelligentinvestor.com.au/articles/Allco-Finance-Group-Limited-AFG/Hangover-hits-Allco.cfm?articleID=390774 accessed May 5, 2011.

Jones, B. (1993) 'Insolvency and the Balance Sheet', *Insolvency Law and Practice,* Vol.9, No.5, pp.133–136.

Jones, S. and Aiken, M. (1994) 'The Significance of the Profit and Loss Account in Nineteenth-Century Britain: A reassessment', *Abacus,* Vol.30, No.2, pp.196–230.

Karvel, G. R. (1979) 'An Empirical Investigation of Auditor Communication: Connotative meaning of the auditor opinion paragraph', unpublished DBA dissertation, University of Colorado, Boulder, in Bagranoff *et al.* (1994).

Katz, D. and Kahn, R. L. (1966/1978) *The Social Psychology of Organisations,* John Wiley and Sons Inc., New York.

Keay, A. R. (1995) 'The Insolvency Factor in the Avoidance of Antecedent Transactions in Corporate Liquidations', *Monash University Law Review,* Vol.21, No.2, pp.305–333.

Kehl, D. (1941/1976) *Corporate Dividends*, reprinted Arno Press, New York, 1976.

Kelly, P. (1801) *The Elements of Book-Keeping,* Johnson and Others, London.

Kendall, N. and Kendall, A. (1998) *Real-World Corporate Governance: A programme for profit-enhancing stewardship*, FT Pitman Publishing, London.

Keynes, J. N. (1917) *The Scope and Method of Political Economy,* Macmillan, London, 4th edition.

Khan, A. (2007) 'Watchdog on Mat over Fincorp Collapse', *The Australian,* May 7.

Kirk, N. (2006) 'Perceptions of the True and Fair View Concept: An empirical investigation', *Abacus,* Vol.42, No.2, pp.205–235.

Klan, A. (2007) 'Retirees Lose All in Fincorp Collapse', *The Australian,* March 30.

Kohler, E. L. and Morrison, P.L., (1926) *Principles of Accounting,* Shaw, Chicago.

Kohn, A. (1989) *Fortune or Failure: Missed opportunities and chance discoveries,* Blackwell, Oxford, UK.

KordaMentha (2007) 'Fincorp Group of Companies', *Summary Report to Noteholders by the Administrators*, July 16.

Korzybski, A. (1933/1958) *Science and Sanity: An introduction to non-aristotelian systems and general semantics,* The International Non-Aristotelian Library Publishing Company, 2nd edition by the Science Press Printing Company, Distributors, PA.

Krasnoff, S. and Ansett, R (1999) *The Meaning of Success,* Shala Press, Tewantin, Queensland.

LaFrenz, C. (2009) 'Bargain Buyers Rush Felled Timbercorp', under 'Branching Out—History of Timbercorp' *AFR,* April 24.

Lamont, L. (2011) 'Fincorp "Spotter's Fee" a Sham, Court Told', *Brisbane Times,* May 3, available at www.brisbanetimes.com.au/action/printArticle?id=2339463

Lannin, S. (2010) 'The Allco Show Comes to Town', March 25, available at http://www.abc.net.au/news/stories/2010/03/24/2854636.htm accessed June 6, 2011.

Laverty, S. M. (2003) 'Hermeneutic Phenomenology and Phenomenology: A comparison of historical and methodological considertions', *International Journal of Qualitative Methods,* pp.21–35.

Lennard, A., and Thompson, S. (1995) *Provisions: Their Recognition, Measurement And Disclosure In Financial Statements, Australian Accounting Standards Board, Canadian Accounting Standards Board, International Accounting Standards Committee, United Kingdom Accounting Standards Board, United States Financial Accounting Standards Board.*

Lewis, P.J. (2010) 'Insolvent trading defences after Hall v Poolman', *Company and Securities Law Journal*, Vol.28, pp. 396–410.

Lincoln, Y. S. and Guba, E. G. (1985) *Naturalistic Inquiry,* Sage, Newbury Park, CA.

Linsmeier, T. J., Boatsman, J. R., James, R., Herz, R. H., Jennings, R. G., Jonas, G. J., Lang, M. H., Petroni, K. R., Shores, D., and Wahlen, J. M. (1998) 'Provisions, Contingent Liabilities and Contingent Assets', Response to IASC Exposure Draft, *Accounting Horizons,* Vol.12, No.2, June, pp.192–200.

Lisle, G. (1899) *Accounting in Theory and Practice,* Vol.1, Green, Edinburgh, in Chambers R. J. (1995) *An Accounting Thesaurus: 500 years of accounting,* Pergamon, Elsevier Science Ltd., Oxford, UK.

Lisle, G. (ed) (1903–1904) *Encyclopaedia of Accounting,* 6 Vols., Green, Edinburgh. Selections from *Encyclopaedia of Accounting* 1903 edited by Richard Brief (1978), Arno Press, New York.

Littleton, A. C. (1956) 'Choice Among Alternatives', *The Accounting Review,* Vol.31, No.3, July, pp.363–370.

Loftus, J. A. and Miller, M. C. (1996) 'Solvency Assessment and Financial Reporting', *Accounting Forum*, Vol.20, No.2, September, pp.97–132.
Loftus, J. A. and Miller, M. C. (2000) *Reporting on Solvency and Cash Condition,* Accounting Theory Monograph, Australian Accounting Research Foundation, Sydney, Australia.
Longo, J. (1999) 'Corporate Ethics: More honest or more careful?', *Australian CPA,* October, pp.19–21.
Ma, R. and Mathews, R. L. (1971/1979) *The Accounting Framework: A contemporary emphasis,* Longman Cheshire Pty. Limited, Melbourne.
Ma, R., Mathews, R. L., and Macmullen, J. (1987) *The Accounting Framework,* revised edition of 1971/1979, Longman Cheshire Pty. Limited, Melbourne.
Ma, R., Parker, R. H., and Whittred, G. (1991) *Consolidation Accounting,* Longman Cheshire Pty. Limited, Melbourne.
MacNeal, K. (1939) *Truth in Accounting,* University of Pennsylvania Press, Philadelphia.
Macve, R. (1981/1997) *A Conceptual Framework for Financial Accounting and Reporting: Vision, tool or threat?* The Institute of Chartered Accountants in England and Wales, London. Published in *New Works in Accounting History,* edited by Richard Brief, Garland Publishing, Inc., 1997.
Main, A. (2003) *Other People's Money,* Harper Collins Publishers, Pymble, NSW.
Mair, J. (1748/1800) *Book-Keeping Moderniz'd,* Isaac Jackson, Dublin, 1748; Bell, Bradfrute and Creech, Edinburgh, 1800.
Malcolm, A. (1731/1986) *A Treatise of Book-Keeping, or Merchant's Accounts,* London, reprinted Garland Publishing Inc., edited by Richard P. Brief.
Manly, G. (1973) 'Gerard Lee Bevan and the City Equitable Companies', *Abacus,* Vol.9, No.2, December, pp.107–115.
Mannix, E. F. and Mannix, J. E. (1982) *Professional Negligence*, Butterworths, Sydney, 3rd edition.
March, J. G. and Simon, H. A. (1958) *Organizations,* John Wiley and Sons Inc., New York.
Margenau, H. (1950) *The Nature of Physical Reality,* McGraw-Hill, New York.
Margenau, H. and Murphy, G. M. (1943/1956) *The Mathematics of Physics and Chemistry,* D. Van Nostrand Company, Inc., Princeton, NJ.
Margret, J. E. (2002) 'Insolvency and Tests of Insolvency: An analysis of the "Balance Sheet" and "Cash Flow" Tests', *Australian Accounting Review,* Vol.12, No.2, pp.59–72.
Margret, J. (2005) 'Surviving Financial Distress: The Case of Too Many Herbs and Spices', *Journal of Applied Management Accounting Research* (*JAMAR*), Vol.3, No.2, pp.51–67.
Marley, C. (1970) *Journal of Business Finance,* Winter, in Chambers, R. J. (1995) *An Accounting Thesaurus: 500 years of accounting,* Pergamon, Elsevier Science Ltd., Oxford, UK.
Martin, C. (1984) *An Introduction to Accounting,* McGraw-Hill, Sydney.
Mason, P., Davidson, S., and Schindler, J. S. (1959) *Fundamentals of Accounting,* Holt Rinehart, New York.
Mathews, R. L. (1962) *Accounting for economists*, Cheshire, Melbourne.
Maxwell, P. B. (1883) *On the Interpretation of Statutes*, Maxwell and Son, London, in Chambers, R. J. (1995) *An Accounting Thesaurus: 500 years of accounting,* Pergamon, Elsevier Science Ltd., Oxford, UK.
May, G. O. (1936) 'The Influence of Accounting on the Development of an Economy', *The Journal of Accountancy,* Vol.61, No.1, January, pp.11–22.

McCracken, H. L. (1948) *American Economic Review,* May, in Chambers, R. J. (1995) *An Accounting Thesaurus: 500 years of accounting,* Pergamon, Elsevier Science Ltd., Oxford, UK.

McGregor, A. (chairperson) (1997) *Speech at the Burns Philp AGM,* November 5.

Mead, G. H. (1934/1962) *Mind, Self and Society,* University of Chicago Press, Chicago.

Mescher, B. (1996) 'Personal Liability for Company Directors for Company Debts', *The Australian Law Journal,* Vol.70, October, pp.837–850.

Metcalf, L. (1977) *The Accounting Establishment,* US Government Printing Office, Washington, DC.

Montgomery, R. (1927) 'Accountants' Limitations', *The Journal of Accountancy,* AIA, AICPA, Vol.44, No.4, October, pp.245–266.

Montgomery, R. (1938) in *Origin and Evolution of Double Entry Bookkeeping,* edited by E. Peragallo, American Institute Publishing, New York.

Moonitz, M. (1961) *The Basic Postulates of Accounting,* Accounting Research Study No.1, American Institute of Certified Public Accountants, New York.

Moonitz, M. and Staehling, C. C. (1952) *Accounting, an Analysis of Its Problems,* Brooklyn Foundation Press, Brooklyn, NY.

Most, K. S. (1977) *Accounting Theory,* Grid Inc., Columbus, OH.

Mullighan, J. (1998) Court Transcript: *Duke Group Ltd. (in Liq) v. Pilmer & Ors,* Judgment of the Honourable Justice Mullighan, January 30, Supreme Court of South Australia.

Munhall, P. (1989) 'Philosophical Ponderings on Qualitative Research Methods in Nursing', *Nursing Science Quarterly,* Vol.2, No.1, pp.20–28.

Ogden, C. K. and Richards, I. A. (1923/1960) *The Meaning of Meaning,* Routledge, London.

O'Malley, S. (chairperson) (2000) *The Panel on Audit Effectiveness,* US inquiry into the effectiveness of auditing initiated by the Public Oversight Board of the American Institute of CPAs, available at www.pobauditpanel.org

One.Tel Limited (2000) Annual Report.

Osgood, C. E., Suci, G. J., and Tannenbaum, P. N. (1957) *The Measurement of Meaning,* University of Illinois Press, Chicago.

Oxford Benefit and Building Society (1886/1986) *Law and Accounting, pre-1889 British Legal Cases*, edited by J. M. Reid, Garland Publishing Inc., New York.

Pacioli, L. (1494) "Particularis de computis et scripturis" in Brown, R. G. and Johnston K. S. (1963) *Paciolo on Accounting*, McGraw-Hill, New York. Listed in Chambers, R. J. (1995) *An Accounting Thesaurus: 500 years of accounting*, Pergamon, Elsevier Science Ltd., Oxford, UK.

Pareto, V. (1916/1963) *The Mind and Society,* translated by A. Bongiorno and A. Livingston, Dover, New York.

Parker, L. D. (1999) 'Historiography for the New Millennium: Adventures in accounting and management', *Accounting History,* NS, Vol.4, No.2, November, pp.11–42.

Parker, R. H. (1994) 'Finding English Words to Talk about Accounting Concepts', *Accounting, Auditing & Accountability Journal*, Vol.7, No.2, pp.70–85.

Paton, W. A. (1917) *The Journal of Accountancy,* AIA, AICPA, January, in Chambers, R. J. (1995) *An Accounting Thesaurus: 500 years of accounting,* Pergamon, Elsevier Science Ltd., Oxford, UK.

Paton, W. A. (1922/1962) *Accounting Theory,* Ronald Press, New York, reprinted Accounting Studies Press, Chicago, 1962.

Paton, W. A. (1931) 'Economic Theory in Relation to Accounting Valuations', *The Accounting Review,* Vol. VI, No.2, June, pp.89–96.

Paton, W. A. (1943) 'Adaptation of the Income Statement to Present Conditions', *The Journal of Accountancy,* Vol.75, No.1, January, pp.8–15.

Paton, W. A. (1949) *Essentials of Accounting,* Macmillan, New York.

Peat, Marwick, Mitchell and Co. (1987) *Survey of Financial Institutions.* Peat, Marwick, Mitchell & Co., 1985–1988 Nedlands, W.A

Peloubet, M. E. (1935) 'Is Value an Accounting Concept', *The Journal of Accountancy,* Vol.59, No.3, March, pp.201–209.

Pfiffner, J. M. and Sherwood, F. (1960) *Administrative Organization,* Prentice-Hall, Englewood-Cliffs, NJ.

Pixley, F. W. (1881/1976) *Auditors: Their duties and responsibilities,* Effingham Wilson, London, reprinted Arno Press, New York, 1976.

Pixley, F. W. (1926) *The Accountant's Dictionary,* Vol.1, Pitman, New York, 2nd edition.

Planck, M. (1950/1968) *Scientific Autobiography and Other Papers,* translated F. Gaynor, Greenwood Press Publishers, New York. Copyright 1949, Philosophical Library, New York.

Potter, B. (1999) 'The Power of Words: Explaining recent accounting reforms in the Australian public sector', *Accounting History,* NS, Vol .4, No.2, November, pp.43–72.

Potter, C. C. (1951) 'The Economic Consequences of Business Accountancy: The need for research by Calvin Potter', *Accounting Research,* UK, Vol.2, No.3, July, pp.308–313.

Pratten, C. (1991) *Company Failure,* Institute of Chartered Accountants of England and Wales, London.

Previts, G. J., Roybark, H. M., and Coffman, E. N. (2003) 'Keeping Watch! Recounting Twenty-Five Years of the Office of Chief Accountant, U.S. Securities and Exchange Commission, 1976–2001', *Abacus,* Vol.39, No.2, pp.147–185.

Quinn, J. B. (1980) *Strategies for Change, Logical Incrementalism,* Richard D. Irwin, Inc., Homewood, IL.

Ramsay, I. (1997) *Corporate Governance and the Duties of Company Directors,* Centre for Corporate Law and Securities Regulation, Faculty of Law, The University of Melbourne.

Ramsay, I. and Hoad, R. (1997) 'Disclosure of Corporate Governance Practices by Australian Companies', *Company and Securities Law Journal,* Vol.15, November, pp.454–470.

Ramsay, I. and Stapledon, G. (1998) *Corporate Groups in Australia,* Centre for Corporate Law and Securities Regulation, The University of Melbourne.

Ramsay, I. and Stapledon, G. (2001) 'Corporate Groups in Australia', *Australian Business Law Review,* Vol.29, No.1, February, pp.7–32.

Rescher, N. (1996) *Process Metaphysics: An introduction to process philosophy,* SUNY Press, New York.

Rescher, N. (2000) *Process Philosophy: A survey of basic issues,* University of Pittsburgh Press, Pittsburgh.

Rescher, N. (2002) 'Process Philosophy', *The Stanford Encyclopaedia of Philosophy (Summer 2002 Edition),* Edward N. Zalta (ed), available at http://plato.stanford.edu/archives/sum2002/entries/process-philosophy/

Roach, M. (2010) 'Combating the Phoenix Phenomenon: An analysis of international approaches', *eJournal of Tax Research,* Vol.8, No.2, December, pp.90–127.

Salsbury, S. (1982) *No Way to Run a Railroad: The untold story of the Penn Central crisis,* McGraw-Hill, New York.

Sarre, R. (2001) 'Risk Management and Regulatory Weakness', in *Collapse Incorporated: Tales, safeguards and responsibilities of corporate Australia,* Part V, Chapter 10, CCH Australia Limited, North Ryde, NSW, pp.292–323.

Scheutze, W. (1991) 'Keep it Simple', *Accounting Horizons,* Vol. 5, No.2, June, pp.113–117.

Scheutze, W. (1993) 'What Is an Asset?', *Accounting Horizons,* Vol.7, No.3, September, pp.66–70.

Scheutze, W. (2001a) 'A Memo to National and International Accounting and Auditing Standard Setters and Securities Regulators', *The R.J. Chambers Research Lecture*, The University of Sydney, November 27, pp.1–14.

Scheutze, W. (2001b) 'What Are Assets and Liabilities? Where Is True North? (Accounting That My Sister Would Understand)', *Abacus,* Vol.37, No.1, February, pp.1–25.

Schumpeter, J. A. (1947) *Capitalism, Socialism and Democracy,* Allen and Unwin, London.

Securities and Exchange Commission, US (2003) *SEC Staff Study on Principles-Based Accounting Systems,* Pursuant to s.108(d) of the Sarbanes-Oxley Act of 2002 on the adoption of the United States Reporting System of a Principles-Based Accounting System, available at www.sec.gov/news/studies/principles-basedstand.htm accessed July 23, 2003.

Shackle, G. L. S. (1959/1962) *Economics for Pleasure,* Cambridge University Press, London.

Shackle, G. L. S. (1970) *Expectation, Enterprise and Profit,* Allen and Unwin, London.

Shakespeare, W. (1602) *Troilus and Cressida,* 11:ii; in Chambers, R. J. (1995) *An Accounting Thesaurus: 500 years of accounting,* Pergamon, Elsevier Science Ltd., Oxford, UK.

Shakespeare, W. (1608) *Timon of Athens,*11:ii; in Chambers, R. J. (1995) *An Accounting Thesaurus: 500 years of accounting,* Pergamon, Elsevier Science Ltd., Oxford, UK.

Shakespeare, W. (17th Century) *Macbeth,* first recorded performance at court (1606), quotation from the Shakespeare parallel text series, edited by Daniel Leary, The City College of New York, 1998 Perfection Learning Corporation, US, copyright 1975 by Simon and Schuster, Inc.

Sharma, D. (1996) 'Analysing the statement of cash flows', *Australian Accounting Review*, Vol.6, September, pp.37–44.

Simon, H. A. (1949) *Administrative Behavior,* Macmillan, New York.

Smith, T. (1992) *Accounting for Growth: Stripping the camouflage from company accounts,* Century Business, London.

Solomons, D. (1989) *Guidelines for Financial Reporting Standards,* Institute of Chartered Accountants of England and Wales. Reprinted (1997) in New Works in Accounting History, edited by Richard P. Brief, Garland Publishing, Inc., New York and London.

Sprague, C. E. (1907/1972) *The Philosophy of Accounts*, reprinted by Scholars Book Company, Houston, TX, 1972.

Sprague, C. E. (1984) *The General Principles of the Science of Accounts and the Accountancy of Investment,* Garland Publishing, Inc., New York and London.

Sprouse, R. T. and Moonitz, M. (1962) *A Tentative Set of Broad Accounting Principles for Business Enterprises,* Accounting Research Study No.3, American Institute of Certified Public Accountants, New York.

Stempf, V. H. (1943) 'Facilitating the Independent Accountant's Review of Internal Accounting Control', *The Journal of Accountancy,* Vol.75, No.1, January, pp.49–57.

Sterling, R. R. (1968a) *The Accountants Magazine,* November, in Chambers, R. J. (1995) *An Accounting Thesaurus: 500 years of accounting,* Pergamon, Elsevier Science Ltd., Oxford, UK.

Sterling, R. R. (1968b) 'The Going Concern: An examination', *Accounting Review*, July, pp.481–502.
Sterling, R. R. (1970) *Theory of the Measurement of Enterprise Income,* University Press of Kansas, Lawrence.
Sterling, R. R. (1979) *Toward a Science of Accounting,* Scholars Book Company, Houston, TX.
Sterling, R. R. (1982) in *Research to Support Standard Setting in Financial Accounting: A Canadian perspective,* edited by S. Basu and J. A. Milburn, Clarkson Gordon Foundation, Toronto.
Stevens, S. S. (1946) 'On the Theory of Scales and Measurement', *Science,* Vol.103, No. 2684, American Association for the Advancement of Science, June 7, pp.677–684.
Stone, W. E. (ed) (1971) *Foundations of Accounting Theory,* University of Florida Press, Gainesville.
Storey, R. K. (1959) 'Revenue Realization, Going Concern and Measurement of Income', *Accounting Review,* April, pp.232–238.
Sweeney, H. W. (1936/1964) *Stabilized Accounting,* Harper and Row, New York, reprinted Holt, Rinehart & Winston, New York, 1964.
Switzer, P. (2010) 'Solvency Statement Would Bury Phoenix', *The Australian,* July 17.
Tabart-Gay, J. M. and Wolnizer, P. W. (1997) 'Business Firms as Adaptive Entities: The case of the major Australian banks 1983–1994', *Abacus,* Vol.33, No.2, pp.186–207.
Thomas, A. L. (1975) 'The FASB and the Allocation Fallacy', *The Journal of Accountancy,* Vol.140, No.5, November, pp.65–69.
Thompson, A. P. (1974) *The Accountant,* January, in Chambers, R. J. (1995) *An Accounting Thesaurus: 500 years of accounting,* Pergamon, Elsevier Science Ltd., Oxford, UK.
Thompson, W. (1777/1984) *The Accomptant's Oracle, or, Key to Science*, Vol.11, N. Nickson, York, UK, reprinted Garland Publishing Inc., New York, 1984.
Thomson, J. (2011) 'Founder of Collapsed Property Company Fincorp Facing Jail After Being Found Guilty of Dishonest Payments', February 17, available at www.smartcompany.com.au/financial-services-and-insurance/20110217 accessed May 12, 2011.
Tomkins, C. and Vass, P. (1998) *Governance Processes for Public Services,* Chartered Institute of Management Accountants, available at www.cimaglobal.com
Tomlins, T. E. (1820) *The Law Dictionary,* Payne and Foss, London, 3rd edition.
Troy, G. (1982) 'Premise of Continuity Obsolete', *The Chartered Accountant in Australia,* Vol.53, No.5, November, p.3.
Trumbull, W. (1958) 'Price-Level Depreciation and Replacement Cost', *The Accounting Review,* Vol.33, No.1, January, pp.26–34.
Trumbull, W. P. (1958) 'Book Review of "Effects of Price Level Changes on Business Income, Capital, and Taxes" by Ralph Coughenour Jones', *The Accounting Review,* Vol.33, Issue 2, April, pp.342–343.
Tweedie, D. P. and Whittington, G. (1984) *The Debate on Inflation Accounting,* Cambridge University Press, New York.
US Steel Corporation (1902/1986) *Corporate Financial Reporting and Analysis in the Early 1900s,* Richard P. Brief (ed), Garland Publishing Inc., New York.
Vickers, D. (1981) 'The Marginal Efficiency of (Money) Capital', *Journal of Business Finance and Accounting,* Vol.8, No.2, pp.165–176.
Vickrey, D. W. (1970) 'Is Accounting a Measurement Discipline?', *The Accounting Review,* Vol.XIV, No.4, October, pp.731–742.
Walker, R. G. (1978) *Consolidated Statements,* Arno Press Inc., New York.

Walker, R. G., Clarke, F. L., and Dean, G. W. (2000) 'Options for Infrastructure Reporting', *Abacus,* Vol.36, No.2, June, pp.123–159.

Wallis, S. (2000) 'Corporate Governance—Conformance or Performance', *Journal of Banking & Financial Services,* Australasian Institute of Banking and Finance, Vol.114, No.4, August, pp.14–19.

Walters, R. M. (1967) *The Accountant* (UK), August, in Chambers, R. J. (1995) *An Accounting Thesaurus: 500 years of accounting,* Pergamon, Elsevier Science Ltd., Oxford, UK.

Watts, R. L. and Zimmerman, J. L. (1978) 'Towards a Positive Theory of the Determination of Accounting Standards', *The Accounting Review,* January, pp.112–134.

Watts, R. L. and Zimmerman, J. L. (1990) 'Positive Accounting Theory: A ten year perspective', *The Accounting Review,* Vol.65, No.1, January, pp.131–156.

Webster, G. R. (1919) *The Journal of Accountancy,* October, in Chambers, R. J. (1995) *An Accounting Thesaurus: 500 years of accounting,* Pergamon, Elsevier Science Ltd., Oxford, UK.

Weiss, P. A. (1971) *Hierarchically Organized Systems in Theory and Practice,* Hafner Publishing Company, New York.

Werntz, W. W. (1941/1968) *W W Werntz, His Accounting Thought,* R. M. Trueblood and G. H. Sorter (eds), American Institute of Certified Public Accountants, New York.

West, B. P. (2003) *Professionalism and Accounting Rules,* Routledge/Taylor and Francis Group, New York.

Whatmough, J. (1957) *Language, a Modern Synthesis,* New York. A Mentor book published by the New American Library, first printing October 1957.

Whitehead, A. N. (1933/1948) *Adventures of Ideas,* Cambridge University Press, Cambridge, UK.

Whorf, B. L. (1956/1962) *Language, Thought, and Reality,* edited (and introduction) by John B. Carroll, foreword by Stuart Chase, MIT Press, Cambridge, MA.

Wilcox, E. B. and Hassler, R. H. (1941) 'A Foundation for Accounting Principles', *Journal of Accountancy,* Vol.72, No.4, October, pp.308–314.

Williams, S. J. (2003) 'Assets in Accounting: Reality lost', *The Accounting Historians Journal,* Vol.30, No.2, December, pp.133–174.

Wixon, R. (ed) (1962) *Accountants' Handbook,* The Ronald Press Company, New York, 4th edition.

Wolk, H. I., Francis, J. R., and Tearney, M. G. (1984) *Accounting Theory,* Kent Publishing, Boston.

Wolnizer, P. W. (1987) *Auditing as Independent Authentication*, Sydney University Press, Sydney.

Wright, M. (1994) 'Accounting, Truth and Communication: The case of a bank failure', *Critical Perspectives on Accounting,* Vol.5, No.4, December, pp.361–388.

Wyatt, A. and Mason, R. (1998) 'Legal and Accounting Regulatory Framework for Corporate Groups: Implications for insolvency in group operations', *Company and Securities Law Journal,* Vol.16, September, pp.424–450.

Yamey, B. S. (2000) 'The "Particular Gain or Loss Upon Each Article We Deal In": An aspect of mercantile accounting, 1300–1800', *Accounting, Business and Financial History,* Vol,10, No.1, March, pp.1–12.

Yamey, B. S., Edey, H. C., and Thompson, H. W. (1963) *Accounting in England and Scotland 1543–1800,* Sweet and Maxwell, London.

Yu, S. C. (1971) 'A Reexamination of the Going Concern Postulate', *International Journal of Accounting,* Spring, pp.37–58.

Zeff, S. A. (2000) 'John B. Canning: A view of his academic career', *Abacus,* Vol.36, No.1, pp.4–39.

TRANSCRIPT

Duke Group Ltd. (in Liq) v. Pilmer & Ors, Judgment of the Honourable Justice Mulligan, January 30, 1998, Supreme Court of South Australia (Civil), Judgement No. S6529.

REPORT OF THE COMMISSION

HIH Royal Commission (2001–2002) at the time available at www.hihroyalcom.gov.au

NEWSPAPER ARTICLES

Baskett, B. (2001) 'Cleaning up the HIH Mess', *The Press,* Section: Business, 2nd edition, Canterbury, New Zealand, May 21, p.20.

Behr, P. and Witt, A. reported 'The Fall of Enron' in the *Washington Post,* as 'Visionary's Dream Led to Risky Business', Sunday July 28, 2002; 'Dream Job Turns into a Nightmare', Monday July 29, 2002; 'Concerns Grow Amid Conflicts', Tuesday July 30, 2002; 'Losses, Conflicts Threaten Survival', Wednesday July 31, 2002; 'Hidden Debts, Deals Scuttle Last Chance', Thursday August 1, 2002, available at www.washingtonpost.com

Boyd, T. (2008) 'Allco's Biggest Losers' available at http://www.businessspectator.com.au/bs.nsf/Article/Allcos-biggest-losers-L3E6G?OpenDocument accessed May, 2011.

Brammall, B. (2001) 'Ship Sank Fast as Firm Assured Shareholders', *Courier-Mail,* Brisbane, Australia, May 21, p.4.

Brammall, B. (2001) 'Anatomy of a Disaster', *Herald Sun,* Melbourne, Australia, May 21, p.7.

Brammall, B. and Bissett, K. (2001) 'Collapse Reaches Overseas—International Fallout', *Daily Telegraph,* Sydney, Australia, May 21, p.4.

Breusch, J. (2001) 'HIH Collapse Signs "Relatively Clear" ', *Australian Financial Review,* Tuesday December 4, p.1, continued p.4.

Bushnell, N. (1990) 'How Budget Was Driven to the Wall', *Australian Business,* May 9, p.16.

Charles, M. (2001) 'News, PBL Bail Out One.Tel', *Herald-Sun,* Melbourne, Australia, May 18, p.37.

Chenoweth, N. and staff reporters. (1990) 'Cash, not Cars, the Future for Budget', *Australian Business,* March 7, pp.22–23.

Daly, M. (1997) 'Ansett's Agony', *The Age and Sunday Age,* Melbourne, August 16, p.21.

Dunn, M. and Ferguson, J. (2001) 'Directors in Hot Seat Over Company Crash', *Herald Sun,* Melbourne, Australia, May 21, p.5.

Easdown, G. and Dunn, M. (2001) 'Paris Night-Life, Luxury Greek Island Cruises for HIH's High-Fliers', *The Advertiser,* Adelaide, Australia, May 21, p.4.

Farr, M. and McDougall, B. (2001) 'Unmasking the $4bn Man: Neville Owen given the job to track HIH culprits', *The Daily Telegraph,* Sydney, Australia, June 19, p.1.

Ferguson, A. (2010) 'Insolvency report is in, now for some action', *Business Day—The Age,* 15 September, available at http://www.businessday.com.au/business/insolvency-report-is-in-now-for-some-action-20100914-15b0p.html

Financial Review, January 31-February 1, 1998, p.3 as reported in the court transcript: *Duke Group Ltd. (in Liq) v. Pilmer and Ors,* Judgment of the Honourable Justice Mullighan, January 30, 1998, Supreme Court of South Australia.

Frith, B. (2009) 'One.Tel good faith issue still far from settled', *The Australian,* November 26, available at http://www.news.com.au/onetel-good-faith-issue-still-far-from-settled/story-e6frg8zx-1225803960240

Gottliebsen, R. (1990) 'Bob Ansett's Life as a Bankrupt', *Business Review Weekly,* October 12, pp.24–27.

Gottliebsen, R. (2001) 'One.Tel Just theTicket for PBL', *Australian,* May 18, p.23.

Kohler, A. (2004) 'Who Would Have Believed It? French Revolt Comes to the Aid of Australia's Intangible Intransigents', Business and Money, *Age,* March 20, pp.1, 2.

Koutsoukis, J. and Main, A. (2003) *Australian Financial Review,* July 4, p.1.

Lampe, A. (1989) 'Ansett, Hamley: Budget charges', *Sydney Morning Herald,* December, p.34.

Lampe, A. (1994) 'Case to Answer for Budget Pair', *Business Age,* October 22, p.31.

Lampe, A. (1994) 'Ansett Sent to Trial over Budget Float', *Business Age,* November 11, p.21.

Lampe, A. (1997) 'Prosecution Wasted Nine Years of My Life, says Ansett', *The Age and Sunday Age,* August 8, p.7.

Lampe, A. (2005) 'One.Tel case close to resumption', *Business—Sydney Morning Herald,* June 16, available at http://www.smh.com.au/news/Business/OneTel-case-close-to-resumption/2005/06/15/1118645867306.html#

MacDougall, B. (2001) 'Court to Check $10 Million Deal', *Daily Telegraph,* Sydney, Australia, 2nd edition, Section: Local, July 3, p.9.

MacDougall, B. (2001) 'Crime Probe on $10m HIH Funds', *Herald Sun,* Melbourne, Australia, July 3, p.24.

Main, A. (2004) 'One.Tel Wrangle Worsens', *Australian Financial Review,* March 19, p.16.

McCrann, T. (2009) 'Corporate law's the disaster', *Herald-Sun,* Melbourne, November, available at http://www.heraldsun.com.au/business/terry-mccranns-column/corporate-laws-the-disaster/story-e6frfig6-1225799515611

Moran, S. (2010) 'One.Tel case cancelled rights issue gets the go-ahead', *The Australian,* May 21; available at http://www.theaustralian.com.au/business/onetel-case-over-cancelled-rights-issue-gets-go-ahead/story-e6frg8zx-1225869363876

Mitchell, S. (1990) 'Hamley Says Accounting Problems Are to Blame', *The Australian Financial Review,* May 13, p.19.

Parker, J., Manson, J., and McIlwraith, J. (1990–1991) 'Fallen Idols', *Australian Business,* December 19/January 9, pp.14–21.

Pheasant, B. (1992) 'Ex-Budget Car Rental Operators Take Class Action', *Australian Financial Review,* July 15, p.5.

Pheasant, B. (1994) 'Bankruptcy Trustee Queries Bob Ansett', *Australian Financial Review,* February 17, p.4.

Potter, B. (1990) 'Budget Corp Takes Ansett, Hamley to Court', *Sydney Morning Herald,* February 3, p.35.

Stark, D. (2001) 'One.Tel's Black Hole Deepens', *Courier-Mail,* Brisbane, Australia, June 21, p.25.

Trute, P. and Gosnell, P. (2001) 'Rich, Keeling out of One.Tel', *Daily Telegraph,* Sydney, Australia, May 18, p.101.

Turner, B. (1993) 'Ansett, Hamley to Run Own Defence on Budget Charges', *Australian Financial Review,* April 6, p.9.

Turner, B. (1993) 'Budget Advisers "Misled ASX" ', *Australian Financial Review,* April 14, pp.1, 2.

Westfield, M. (2001) 'PM Lets Genie Out of the Bottle—HIH Royal Commission', *Australian,* May 22, p.2.

Westfield, M. (2001) 'Howard Wants the Truth to Take Its Time—HIH Royal Commission', *Australian,* June 19, p.4.

AUTHOR'S NAME NOT AVAILABLE (PRE 2005)

'James, Lachlan to be Quizzed', *Australian Financial Review*, March 13–14, 2004, p.4.
'Road to Disaster', *Australian,* April 17, 2003.
'HIH "Too Late to Sue FAI Over Dud Sale" ', *Australian,* December 6, 2001, p.4.
'HIH Figures Were "Adjusted" ', *Townsville Bulletin,* Queensland, Australia, December 20, 2001, p.29.
Australian Associated Press, *AAP General News*, Australia, July 16, 2001.
Australian Associated Press, 'FED: HIH in Trouble Six Years Ago', *AAP General News*, Australia, July 2, 2001, available at www.education.elibrary.com.au
'Williams Warned About HIH's Financial Problems in a Letter From British Branch's Chief', *Herald Sun,* Melbourne, Australia, May 21, 2001, p.4.
'The HIH Insurance Collapse', *Herald Sun,* Melbourne, Australia, May 21, 2001, p.4.

PRIMARY WEBSITE REFERENCES

Australian corporate news (2003): www.cch.com.au
Australian News: www.newsstore.f2.com.au/apps/newsSearch.ac
Australian Prudential Regulatory Authority: www.apra.gov.au
Australian Securities and Investment Commission: www.asic.gov.au
Australian Treasury: www.treasury.gov.au
Canada Corporation's Act and Canada Business Corporations Regulations: http://laws.justice.gc.ca/en/c-44/9507.html
Center for Advanced Research in Phenomenology: www.phenomenologycenter.org/phenom.htm
Chartered Institute of Management Accountants: www.cimaglobal.com
Corporations and Markets Advisory Committee: www.camac.gov.au
Court transcripts—Australia: www.austlii.edu.au
DatAnalysis database—through La Trobe University Library: www.latrobe.edu.au/library
Dun and Bradstreet—Australia: http://dnb.com.au
Electronic Library—Australia: www.education.elibrary.com.au
HIH Royal Commission: www.hihroyalcom.gov.au
Price Waterhouse Coopers: www.pwcglobal.com.au/Extweb/manissue.nsf
Proceedings of the Water Wheel case: www.millsoakley.com.au
Public Oversight Board of the American Institute of CPA's: www.pobauditpanel.gov
The Sarbannes–Oxley Act: http://www.soxlaw.com
Securities Exchange Commission, US: www.sec.gov/rules and www.sec.gov and www.sec.gov/news/studies/principlesbasedstand.html
The Emmanuel Saxe Distinguished Lectures in Accounting, City University of New York, February 18, 1975: http://newman.baruch.cuny.edu/digital/saxe/saxe_1974/burton_75.htm
University of South Australia, the Corporate Social Responsibility: www.business.unisa.edu.au/cobar/corpresp
US Blue Ribbon Committee: www.nyse.com
US Washington Post: www.washingtonpost.com

LEGISLATIVE INSTRUMENTS

Australian Accounting Standards (2002) authorised versions available in hard copy from the AASB alternatively, from www.aasb.com.au

Australian Accounting Handbook (2010, 2011) incorporating Australian Accounting Standards and the International Financial Reporting Standard (IFRS) equivalents, *CPA Australia,* Pearson Australia.

Australian Bankruptcy Act (1966) Commonwealth of Australia.

Australian Corporations Act (2001) *Butterworths*, Sydney.

Australian Corporations and Securities Legislation, Vol.1, incorporating *Corporations Act 2001,*, the ASIC Act 2001 and related regulations (2010, 2011), CCH Australia Limited,

British Companies Legislation, *The Companies Act 1985 and Insolvency Act 1986 and Related Legislation*, 4th edition, CCH Editions Limited, Oxfordshire.

Canada Corporation's Act and Canada Business Corporations Regulations available at http://laws.justice.gc.ca/en/c-44/9507.html

New Zealand Companies Act, 1993, Part 1, section 4, Part V1 sections 70 & 77, Part X11 *Disclosure Regulations.*

Ontario Business Corporations Act (1990) annotated by Ames, J. and Lettner, M., Butterworths, Canada.

Sarbanes-Oxley Act (2002) 'Goals, Content, and Status of Implementation', Speech by the SEC Commissioner Paul S. Atkins, by invitation from the editors of the *International Financial Law Review,* March 25, 2003, available at www.sec.gov./news/speech/spch032503psa.htm

AUTHORITATIVE LITERATURE

Accounting Standards Committee (UK), (1978) *SSAP14 Group Accounts.*

American Accounting Association's Financial Accounting Standards Committee, FASB, (1998) Response to IASC Exposure Draft, 'Provisions, Contingent Liabilities and Contingent Assets', *Accounting Horizons,* Vol.12, No.2.

American Accounting Association's Financial Accounting Standards Committee, FASB, (1984) SFAC1: *Objectives of Financial Reporting by Business Enterprises*; SFAC5: *Recognition and measurement in financial statements of business enterprises.*

American Institute of Accountants, AIA, (1932/1943) 'Report of the Special Committee on Cooperation with the Stock Exchanges of the American Institute of Accountants', September, source cited May 1943.

American Institute of Accountants, AIA, (1940) *Accounting Research Bulletin*, No.7.

American Institute of Certified Public Accountants, AICPA, (1959/1961) *Accounting Research Bulletin 51,* 'Consolidated Financial Statements', source cited American Institute Certified Public Accountants, 1961.

American Institute of Certified Public Accountants, AICPA, (1963) 'Statements on Auditing Procedures, No.33', SAP33, *Committee on Auditing Procedures.*

American Institute of Certified Public Accountants, AICPA, (1970) 'Basic Concepts and Accounting Principles Underlying Financial Statements of Business Enterprises', APBS4.

Australian Prudential Regulatory Authority, APRA, (2002) *Submission to the HIH Royal Commission,* available at www.hihroyalcom.gov.au and www.apra.gov.au

Australian Prudential Standards (2002) GPS110: *Capital Adequacy for General Insurers* and GPS210: *Liability valuation,* Australian Prudential Regulatory Authority (APRA).

Australian Prudential Standards (2003) *Discussion Paper on Stage 2 Reforms of General Insurance Industry,* available at www.apra.gov.au

Australian Securities and Investment Commission, ASIC, (2002) 'Stage one results of accounting surveillance', Media Release 02/460, Wednesday 18 December.

Australian Securities and Investment Commission, ASIC, (2003) 'Stage two results of accounting surveillance', Media Release 03/125, Thursday 10 April.

Australian Securities and Investment Commission, ASIC, (2010) 'National Insolvent Trading Program Report 213', Australian Securities and Investment Commission, October 2010.

Australian Securities Exchange, ASX, (2003) *Principles of Good Corporate Governance and Best Practice Recommendations,* Corporate Governance Council, March and *Corporate Governance Listing Rule 4.10.3,* available at www.asx.com.au

Australian Securities Exchange, ASX, (2007) *Corporate Governance Principles and Recommendations,* 2nd edition, ASX Corporate Governance Council, August. To take effect January 2008—in Foreword.

Australian Securities and Investments Commission, ASIC, (1998/1999) *The Report of the Investigation into Burns Philp & Company Limited, December 1998,* Commonwealth of Australia, 1999.

Australian Securities and Investment Commission, ASIC, (2002) *Ethics and Governance,* Annual Report. ASIC Media Releases (2002 and 2003), available at www.asic.gov.au

Australian Securities and Inveestment Commission, ASIC, (2002–2010) *Annual Reports,* available at www.asic.gov.au

Australian Securities and Investment Commission, ASIC, (2010) *Statement on Fincorp,* by Mr Tony D'Aloisio, Chairman ASIC to the Senate Standing Committee on Economics, May, available at www.asic.gov.au

Australian Securities and Investment Commission, ASIC, (2009) *Duty to Prevent Insolvent Trading: Guide for directors,* Consultation Paper 124, November.

Australian Securities and Investment Commission, ASIC, (2010) *National Insolvency Trading Program* (NITP), Report 213, October.

Australian Securities and Investment Commission, ASIC, (2010) *Australian Insolvency Statistics,* Series 3: External administrators' reports, 3.3 time series for July 1, 2004, to June 30, 2010, available at www.asic.gov.au

Australian Securities and Investment Commission, ASIC, (2010) *ASIC Insolvency Update,* available at www.asic.gov.au/insolvency

Australian Society of Accountants and the Institute of Chartered Accountants in Australia (1985) *"A True and Fair View" and the Reporting Obligations of Directors and Auditors: Submission to the National Companies & Securities Commission on the Consultative Document,* Australian Society of Accountants, Melbourne.

Australian Society of Accountants, The Institute of Chartered Accountants in Australia and Accounting Standards Review Board, Statement of Accounting Concepts: SAC2: *Objective of General Purpose Financial Reporting*; SAC3: *Qualitative Characteristics of Financial Information;* SAC 4, *Definition and Recognition of the Elements of Financial Statements.*

Blue Ribbon Committee on Improving the Effectiveness of Corporate Audit Committees (1999) *Report and Recommendation of the Blue Ribbon Committee on Improving the Effectiveness of Corporate Audit Committees,* available at www.nyse.com

Cadbury Committee (1991/1992) *Report of the Committee on the Financial Aspects of Corporate Governance* and the *Code of Corporate Governance—Final and Interim Reports,* Gee, London.

Cole Royal Commission, Royal Commission into the Building and Construction Industry (1915), *Final Report,* Vol.8, 'Reform—National Issues, Part 2', Chapter 12, "Phoenix Companies".

Companies & Securities Advisory Committee, CASAC, (1998) 'Corporate Groups', Discussion Paper, December.

Companies & Securities Advisory Committee, CASAC, (2000) 'Corporate Groups Final Report', *Australian Securities and Investment Commission,* May, available at www.asic.gov.au/publications

Corporations and Markets Advisory Committee, CAMAC, (2003) *Discussion Paper: Rehabilitating large and complex enterprises in financial difficulties,* Sydney, NSW, September, available at www.camac.gov.au

Corporations and Markets Advisory Committee, CAMAC, (2010) *Guidance for Directors,* Report, April, available at www.camac.gov.au.

Corporate Law Economic Reform Program, Proposals for Reform—CLERP3 (1997) *Directors' Duties and Corporate Governance: Facilitating innovation and protecting investors,* CLERP9 (2002) *Corporate Disclosure* and the CLERP Bill (2003) *Audit Reformed Corporate Disclosure,* Australian Government Publishing Service, available at http://www.treasury.gov.au

Hansard, *Proof* Committee Hansard (2004) 'Joint Committee on Corporations and Financial Services', Reference: CLERP (Audit Reform and Corporate Disclosure) Bill, March, Canberra, *[Proof Copy].*

International Accounting Standards Committee (2002) *International Accounting Standards Handbook,* London, UK, available at www.iasc.org.uk

International Bar Association, IBA, (1994) Bankruptcy Legislation Sub-Committee, Tests for Insolvency, 25th Biennial Conference, Committee J.

Jowitt's Dictionary of English Law (1977) J. Burke (ed), Vol.1, 2nd edition, Sweet and Maxwell, London.

National Companies and Securities Commission, NCSC, (1984) *"A True and Fair View" and the Reporting Obligations of Directors and Auditors,* Australian Government Publishing Service, Canberra.

NYSE Blue Ribbon Committee (1999) *Report and Recommendation of the Blue Ribbon Committee on Improving the Effectiveness of Corporate Audit Committees,* available at www.nyse.com

Owen, Justice Neville (2003) *HIH Royal Commissioner's Final Report,* HIH Royal Commission, Commonwealth Government, Australia, available at www.hihroyalcom.gov.au

Oxford Illustrated Dictionary (The) (1962/1979) edited by J. Coulson, C. T. Carr, L. Hutchinson, and D. Eagle, Clarendon Press, Oxford.

Oxford English Dictionary (The Shorter): On historical principles (1933/1975) prepared by W. Little, H. W. Fowler, and J. Coulson; revised and edited by C. T. Onions, 3rd edition, Vol.1, Clarendon Press, Oxford.

Oxford Dictionary of Business English (1993) edited by A. Tuck, Oxford University Press, Oxford.

Pocket Oxford English Dictionary (1970), Clarendon Press, Oxford.

Compact Oxford English Dictionary (2000/2008) edited by C. Soames and S. Hawker, Oxford University Press.

Securities Exchange Commission (US), SEC, (2002), *Study Pursuant to Section 108(d) of the Sarbanes-Oxley Act of 2002 on the Adoption by the United States Financial Reporting System of a Principles-Based Accounting System,* July 25, available at http://www.sec.gov/news/studies/studiesarchive/2003archive.shtml

Securities Exchange Commission (US), SEC, (2005), *Report and Recommendations Pursuant to Section 401(c) of the Sarbanes-Oxley Act of 2002 On Arrangements with Off-Balance Sheet Implications, Special Purpose Entities, and Transparency of Filings by Issuers,* June 15, at http://www.sec.gov/news/studies/studiesarchive/2003archive.shtml

Securities Exchange Commission (US), SEC, (2008), *Report and Recommendations Pursuant to Section 133 of the Emergency Economic Stabilization Act of*

2008: Study on Mark-To-Market Accounting, December 30, available at http://www.sec.gov/news/studies/studiesarchive/2003archive.shtml

Securities Exchange Commission (US), SEC, (2009), *Study of the Sarbanes-Oxley Act of 2002 Section 404 Internal Control over Financial Reporting Requirements*, October 30, available at http://www.sec.gov/news/studies/studiesarchive/2003archive.shtml

PARLIAMENTARY REPORTS

Joint Standing Committee on Public Accounts and Audit, JCPAA, (2002) *Report 391, Review of Independent Auditing by Registered Company Auditors,* Bob Charles MP (chairman), The Parliament of the Commonwealth of Australia, Australian Government Press, August.

CASE REFERENCES

A Debtor (No.17 of 1966) [1967] 1 All E.R. 668
ASIC v. Plymin [2003] 46 ACSR 126
Associated Gas and Electric Company [1942] 11 SEC 974
Australian Co-Operative Development Society [1977] QD.R 66; (1976) 2 ACLR 207,218
*Australian Securities and Investment Commission v Ric*h [2009] NSWSC 1229
Australian Securities Commission v. Fairlie [1993] 11 ACLC 669; BC9300067—TASSC—25/06/1993.
AWA Ltd. V. Daniels [1992] 7 ACSR 759
Bank of Australasia v. Hall [1907] 4 C.L.R. 1514
Bond Corporation Holdings Ltd. [1990] 1 ACSR 350
Chew v. R [1991] 4 WAR 21
City Equitable Fire Insurance Company Limited [1924] No.0048 of 1922, C.A.
City of Glasgow Bank v. MacKinnon [1882] 9 Court Sessions Cases, 4th Series, 535
Commonwealth Bank of Australia v. Friedrich [1991] 9 ACLC 946
Continental Vending [*U.S. v. Simon*, 425 F.2d 796 (2d Cir. 1969)]
Cornhill Insurance plc v. Improvement Services Ltd. [1986] 1 W.L.R. 114
Cuff v. London and County Land and Building Company Ltd. [1912] 1 Ch.440
Daniels v. Anderson [1995] 37 NSWLR 438
David Grant & Co. Pty. Ltd v. Westpac Banking Corporation [1995] 184 C.L.R. 265
Dent v. The London Tramways Company (Ltd.) [1881] 16 L.R. Ch.344
D'Onofrio [1983] 76 FLR 136
Duke Group Ltd. (in liq) v. Pilmer & Ors [1998] Supreme Court S.A., Judgement No.S6529
Dumbell's Banking Company Ltd. [1900] 26 Acc L.R. 181
Dunn v. Shapowloff [1978] 2 NSWLR 235
Escott et al. v. Bar Chris Construction Corp.et al. 283 F. Supp. 643 (S.D.N.Y. 1968). (The Bar Chris Case)
European Life Assurance Co [1869] L.R. 9Eq.122
Expo International Pty. Ltd. (in liq) v. Chant [1979] 2 NSW. L.R. 820; C.L.C. 40–608
Hall v.Poolman [2007] 215 FLR 243; 65 ACSR 123
Howship Holdings Pty. Ltd. [1996] 14 ACLC 1549
Knightswood Nominees Pty. Ltd. V. Sherwin Pastoral Co Ltd [1989] 7 ACLC 536
Leeds Estate Building and Investment Society Ltd. v. Shepherd [1887] 36 Ch. D. 787
Leslie & Anor v. Howship Holdings Pty. Ltd. [1997] 133 FCA 459

London & Counties Assets Co. Ltd. V. Brighton Grand Concert Hall and Picture Palace Ltd [1915] 2 K.B. 493, 501
London and General Bank [1895] (No.2) 2 Ch. 673
London Oil Storage Company Ltd. (The) v. Seer, Hasluck and Co. [1904] 31 Acc L.R.1
Melbase Corporation Pty. Ltd. V. Legenhoe Pty. Ltd. [1995] 17 ACSR 187
Minion v. Graystone [1986] 1 QD.R 66; QD.R. 157, 169
Newark Pty. Ltd. (in liq) [1993] 1Qd R409.
Oxford Benefit Building and Investment Society [1886] 35 L.R. Ch. 502
Pacific Acceptance Corporation Ltd. V. Forsyth and Others [1970] 92 WN (NSW) 29
Parker v. Gosage [1835] 2 C.M. & R.617; 150 E.R.262
Pinner v. Everett [1969] 3 All E.R. 257
Rees v. Bank of NSW [1964] 111 C.L.R.
Rex v. Lord Kylsant and Another [1931]
Roy Morgan Research Centre (The) v. Wilson Market Research Pty. Ltd. [1996] 39 NSW L.R.
Salomon v Salomon & Co Ltd [1897] AC 22
Sandell v. Porter [1966] 115 C.L.R.
Sheahan v. Hertz Australia Pty Ltd [1995] 16 ACSR 765
Sons of Gwalia Ltd v. Margaretic ING Investment Management LLC v.Margaretic [2007] HCA 1 31 January 200
Standard Chartered Bank v. Antico [1995] 18 ACSR 1
Standard Chartered Bank of Australia Ltd. v. Antico & Ors [1995] 38 NSWLR 290
The Trustee of the Property of Apfel v. Annan, Dexter and Co. [1926] 70 Acc L.R. 57
Timbertec Pty .Ltd. [1974] 24 F.L.R.
Trade Practices Commission v. Arnotts Ltd. (No.5) [1990] 21 FCR 324
Turquand v. Marshall [1868] L.R. 6 Eq. 112 Master of the Rolls—Chancery 20 L.T. 766(1869)
United States v. Carl J. Simon et al. [1969] 425 F. 2d. 796
Verner v. General and Commercial Investment Trust Ltd. [1894] 2 Ch.239
Warburton v. Loveland [1982] 6Bli. N.S.1; 2 Dow. & C1.480; 5 E.R. 499

Index

D

E

F